Entrepreneurship in the BRICS
Economic Development and Growth in the Post-Pandemic World

Edited by Ndivhuho Tshikovhi, Fulufhelo Netswera and Ravinder Rena

NEW YORK AND LONDON

First published 2025
by Routledge
605 Third Avenue, New York, NY 10158

and by Routledge
4 Park Square, Milton Park, Abingdon, Oxon, OX14 4RN

Routledge is an imprint of the Taylor & Francis Group, an informa business

© 2025 selection and editorial matter, Ndivhuho Tshikovhi, Fulufhelo Netswera and Ravinder Rena; individual chapters, the contributors

The right of Ndivhuho Tshikovhi, Fulufhelo Netswera and Ravinder Rena to be identified as the authors of the editorial material, and of the authors for their individual chapters, has been asserted in accordance with sections 77 and 78 of the Copyright, Designs and Patents Act 1988.

All rights reserved. No part of this book may be reprinted or reproduced or utilised in any form or by any electronic, mechanical, or other means, now known or hereafter invented, including photocopying and recording, or in any information storage or retrieval system, without permission in writing from the publishers.

Trademark notice: Product or corporate names may be trademarks or registered trademarks, and are used only for identification and explanation without intent to infringe.

ISBN: 978-1-032-75508-3 (hbk)
ISBN: 978-1-032-75776-6 (pbk)
ISBN: 978-1-003-47560-6 (ebk)

DOI: 10.4324/9781003475606

Typeset in Times New Roman
by KnowledgeWorks Global Ltd.

This work is based on the research project supported by the NIHSS, South Africa

Contents

List of Figures   x
List of Tables   xi
List of Contributors   xiii

Introduction   1
NDIVHUHO TSHIKOVHI, FULUFHELO NETSWERA, RAVINDER RENA
AND LILLIE FERRIOL PRAT

PART I
Implications and Consequences during COVID-19 Pandemic in BRICS Nations   7

1 **The Impact of COVID-19 Pandemic on SMMEs in BRICS Economies: Policy Responses and Combating Strategies**   9
FRANK RANGANAI MATENDA, MABUTHO SIBANDA,
AND JUSTIN CHIRIMA

2 **Policies and Strategies for the Mitigation of COVID-19 Impact on SMMEs in South Africa**   31
FIONA LANGRY

3 **COVID-19 and Sustainability of Indian MSMEs in Crisis: The Role of Government of India**   41
ROLI RAGHUVANSHI AND RAVINDER RENA

4 **The Impact of COVID-19 on Entrepreneurship Focusing on Small and Medium Enterprises in South Africa**   58
ZAMASWAZI CELE, NDIVHUHO TSHIKOVHI,
AND FULUFHELO NETSWERA

Contents

5 China's SMEs in the Scope of COVID-19: Strategies and Prospects for Survival and Development 75
XI CHEN, JAI KUMAR, AND CHENSI LI

6 Emerging Trends among Indian Entrepreneurs: A Post COVID-19 Outlook 95
S. YAVANA RANI AND RAVINDER RENA

7 The Future of Entrepreneurship in a Post-COVID-19 Era in South Africa 108
NJABULO NDLOVU AND RICHARD SHAMBARE

8 Restaurants and COVID-19: A Focus on the Learning Experiences of Restaurant Entrepreneurs Amidst COVID-19 in South Africa 127
KNOWLEDGE SHUMBA, WELLINGTON CHAKUZIRA, RICHARD SHAMBARE, AND NTSWAKI PETUNIA MATLALA

PART II
Challenges and Opportunities in BRICS Countries 145

9 Importance of Governance in Entrepreneurship 147
NAMRATA DHASMANA

10 The Impact of Entrepreneurship on Economic Growth in Emerging Economies: Evidence from BRICS Countries 161
FRANK RANGANAI MATENDA AND MABUTHO SIBANDA

11 Does the Mixed Ownership Reform Promote the Innovation Level of State-Owned Enterprises?: A Dual Analysis of Equity Balance and Top Management Governance 181
ZHE SUN, ZHE WANG, XIAOMING WANG, AND LIANG ZHAO

12 Strategic Development Opportunities through BRICS Innovation Cooperation Action Plans: Innovative Exchange as a Path to Integration 204
ARTHUR CHAGAS DOS SANTOS

Contents ix

13 Industry, Innovation, and Infrastructure:
Contribution of SMEs in the Developing Economies   218
ZAKIA TASMIN RAHMAN, RUHI LAL, AND RAVINDER RENA

PART III
Individual BRICS Nations' Perspectives on
Entrepreneurship   249

14 Exploring the Urban Economics of Street Markets
in BRICS Nations: The Case Study of Rolêfeira in
Araraquara, Brazil   251
RENAN AUGUSTO RAMOS AND NDIVHUHO TSHIKOVHI

15 Entrepreneurship for Economic Development
and Growth: The Case of Russia in BRICS   262
SERGEI SMIRNOV AND NDIVHUHO TSHIKOVHI

16 Technological Entrepreneurship and Peculiarities of Its
Development in Russia   277
NIKOLAI O. YAKUSHEV

17 Entrepreneurial Lens into Creative Industries in Russia
Post-COVID-19: The Case of Urals Region   299
ANNA KURUMCHINA

18 The Influence of Entrepreneurship Education on Higher
Education Students' Entrepreneurial Intentions and
Motivation in South Africa   317
ANKIT KATRODIA

19 Towards an Aggressive Economic Growth: Promoting
Entrepreneurship as a Catalyst for Development
in South Africa   326
GILBERT MOTSAATHEBE AND RAVINDER RENA

Index   345

Figures

1.1	Number of studies per country	16
1.2	Study types	16
3.1	Activity-based percentage share of MSMEs in India	44
3.2	Contribution of MSMEs in Indian economy	45
3.3	Use-based category-Index of industrial production, 2019–2020 to 2020–2021	45
3.4	IIP in manufacturing category, India, 2019–2020 to 2020–2021	47
3.5	Monthly IIP growth rate, India, April 2020–December 2021	48
3.6	Source, annual report 2020–2021, MSME, GOI, Authors calculations	48
3.7	Negative growth rate in total exports April 2019–December 2019 vs. April 2020–December 2020	50
3.8	Positive growth rate in total exports January 2020–December 2020 vs. January 2021–December 2021	50
3.9	Commodities Export Growth Rate 2019–2020 vs. 2020–2021	51
3.10	Growth rate; macro-economic aggregates	52
5.1	Chart of SMEDI trend of SMEs in China since the beginning of 2021	87
7.1	The entrepreneurial process	110
7.2	The entrepreneurial cycle	111
7.3	Dual breakeven analysis in the post-COVID-19 era	120
8.1	Strategic recommendations	140
9.1	Anarchy and prosperity in the global sphere	158
12.1	Text mining of keyword frequency in presidential declarations until innovation cooperation action plan.	209
13.1	Model for goals of sustainable development and objectives	232
15.1	Entrepreneurial activity in Russia	269
17.1	Souvenirs, Chernoistochinsk	308
19.1	The general trend of GDP from the year 2000 to 2018	333

Tables

1.1	Database research results	13
1.2	Features of the reviewed articles	14
2.1	Summary of Africa COVID-19 detect data by country as at March 2022	32
3.1	Composite criteria: Investment in plant and machinery/equipment and annual turnover	42
3.2	Employment status in MSMEs, India, rural and urban (lakhs)	46
3.3	Survey on employment, sales, and cash flow of firms in India	49
4.1	Metrics for running a beauty salon and nail bar table	70
5.1	Statistical Methods for the Division of Chinese Large, Medium, and Small Enterprises (2017)	76
6.1	Existing and revised classification of MSME's	96
6.2	Contribution of MSMEs in India's GDP (in rupee crores)	96
6.3	Private sectors/social entrepreneurs effort to uplift MSME industry after COVID-19	97
6.4	Schemes introduced by government of India to uplift MSME industry post COVID-19	98
6.5	Negative growth of commodities during July 2020 compared to July 2019	101
6.6	Forecast for Asian countries' GDP growth (as of September 2020)	101
7.1	COVID-19 SME rescue packages	117
7.2	Gumi Breakeven analysis in post-COVID-19	121
7.3	SME opportunities	123
8.1	Criteria for determining alert levels (Disaster Management Act, 2020)	135
10.1	Entrepreneurial indicators	168
10.2	Descriptive statistics	170
10.3	Correlation matrix for entrepreneurial indicators	171
10.4	Principal component analysis indexes	172
10.5	Regression results	174

11.1	Variable definitions	189
11.2	Descriptive statistics	190
11.3	Correlation matrix	191
11.4	Mixed ownership reform and enterprise innovation	192
11.5	Robustness test	194
11.6	The empirical analysis of monopolistic versus competitive SOEs	196
11.7	The empirical analysis of regional marketisation development	197
11.8	The empirical analysis of technological versus non-technological SOEs	198
12.1	keyword frequency table.	210
12.2	Diagnosis of BRICS members in the area of ST&I in 2016	215
13.1	Difference of objectives between medium-sized and small businesses (SMBs) and micro, little, and medium-sized businesses (MSMEs) (SMEs)	220
13.2	Contribution of SMEs in developing nations	225
13.3	SMEs are crucial for fostering globalisation and growth that is more inclusive	227
13.4	Goal 9 of the UN's sustainable development agenda, "Industry, Innovation, and Infrastructure", outlines its objectives	231
13.5	SME's contribution to SDG No. 9	233
13.6	Differentiation of SMEs in China and India	236
13.7	Futuristic approach of SMEs in developing economies	239
14.1	Types of goods traded	256
14.2	Level of stallholders' registration	256
14.3	Results of economic practices	257
14.4	Meanings of economic practices	258
15.1	The evolution of private entrepreneurship in Russia	264
15.2	Entrepreneurship development indicators in Russia, Belarus, and Ukraine	267
15.3	GEM's entrepreneurship indicators for particular CEEC, Former Soviet Union countries [FSU], and BRICS countries	269
19.1	Number of SMMEs per Province in South Africa	335
19.2	Schedule of SMMEs by the NSB Act of 1996	336
19.3	Table of Mineral Resources in South Africa	338

Contributors

Zamaswazi Cele – Durban University of Technology, South Africa

Arthur Chagas dos Santos – Escola Superior de Guerra (Superior War College), Brazil

Wellington Chakuzira – University of South Africa, South Africa

Xi Chen – Assistant Professor at the School of International and Public Affairs, Jilin University, China. She is also a researcher at the Institute of National Development and Security Studies at the same university.

Justin Chirimab – Department of Mathematics and Computer Science, Great Zimbabwe University, Zimbabwe

Namrata Dhasmana – Major, Economist, Columnist, Senior Industry Expert, Indian Institute of Management, India

Ankit Katrodia – Senior Lecturer in North West University, School of Management Sciences, South Africa

Jai Kumar – PhD student majored in International relation at the School of International and Public Affairs, Jilin University, China

Anna Kurumchina – holds a PhD from the Ural Federal University, Russia

Ruhi Lal – Associate Professor/Head Student Support, Amity School of Communication, Amity University, India

Fiona Langry – Durban University of Technology, South Africa

Chensi Li – junior student majored in diplomacy at the School of International and Public Affairs, Jilin University, China

Frank Ranganai Matendaa – School of Accounting, Economics, and Finance, University of KwaZulu-Natal, South Africa

Ntswaki Petunia Matlala – University of the Western Cape, South Africa

Gilbert Motsaathebe – Research Professor: Indigenous Language Media in Africa, North-West University, South Africa

Njabulo Ndlovu – Lupane State University, Zimbabwe

Fulufhelo Netswera, Executive Dean Faculty of Management Sciences at Durban University of Technology (DUT) tasked to develop the DUT Business School.

Lillie Ferriol Prat – Durban University of Technology, South Africa

Roli Raghuvanshi – Department of Commerce, Shyamlal College (eve.), University of Delhi, Delhi, India

Zakia Tasmin Rahman – Assistant Professor, Amity School of Communication, Amity University, India

Renan Augusto Ramos – State University of Campinas, Brazil

Ravinder Rena – Professor of Economics, DUT Business School, Faculty of Management Sciences, Durban University of Technology, South Africa

Knowledge Shumba – University of the Western Cape, South Africa

Mabutho Sibandaa – School of Accounting, Economics, and Finance, University of KwaZulu-Natal, South Africa

Zhe Sun – Center for China Public Sector Economy Research, Jilin University, China

Richard Shambare – University of Fort Hare, South Africa

Sergei Smirnov – Professor in Saint Petersburg State University, Russia

Yavana Rani Subramanian – Associate Professor, Faculty of Management Studies, Jain University, India

Ndivhuho Tshikovhi – Durban University of Technology, South Africa

Nikolai O. Yakushev – Researcher at the Vologda Research Center of the Russian Academy of Sciences, Russia

Xiaoming Wang – Party School of Inner Mongolia Autonomous Region Committee of CPC, China

Zhe Wang – Economics School, Jilin University, China

Liang Zhao – Hunter Center for Entrepreneurship, Strathclyde Business School, University of Strathclyde, United Kingdom

Introduction

Ndivhuho Tshikovhi, Fulufhelo Netswera, Ravinder Rena and Lillie Ferriol Prat

Macro-economic indicators worldwide suggest that there is a direct relationship between entrepreneurship intensity and economic growth. Essentially, entrepreneurship is a driver of economic growth. It exploits the new methodologies and opportunities to address an existing gap within an economic system and thereby directly impact positively on the creation of new employment opportunities. Entrepreneurship contributes to economic stability by offering new innovation, products and services through cost-effective mechanisms. In turn, economic stability leads to increased investment in manufacturing and service sectors, among others. For many countries across the globe, the entrepreneurship is a tool of innovation promotion that supports sound economic environment as it stimulates economic growth and development. The BRICS nations, i.e., Brazil, Russia, India, China and South Africa, which are a group of emerging countries comprises the highest developmental block of the emerging nations. Without clear entrepreneurship promotion policies, the growth and development of the BRICS nations as well as their influence on the development and growth of the global economy would be insignificant. Therefore, it is imperative to assess the entrepreneurship policies, strategies, promotional programmes and their implications, on among others, entrepreneurship funding, economic growth and employment trends are important. Undoubtedly, the COVID-19 pandemic has impacted the entrepreneurship environment and equally steered state funding priorities away from entrepreneurship development support worldwide. This research book is aimed at assessing the effect that COVID-19 has had on among others, government funding priority, policy interventions and resultant implications on the entrepreneurship environment, economic growth and employment.

The next set of chapters described below will take the reader though a journey divided into three different themes covering: Implications and Consequences during COVID-19 pandemic in BRICS nations, Challenges and Opportunities in BRICS countries and Individual BRICS nations' perspectives on Entrepreneurship.

DOI: 10.4324/9781003475606-1

PART I: Implications and Consequences during COVID-19 Pandemic in BRICS Nations

Chapter 1 starts by looking at BRICS economies, government policy interventions and combating strategies during and after the COVID-19 that can augment the resilience of SMMEs. The authors Frank Ranganai Matenda, Mabutho Sibanda and Justin Chirima provide a systematic literature review that concludes with a multiplicity of policy responses and combating strategies to enhance the resilience of SMMEs as well as disclosing some research gaps to be explored in this study area.

The next set of chapters within Part I provide individual focus on South Africa, India and China highlighting struggles met during the pandemic as well as trends and outlooks resulting from the catastrophic world-wide event. Chapters 2 and 3, *"Policies and strategies for the mitigation of COVID-19 impact on SMMEs in South Africa,"* by Fiona Langry and *"COVID-19 & Sustainability of Indian MSME's in Crisis: The Role of Government of India,"* by Roli Raghuvanshi and Ravinder Rena, assess the impact caused by COVID-19 pandemic in South Africa and India respectively and recommend policy approaches to improve how SMMEs will operate in the wake of COVID-19. The chapters can be seen as complemental in that it allows the reader to identify potential synergies by noting similarities and differences.

Chapter 4 authored by Zamaswazi Cele, Ndivhuho Tshikovhi and Fulufhelo Netswera, *"The Impact of COVID-19 on Entrepreneurship focusing on Small- Medium Enterprises in South Africa,"* brings the attention back to South Africa emphasising the practical aspect of impact on formal and informal businesses relying solely on physical contact. By looking at how these businesses have been impacted, the importance of business metrics becomes evident as a basis for business decision-making in the face of uncertainty. Chapter 4 reminds the reader of the detrimental effect caused by the poor relationship between the lack of business metrics and policies, aggravated in turn by uncertainty.

Chapter 5, *"China's SMEs in the scope of COVID-19: Strategies and prospects for Survival and Development,"* by Xi Chen, Jai Kumar and Chensi Li, concentrates in the analysis on strategies and policies applied during the COVID-19 pandemic in the Chinese context, which is not only informative in and of itself but also helps the reader to further expand the comparative context gained in Chapters 1 and 2.

Chapters 6 *"Emerging trends among Indian entrepreneurs – A post COVID-19 outlook,"* by Yavana Rani Subramanian and Ravinder Rena and Chapter 7, *"The future of entrepreneurship in a post-covid-19 era in South Africa,"* by Njabulo Ndlovu and Richard Shambare, look at trends in India and South Africa *after* COVID-19, a parameter equally important to the holistic understanding of future and current entrepreneurship policies.

Last but not least, this first section closes with Chapter 8, "*Restaurants and COVID-19: a focus on the learning experiences of restaurant entrepreneurs amidst COVID-19 in South Africa,*" by Knowledge Shumba, Wellington Chakuzira, Richard Shambare and Ntswaki Petunia Matlala, explores South African restaurant entrepreneur's experiences, with a focus on the challenges and the strategies they implemented to recover from the impact of COVID-19. Together, Chapters 4 and 8 provide a more detailed micro-analysis perspective on the implications at quasi-individual level. As the collective is a sum of individuals, it is therefore an essential part of the analysis, which seeks to provide an accurate description of reality.

PART II: Challenges and Opportunities in BRICS Countries

The second part remains more macro-centric yet manages to provide a great deal of detail. This is helpful when looking at the mechanisms behind the possible metamorphosis of a challenge into an opportunity. For instance, Chapter 9, "*Importance of Governance in Entrepreneurship,*" by Namrata Dhasmana, observes that in India there is an imperative need to keep compliance and governance in check and highlights the importance of governance in entrepreneurship as a means and opportunity to align the sentiments of public interest and keep all the stakeholder's interests in place.

Chapter 10, "*The impact of entrepreneurship on economic growth in emerging economies: Evidence from BRICS countries,*" by Frank Ranganai Matenda and Mabutho Sibanda, revisits the very essence of the matter which is to define how entrepreneurship has actually been measured in the first place and how it may be improved. The chapter goes on to provide detailed study results, which have extensive policy implications concerning the imperativeness of entrepreneurship in inspiring economic growth in BRICS economies.

Chapter 11, by Zhe Sun, Zhe Wang, Xiaoming Wang and Liang Zhao "*Does the mixed ownership reform promote the innovation level of state-owned enterprises? A dual analysis of equity balance and top management governance,*" takes on an equally interesting as complex question in the Chinese setting, which is evaluating whether mixed ownership reform promotes the innovation level of state-owned enterprises.

Chapter 12 "*Strategic Development Opportunities through BRICS Innovation Cooperation Action Plans: Innovative Exchange as a Path to Integration*" by Arthur Chagas dos Santos, seeks to understand the mechanisms that have encouraged BRICS, at a macro-level, to become more integrated in fostering and sharing knowledge.

The second book section is wrapped up with Chapter 13, "*Industry, Innovation & Infrastructure: Contribution of SMEs in the Developing Economies*" by Zakia Tasmin Rahman, Ruhi Lal and Ravinder Rena, which emphasises the future outlook of SMES having the ability to eradicating poverty.

While studying the differences between India and China, the chapter also delves into the mechanisms and opportunities, which allow strategies for developing economies and emerging nations of the world, to take the full advantage of increase in employment, capital formation, income generation, boost in foreign exchange, infrastructural development, sustainable growth and development, derived from SME activity.

PART III: Individual BRICS Nations' Perspectives on Entrepreneurship

This third and final section of the book focuses on particular questions and aspects relevant to the nations of Brazil, Russia and South Africa. It can be said that while the study of common issues between countries is of excellent value, it is equally important to pay attention to the current individual characteristics which are unique to the different nations conforming to the BRICS. Although the chapters may bring, at first glance, less immediately obvious synergies to light, they are by no means less valuable to the overall multilateral context.

In Chapter 14, *"Exploring the urban economics of street markets in BRICS nations: the case study of "Rolêfeira" in Araraquara, Brazil,"* by Renan Augusto Ramos explores urban economic geography to assess which processes produce economic diversity in BRICS cities and how local governments respond to them at a local scale. The Brazilian city of Araraquara was chosen as the research location while the study was carried out at the street market named "Rolêfeira" during the years 2020 and 2021.

Chapter 15, *"Entrepreneurship for Economic Development and Growth: The Case of Russia in BRICS,"* by Sergei Smirnov and Ndivhuho Tshikovhi, takes on the simple yet complex question of: How many entrepreneurs (and what quality) are desirable for Russia? The chapter goes on to examine this question in the context of the distinctive features of Russian entrepreneurship using data analysis and literature review.

In Chapter 16, *"Technological entrepreneurship and peculiarities of its development in Russia,"* by Nikolai O. Yakushev, the relevance of technology in entrepreneurship is highlighted and seeks to evaluate whether technological entrepreneurship in Russia should be framed as a separate sector of the economy. This is a relevant question in the Russian context necessary to resolve priority problems in Russia in terms of stimulating the development of technological entrepreneurship.

In Chapter 17, *"Entrepreneurial lens into creative industries in Russia post COVID-19: The case of Urals Region"* by Anna Kurumchina, she explores creative industries development and perspectives in the Russian Ural region. While COVID-19 has largely been a disrupting factor with negative consequences, it has provided some entrepreneurial opportunities.

Chapter 18, *"The influence of Entrepreneurship Education on Higher Education Students' Entrepreneurial Intentions and Motivation in South Africa,"* by Ankit Katrodia, seeks to review existing studies and programmes to determine the effectiveness of high school entrepreneurship education in determining entrepreneurial foci and stimuli in South Africa. It is interesting to note that while results indicate that entrepreneurship training is valuable in skills development and confidence building, a plethora of factors, including personality traits, have been barriers to the effectiveness of higher education entrepreneurship training.

Chapter 19, *"Towards an aggressive economic growth: Promoting Entrepreneurship as a Catalyst for Development in South Africa,"* by Gilbert Motsaathebe and Ravinder Rena, goes through the challenges of corruption, failure to address the triple legacy of poverty, inequality and unemployment in South Africa. The conceptual chapter uses a systems approach and draws on the example of the Asian Tigers to offer a comprehensible model for implementing what it sees as the key catalysts of economic growth and development in a more systematic way. It highlights the significance of well-functioning parastatals and thriving SMMEs in growing the economy aggressively and ultimately recommends a more systematic approach to growing the economy and addressing the triple challenge of poverty, unemployment and inequality.

As of January 2024, Iran, Egypt, Ethiopia, Saudi Arabia and the United Arab Emirates officially accepted the invitation to join BRICS. In order to understand the incredible potential that bilateral and multilateral agreements will likely unleash, it is important to have a thorough understanding of how the entrepreneurship scenario is looking in BRICS+ today. The chapters in this book ultimately allow the reader to be embarked in a journey where multiple dimensions of entrepreneurship are explored within the BRICS context. This holistic experience seeks to bring the reader's understanding closer to a more accurate description of reality in terms of what entrepreneurship in BRICS countries currently entail. As the Roman philosopher Seneca famously said "Luck is when preparation meets opportunity," and preparation is indeed very much underway.

Part I
Implications and Consequences during COVID-19 Pandemic in BRICS Nations

1 The Impact of COVID-19 Pandemic on SMMEs in BRICS Economies

Policy Responses and Combating Strategies

Frank Ranganai Matenda, Mabutho Sibanda, and Justin Chirima

Introduction

Small, micro, and medium enterprises (SMMEs) are the backbone of developing economies (Behera *et al.*, 2021; Suguna *et al.*, 2022). They promote economic growth and development and technological and financial innovations, open new markets, and create jobs, among other things (Khan *et al.*, 2021; Suguna *et al.*, 2022; World Bank Group, 2022). Further, Njanike and Edomah (2020) indicated that SMMEs are dominant enterprises in developing economies. Not surprisingly, they are the majority of corporates in BRICS economies and are spread in urban and rural areas. BRICS is an acronym for the influential alliance of the leading emerging market countries, i.e., Brazil, Russia, India, China, and South Africa. The BRICS alliance intends to encourage security, peace, cooperation, and development among the five economies. Iqbal (2022) articulated that the influence and function of the BRICS economic bloc are substantial to the global economy in terms of GDP (US$16.039 trillion and 25% nominal), population (40%), world trade (18%), land coverage (30%), and global forex (US$4 trillion). The economic significance of SMMEs indicates that they are a significant component of the global economy. As the global economy becomes more interconnected, the globalisation of SMMEs is expected to increase.

Pandemics like COVID-19 are associated with unprecedented effects on economies and untold social order. The COVID-19 pandemic is not just a health problem but the most significant public health catastrophe in living memory and an economic problem. It has adversely affected the global economy, especially businesses. SMMEs have been hit hard by the pandemic, which threatened their survival (Behera *et al.*, 2021; Du, Razzaq, and Waqas, 2023). They are vulnerable to the pandemic due to several factors, which include a lack of financial and managerial resources, fewer research and development sources, lack of preparedness for such disruptions, reliance on central government and local agencies, limited applications of advanced technologies, dependence on a minute number of clients, psychological impact on owners and managers, reliance on routine

DOI: 10.4324/9781003475606-3

business transactions, and their smaller size and scale of operations (Bartik *et al.*, 2020; Du *et al.*, 2023; Hossain, Akhter, and Sultana, 2022; Prasad *et al.*, 2015; Williams and Schaefer, 2013).

The COVID-19 outbreak resulted in chain reactions, such as the collapse of stock markets and trade breakdown, which negatively influenced businesses, especially SMMEs (Behera *et al.*, 2021; Su *et al.*, 2022). For instance, in China, small and medium-sized enterprises (SME)s' total profits for the first quarter (Q1) of 2020 declined by 3.82 billion yuan compared to Q1 of 2019 (Su *et al.*, 2022). The Indian SMME sector witnessed a 55% loss in employment and a 17.2% loss in yearly sales, and on average, its production capacity deteriorated from 75% to 11% (Behera *et al.*, 2021). Hence, given the economic significance of SMMEs, governments in all four corners of the world have introduced myriad policy interventions to improve the resilience of SMMEs during and after the COVID-19 pandemic. Further, SMMEs have adopted numerous combating strategies for them to survive the pandemic. Buzulukova and Sheresheva (2021) opined that for SMMEs to respond to and survive the COVID-19 pandemic, they should adopt multiple measures to improve their resilience instead of waiting for support from governments and their agencies, which is usually delayed and insufficient.

This chapter conducts a systematic literature review to examine government policy interventions and combating strategies that can augment the resilience of SMMEs during and after the COVID-19 pandemic in BRICS economies. Our findings highlight a multitude of policy responses and combating strategies that can enhance the resilience of SMMEs during and after the pandemic in BRICS countries. Moreover, the study's results disclose some research gaps that can be explored in this study area.

Literature Review

A crisis is an unwelcome, often unanticipated, and time-restricted process that evolves, develops in phases, and whose end result is probably vague (Glaesser, 2006). Crises usually lead to firms' failure. Generally, crisis management literature is limited and more restricted in emerging economies. However, with the increase in the number of crises, especially disease pandemics like COVID-19, it is essential, and there is a dire need to perform research related to crisis management.

The COVID-19 pandemic has adversely influenced the operations of corporates, predominantly SMMEs. Compared to big firms, SMMEs are underprivileged in several areas, including innovation and financing (Su *et al.*, 2022). Su *et al.* (2022) postulated that, compared to huge companies, SMEs are associated with a comparatively solitary financing way, and too simple capital chain structure. The pandemic brought misery to many SMMEs and radically changed the business ecosystem. It has exposed numerous SMMEs to many challenges and difficulties threatening their survival (see Xiao and Su, 2022). These challenges include supply chain disruptions, increased costs and declining profitability levels, operational challenges, negative influence on financial performance, damaged firm and stakeholder confidence, restricted access to finance, work non-resumption, fall in market demand and supply, and downfall of consumption.

Although most SMMEs have been affected by the COVID-19 pandemic, diverse SMMEs have been impacted differently by the pandemic. Certain kinds of SMMEs have been at a greater risk than others. Reviewed studies indicated that the influences of the pandemic on SMMEs are self-evident and are both negative and positive. This indicates that not all SMMEs were adversely impacted by the pandemic. Some SMMEs benefitted from the pandemic. The extant evidence indicated that some of the characteristics of the SMMEs are beneficial during crisis periods. For instance, SMMEs are adaptable and flexible due to their small size, relatively flat hierarchical structures, and status of being privately traded. However, reviewed literature indicated that SMMEs are generally less resilient to pandemics than huge corporates.

Interestingly, Su *et al.* (2022) classified SMEs' heterogeneous performance into five categories, i.e., general beneficiaries, beneficiaries, irrelevant, victims, and general victims. The pandemic victims are SMEs that face severe bankruptcy dilemmas and operational difficulties under the influence of the pandemic. Victims (e.g., start-ups and micro-enterprises) are more vulnerable to the pandemic than general victims (e.g., innovative SMEs facing financing constraints). Beneficiaries are "winners" in the pandemic, whose gains are shown by exclusive industry features and business models that generate funds to uphold a profitable or normal business condition. Beneficiaries (e.g., digital and high-tech SMEs) benefit more from the pandemic than general beneficiaries (e.g., SMEs in the computer game industry). Finally, some SMEs are not impacted by the pandemic or the pandemic has a minimum influence on them. These SMEs include those in energy manufacturing and information technology industries.

Even though SMMEs are economically significant, they are associated with a low ability to withstand catastrophes like the COVID-19 pandemic. The government is one of the key exogenous factors influencing the vigorous development of SMMEs (Behera *et al.*, 2021). Against a backdrop of the COVID-19 pandemic increasing the mortality rates of SMMEs, governments have introduced a multiplicity of policy interventions and SMMEs adopted a myriad of coping strategies to alleviate the adverse influences of the pandemic on their operations. In support of this, Su *et al.* (2022) indicated that governments should adopt supportive policies in crisis times like the COVID-19 pandemic to help SMEs overcome their operating challenges and circumvent the crisis of social stability and macroeconomic development brought about by the failure of many SMEs. Bouazza (2015) indicated that legal systems, state policies, and supportive policies significantly influence SME growth. As expected, BRICS governments have been supporting SMMEs through a number of policy interventions, such as reduced taxes, increased credit support, and reduced tax rates

(Behera et al., 2021; Chernova and Neklyudova, 2022). However, it should be noted that some government actions and policies can adversely influence SMME development (see, for instance, Su et al., 2022). Government policies and actions may result in sophisticated legal systems, heavy tax burdens, low trust in the judicial system, and complex administrative procures, which may negatively affect the operations of SMMEs. Some of the coping strategies implemented by SMMEs include modification of business models, motivational support to employees, and adopting technology (Boucas da Silva, Miranda, and Hoffmann, 2021; Fubah and Moos, 2022).

Methodology

This chapter executed a systematic literature review to answer the research question: *What government policy responses and SMME combating strategies can be adopted to improve the resilience of SMMEs during and after the COVID-19 crisis in BRICS countries?* The methodological approach suggested by Tranfield, Denyer, and Smart (2003) and improved by Hansen and Schaltegger (2016) was followed to answer this question. This approach recognises appropriate studies through specific and reproducible selection criteria. The approach is associated with six stages: (1) research identification, (2) designing of exclusion and inclusion criteria, (3) study selection, (4) examination of the quality of studies, (5) data extraction, and (6) synthesis of data.

Data Collection

All appropriate keywords were identified (stage 1) to embrace the whole research field. The identified keywords include the following: "impact," "effect," "COVID-19," "SMMEs," "SMEs," "policies," "policy responses," "combating strategies," "BRICS," "Russia," "Brazil," "China," "South Africa," and "India." Search terms were generated from these keywords. In this study, a pilot test was conducted. The first five studies gathered from Google were reviewed as a pilot test. Four more keywords from the pilot test were identified, i.e., "policy recommendations," "policy interventions," "coronavirus," and "influence." Findings from the pilot test were to fine-tune the search terms over numerous iterations. The following final search terms were applied to gather appropriate studies:

- Policies to support SMEs/SMMEs during and after the COVID-19/coronavirus in BRICS countries/BRICS economies/Brazil/Russia/China/India/South Africa.
- SMEs/SMMEs responses to COVID-19/coronavirus in BRICS countries/BRICS economies/Brazil/Russia/China/India/South Africa.
- Effect/impact/influence of COVID-19/coronavirus on SMEs/SMMEs in BRICS countries/BRICS economies/Brazil/Russia/China/India/South Africa.

The search pooled 41 studies from ScienceDirect, Google Scholar, Google, and Scopus. These databases were chosen because they are the central databases of peer-reviewed articles in the universe (see, for instance, Bockel, Horisch, and Tenner, 2021).

The criteria were developed for inclusion and exclusion to allow the incorporation of all relevant articles (step 2). The only articles reviewed in this current study are journal articles and conference proceedings papers written in English. The aim was to make known the reviewed evidence to the common English-speaking parties. These articles were limited to the articles published from the year 2020 to the year 2022. The start year 2020 is when the COVID-19 pandemic was confirmed a global pandemic by the World Health Organisation. In addition, procedures to restrict COVID-19 spread were first introduced in 2020. The ending year of 2022 is the year this article was designed. In step 3, the authors selected the articles. In the first instance, the titles and abstracts of the potential articles were assessed. After reviewing their titles and abstracts, three articles were excluded; two did not meet the mentioned inclusion criteria, and one was a duplicate. In some instances, the researchers could not decide whether to incorporate or omit an article after assessing its title and abstract. Given this situation, the introduction and/or conclusion were analysed. When the assessment of the article's introduction and/or conclusion is insufficient for the authors to incorporate or omit an article, the authors assess the entire article. Out of the 38 remaining articles, the authors omitted three after the introduction review and another three after the whole article analysis since they were irrelevant. Moreover, two more articles were excluded because they were unattainable. This study's final sample of articles reviewed had 30 studies (see Table 1.1). No additional examination of the quality of the articles was employed since the authors reviewed only peer-reviewed journal articles and conference proceedings papers (step 4). Including conference proceedings papers permitted authors to consider the most current research outcomes and expanded the type of literature incorporated in this recent article. Moreover, including conference proceedings articles guaranteed a "balance between breadth and depth" (Fisch and Block, 2018).

An integrated data extraction sheet was implemented to extricate data from the chosen articles (step 5). The sections of the data extraction sheet were filled

Table 1.1 Database research results

	Omission	Total
Automatic search		41
Duplicate studies	−1	40
Studies not appropriate	−8	32
Studies unattainable	−2	30
Final sample		30

with the pertinent information for each assessed article, i.e., author(s), publication year, the title of the article, article's aim, name of the journal or academic conference, sample, research design, techniques(s) applied, country of focus, and study results. Table 1.2, which is a cutting from the integrated data extraction sheet, outlines some of the features of the reviewed studies.

Table 1.2 Features of the reviewed articles

Author(s)(Year)	Journal title	Country of focus
Chernova and Neklyudova (2022)	SHS Web of Conferences	Russia
Fubah and Moos (2022)	Sustainability	South Africa
Puthusserry et al. (2022)	British Journal of Management	India
Su et al. (2022)	Frontiers of Psychology	China
Sun et al. (2022)	Finance Research Letters	China
Xiao and Su (2022)	Environmental Science and Pollution Research	China
Behera et al. (2021)	Small Enterprises Development, Management and Extension Journal	India
Boucas da Silva et al. (2021)	Brazilian Journal of Tourism Research	Brazil
Buzulukova and Sheresheva (2021)	Proceedings of the European Marketing Academy	Russia
Dai et al. (2021)	China Economic Review	China
Dladla (2021)	Asian Journal of Economics and Finance	South Africa
Ma, Liu, and Gao (2021)	PLoS ONE	India
McLellan and Mzini (2021)	The 6th Annual International Conference on Public Administration and Development Alternatives	South Africa
Mkhonza and Sifolo (2021)	International Journal of Entrepreneurship and Business Development	South Africa
Sajan (2021)	International Journal of Scientific Development and Research	India
Sun et al. (2021)	Economic Research-Ekonomska Istrazivanja	China
Banu and Suresh (2020)	Mukt Shabd Journal	India
Chetia (2020)	International Journal of Humanities and Social Science Invention	India
Dey and Diswas (2020)	International Journal of Creative Research Thoughts	India
Duggappa (2020)	Intercontinental Journal of Marketing Research Review	India
Indrakumar (2020)	Manpower Journal	India
Lal et al. (2020)	International Journal of Multidisciplinary Research and Development	India
Lavanya and Deepika Rani (2020)	International Journal of Innovative Research in Management Studies	India

(Continued)

Table 1.2 (Continued)

Author(s)(Year)	Journal title	Country of focus
Lu et al. (2020)	Environmental Hazards	China
Mahajan (2020)	GIS Science Journal	India
Oni and Omonona (2020)	The Retail and Marketing Review	South Africa
Razumovskaia et al. (2020)	Journal of Open Innovation: Technology, Market, and Complexity	Russia
Roy, Patnaik, and Satpathy (2020)	Eurasian Chemical Communications	India
Sahoo and Ashwani (2020)	Global Business Review	India
Sarkisian-Artamonova and Kalacheva (2020)	Proceedings of ADVED 2020 – 6th International Conference on Advances in Education	Russia

Data Analysis

A two-step process was conducted to synthesise the data (step 6) to answer the research question. Firstly, the study examined government policy influences on the effects of the COVID-19 pandemic on SMMEs in BRICS economies. Then, the combating strategies that SMMEs can adopt to alleviate the adverse influences of the COVID-19 pandemic on their operations in BRICS economies were analysed. Some relevant information is summarised using a table, a chart, and a bar graph. A descriptive-analytical technique to divulge the apposite outcomes of this systematic literature review, i.e., policy responses and combating strategies implemented. Majority of the studies are qualitative; however, this is expected because this is an emerging research stream.

Figure 1.1 indicates that 14/30 articles are devoted to India and only 1/30 study is directed to Brazil. Moreover, the 6/30, 4/30, and 5/30 studies are linked to China, Russia, and South Africa, respectively.

Figure 1.2 shows that 90% of the articles are journal articles and 10% are conference proceedings papers.

Results

The systematic literature review results are presented in three subsections: policy responses, combating strategies, and research gaps.

Policy Responses

This subsection illuminated government policy responses that can be adopted to support SMMEs during and after the COVID-19 pandemic.

16 *Frank Ranganai Matenda, Mabutho Sibanda and Justin Chirima*

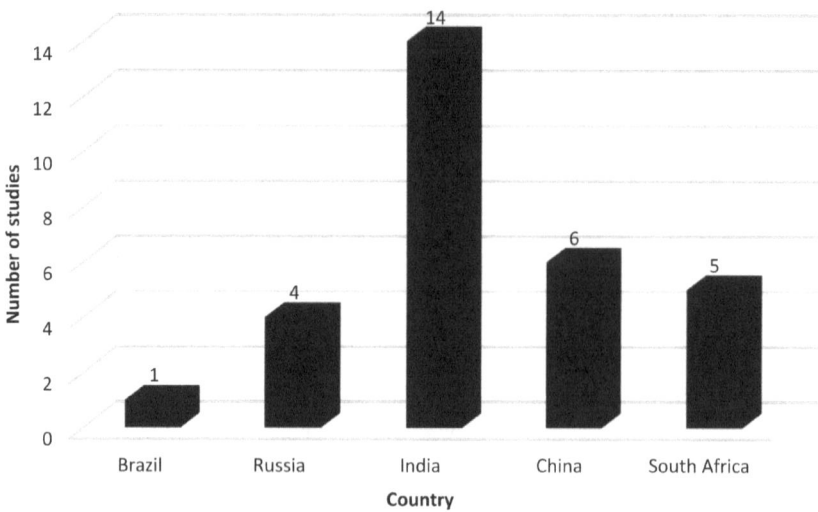

Figure 1.1 Number of studies per country

Financial and Technical Support and Removal of Administrative Barriers

For SMMEs to survive the pandemic, they need financial and technical support (Boucas da Silva *et al.*, 2021; Chernova and Neklyudova, 2022; Dey and Diswas, 2020; Lu *et al.*, 2020; McLellan and Mini, 2021; Oni and Omonona, 2020) at the earliest possible time (Indrakumar, 2020). Generally, the support would

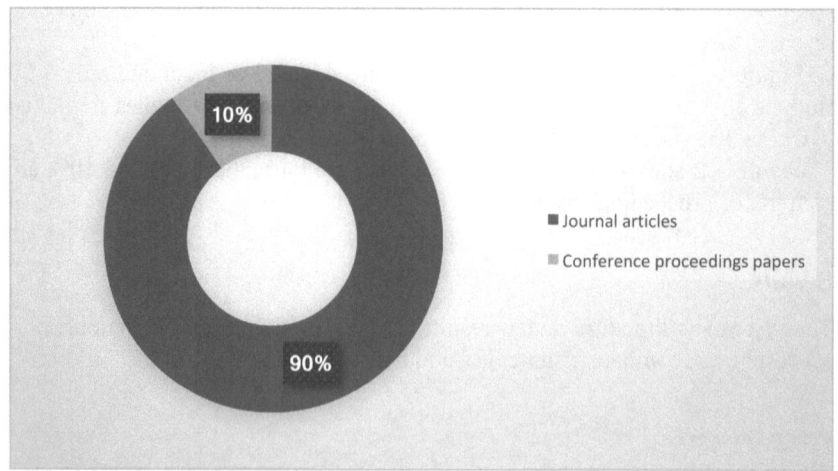

Figure 1.2 Study types

improve trust in the SMME sectors (Mahajan, 2020). Financial support comes in different forms (Duggappa, 2020; Indrakumar, 2020; Sahoo and Ashwani, 2020), and it alleviates the risks of cash flow disruption (Indrakumar, 2020) and reduces finance costs. The pandemic requires methodical, aggressive, and well-targeted fiscal-monetary stimulus packages (Sahoo and Ashwani, 2020). Accommodative and prudent monetary policies need to be designed to increase liquidity levels for both SMMEs and employees to decrease operating costs of businesses and amplify the fiscal policy counter-cyclical adjustment to enlarge the fiscal spending scale (see, for instance, Su et al., 2022). Direct loans, preferential loans, collateral-free loans, and interest-free working capital should be made available, and improved loan renewal policy arrangements must be designed to assist SMMEs so that they can restart their business activities and safeguard jobs (Banu and Suresh, 2020; Behera et al., 2021; Chetia, 2020; Roy et al., 2020; Sahoo and Ashwani, 2020; Sajan, 2021; Sarkisian-Artamonova and Kalacheva, 2020; Su et al., 2022). SMME credit limits should be raised and bank loan service fees need to be reduced to promote the distribution of loans. In the same vein, Sajan (2021) proffered that required reserve ratios for banks must be reduced. Governments should allow SMMEs to pay some of their arrears in instalments (Dey and Diswas, 2020).

Governments need to act as guarantors for SMMEs which take loans from financial institutions (Dey and Diswas, 2020; Roy et al., 2020), create SMME rehabilitation funds to boost SMMEs during difficult times (see, for instance, Lu et al., 2020), and provide different services to SMMEs so that they survive the pandemic (Lu et al., 2020). For instance, governments can design policies that enable SMMEs to access and develop additional skills during a crisis (Banu and Suresh, 2020). Basically, policies should support training and redeployment. Ma et al., 2021) opined that social infrastructure and service-oriented policy responses offer convenience to SMEs that commence production and work and diminish the adverse effects of the pandemic control and prevention, inspection, and supervision of market operations. The restructuring process of the industrial chain and market recovery needs to speed up to promote the recovery of SMMEs (see Ma et al., 2021). McLellan and Mzini (2021) promulgated that new SME markets must be designed. Support institutions promoting SMMEs must be developed and augment the governance of SMME-associated policy responses (Dey and Diswas, 2020; Indrakumar, 2020) and must initiate joint actions which are essential for the survival of firms (Boucas da Silva et al., 2021). Reviewed evidence also indicated that SMMEs must be supported to adopt new work processes and speed up digitisation and innovation.

Sarkisian-Artamonova and Kalacheva (2020) and Sahoo and Ashwani (2020) highlighted that firms in the most influenced sectors should be assisted the most, and Dladla (2021) propounded that devoted interventions should be put in place to guarantee that businesses with the potential to expand are resuscitated. Some businesses have survived the pandemic and need support

(Dladla, 2021). Duggappa (2020) indicated that governments need to support SMMEs that produce products and offer services that are critically required during the pandemic. Irfan *et al.* (2021) postulated that top-down and bottom-up methodologies are required to direct plans to support productive entrepreneurs during the COVID-19 catastrophe. Dladla (2021) indicated that governments should implement deliberate and targeted interventions to ride on the wave of and develop SMEs (e.g., those in the information and technology sector) that exploit new opportunities created by the pandemic and integrate. In addition, government stimulus packages introduced to deal with the influences of the pandemic on SMMEs were inadequate. Therefore, governments of BRICS countries need to introduce adequate stimulus packages to deal with the effects of the pandemic on SMMEs if they are to survive. Further, Su *et al.* (2022) further opined that professionals should be trained especially in the areas of artificial intelligence and big data, an ample system of regulations and laws must be enhanced, and governments must introduce support policies to control and guide the online business content and introduce policies to defend businesses with comparatively weak comparative advantages and circumvent the issue of a dominant corporate to guarantee an orderly and fair market.

Governments should ensure that supply chains are resilient (Mahajan, 2020) and restrict foreign multinational companies' business activities so that SMMEs cannot be exposed to competitive threats (Roy *et al.*, 2020). Also, governments should maintain the employment of SMMEs stable, buy goods and services from SMMEs, evaluate the effects of designed policies timeously and then make modifications, analyse SMMEs to comprehend their challenges and worries and then offer directed assistance, augment the legal system of SMMEs and encourage firms to integrate their capability to alleviate the effects of risks on their operations (Su *et al.*, 2022). Reviewed literature indicated that some definitions of SMMEs are too strict to promote their survival during crisis periods. Behera *et al.* (2021) articulated that the definition of an SMME affects its economic performance. Hence, the definitions of SMMEs can be modified (Duggappa, 2020; Indrakumar, 2020) to boost capital flow to the sector and render the sector more competitive and viable in the global market (Indrakumar, 2020). In India, for instance, SMMEs were redefined to make them competitive and viable (Banu and Suresh, 2020; Behera *et al.*, 2021; Dey and Diswas, 2020; Sajan, 2021). Su *et al.* (2022) further proffered that practical assistance must be given premised on real production requirements, and deregulation must be supplemented by upgraded regulatory efficacy to stabilise employment and safeguard people's livelihoods. Roy *et al.* (2020) promulgated that governments should design relief measures for employees susceptible to job losses, and Sajan (2021) proposed that export activity realisation and repatriation periods can be prolonged. Moreover, bankruptcy filings started by creditors and tax audits should be banned, labour law reforms should be done, and issues such as working hours and security must be addressed.

Administrative burdens for SMMEs should be reduced (Ma *et al.*, 2021). The funding requirements for SMMEs must be less strict, and foreign-owned firms should be allowed to apply for funding (Mkhonza and Sifolo, 2021). Mkhonza and Sifolo (2021) promulgated that the funds provided should be accessible easily and at the earliest possible time, and the time between application and fund payout should be shortened. Further, Mkhonza and Sifolo (2021) suggested that communication between the government and SMMEs must be improved. Banu and Suresh (2020) and Oni and Omonona (2020) highlighted that governments should enhance their information dissemination approaches to guarantee that information associated with small firms' relief schemes arrives to the end-users as early as possible. This is essential since most SMMEs are unaware of the government's measures (Lal *et al.*, 2020). Oni and Omonona (2020) further postulated that relief fund payout procedures for small firms must be seamless and transparent. Moreover, governments should promote the formalisation of the unorganised SMMEs by designing more straightforward registering procedures associated with fewer entry barriers (Lal *et al.*, 2020). This will enable the governments to offer benefits to SMMEs since they will get registered quickly.

Interest Rates and Loan Repayments

During COVID-19-like crises, interest rates must be reduced so financial institutions can advance loans cheaper (Behera *et al.*, 2021; Su *et al.*, 2022). The governments must limit the interest rates and make funds available at lower rates. Chernova and Neklyudova (2022) propounded that reducing interest rates promotes lending and aggregate demand. In addition, Dey and Diswas (2020) opined that interests or penalties for delayed payments can be waived. Moreover, loan repayments by SMMEs should be postponed to lessen the debt burden upon SMMEs during the crisis periods (Indrakumar, 2020; McLellan and Mzini, 2021; Su *et al.*, 2022). Roy *et al.* (2020) proposed that governments can design regulations that could provide a prolonged tenure to repay SMME loans. Low-interest loans characterised by medium-term and long-term repayment periods must be made available.

Payments to SMMEs and Government Procurement Tenders

It has emerged that, in most cases, governments and their agencies take a long to pay SMME dues. This puts SMMEs under much pressure and threatens their survival during crisis periods. Therefore, governments and their agencies should honour all dues to SMMEs within short periods (Banu and Suresh, 2020; Behera *et al.*, 2021; Sajan, 2021). Cash flows from the governments and their agencies must be consistent. Moreover, governments should design public procurement procedures suitable for SMMEs. For instance, in India, the government encouraged SMMEs to participate and supply in government tenders by banning international tenders for government procurement up to a particular amount (Banu and Suresh, 2020; Behera *et al.*, 2021; Duggappa, 2020; Sajan, 2021). Banu and Suresh (2020) and Duggappa (2020) suggested that disallowing global tenders for government procurement up to a specific amount is helpful since it reduces competition from foreign firms. Banning global tenders also promotes the consumption of home-grown goods and services.

Digital Transformation

Governments should promote the digital transformation of SMMEs. Roy *et al.* (2020) suggested that developing countries' governments must assist SMMEs in entering into trade agreements with developed economies to import advanced technological equipment to maximise production. Policies should emphasise altering offline business models for SMMEs to incorporate online business models to acclimate to the pandemic (see Su *et al.*, 2022). Further, Su *et al.* (2022) opined that governments need to offer essential systematic and refined online business training to SMEs that require it. For instance, in India, e-marketing replaced exhibitions and trade fairs (Dey and Diswas, 2020; Duggappa, 2020; Sajan, 2021), and e-market linkages increased sales for SMMEs (Chetia, 2020).

Tax Rates

Governments can cut tax rates to augment the liquidity levels of taxpayers during crisis periods (Behera *et al.*, 2021; Duggappa, 2020). Su *et al.* (2022), Ma *et al.* (2021), Lu *et al.* (2020), and Roy *et al.* (2020) indicated that tax relief policies (general or targeted) are some of the most effective support policies. Ma *et al.* (2021), Dey and Diswas (2020), Oni and Omonona (2020), and Sarkisian-Artamonova and Kalacheva (2020) promulgated that governments should instigate tax exemptions, deferrals and reductions, prolong the tax payment period, and offer tax subsidies. Sarkisian-Artamonova and Kalacheva (2020) further indicated that a deferral of tax and accounting records, a ban on off-site tax inspections, exclusion of fines, and changes in the advance income tax payment are essential to promote the survival of SMMEs.

Demand and Supply

The COVID-19 pandemic adversely affected the demand and supply of goods and services. Hence, policies that promote supply and demand must be designed. Governments must implement structural reforms on the supply side to promote sustainable economic growth (Su *et al.*, 2022). Dai *et al.* (2021) propounded that after the COVID-19 controls were revoked, a lack of demand substituted supply-side problems as the main challenge. Consequently, designing policies aimed at consumers, principally vulnerable and low-income consumers, could benefit SMMEs as domestic demand rises (Dai *et al.,* 2021). Stimulating consumption and increasing demand amplify employment, enhance production, and increase incomes, resulting in a further surge in consumption and attainment of a virtuous circle (Lu *et al.*, 2020; Ma *et al.*, 2021). Governments need to be promotional.

Employee Health and Safety

Governments' efforts must deal with issues related to employee health and safety. Worker health and safety and childcare should be prioritised. Work should resume orderly, and control mechanisms should be efficient and effective to avoid exposing workers to the deadly virus. Ma *et al.* (2021) opined that essential public health needs to be guaranteed. Su *et al.* (2022) articulated that governments need to invest more in public health care to manage the pandemic whilst upholding the "top-down" precision in executing pandemic deterrence, control, and economic recovery.

Subsidies and Obligations

SMMEs expect the government to provide employment, tax, and operating subsidies in times of crisis (Chetia, 2020; Lu *et al.*, 2020; Ma *et al.*, 2021; McLellan and Mzini, 2021; Oni and Omonona, 2020; Sarkisian-Artamonova and Kalacheva, 2020). Operating subsidies can be salaries, research and development, and business-connected utilities, e.g., electricity (Indrakumar, 2020; Ma *et al.*, 2021; Su *et al.*, 2022). Subsidies lessen cash flow pressures on SMMEs since they reduce their expenses. Further, governments can suspend or reduce some of the obligations of SMMEs, e.g., insurance fees, social security, and pension contributions (McLellan and Mzini, 2021; Razumovskaia *et al.*, 2020). SMME rent deferment and relief to commercial properties, deferment of public utility fees, and waiver of administrative fees also reduce SMME expenses (see Sarkisian-Artamonova and Kalacheva, 2020).

Work and Production Commencement and Business Models

Governments must help SMMEs commence production and work as early as possible (Lu *et al.*, 2020; Sun *et al.*, 2022) by enhancing the capacity-building of SMMEs (see Sun *et al.*, 2022) and reducing restrictions to permit an upsurge in the mobility of people and logistics (Lu *et al.*, 2020). The commencement of work and production increases the revenue of SMMEs. Nevertheless, work commencement should be accompanied by effective and efficient control strategies and the unblocking of blocked industrial chains.

General Policy Recommendations

The COVID-19 pandemic significantly affected SMMEs with enormous differential effects across sectors. This implies that SMME policy preferences vary according to sectors and firm types (Lu *et al.*, 2020). Hence, government policy interventions should be sensitive to the diverse kinds of SMMEs instead of embracing a one-size-fits-all method that can lead to regional policy risks. In the short term, policies should promote SMME survival. In the long run, policies should move towards a more structural approach to encouraging the growth and renewal of SMMEs through internationalisation, innovation, and networking. Razumovskaia *et al.* (2020) opined that government support measures must be premised on vibrant economic policy goals. Also, reviewed evidence indicated that SMMEs can only be protected, promoted, and supported when the designed measures are rapidly and adeptly implemented (Lal *et al.*, 2020). Moreover, the adverse influences of new policies on the business models of SMMEs need to be reduced (Su *et al.*, 2022).

Combating Strategies

This subsection illustrates the combating strategies for SMMEs to adopt for survival in pandemics.

Action Plans, Entrepreneurial Mindset, and Entrepreneurial Action

SMMEs must design appropriate action plans to augment their survival rates (Mahajan, 2020). Similarly, Sun *et al.* (2021) promulgated that firms must generate appropriate crisis plans that effectively and efficiently address COVID-19. The forecasted cash inflows and outflows, budgets, commitments, and anticipated risks must be considered when creating action plans (Behera *et al.*, 2021). In addition, Oni and Omonona (2020) indicated that situations must be regularly evaluated and re-evaluated. Moreover, SMMEs need positive entrepreneurial mindsets, identify entrepreneurial opportunities, and take entrepreneurial actions as a coping mechanism during the pandemic (Fubah and Moos, 2022). An entrepreneurial mindset allows businesses to make vital decisions to stay in business. Entrepreneurial actions can manifest through entering new markets, diversifying businesses, altering business models, or recognising novel opportunities (Fubah and Moos, 2022).

Information and Support

SMMEs must seek and access specialised services, knowledge, and technical-financial support from different stakeholders to improve their competitiveness (Boucas da Silva *et al.*, 2021). They need to gather dependable and correct information concerning support and financial relief offered by the governments and their agencies to SMMEs. This information assists them in designing and implementing their financial strategies. Also, SMMEs must be formally registered with the government and its agencies (see, for example, Fubah and Moos, 2022) and must be organised (Indrakumar, 2020; Mkhonza and Sifolo, 2021). Oni and Omonona (2020) promulgated that small firms must register with the government and obey instructions as they come to make it easy for the government to gather data. Further, SMMEs can get support from family members (see Fubah and Moos, 2022) and could get credit from informal channels (Roy *et al.*, 2020).

Strategies

To improve the performance and market value of SMMEs, reliable, flexible, and helpful crisis management strategies and post-crisis strategies must be designed and promoted. Responsive teams that deal with crises can be set up. The management teams of SMMEs must make prudent decisions in real-time and have a positive attitude for SMMEs to survive. Reviewed studies indicated that to survive crises, SMMEs can adopt several resilient strategies and competencies that include agility, adaptability, innovativeness, resourcefulness, positivity, flexibility, and collaboration (Giancotti and Mauro, 2020; Puthusserry *et al.*, 2022). Puthusserry *et al.* (2022) propounded that flexible organisational structures are resilient and are linked to innovative responses to exogenous shocks. Also, strategies for emotional regulation, employee remuneration, pricing, differentiators, goods, product quality, and distribution models should be considered (see Behera *et al.*, 2021; Lavanya and Deepika Rani, 2020; Mahajan, 2020). SMMEs can address the effects of the pandemic through product development, market penetration, and diversification growth strategies. Products must be improved, and SMMEs should negotiate with clients and suppliers (Boucas da Silva *et al.*, 2021; Lavanya and Deepika Rani, 2020). The delivery of products should be strengthened (Boucas da Silva *et al.*, 2021) and SMMEs must enlarge their supply chain and be able to work from home, where possible. New goods and services may be offered (Boucas da Silva *et al.*, 2021). Buzulukova and Sheresheva (2021) promulgated that SMEs should change the range of products and services they provide, and Duggappa (2020) postulated that SMMEs should adopt environmentally conscious sustainable practices. Further, SMMEs should keep operations on track; however, if the worse comes to the worst, they can cease operations.

Marketing, Advertising, and Promotions

To survive the pandemic, SMMEs must fortify their communication, marketing, advertising, and promotion activities (Boucas da Silva *et al.*, 2021; Fubah and Moos, 2022). Boucas da Silva *et al.* (2021) indicated that products and services should be creatively promoted on both traditional channels (e.g., billboards and newspapers) and virtual channels (e.g., Facebook and Instagram). SMMEs should continuously market, advertise, and promote their services and products to prospective clients to create awareness; otherwise, they risk forgetting their services and products as clients' buying behaviour changes. They must adapt their marketing, advertising, and promoting methods to survive the pandemic. In times of crisis, promotional strategies reinforce the image of SMMEs. Also, client and brand loyalty must be reinforced by promoting brand reliability.

Consumer Tastes

The COVID-19 pandemic has changed consumer behaviour and tastes. Behera *et al.* (2021) postulated that, even though discretionary spending is apparent in the behaviour of consumers, there is a change in client tastes that enterprises can exploit. First, SMMEs should understand the new behaviours of customers during and after the pandemic. Second, SMMEs should design strategies to become stable in the "new normal" and discover answers for the pandemic-linked problems influencing their consumers' behaviour.

Technology

New technological innovations are transmuting the business landscape for SMMEs. Therefore, SMMEs should adopt technology to improve their business processes to augment their business performance and survive the pandemic (Chetia, 2020; Duggappa, 2020; Mkhonza and Sifolo, 2021). Technology connects suppliers and buyers in all locations, unlocking business opportunities for SMMEs and allowing SMMEs to engage in social media, have an online presence, and adopt online business models, thereby building online communities. Embracing and strengthening new-age technological innovations assist SMMEs in enhancing the efficiency of their processes, reducing costs, enhancing information visibility, and augmenting worker safety (Behera *et al.*, 2021). Moreover, Behera *et al.* (2021) proffered that SMMEs should work with leaders in the technology areas, such as tech start-ups, research organisations, and students. Organisational cultures that value innovation, proactiveness, creativity, and planning should be promoted. Digital infrastructure accessibility is required to grasp digital transformation and augment skills to access technology and innovation. SMMEs should invest more to improve their technological infrastructure and ecosystem since crises are associated with an unpredictable nature and scale. Generally, there is a dire need to design a robust digital ecosystem in BRICS economies.

Partnerships and Networking

SMMEs need to use partnerships and networks to survive the pandemic and keep on operating (Buzulukova and Sheresheva, 2021; Chetia, 2020; Fubah and

Moos, 2022; Puthusserry *et al.*, 2022). They can partner with huge corporations, other SMMEs, or foreign players. In the same vein, Boucas da Silva *et al.* (2021) and Sarkisian-Artamonova and Kalacheva (2020) indicated that collaborations may be done with competitors, suppliers, students, and graduates to generate ideas, abilities, and skills that address the pandemic. Partnerships help SMMEs to penetrate different markets and create low-cost production bases. Existing literature also revealed that networking and inter-organisational partnerships offer opportunities for sharing and raising resources (e.g., information and knowledge) from partners, decreasing uncertainties, increasing adaptive response to externalities, attaining economies of scale, and obtaining joint financing. Moreover, alliances with competitors may put governments and their agencies under pressure to help SMMEs (Boucas da Silva *et al.*, 2021).

Costs and Revenue Schemes

SMMEs must reduce their costs to increase their chances of survival in a crisis period (Lavanya and Deepika Rani, 2020). Boucas da Silva *et al.* (2021) indicated that costs must be managed. Xiao and Su (2022) and Sun *et al.* (2021) indicated that firms must examine their fixed and variable costs precisely. Cost reduction can increase the profits and revenues of SMMEs. Sun *et al.* (2021) stressed that revenue schemes must be appropriately altered where needed. Altering costs and revenues helps firms create robust plans, make informed decisions, and reduce the pandemic impact on firms' profitability. This implies that SMMEs need to adopt financial adaptability measures.

Business Models

SMMEs must examine the feasibility of their current business models, considering their costs and revenues and the rapid changes happening in the markets (see Sun *et al.*, 2021; Xiao and Su, 2022). Business models must be altered to survive crisis periods (Fubah and Moos, 2022) since crisis periods present chances for modification and time for training and designing operational safety measures. Evidence indicates that SMMEs must develop skills to survive crises and promote recovery (Mkhonza and Sifolo, 2021; Sarkisian-Artamonova and Kalacheva, 2020). (Puthusserry *et al.* (2022) proffered that SMMEs should adopt knowledge management research to acquire the required knowledge to deal with the crisis.

Employee Well-Being and Welfare

SMMEs should guarantee that the well-being and welfare of their employees is safeguarded. Employees must be cared for (Boucas da Silva *et al.*, 2021). SMMEs must adhere to the measures and procedures put in place by the responsible authorities to avert the spread of COVID-19 (Banu and Suresh, 2020; Mahajan, 2020). Also, clear lines of communication with workers must be designed to overcome the anxiety and worries associated with the pandemic. Open and transparent communication lines assure employees of job security (Puthusserry *et al.*, 2022). Banu and Suresh (2020) propounded that continuous communication with employees is required so that they can get back to work. In addition, employees should be given motivational support (Boucas da Silva *et al.*, 2021). Oni and Omonona (2020) proposed that workers should be adequately motivated to promote organisational citizenship, leading to organisational sustainability and profitability. In the same vein, Puthusserry *et al.* (2022) promulgated that open discussions concerning strategies and plans of the firm are essential in promoting worker motivation, which helps the firm to keep operating. Moreover, SMMEs should respond to employee issues with flexibility and human-centric aptitudes. They should also help their employees by informing them about government incentives and labour issues (Boucas da Silva *et al.*, 2021).

Retrenchments, Unpaid Vacations, and Existential Issues

For SMMEs to survive, they may need to retrench workers or give them unpaid leave (Boucas da Silva *et al.*, 2021). In support of this, Fubah and Moos (2022) posited that firms retrench workers to decrease costs. This implies that employment relationships for SMMEs must be flexible. Further, during crisis periods, owners of SMMEs can downsize to reduce operating costs or sell their companies to save them. If the worse comes to the worst, SMMEs can exit the market.

Research Gaps

In practice, there is a dire need to design monitoring or tracking mechanisms to examine the efficacy and implementation of the measures introduced by the governments (Lal *et al.*, 2020; Mahajan, 2020; Razumovskaia *et al.*, 2020). To successfully deal with extended external shocks, inventive and speedy crisis responses should balance structured and planned activities with impromptu entrepreneurial activities (Puthusserry *et al.*, 2022). Puthusserry *et al.* (2022) further indicated that these activities must be suggested depending on the firm life cycle phases. Further review of the literature discovers that governments design general and directed policies and procedures to lessen the negative influences of the pandemic on SMMEs. However, the effect of general and targeted policies on SMMEs is not apparent (Dai *et al.*, 2021). Hence, the impact of general and targeted policies on SMMEs must be rigorously analysed in practice, implementing data from several economies (Dai *et al.*, 2021). Further research is required to examine the efficacy of government policies to support the redevelopment and recovery of SMMEs.

Reviewed literature indicated that, in practice, there is scanty prior research concerning the post-disaster policy needs of SMMEs impacted by the pandemic. As a result, more research on the post-disaster policy needs of SMMEs affected by the pandemic should be executed. Learning from the pandemic, suitable crisis management strategies that deal with short-term and long-term after-effects must be crafted. Puthusserry *et al.* (2022) articulated that research that adopts quantitative techniques (incorporating quasi-experimental research designs) that deal with changes in economy/industry or more granulated echelons must be conducted. Using quantitative techniques helps draw causal intuitions into various areas of the study that assist corporates in navigating the COVID-19 pandemic and other forthcoming crises. Moreover, more research is required to recognise the "survival patterns" of SMMEs that will seem robust in the long term and lead to modifications of the business models of SMMEs (Buzulukova and Sheresheva, 2021).

Conclusions

The chapter presented a systematic literature review analysing government policy interventions and combating strategies that can improve SMME resilience during and after the COVID-19 pandemic in BRICS economies. The findings underscored myriad policy responses and combating strategies that can enhance SMME resilience during and after the pandemic in BRICS countries. Further, the study results illuminated some research gaps that can be exploited in this research area. These results could assist diverse stakeholders in comprehending the subject matter at hand. The study recommends that policymakers and SMMEs incorporate the stated policy responses and combating strategies when reacting to COVID-19-like pandemics and future multistage and multiheaded black swan crises on SMMEs. Policymakers should also design business incubators and promote the establishment of business houses to support the development of early-stage SMEs. Systematic literature reviews to examine policy responses and combating strategies for big corporates in BRICS economies can be conducted for future research. Although the study might have omitted some relevant studies, it can be enhanced by incorporating grey literature, probing other databases, and including studies published in other languages besides English. The study can be extended by incorporating articles on other emerging markets for more insights.

References

Banu, S., and Suresh, B. H. (2020) COVID-19 and its impact on micro, small and medium enterprises in India. Mukt Shabd Journal IX (X): 606–617.

Bartik, A., Bertrand, M., Cullen, Z. B., Glaeser, E. L., Luca, M., and Stanton, C. (2020) How are small businesses adjusting to COVID-19? Early evidence from a survey. Harvard Business School Working Paper 20 (102): 1–37.

Behera, M., Mishra, S., Mohapatra, N., and Behera, A. (2021) COVID-19 pandemic and micro, small and medium enterprises (MSMEs): Policy response for revival. Small Enterprises Development, Management & Extension Journal 47 (3): 213–228.

Bockel, A., Horisch, J., and Tenner, I. (2021) A systematic literature review of crowdfunding and sustainability: Highlighting what really matters. Management Review Quarterly 71 (2): 433–453.

Bouazza, A. M. (2015) Establishing the factors affecting the growth of small and medium-sized enterprises in Algeria. American International Journal of Social Science 4 (2): 101–115.

Boucas da Silva, D. L., Miranda, A. L., and Hoffmann, V. E. (2021) Live or let die: Strategies for coping with COVID-19 from a business perspective in Sao Luis do Maranhao, Brazil. Revista Brasileira de Pesquisa em Turismo, Sao Paulo 15 (1): 2203.

Buzulukova, E., and Sheresheva, M. (2021) SME strategies to meet COVID-19 crisis and to stay competitive in post-pandemic time: the evidence from Russia. In: Proceedings of the European Marketing Academy, 50th (94703).

Chernova, C., and Neklyudova, N. (2022) The impact of the coronavirus pandemic on small and medium-sized enterprises in Russian Federation. SHS Web of Conferences 135: 01005.

Chetia, M. (2020) The impact of COVID-19 pandemic on MSME sector of India – Challenges and prospects. International Journal of Humanities and Social Science Invention 9 (7): 59–63.

Dai, R., Feng, H., Hu, J., Jin, Q., Li, H., Ranran, W., Wang, R., Xu, L., and Zhang, X. Z. (2021) The impact of COVID-19 on small and medium-sized enterprises: Evidence from two-wave phone surveys in China. China Economic Review 67 (C): 101607.

Dey, M., and Diswas, P. (2020) A review on the impact of COVID-19 on MSMEs in India. International Journal of Creative Research Thoughts 8 (12): 3061–3069.

Dladla, L. G. (2021) The economics of the COVID-19 pandemic and its effects on small businesses in South Africa. Asian Journal of Economics and Finance 3 (1): 59–69.

Du, L., Razzaq, A., and Waqas, M. (2023) The impact of COVID-19 on small- and medium-sized enterprises (SMEs): Empirical evidence for green economic implications. Environmental Science and Pollution Research 30: 1540–1561.

Duggappa, V. (2020) Impact of COVID-19 on Indian MSME sector – Issues and challenges. Intercontinental Journal of Marketing Research Review 8 (7): 1–11.

Fisch, C., and Block, J. (2018) Six tips for your (systematic) literature review in business and management research. Management Review Quarterly 68 (2): 103–106.

Fubah, C. N., and Moos, M. (2022) Exploring COVID-19 challenges and coping mechanisms for SMEs in the South African entrepreneurial ecosystem. Sustainability 14 (4): 1944.

Giancotti, M., and Mauro, M. (2020) Building and improving the resilience of enterprises in a time of crisis: From a systematic scoping review to a new conceptual framework. Economia Aziendale Online 11 (3): 307–339.

Glaesser, D. (2006) Crisis management in the tourism industry (2nd ed.). Butterworth Heinemann, Oxford.

Hansen, E. G., and Schaltegger, S. (2016) The sustainability balanced scorecard: A systematic review of architectures. Journal of Business Ethics 133 (2): 193–221.

Hossain, M. R., Akhter, F., and Sultana, M. M. (2022) SMEs in COVID-19 crisis and combating strategies: A systematic literature review (SLR) and a case from emerging economy. Operations Research Perspectives 9: 100222.

Indrakumar, D. (2020) COVID-19 and its impact on micro, small, and medium enterprises in INDIA. Manpower Journal LIV (3 & 4): 75–88.

Iqbal, B. A. (2022) BRICS as a driver of global economic growth and development. Global Journal of Emerging Market Economies 14 (1): 7–8.

Irfan, M., Razzaq, A., Suksatan, W., Sharif, A., Elavarasan, R. M., Yang, C., Hao, Y., and Rauf, A. (2021) Asymmetric impact of temperature on COVID-19 spread in India: Evidence from quantile-on-quantile regression approach. Journal of Thermal Biology 104: 103101.

Khan, I., Hou, F., Irfan, M., Zakari, A., and Phong, H. (2021) Does energy trilemma a driver of economic growth? The roles of energy use, population growth, and financial development. Renewable and Sustainable Energy Reviews 146 (C): 111157.

Lal, B. S., Sachdeva, P., Simran, and Mittal, T. (2020) Impact of COVID-19 on micro small and medium enterprises (MSMEs): An overview. International Journal of Multidisciplinary Research and Development 7 (12): 5–12.

Lavanya, G., and Deepika Rani, Ms. K. (2020) A study on impact of COVID-19 on small scale industries in Bangalore city. International Journal of Innovative Research in Management Studies 4 (12): 211–217.

Lu, Y., Wu, J., Peng, J., and Lu, L. (2020) The perceived impact of the COVID-19 epidemic: Evidence from a sample of 4807 SMEs in Sichuan Province, China. Environmental Hazards 19 (4): 323–340.

Ma, Z., Liu, Y., and Gao, Y. (2021) Research on the impact of COVID-19 on Chinese small and medium-sized enterprises: Evidence from Beijing. PLoS ONE 16 (12): e0257036.

Mahajan, Y. D. (2020) Study of impact of coronavirus pandemic on small and medium enterprises (SMEs) in India. GIS Science Journal 7 (9): 1–6.

McLellan, N. F., and Mzini, L. B. (2021) The effect of COVID-19 pandemic among local small-medium enterprises: a case of Johannesburg, region G. The 6th Annual International Conference on Public Administration and Development Alternatives 06–08 October 2021, Virtual Conference, pp. 479–488.

Mkhonza, V. M., and Sifolo, P. P. S. (2021) COVID-19 effect on business performance: SMMEs perspectives in a South African context. International Journal of Entrepreneurship and Business Development 4 (5): 727–743.

Njanike, K., and Edomah, N.(Eds.) ((2020) The factors influencing SMEs growth in Africa: A case of SMEs in Zimbabwe. In Regional Development in Africa. IntechOpen Limited.

Oni, O., and Omonona, S. (2020) The effect of COVID-19 on small retail businesses in Alice Town, South Africa. The Retail and Marketing Review 16 (1): 48–57.

Prasad, S., Su, H.-C., Altay, N., and Tata, J. (2015) Building disaster-resilient microenterprises in the developing world. Disasters 39 (3): 447–466.

Puthusserry, P., King, T., Miller, K., and Khan, Z. (2022) A typology of emerging market SMEs' COVID-19 response strategies: The role of TMTs and organizational design. British Journal of Management 33: 603–633.

Razumovskaia, E., Yuzvovich, L., Kniazeva, E., Klimenko, M., and Shelyakin, V. (2020) The effectiveness of Russian government policy to support SMEs in the COVID-19 pandemic. Journal of Open Innovation: Technology, Market, and Complexity 6: 160.

Roy, A., Patnaik, B. C. M., and Satpathy, I. (2020) Impact of COVID-19 crisis on Indian MSME sector: A study on remedial measures. Eurasian Chemical Communications 2 (9): 991–1000.

Sahoo, P., and Ashwani (2020) COVID-19 and Indian economy: Impact on growth, manufacturing, trade and MSME sector. Global Business Review 21 (5): 1159–1183.

Sajan, E. L. (2021) A study on the impact of the COVID-19 crisis on the Indian micro, small and medium enterprises. International Journal of Scientific Development and Research 6 (2): 267–274.

Sarkisian-Artamonova, A. A., and Kalacheva, O. N. (2020) Impact of the COVID-19 pandemic on the small and medium-sized business economy in Russia as an educational tool. In: Proceedings of ADVED 2020 – 6th International Conference on Advances in Education 5–6 October 2020, pp. 414–421.

Su, W., Guo, X., Ling, Y., and Fan, Y.-H. (2022) China's SMEs developed characteristics and countermeasures in the post-epidemic era. Frontiers of Psychology 13: 842646.

Suguna, M., Shah, B., Sivakami, B. U., and Suresh, M. (2022) Factors affecting repurposing operations in micro small and medium enterprises during COVID-19 emergency. Operations Management Research. https://doi.org/10.1007/s12063-022-00253-z

Sun, Y., Zeng, X., Zhao, H., Simkins, B., and Cui, X. (2022) The impact of COVID-19 on SMEs in China: Textual analysis and empirical evidence. Finance Research Letters 45 (C): 102211.

Sun, T., Zhang, W.-W., Dinca, M. S., and Raza, M. (2021) Determining the impact of COVID-19 on the business norms and performance of SMEs in China. Economic Research-Ekonomska Istrazivanja. https://doi.org/10.1080/1331677X.2021.1937261

Tranfield, D., Denyer, D., and Smart, P. (2003) Towards a methodology for developing evidence-informed management knowledge by means of systematic review. British Journal of Management 14 (3): 207–222.

Williams, S., and Schaefer, A. (2013) Small and medium-sized enterprises and sustainability: managers' values and engagement with environmental and climate change issues. Business Strategy and the Environment 22 (3): 173–186.

World Bank Group (2022) Small and medium enterprises (SMEs) finance. World Bank, Washington, DC.

Xiao, D., and Su, J. (2022) Macroeconomic lockdown effects of COVID-19 on small business in China: Empirical insights from SEM technique. Environmental Science and Pollution Research. https://doi.org/10.1007/s11356-022-20071-x

2 Policies and Strategies for the Mitigation of COVID-19 Impact on SMMEs in South Africa

Fiona Langry

Introduction

Coronavirus disease 2019 (COVID-19) was first identified in Wuhan, China, in December 2019, transmuting into a highly contagious respiratory disease and effectively leading to a global pandemic (WHO, 2023). Exponential rises in the number of infections led to government-sanctioned lockdowns, the subsequent curtailing of people movement, and the forcible imposition of social distancing, all converged to create a state of disaster for economies around the world (Javed, 2020). The African continent experienced the first confirmed case of COVID-19 in Egypt in February 2020, sparking fears that the rudimentary healthcare systems would be ill-equipped to cope with the devastating effects placed on the national healthcare systems (Gilbert *et al.*, 2020).

Despite this doomsday prediction, Africa accounted for less than 4% of COVID-related infection rates worldwide (Worldometer, 2020). Worldometer statistical data as of March 2022 denote the following statistics: Europe has the highest number of infection cases at 36%, Asia at 28%, North America at 20%, and South America at 12%. Similarly, the trends follow the same pattern when detailing the total death cases, with Africa accounting for just 4% of the cumulative death count of over six million people worldwide. A notable exception to this count lies with South Africa, representing 32% of the confirmed cases and 40% of total deaths on the African continent (Table 2.1). Table 2.1 shows the statistical data for the most affected countries on the African continent, highlighting South Africa as the forerunner in infection cases and deaths.

A National State of Disaster was declared by President Cyril Ramaphosa on 15 March 2020 in South Africa due to the COVID-19 pandemic and efforts to curtail the spread of the virus (Government Gazette, 2020). The lockdown regime implemented in South Africa in March 2020 included the national lockdown of border posts, major industries such as the alcohol and tobacco industries, and the closing of all schools and many businesses, effectively enforcing social distancing to curb the spread of COVID-19 (Gondwe, 2020). The South African government implemented a bold R500bn economic stimulus package

DOI: 10.4324/9781003475606-4

Table 2.1 Summary of Africa COVID-19 detect data by country as at March 2022

No	Country	Total Cases	Total Deaths	Tot Cases/1M pop	Deaths/1M pop	Total Tests	Tests/1M pop	Population
1	South Africa	3,704,218	99,881	61,137	1,649	23,585,561	389,272	60,588,931
2	Morocco	1,162,497	16,052	30,869	426	11,237,010	298,384	37,659,611
3	Tunisia	1,029,762	28,065	85,597	2,333	4,475,031	371,978	12,030,364
4	Libya	501,135	6,377	71,272	907	2,464,710	350,536	7,031,257
5	Egypt	495,373	24,277	4,689	230	3,693,367	34,963	105,637,902
6	Ethiopia	469,455	7,489	3,917	62	4,601,985	38,402	119,835,892
7	Kenya	323,289	5,647	5,794	101	3,473,702	62,255	55,798,153
8	Réunion	318,695	689	351,662	760	1,535,875	1,694,753	906,253
9	Zambia	315,623	3,962	16,383	206	3,322,571	172,469	19,264,712
10	Algeria	265,550	6,871	5,874	152	230,861	5,107	45,206,370
11	Botswana	263,950	2,619	108,492	1,076	2,026,898	833,124	2,432,889
12	Nigeria	255,103	3,142	1,187	15	4,589,725	21,359	214,881,328
13	Zimbabwe	244,519	5,427	16,052	356	2,156,817	141,585	15,233,322
14	Mozambique	225,210	2,200	6,876	67	1,289,244	39,362	32,753,427
15	Uganda	163,768	3,595	3,397	75	2,527,540	52,426	48,211,698
16	Ghana	160,819	1,445	4,997	45	2,387,305	74,179	32,182,951
17	Namibia	157,523	4,016	60,131	1,533	975,199	372,261	2,619,666
18	Rwanda	129,647	1,458	9,602	108	5,024,291	372,127	13,501,562
19	Cameroon	119,544	1,927	4,319	70	1,751,774	63,295	27,676,452
20	Angola	99,003	1,900	2,860	55	1,473,371	42,565	34,614,921
21	DRC	86,461	1,335	918	14	846,704	8,987	94,218,722
22	Senegal	85,831	1,964	4,905	112	1,033,634	59,069	17,498,815
23	Malawi	85,561	2,626	4,283	131	557,258	27,897	19,975,683
24	Ivory Coast	81,655	796	2,970	29	1,455,273	52,927	27,495,892
25	Eswatini	69,552	1,392	58,906	1,179	494,417	418,738	1,180,732
26	Madagascar	63,928	1,380	2,211	48	407,670	14,102	28,908,966
27	Sudan	61,775	4,888	1,355	107	562,941	12,345	45,601,119
28	Mauritania	58,662	981	12,073	202	769,026	158,276	4,858,752
29	Cabo Verde	55,925	401	98,750	708	400,982	708,040	566,327
30	Gabon	47,570	303	20,543	131	1,584,243	684,161	2,315,598

(Continued)

Table 2.1 (Continued)

No	Country	Total Cases	Total Deaths	Tot Cases/1M pop	Deaths/1M pop	Total Tests	Tests/1M pop	Population
31	Seychelles	39,761	163	400,050	1,640			99,390
32	Burundi	38,308	38	3,065	3	345,742	27,667	12,496,550
33	Togo	36,878	272	4,283	32	708,953	82,334	8,610,730
34	Mayotte	36,745	187	129,348	658	176,919	622,783	284,078
35	Guinea	36,435	440	2,651	32	660,107	48,035	13,742,206
36	Mauritius	35,380	934	27,741	732	358,675	281,229	1,275,382
37	Tanzania	33,773	800	539	13			62,644,755
38	Lesotho	32,775	697	15,094	321	415,510	191,362	2,171,329
39	Mali	30,453	727	1,433	34	640,225	30,130	21,248,603
40	Benin	26,952	163	2,128	13	604,310	47,709	12,666,461
41	Somalia	26,400	1,348	1,585	81	400,466	24,049	16,651,755
42	Congo	24,059	383	4,184	67	347,815	60,485	5,750,478
43	Burkina Faso	20,751	375	948	17	248,995	11,378	21,883,842
44	South Sudan	17,093	138	1,497	12	351,877	30,817	11,418,421
45	Equatorial Guinea	15,899	183	10,729	123	295,501	199,418	1,481,816
46	Djibouti	15,573	189	15,379	187	292,984	289,339	1,012,596
47	CAR	14,649	113	2,945	23	81,294	16,345	4,973,503
48	Gambia	11,973	365	4,727	144	155,686	61,468	2,532,811
49	Eritrea	9,723	103	2,678	28	23,693	6,526	3,630,451
50	Niger	8,788	308	342	12	235,282	9,153	25,704,992
51	Guinea-Bissau	8,113	169	3,962	83	127,492	62,264	2,047,590
52	Comoros	8,076	160	8,960	178			901,301
53	Sierra Leone	7,674	125	930	15	259,958	31,492	8,254,605
54	Liberia	7,397	294	1,406	56	139,824	26,577	5,261,087
55	Chad	7,267	190	422	11	191,341	11,104	17,232,144
56	Sao Tome and Principe	5,941	73	26,273	323	29,036	128,407	226,125
57	Western Sahara	10	1	16	2			622,467
58	Saint Helena	2		327				6,108
	Total:	11,658,451	252,043					

to counter the negative impact on the economy in the wake of harsh lockdown measures, instituting macroeconomic policy measures that reduced the interest rates while also providing business relief packages.

Small, Medium, and Micro Enterprises (SMMEs), informal traders and individuals in low-income households were the most impacted (Casale and Posel, 2020), with unemployment declining 18% in the period February to April 2020, resulting in the loss of three million jobs from (Ranchhod and Daniels, 2020). Extant literature denotes that Small, Medium, and Micro Enterprises (SMMEs) are integral towards driving economic growth in developing countries by reducing unemployment and contributing to the overall Gross Domestic Product (GDP) (Surya et al., 2021). The adverse effects of strict lockdown measures and the subsequent unprecedented challenges faced by the self-employed, informal traders and the inability of many SMMEs to work remotely resulted in the downsizing and closure of many businesses (Belitski *et al.*, 2022). The continued survival of the SMME sector is an integral driver of economic growth and recovery in South Africa, and this paper seeks to identify mitigating policies and strategies that can be deployed in the context of the ongoing COVID-19 pandemic. This paper consists of four sections: A literature review to document the economic impact of the COVID-19 pandemic, the Impact of COVID-19 on the SMME sector, and a discussion and recommendations for the South African SMME sector, with the last section providing concluding remarks.

Literature Review

Economic Impact of COVID-19

The onset of the COVID-19 pandemic on the South African economy came when the economy was under heavy pressure and the country was in a technical recession (Chitiga-Mabugu et al., 2021). The reactionary lockdown measures instituted by the government to protect public health systems led to a sharp contraction of an already fragile economy. Despite government intervention to absorb the negative economic impact and protect certain industries and businesses, the resultant fallout detracted the economy to a 7.2% contraction in 2020 (Sekyere et al., *2020*). An already beleaguered economy was further impacted by Moody's downgrade in the first quarter of 2020, effectively rendering the South African economy to junk status and increasing the cost of borrowing from international financial markets.

Declining GDP Growth

The domestic economy was forecasted to contract by 7.2% in 2020, compounded by a deteriorating fiscal position which saw GDP realisation fall to 17.9% (National Treasury, 2020). Unemployment reached an 11-year high of

29.1%, exacerbated by COVID-19, which saw alarming increases in job losses due to government-sanctioned lockdowns (Arndt *et al.*, 2020). Government stimulus packages implemented to counter the harsh lockdown measures saw the debt to GDP burden increase to an estimated 81.8% for the 2020/2021 period (National Treasury, 2020), leading to a further decline in the per capita income and having a detrimental effect on the livelihoods of the South African populace.

Declining Trade Volume

The World Trade Organisation (WTO, 2020) predicted a sharp decline for 2020 in the global economy as the COVID-19 pandemic upended major industries due to enforced lockdowns. Extreme disruptions in global supply chains and regional trade due to extensive containment measures to stop the spread of the virus contributed to a contraction of the export demand and supply with various trading partners (Erero and Makananisa, 2021). Closed borders, reduced or cancelled imports of non-essential items, and the disruption to the agri-food supply chains were catalysts to an already strained South African economy in the middle of a recession (Sekyere *et al.*, 2020).

Context of the SMME Sector in South Africa

Classifying Small, Micro and Medium Enterprises

SMMEs are widely regarded as the growth drivers for the economy as they create employment, assist in poverty alleviation, and contribute towards the socioeconomic development of a country (Tambunan, 2021). The Small Enterprise Development Agency (SEDA) in South Africa categorises the SMME sector into the formal, informal, and non-VAT registered business sectors. It declares that the number of SMMEs grew by 2.5% to 2.61 million for the fiscal year 2020Q1, of which 1.7 million can be attributed to the informal sector. The majority of the SMME businesses in South Africa operate from the informal sector, encompassing street trading, backyard manufacturing, and home-based enterprises, and, according to Berry et al. (2002), can be classified as "survivalist self-employed persons from the poorest layers of the population". Extant literature (Kamunge, Njeru and Tirimba, 2014; Fatoki, 2014) denote that the survival rate is very poor for many small businesses, especially in the first five years, which is attributed to a lack of finance, technology knowledge, and economic uncertainty cited as some factors impeding the viability of the business operations and growth (Islam and Abd Wahab, 2021). It is prudent to note that these survivalist SMME entities are highly susceptible to economic shocks, as evidenced in the wake of the COVID-19 pandemic (Bimha and Primrose, 2021).

Factors Affecting the Survival and Growth of SMMEs

Internal and external factors play an integral role in the viability and sustainability of small businesses (Bashir, Wadari and Ibrahim, 2021). The internal environment challenges comprise poor management competency and business management training, lack of financial knowledge, the subsequent hindrance of access to finance, and a poor understanding of technological capabilities (Sitharam and Hoque, 2016). Macro-environmental factors in the South African economic climate, such as interest rates, inflation, and high unemployment, compounded by the weak rand, are all determinants in the factors that negatively impact the growth of small businesses according to Sitharam and Hoque (2016). Global Market Research Company (IPSOS, 2020), in an online survey undertaken in September 2020, postulated that over 55% of SMME business owners in South Africa expressed concern over the viability and sustainability of their business as a direct result of the COVID-19 pandemic.

Government Support Initiatives for SMMEs in South Africa

In its awareness that the SMME sector is a key determinant towards promoting growth, creating job opportunities, and effectively alleviating poverty, the South African government established the National Small Business Act (102 of 1996). The National Development Plan (NDP) of South Africa, adopted by the Cabinet in 2012, is a blueprint to reduce inequality and alleviate poverty by 2030. The SMME sector was identified as a potential driver in achieving these outcomes, as 90% of the projected 11 million jobs to be created were expected to be generated by SMMEs. Proposed support for SMMEs in the form of easing of rules for small businesses, the development of finance institutions, and public and private incubators were some of the initiatives outlined in the NDP. This was further solidified when the government introduced the Ministry of Small Business Development in 2014, primarily assisting the small business sector (SEDA, 2016).

Impact of COVID-19 on the SMME Sector

The Disaster Management Act, 2002 (Act No. 57 of 2002) dictates that all SMME businesses providing essential economic goods and services are allowed to trade. COVID-19 had far-reaching consequences for many SMME entities, notably for businesses with no paperwork to substantiate their claim as a legitimate SMME provider and doubly so for the informal sector, which was left with no consumer to trade with due to lockdown restrictions. Small businesses that did not register their businesses or employees for UIF or paid taxes were suddenly left with no income resources. This micro-trading space, which fuels the economic landscape for South Africa, was forced to lay off hundreds of employees and close their business. According to FinFind (2020) in their

November 2020 report, 42% of SMMEs closed due to the COVID-19 pandemic and resultant lockdown. The sectors hardest hit by the lockdown and with the most closures were: Construction (14.2%), Food and beverage (9.9%) and Hospitality (9.7%), resulting in a 60% loss of employment across all SMMEs (FinFind, 2020).

Methods

This study was undertaken via a secondary data collection method, encompassing external sources that provided integral insights and knowledge on the impact of COVID-19 on the SMME sector in South Africa. Extant literature was analysed from government-published data and statistical analysis referenced from credible sources, further explored to corroborate the themes identified by the literature. Wahono (2015) proclaims literature review as a "process of identifying, assessing, and interpreting all available research evidence of providing answers for specific research questions". The results and findings identified provide credibility to the negative impact of COVID-19 on the SMME sector in South Africa, which allows for the discussion and recommendations that will be unpacked.

Discussion and Recommendations

The COVID-19 pandemic continues to affect global economies and SMMEs, and South Africa is no exception. The enforced lockdown measures implemented during the early stages of the pandemic, coupled with restrictions on people's movement within the country, created major disruptions to all economic sectors within South Africa, resulting in the closure of many SMMEs. This statement is supported by a survey undertaken by Beyond Covid Business from the period July 2020 to March 2021, incorporating almost 4,500 companies, which denotes a bleak picture for the future of SMMEs:

- 56% were micro employers with a staff contingent of ten or less or small businesses with a staff contingent of 11 to 50.
- 26% of businesses across all categories reported closure.
- SMMEs planned to retrench an average of 13% of their staff contingent, equivalent to 1.2 million people.
- Of the business categories most affected, the hardest hit were the construction, hospitality, and manufacturing sectors.

Despite government intervention to assist SMMEs impacted by the pandemic and not being essential service providers, this initiative didn't extend to the micro-businesses and informal traders due to the administrative red tape involved, compounded with the lack of registration or formal business documents from these businesses (Khumalo, 2020). SEFA (2020) declared that unregistered companies were not eligible for assistance, and those submitting claims for financial reprieve must prove that COVID-19 has a material impact on business operations. The catalyst from this fallout resulted in mass unemployment, creating further dependencies on an already overburdened and over-extended government. SMMEs faced further challenges as most businesses operate in the services sector, which entails personal contact, which was disallowed by the level 5 and 4 lockdown measures, resulting in a lack of demand for production and services, leading to a considerable reduction in operational cash flow. Many SMMEs didn't have liquidity reserves, and for those that did, they did not extend to more than a few months at the least.

To ensure operational viability and sustainability during the rest of the pandemic and post-COVID-19, SMMEs must incorporate changes to their business model in conjunction with government and private sector assistance. Embracing digital technologies for SMMEs that can adopt going digital creates a platform for marketing services and selling products online, creating awareness and having social media engagement by word of mouth for the business (Amankwah-Amoah et al., 2021). A key premise of this model centres around implementing a digital adoption strategy and increasing the technological knowledge and skills of SMME business owners and employees.

Government and private sector assistance provided grants and tax exemptions while also providing much-needed abolition of red tape for informal businesses without required registration and financial documents. This can be established by including the informal sector in the SEFA blueprint document, providing financial relief in the form of a business grant, effectively investing in the informal sector. Government suspension or reduction in taxes promotes localisation of manufacturing, reducing the need to import the majority of textiles. Private sector funding in relief funds or deferred payment options for loans or rent payable can be implemented, giving the business a breather to gather liquidity reserves for the short term. The government and the private sector must align and implement initiatives that drive innovation and incorporate and build training and development centres that promote digital technologies and skill enhancement opportunities to manage a business.

Conclusion

The key premise of this paper was to identify mitigating policies and strategies that can be deployed in the context of the ongoing COVID-19 pandemic in the SMME sector in South Africa. The deteriorating fiscal position of the South African economy was further impacted due to the COVID-19 pandemic, increasing the debt burden to 81.8% for the 2020/2021 period. South Africa has to look to the future, post-COVID-19, to stimulate economic growth to increase the debt-to-GDP ratio. SMMEs are growth drivers for the economy, as they interact directly with the community and can thrive despite economic uncertainty due to many businesses' services. SMMEs also play an integral role in reducing unemployment, and government policies that promote the sustainability of SMMEs are required. Furthermore, long-term support from government policies that are geared towards lessening the technological skills gap and adoption of digital technologies, broadening the business management knowledge of how to operate an SMME, removing many administrative red tape hindrances for SMME operation and creating new markets via partnerships with bigger businesses are needed.

References

Amankwah-Amoah, J., Khan, Z., Wood, G. and Knight, G. (2021) COVID-19 and digitalisation: The great acceleration. *Journal of Business Research 136*: 602–611.

Arndt, C., Davies, R., Gabriel, S., Harris, L., Makrelov, L., Modise, B., Robinson, S., Simbanegavi, W., Seventer, V.D. and Anderson, L. (2020) Impact of Covid-19 on the South African economy. An initial analysis. Southern Africa – Towards Inclusive Economic Development.

Bashir, D., Wadari, S. and Ibrahim, Y. (2021). *Factors Affecting The Growth Of Small And Medium Scale Enterprises In Jigawa State Of Nigeria*. [online] Available at: https://www.ijiras.com/2021/Vol_8-Issue_4/paper_13.pdf (Accessed 25 Aug. 2021)

Belitski, M., Guenther, C., Kritikos, A.S. and Thurik, R. (2022) Economic effects of the COVID-19 pandemic on entrepreneurship and small businesses. *Small Business Economics 58*(2): 593–609.

Berry, A., Von Blottnitz, M., Cassim, R., Kesper, A., Rajaratnam, B. and van Seventer, D.E., 2002. The economics of SMMES in South Africa. *Trade and Industrial Policy Strategies*, *1*(1): 1–110.

Bimha, H. and Primrose, Z.J., 2021. The impact of Covid-19 on the small, medium and micro enterprises sector in Cape Town, South Africa. *International Journal of Research in Business, Economics and Management*, 5(5): 1–22.

Casale, D. and Posel, D., 2020. Gender and the early effects of the COVID-19 crisis in the paid and unpaid economies in South Africa. *National Income Dynamics (NIDS)-Coronavirus Rapid Mobile Survey (CRAM) Wave*, *1*, pp. 1–25.

Chitiga-Mabugu, M., Henseler, M., Mabugu, R. and Maisonnave, H. (2021) Economic and distributional impact of COVID-19: Evidence from macro-micro modelling of the South African economy. *South African Journal of Economics* 89(1): 82–94.

Erero, J.L. and Makananisa, M.P. (2021) Impact of covid-19 on the South African economy: A CGE, Holt-winter and SARIMA model's analysis. *Turkish Economic Review* 7(4): 193–213.

Fatoki, O. (2014) The impact of managerial competencies on the performance of immigrants owned enterprises in South Africa. *Mediterranean. Journal of Social Science* 5(6): 141–144.

Finfind (2020.) SA SMME COVID-19 Impact Report. https://knowledge.finfind.co.za/the-sa-smme-covid-19-impact-report (Accessed 23 March 2022).

Gilbert, M., Pullano, G., Pinotti, F., Valdano, E., Poletto, C., Boëlle, P.-Y., D'Ortenzio, E., Yazdanpanah, Y., Eholie, S.P., Altmann, M., Gutierrez, B., Kraemer, M.U.G. and Colizza, V. (2020) Preparedness and vulnerability of African countries against importations of COVID-19: A modelling study. *Lancet* 395(10227): 871–877.

Gondwe, G. (2020) Assessing the impact of COVID-19 on Africa's economic development. United Nations, Trade and Development. https://unctad.org/system/files/official-document/aldcmisc2020d3_en.pdf (21 March 2022).

Government Gazette. (2020) Declaration of Disaster Management Act, No. 43096, 15 March. https://www.gov.za/issues/national-development-plan-2030 (Accessed 23 March 2022).

IPSOS. (2020) SMME's – Understanding the impact of Covid-19 [online]. https://www.ipsos.com/en-za/smmes-understanding-impact-covid-19 (Accessed 23 March 2022).

Islam, A. and Abd Wahab, S. (2021) The intervention of strategic innovation practices in between regulations and sustainable business growth: A holistic perspective for Malaysian SMEs. *World Journal of Entrepreneurship, Management, and Sustainable Development* 11(1): 1–26.

Javed, A. (2020) Impact of COVID-19 on Pakistan's services sector. *Jurnal Inovasi Ekonomi* 5(3): 107–116.

Kamunge, M.S., Njeru, A. and Tirimba, O.I. (2014) Factors affecting the performance of small and micro enterprises in Limuru Town Market of Kiambu County, Kenya. *International Journal of Scientific and Research Publications* 4(12): 1–20.

Khumalo, S. (2020) First batch of govt's coronavirus relief funding to roll out to small businesses next week. https://www.fin24.com/Economy/first-batch-of-govts-coronavirus-relieffunding-to-roll-out-to-small-businesses-next-week-20200410 (Accessed 27 March 2022).

National Treasury. (2020) Supplementary Budget. National Treasury. http:www.treasury.gov.za/documents.national

Ranchhod, V. and Daniels, R.C., 2020. Labour market dynamics in South Africa in the time of COVID-19: Evidence from wave 1 of the NIDS-CRAM survey.

SEDA. 2016. *The Small, micro and medium enterprise sector of South Africa*. Available: seda.org.za/Publications/Publications/The Small, Medium and Micro Enterprise Sector of South Africa Commissioned by Seda.pdf . (Accessed 7 March 2022).

Sekyere, E., Bohler-Muller, N., Hongoro, C. and Makoae, M. (2020) The Impact of COVID-19 in South Africa. http://www.seda.org.za/Publications/Publications/SMME%20Quarterly%202020%20Q1.pdf (Accessed 22 March 2022).

Sitharam, S. and Hoque, M. (2016) Factors affecting the performance of small and medium enterprises in KwaZulu-Natal, South Africa. *Problems and Perspectives in Management* 14(2): 277–288.

Small Enterprise Finance Agency (SEFA). (2020) COVID-19 Response Programme [Online]. https://www.sefa.org.za/services/covidfunds (Accessed 27 March 2022).

Surya, B., Menne, F., Sabhan, H., Suriani, S., Abubakar, H. and Idris, M. (2021) Economic growth, increasing productivity of SMEs, and open innovation. *Journal of Open Innovation: Technology, Market, and Complexity* 7(1): 20.

Tambunan, T. (2021) Micro, small and medium enterprises in times of crisis: Evidence from Indonesia. *Journal of the International Council for Small Business* 2(4): 278–302.

Wahono, R.S. (2015) A systematic literature review of software defect prediction. *Journal of Software Engineering* 1(1): 1–16.

WHO (2023) Coronavirus disease (COVID-19). https://www.who.int/emergencies/diseases/novel-coronavirus-2019/advice-for-public (Accessed 9 December 2023).

World Trade Organisation (WTO). (2020) World Trade Outlook. https://www.wto.org/english/news_e/pres20_e/pr855_e.htm (Accessed on 23 March 2022).

Worldometer (2020) COVID Live – Coronavirus Statistics. https://www.worldometers.info/coronavirus/ (Accessed 9 December 2023).

3 COVID-19 and Sustainability of Indian MSMEs in Crisis

The Role of Government of India

Roli Raghuvanshi and Ravinder Rena

Introduction

The social and economic life of the world economies came to a standstill in lieu of the Coronavirus-19 outbreak. The economies, which used to be busy in enormous sectors and productivity, suddenly started looking forward to solutions to the never experienced problems before and started diverting resources to the required aspects. The impact of the COVID-19 outbreak was realised in all sectors of the economies, and the most affected was the manufacturing sector on which the developing and the emerging economies rests a lot. International Monetary Fund (IMF) stated that this crisis was worse than the great depression of 1929.

The Government of India (GOI) ordered a nationwide lockdown on 24 March 2020 for 21 days to fight the coronavirus pandemic. In a phased manner, the GOI and National Disaster Management Committee extended the lockdown several times, and later on, the lockdown was eased down in phases based on the circumstances in the containment zones.

Throughout the lockdown, the economy experienced a severe impact on various sectors, but the manufacturing sector was the hardest hit. The medium, small and micro enterprises suffered the most due to their size, lack of capital, and inability to prepare for any such shock, which came as a surprise, and they had no time to defend themselves.

The supply side is affected by a labour shortage and an interrupted supply chain in terms of a reduced supply of intermediate goods and raw materials. Capacity utilisation was therefore at stake when this all started, and on the other hand, the demand suffered due to the loss of jobs and reduced wages. Though the impact of coronavirus is inevitable on both large and small firms since medium and small enterprises are more susceptible to the tremors, it is important to know what will happen to their sustainability in the long run.

In India, the Ministry of Micro, Small, and Medium Enterprises is the apex authority forming the rules and regulations. As per the latest definition of MSMEs in India, the investment in equipment or machinery and plant defines the categories for the same (Table 3.1).

DOI: 10.4324/9781003475606-5

Table 3.1 Composite criteria: Investment in plant and machinery/equipment and annual turnover

Criterion	Manufacturing		Services	
	Turnover	Investment	Turnover	Investment
Micro	Rs. 5 crore (US$ 0.6 million)	Less than Rs. 25 lakh (US$ 0.03 million)	Rs. 5 crore (US$ 0.6 million)	Less than Rs. 10 lakh (US$ 0.01 million)
Small	Rs. 50 crore (US$ 6.8 million)	More than Rs. 25 lakh (US$ 0.03 million) but less than Rs. 5 crore (US$ 0.6 million)	Rs. 50 crore (US$ 6.8 million)	More than Rs. 10 lakh (US$ 0.01 million) but less than Rs. 2 crore (US$ 0.3 million)
Medium	Rs. 250 crore (US$ 34 million)	More than Rs. 5 crore (US$ 0.6 million), but less than Rs. 10 crore (US$ 1.4 million)	Rs. 250 crore (US$ 34 million)	More than Rs. 2 crore (US$ 0.3 million) but does not exceed Rs. 5 crore (US$ 0.6 million)

Source: Ministry of Micro, Small, and Medium Enterprises

Literature Review

The economic and social devolvement in economies is a contribution made by Medium and Small-Scale enterprises as MSMEs have an important role to play in the upliftment of the economies (Shaikh & Pahore, 2010; Toma et al., 2014; Ahmedova, 2015). Noteworthy importance is accepted worldwide for medium and small-scale enterprises as it contributes to the progress of nations. Gradually the MSMEs are making their mark in the progress of the nation and are garnering a lot of limelight throughout the world (Carrier, 1999). Multilateral agencies, governments, economists, and strategists are acknowledging the importance of MSMEs worldwide. They are considered to be one of the powerful means for the development of rural areas and the eradication of poverty.

As per the Annual Report on MSMEs, 2021, the small and Medium Enterprise sector employs approximately 40% of India's workforce and contributes almost 45% to India's manufacturing output. The contribution of Small and Medium Enterprises in total exports from the country stands to be around 40% (Liu, 2008). In the case of China, it states that the growth and development of small and medium enterprises have continuously supported Chinese economic growth. The share of medium and small-scale enterprises stands to be approximately 90% of the total SMEs in China, and the contribution of the same to the country's GDP stands to be approximately 60%, creating 82% of employment opportunities in the country. Thus, the importance of SMSEs is emphasised and it may become inevitable to consider it an important point of discussion in these troubled times.

The COVID-19 pandemic has made the MSME sector most vulnerable due to its small size, lower scale of operations, and limited financial resources, as they are not ready to deal with this unexpected situation (Sipahi, 2020). The revenue generation has suffered amply because of the problem of disruption in demand and production as they suffered due to raw materials and labour unavailability (Singh, 2020). COVID-19 compelled the enterprises to curtail their production due to a lack of labour, raw materials, and finances, or they had to switch to producing PPE kits, masks, and other essential items with little time to adjust (Tripathy, 2020). All India manufacturers conducted a survey on the Indian enterprises and concluded that self-employed MSMEs had no chance to recover and, therefore, initiated shutting down their units in distress. (Tripathy & Bisoyi, 2021). In the export sector, the units which were into manufacturing of garments accounted for approximately 150 crores in the period of March 2020 to May 2020 (Roy, 2020). $1.5 billion is the estimated loss for the leather-based MSMEs in India, and they are suffering regarding payment to labourers, overhead payments, inadequate supply of raw material, forced labour migration, etc. (Tripathy & Bisoyi, 2021).

Though the Indian government adopted various measures to drive their MSMEs, some studies identified gaps in the strategies formulated to revive this sector (Sipahi, 2020). The GOI has taken stimulus measures and liquidity support to safeguard the interests of MSMEs so that the continuation of business does not break and their capacities are safeguarded (Chauhan, 2020; WTO, 2020). However, there are problems related to informal MSMEs accounting for approximately 63.4 million enterprises, mainly the micro-ones. It was also revealed that the correction measures taken by GOI were trying to revive the MSMEs indirectly. Hence, a proper comprehensive policy is needed to downsize the effect of COVID-19 on small and medium enterprises. The measures taken by the GOI so far are not enough, and more measures must be considered for the revival of the sector (Raney, 2020). It is important and inevitable to have a proper policy to revive the sector and safeguard the stakeholders' interests in the MSME sector (Ghosh, 2020).

Technological innovation, employment generation, and improvement in people's standard of living are the spillover effects of MSMEs in the Chinese economy (Lingli, 2020). According to ILO (International Labour Organisation) data from 99 economies reveals that the MSMEs generate 70% of employment and self-employment opportunities. At the same time, the "2020 China's Small and Medium-sized Enterprise Market Status Survey and Development Trend Forecast Analysis Report" released by China Industry Research Network shows that by the end of 2019, Chinese Small, Micro, and Medium-sized enterprises accounted for 99.7% of the total number of enterprises in the country. Among them, small and micro enterprises accounted for 97.3%. Chinese SMEs contribute more than 50% of taxation, more than 60% of GDP, more than 70% of technological innovation, more than 80% of urban labour employment, and more than 90% of the number of enterprises. Data from 1993 to 1998 reveals that the MSMEs are better than those large enterprises in terms of value addition and better operating capabilities (Yifu & Yongjun, 2001).

As the literature review states various examples of MSMEs' contribution to different sectors of the economy, it is imperative to understand the role of MSMEs in the Indian context.

Role of MSMEs in India

Activity based percentage share of MSME's in India

- Manufacturing
- Trade
- Services
- All

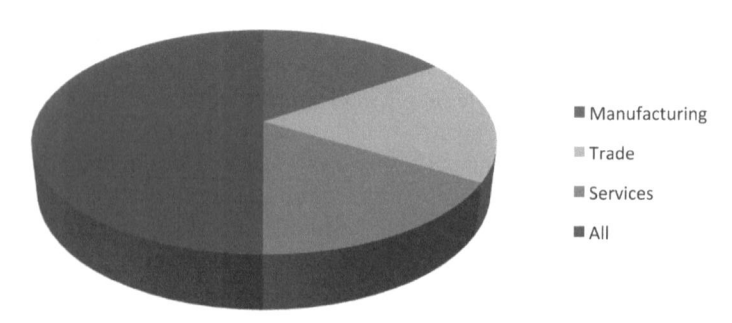

Figure 3.1 Activity-based percentage share of MSMEs in India

Contribution of MSMEs to the Indian Economy

The Central Statistics Office, Ministry of Statistics and Programme Implementation, has revealed that the gross value added by the Share of Micro, Small, and Medium enterprises in the country's GDP in 2019–2020 was 30%. Gross value added (GVA) in All India Gross Domestic Product at current prices (2011–2012, 2019–2020) was 30.0%. In the country's total manufacturing, the MSME share stood at approximately around 36.9%. Directorate General of Commercial Intelligence and Statistics (DGCIS) data revealed that in 2019–2020, the share of MSME in total exports of India was 49.8%, and in the year 2020–2021, the share stood to be 49.5% (Figure 3.1).

Impact of COVID-19 on the MSMEs: Case of India

The Index of Industrial Production (IIP), which is considered an important and relevant parameter for analysis of the status of industrial output, is taken here to see the movements in IIP from April 2020 to December 2020 compared with its counterpart previous year data, i.e., 2019, on IIP in Use-Based Category (Figure 3.2 and 3.3).

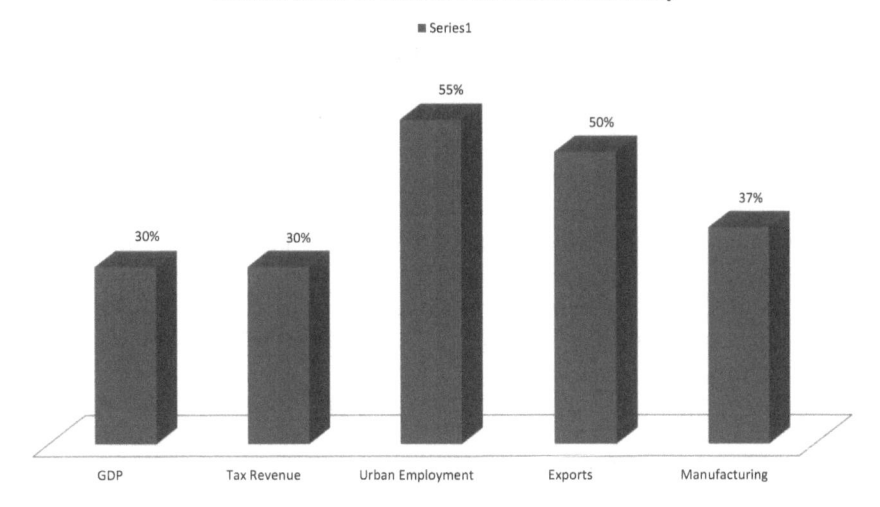

Figure 3.2 Contribution of MSMEs in Indian economy
Source: CSO, MOSPI, GOI

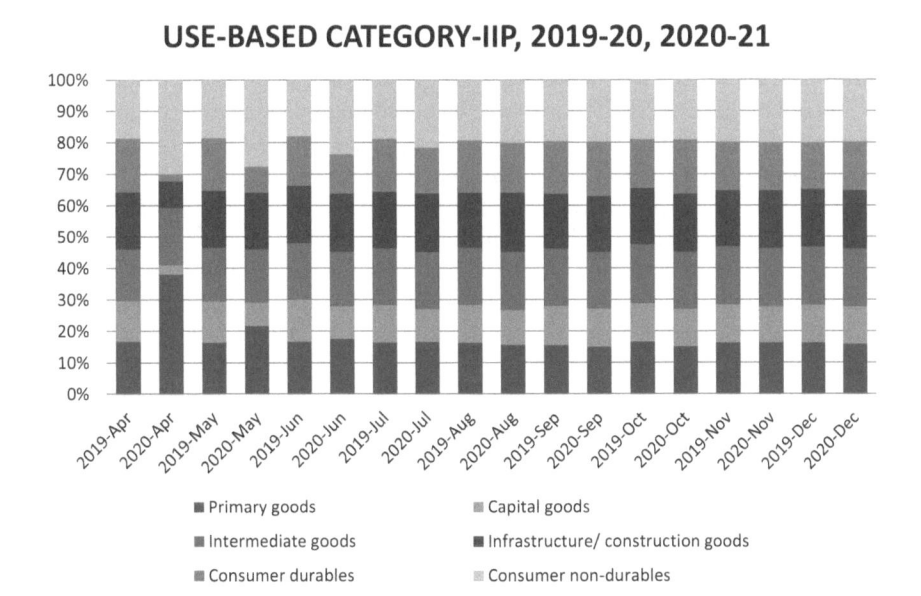

Figure 3.3 Use-based category-Index of industrial production, 2019–2020 to 2020–2021

The data analysis reveals that the year 2020, post-lockdown, has hampered the IIP of the nation, as shown in Figure 3.5. It could be understood that IIP data, though majorly considers the data of registered firms, as the growth of MSMEs, depends upon the growth of industrial production, we can understand that the MSMEs did get affected because of a downturn in the IIP when compared to the IIP 2020–2021 with the previous IIP 2019–2020.

The manufacturing sector constitutes 77.63% of the IIP in India, and the contribution of MSMEs in manufacturing is 31% as per the Ministry of Micro, Small, and Medium Enterprises, GOI, in their Annual Report 2020–2021. Therefore, it is inevitable to discuss the IIP of the manufacturing sector, which plays a vital role in the economy in terms of productivity and employment. Comparing the data of 2019–2021 with 2021–2022, we understand the dip in the manufacturing sector's performance due to the coronavirus pandemic.

Analysing the monthly growth rate data for April 2020–December 2021, we see that from April 2020 to September 2020, the growth rate was devastating and negative. It started recovering from October 2021 onwards but, more or less, remained at an extremely low level. March 21 saw a positive increase, but only to slump later on April 21. Since May 21, the trend has been a declining growth rate, which is a matter of concern for medium, small, and micro enterprises as they will be facing severe consequences.

No. of Persons Employed by MSMEs in India

Small, micro, and medium enterprises have played a major role in the employment generation of the country. The data in Table 3.2 reveals the registered firms' and employment generation statuses. The Urban MSMEs have a share of 55%, and the rural MSMEs contribute 45%. Micro units play a very important role as we can see that 1,076.19 lakh people are engaged in the micro units, which displays the contribution of the same for the economy.

The distribution of workforce in the MSMEs in India is of utmost importance as after agriculture; it is the medium, micro and small enterprises which give a maximum number of employments. Any downturn in the MSME post-COVID-19 will severely affect the employment rate also in a negative manner both in rural and urban areas.

Table 3.2 Employment status in MSMEs, India, rural and urban (lakhs)

Sector	Micro	Small	Medium	Total	Share (%)
Rural	489.30	7.88	0.60	497.78	45
Urban	586.88	24.06	1.16	612.10	55
All	1,076.19	31.95	1.751	109.89	100

Source: Annual Report: 2020–2021, Ministry of Micro, Small, and Medium Enterprises, Government of India

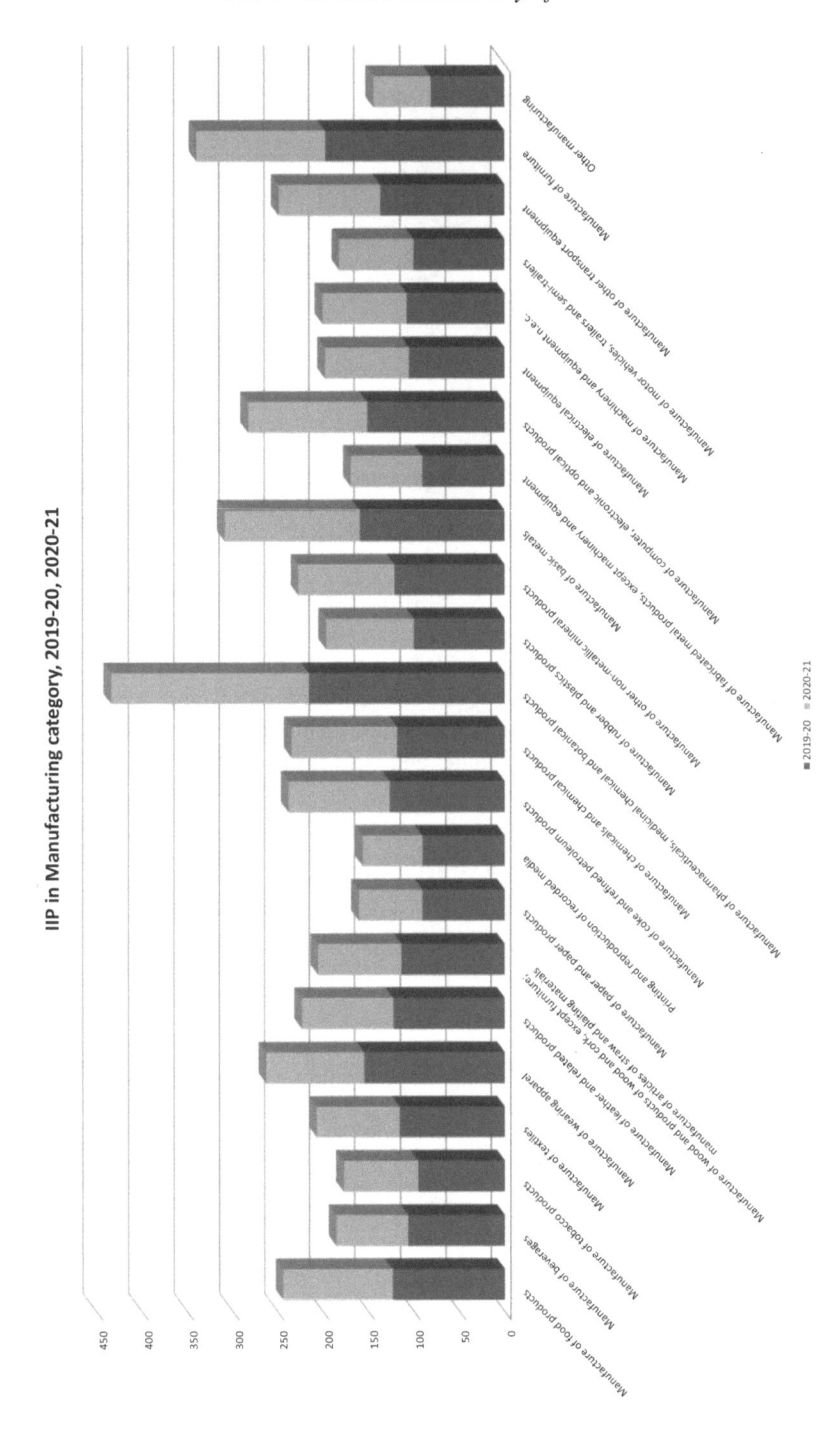

Figure 3.4 IIP in manufacturing category, India, 2019–2020 to 2020–2021

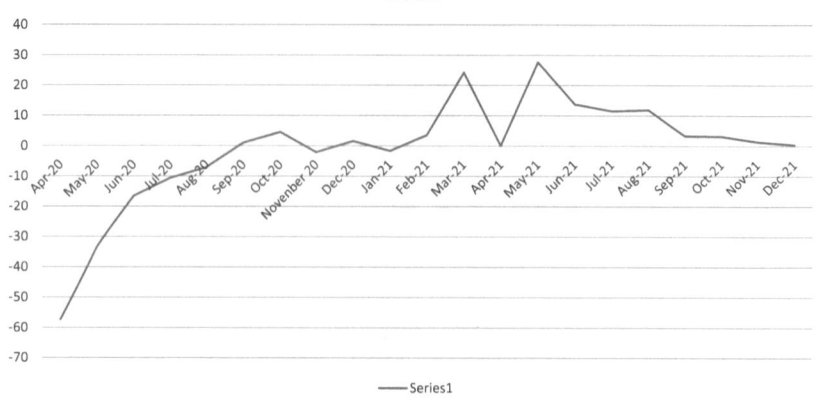

IIP Monthly growth rate in India, April 2020 to December 2021

Figure 3.5 Monthly IIP growth rate, India, April 2020–December 2021
Source: CEIC Database, Authors calculation

A firm-level survey conducted by the Asian Development Bank Institute on MSMEs in Asia reveals that on the employment front, the workforce will face dampening consequences because of closures and layoffs of employees. The survey was conducted in eight Asian Economies, including India, and data was collected on employment, sales revenue, and cash flows. The data on India is mentioned in the table given below.

Employment status of MSME's in India (%)

	Micro	Small	Medium
All	1076.19	31.95	1.751
Urban	586.88	24.06	1.16
Rural	489.3	7.88	0.6

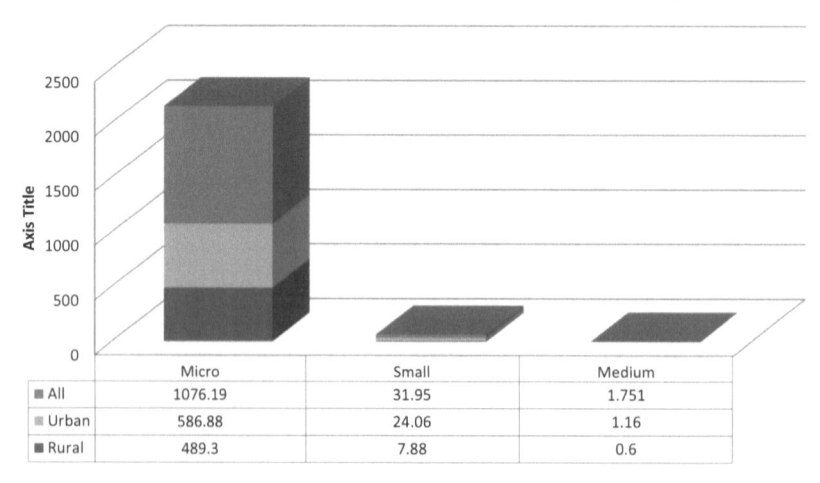

Figure 3.6 Source, annual report 2020–2021, MSME, GOI, Authors calculations

Table 3.3 Survey on employment, sales, and cash flow of firms in India

Sl. No	Analysis base (Survey of MSME firms)	Corresponding response (%)
1	Percentage of firms that reduced permanent employees	49%
2	Percentage of firms that reduced permanent employees by more than 40%	17%
3	Percentage of firms that reduced temporary employees	60%
4	Percentage of firms that reduced temporary employees by more than 40%	22%
5	Percentage of firms that experience sales decline	78%
6	Percentage of firms who experienced more than 40% of decline in sales	36%
7	Percentage of firms with cash shortage	46%
8	Percentage of firms that experienced temporary exit	26%
8	Percentage of firms with both cash shortage and exit experience	12%

Source: Asian Development Bank Institute, Working paper series, No. 1241, March 2021

Table 3.3 reveals the percentage of decline in employment of permanent and temporary workers due to the COVID-19 effect. The firms in the MSME sector faced challenges regarding employment and a cash shortage, and many were bound to exit from the business, as revealed in the table.

Impact of COVID-19 on Indian Exports

The data collected from DGFT and GOI reveals a sharp decline in the total exports of India when the 2019–2020 data was compared with 2020–2021 data on total exports from India on a month-on-month basis. The growth rate calculated for the same revealed a negative growth overall, as can be seen from Figure 3.8, due to the COVID-19 impact, and it was only after January 2021 that the economy started experiencing a positive growth rate, although a lower growth rate than the previous counterpart year, as visible from Figure 3.9.

Figure 3.8 reveals that the February to April 2021 export growth rate brought some hope for the industries and economy. However, the sharp decline thereafter crowded out the scenario. Till December 2021, the growth rate of Indian exports has been somewhat at a very low level, which confirms the devastating bearing of the pandemic on Indian exports.

The commodities with a dynamic role in the impressive performance of Indian Exports were also analysed. The commodities selected were decided based on their weightage in the total exports from India. The considered commodities

India's total export growth rate on monthly basis, April to December, 2019, & 2020

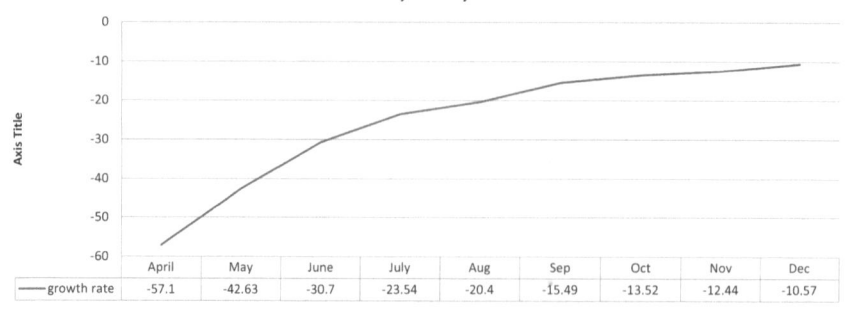

	April	May	June	July	Aug	Sep	Oct	Nov	Dec
growth rate	-57.1	-42.63	-30.7	-23.54	-20.4	-15.49	-13.52	-12.44	-10.57

Figure 3.7 Negative growth rate in total exports April 2019–December 2019 vs. April 2020–December 2020

Source: DGFT, Department of Commerce, Ministry of Commerce and Industry, GOI, Authors calculations

were the ones that had two or more weights. For instance Cereals (3.4637), Minerals fuels, mineral oils and products of their distillation, bituminous substances, mineral wax (9.2204), and pharmaceutical products (6.1666), plastic articles thereof (6.6575), Articles of apparel and clothing accessories, knitted or crocheted (2.3624), Articles of apparel and clothing accessories, not knitted or crocheted (2.1721), Natural or cultured pearls, precious or semi-precious stones, pre metals, clad with pre metals (2.0321), Iron and steel (8.9377), Articles of Iron and steel (4.1652), Nuclear Reactors, boilers, machinery and mechanical appliances thereof (2.2585), Electrical machinery and equipment and

Growth rate of India's total exports, monthly basis, Jan 2020-Dec 2020 vs. Jan 2021-Dec 2021

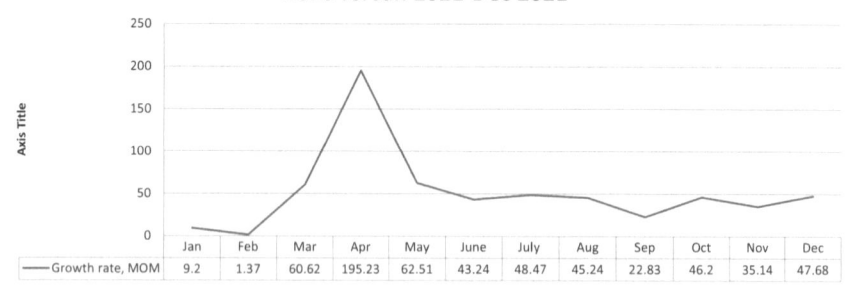

	Jan	Feb	Mar	Apr	May	June	July	Aug	Sep	Oct	Nov	Dec
Growth rate, MOM	9.2	1.37	60.62	195.23	62.51	43.24	48.47	45.24	22.83	46.2	35.14	47.68

Figure 3.8 Positive growth rate in total exports January 2020–December 2020 vs. January 2021–December 2021

Source: DGFT, Department of Commerce, Ministry of Commerce and Industry, GOI, Authors calculations

Figure 3.9 Commodities Export Growth Rate 2019–2020 vs. 2020–2021
Source: DGFT, Department of Commerce, Ministry of Commerce and Industry, GOI, Authors calculations

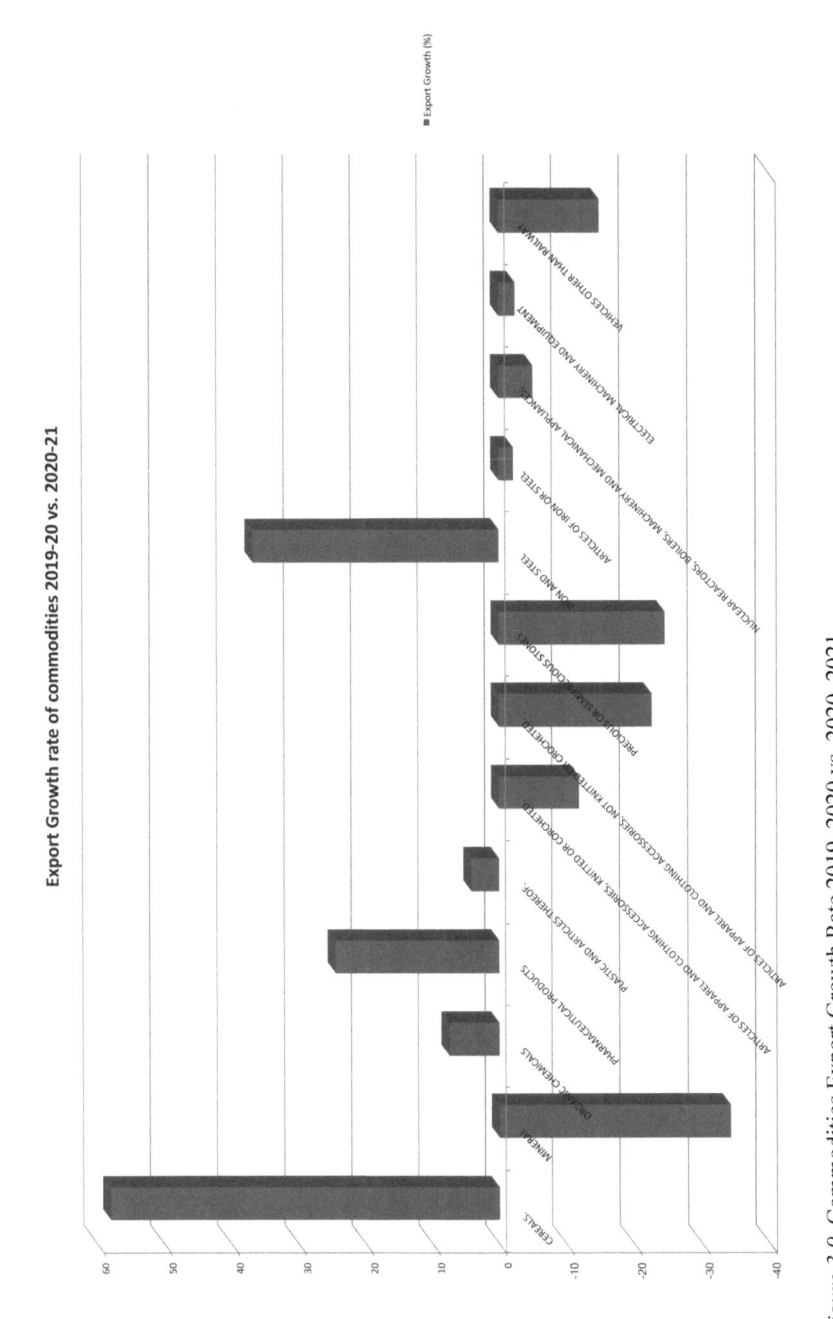

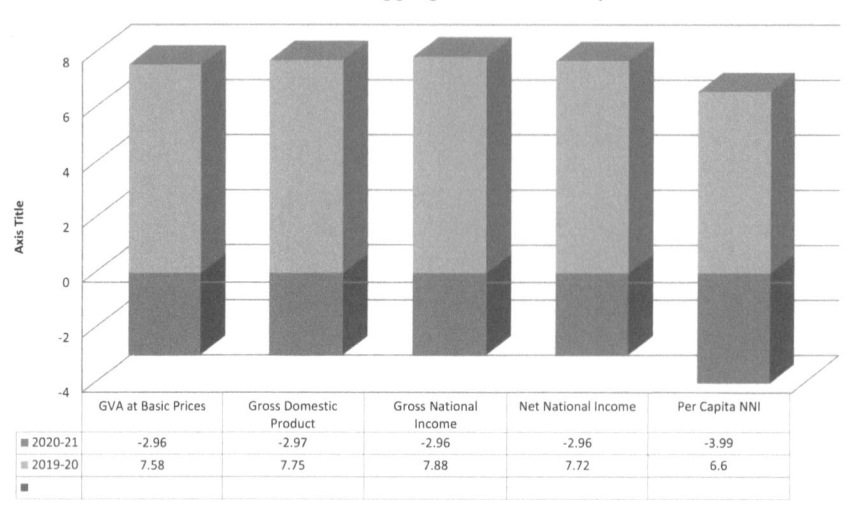

Macro economic aggregates at current prices

	GVA at Basic Prices	Gross Domestic Product	Gross National Income	Net National Income	Per Capita NNI
2020-21	-2.96	-2.97	-2.96	-2.96	-3.99
2019-20	7.58	7.75	7.88	7.72	6.6

Figure 3.10 Growth rate; macro-economic aggregates

Source: RBI handbook on statistics, Authors calculation, Data for 2020–2021 is provisional estimates.

parts thereof, sound recorders and reproducers, Television (6.4919), Vehicles other than railway or tramway rolling stock and parts and accessories thereof (4.8649).

The Indian Economy's Macroeconomic aggregates also reveal that COVID-19 has negatively impacted the same, as can be seen from Figure 3.10; the considered aggregates are gross value added at basic prices, gross domestic product, gross national income, net national income, and per capita net national income. Comparison between 2019–2020 and 2020–2021 reveals the negative growth rates for 2020–2021, as the impact of COVID-19 had brought a severe decline in the Macroeconomic aggregates.

Sustainability in Crisis: Policy Initiatives by Government of India

Aatmanirbhar Bharat Abhiyaan: A special measure due to the ample contribution of medium- and small-scale enterprises to economic development, the GOI realised that the pandemic-hit economy could be revived only if special consideration would be provided to the small- and medium-scale enterprises, as they play a vital role in building the nation. The Aatmanirbhar Bharat Abhiyaan package announced by the GOI allocated a substantial amount to the MSMEs. It ensured that the implementation was also taken care of so that the actual impact of the package could be realised and not only remain a mere announcement.

Apart from the ongoing credit schemes, the Ministry of Medium and Small-scale Enterprises made the following announcement to revive the sector. The actions comprise a move to bail out 200,000 suffering small- and medium-sized firms. The following are the measures:

- On 13 May, 2020, Under the Emergency Credit Line Guarantee Scheme (ECLGS), a collateral-free loan of up to 30,000 was announced as an additional credit facility to fulfil small- and medium-sized firms' revival and operational needs. An estimated number of beneficiary firms is approximately 45 lakhs of small- and medium-scale enterprises.
- To finance the working capital of street vendors, a provision of Rs. 10,000 was made. On 14 May 2020.
- On 17 May 2020, the GOI declared a reform of the IBC (Insolvency and Bankruptcy Code), and it stated that the insolvency proceedings have been suspended for one year. Also, it was decided that the debt that has emerged due to COVID-19 will not be considered a part of default, relieving many MSMEs. Also, there was an increase in the limit of a minimum threshold of up to Rs. 10 million to start the process of insolvency of firms.
- On 22 May 2020, a decision to reduce the rate of interest from 5.5% to 4% was taken to provide cheap loans to medium- and small-scale enterprises
- Announcement of credit facilities for MSMEs and vendors under the MUDRA scheme was made. An interest subsidy of 2% on small loans of up to 50,000 for 12 months was made.
- Equity infusion through fund of funds of Rs. 50,000 for capacity augmentation. It will uplift the spirit of MSMEs and help them get listed on the stock exchange.
- For women self-help groups, which form an important part of micro-enterprises, the collateral-free lending limit was increased from Rs. 10 lakhs to Rs. 20 lakhs with an estimation of supporting 2.5 lakh households.
- Refinancing facilities of Rs. 50,000 crores were announced for the National Bank for Rural Development (NABARD), the Small-Scale Development Bank of India (SIDBI) and the National Housing Bank at the policy repo rate.
- The GOI announced a provision of Rs. 20,000 crores as subordinate debt to support stressed medium- and small-scale enterprises that will need equity support. It was estimated that around two lakh units would benefit from this provision. Any functioning medium, small, and micro-enterprises which are stressed will get support.
- Government will provide support of Rs. 4,000 crores to Credit Guarantee Fund Trust to Medium and Small Enterprises (CGTMSE), which will provide partial Credit Guarantee support to Banks and the Promoters of the Medium, Small and Micro Enterprises will be given debt by banks, which the promoter will then infuse as equity in the unit.

- The Reserve Bank of India decided to decrease the repo rate, and the financial institutions could lend more to the stressed MSMEs and targeted to allocate more funds to the units. For example, the SBI in Mumbai targeted to allocate approximately Rs 700 crores to medium, small, and micro enterprises.
- A period of 45 days was decided for the GOI and central public sector undertaking to clear all dues of the MSMEs so that they do not face severe financial crunch.
- The global tenders of up to Rs. 200 crores were banned from participating in government procurement so that the interest of the domestic players could be safeguarded.
- Due to COVID-19, the platforms for MSMEs were out of the question to showcase their product; therefore, to offset the impact of not having trade fairs and exhibitions, e-platforms were arranged, and the units were linked to e-markets. This was supported by FINTECHS so that smooth transactions could take place.
- All the establishments that were situated under the Employees Provident Fund Organisation were provided with a relief package of Rs. 6,750 crores as the contribution of employees and employers was brought down to 10% from 12% to facilitate more liquidity. It was expected that around 3.4 crore employees and around 6.5 lakh employers would have the relief.
- For small and medium enterprises and non-banking financial institutions, the TDS was brought down by 25%, and for medium enterprises and non-banking financial institutions, the TDS was brought down by 25%, and the income tax return filing time limit was increased until 30 November 2020.

Challenges Ahead and Policy Recommendations

After going through the measures taken by the GOI, it was found that certain gap areas need to be filled. The major challenge faced by the Indian Small and medium enterprises is the upliftment of the MSMEs lying in rural areas. Financial accessibility and marketing their products is a major cause of concern. The struggle of small and medium enterprises could be seen in arranging for their electricity bills, disbursement of salaries, Internet and telephone charges, local taxes, and non-accessibility to easy bank loans. Apart from their daily struggle to arrange their overhead expenses, they also suffer because of their non-inclusivity in the system. The unregistered firms are the biggest sufferers as they are not eligible to access many government benefits. The registration issue intensifies their struggle for credit, marketing, technological upliftment, and non-accessibility to other infrastructural facilities.

The major area of concern is the identification of appropriate beneficiaries. The reason behind the ineffectiveness of the revival packages is the lack of adequate datasets, because of which the bottlenecks prevent the policies from getting implemented effectively; rather, these hurdles worsen the prospects of small and medium firms. A census on medium, small and micro enterprises was conducted in 2006–2007 and it was observed that the dataset was scattered and lacked uniformity.. The MSME databank, UAM (Udyog Aadhar Memorandum) and GSTN (Goods and Services Tax Network. Most of the data is gained through voluntary disclosures. In some cases, like GSTN, there is a mandatory requirement that only units with more than 4 million of turnover can register. These shortcomings deprive the economy of a comprehensive dataset. Even RBI's expert committee on MSMEs has disclosed a lack of a proper dataset on MSMEs in the economy. Therefore, an arrangement for a reliable and structured dataset is of utmost importance so that the benefits of packages reach the true beneficiaries in time; this states that the inclusiveness of unregistered MSMEs is very important.

On the financial aspect, as small and medium enterprises are more likely to be impacted severely as they are cash-strapped whenever hit by the crisis, providing emergency funding is a must. It will not only help the cash-strapped MSMEs but will also give a platform for their revival. So, funding programmes for emergencies is a must to do. Decreased interest rates, tax breaks, tax holidays, and provisions for conducive lending policies will greatly help.

Technological assistance is very important to help the SMEs survive in a crisis. It will train them to explore diversified business platforms to sell their product and help them build a strong network. The virtual platform has been of great help for businesses to survive across the globe as the economies have witnessed the same. Adequate training is of utmost importance so that the benefits of technological advancements could also help them sustain in crisis. As in India, the population distribution is biased towards the rural areas, where the majority of the Indian population resides, if technological inclusiveness is not worked upon then it is doubtful that the MSMEs could be revived as, the majority of them will be deprived to benefit and as a result, the sustainability of the entire MSME sector will be under question.

The implementation of well-conceptualised policies and their penetration among all MSMEs is another major area of concern. An effective and efficient transparency mechanism has to be in place so that the benefits reach out to the really in need. The direct cash transfer arrangements through Jan-Dhan, Aadhaar, and Mobile have definitely brought changes in the previous practices and have helped in making the system more transparent, but still, the loopholes could be seen because many people are still not part of financial inclusion, and the effective implementation still needs to be addressed. It is indeed a very effective platform for uplifting the marginalised communities and daily wage workers, but the government needs to speed up the process of financial inclusion. ILO, in its recent report, has mentioned clearly that financial assistance is very much required in the countries where majorly the workforce is in the informal sector. ILO very specifically quoted India, Nigeria, and Brazil that they must have a good mechanism of cash transfers in place so that the deprived section's upliftment could occur.

Post-pandemic, one more area of concern will be increasing NPA levels. The MSMEs have got support from the financial institutions for revival and are in a collateral-free mode. The responsibility of the government and financial institutions becomes more in terms of looking into this matter. Apart from financial assistance, the GOI must adopt the provision of deferment payments in case of utilities, and it will help the MSME units to survive, giving them more space to accommodate. Many countries such as China, Singapore, Taiwan, and Europe economies have adopted these measures, which have certainly given a big relief to cash-struck small and medium units.

Conclusion

Although the COVID-19 pandemic has made life difficult for everyone, especially small- and medium-scale enterprises, to overcome the situation, the GOI has made several provisions to address the situation. Though it is quite understood that the revival process is full of challenges and will take time to get everything back in place as the government and businesses are working together for the revival process, as is quite evident also from the policy initiatives, we hope that the MSME sector will be back on track in some period. After analysing the policy initiatives taken so far by the government and understanding the underlying challenges, the strategy will seek coordination between all stakeholders. Rebuilding of effective means to overcome the post-COVID-19 impact is inevitable. Rethinking the strategies related to diversification, marketing of products, market access and proper penetration, financial inclusion, transparency, and other related policies are the areas of concern. As businesses are being transformed by the new age digital era, there is indeed a need to create digital platforms and train businesses. The adoption of new-age technology will help small and medium firms to optimise cost and enhance opportunities for product development and diversification. Experiencing the present COVID-19 crisis, it is important to chalk up a conducive predicament supervision strategy that is capable of addressing both instantaneous and enduring costs.

References

Ahmedova, S. (2015) Factors for increasing the competitiveness of small and medium-sized enterprises (SMEs) in Bulgaria. *Procedia-Social and Behavioural Sciences*, *195*:1104–1112.

Carrier, C. (1999) The training and development needs of owner-managers of small businesses with export potential. *Journal of Small Business Management*, 37(4):30.

Chauhan, J. P. (2020) An impact of COVID-19 on Indian economy: A brief view of selected sectors. *EPRA International Journal of Multidisciplinary Research (IJMR)*, 6(6):9–12.

Financial Express (19 March 2020) Govt considers easier loan, tax rules for SMEs to help economy amid coronavirus. https://www.financialexpress.com/industry/sme/govt-considers-easier-loan-tax-rules-for-smes-to-help-economy-amid-coronavirus/1903106/ (Accessed 2 March 2023).

Ghosh, S. (2020) Examining the COVID-19 relief package for MSMEs. *Economic & Political Weekly*, *LV* (22):10–12.

Lingli, Y. (2020) The impact of COVID-19 on SMEs in province and the countermeasures. *Journal of Hubei University of Economics (Humanities and Social Sciences Edition)*, *17*(10):47–49+52.

Liu, X. (2008) SME development in China: A policy perspective on SME industrial clustering, in: Lim, H. (ed.), SME in Asia and Globalization, ERIA Research Project Report – 5: 37–68.

Singh, A. (12 June 2020). What about India's MSME Sector: COVID-19 pandemic and Indian MSMEs sector outlook. http://dx.doi.org/10.2139/ssrn.3696778

Shaikh, F. M., & Pahore, N. A. (2010) Performance review of export potential of Pakistani SMEs compared with developing countries. *Journal of Business Strategies*, *4*(2):10.

Sipahi, E. (2020) COVID-19 and MSMEs: A revival framework. *Research Journal in Advanced Humanities*, *1*(2):7–21.

Toma, S. G., Grigore, A. M., & Marinescu (2014) Economic development and entrepreneurship. *Procedia Economics and Finance*, *8*(0):436–443.

Tripathy, A. (2020) COVID-19 affect and micro, small, and medium enterprises (p. 5). *The Times of India* (Print).

Tripathy, S., & Bisoyi, T. (2021) Detrimental impact of COVID-19 pandemic on micro, small and medium enterprises in India. *Jharkhand Journal of Development and Management Studies*, *19*(1):8651–8660.

WTO. (2020) Helping MSMEs navigate the COVID-19 crisis. *World Trade Organisation*, *LXV* (12):1–8.

Yifu, L., & Yongjun, L. (2001) The development of small and medium-sized financial institutions and the financing of SMEs. *Economic Research*, (01):10–18+53–93.

4 The Impact of COVID-19 on Entrepreneurship Focusing on Small and Medium Enterprises in South Africa

Zamaswazi Cele, Ndivhuho Tshikovhi, and Fulufhelo Netswera

Introduction

The effects of the pandemic on SMEs were felt throughout the globe. For instance, the pandemic crisis negatively affected the hospitality and tourism industries in Kuwait by forcing small and medium enterprises (SMEs) in Kuwait to curtail much of their businesses (Al-Fadly, 2020). In March 2020, 45% of business owners indicated they had to suspend or shut down their businesses. A Kuwait COVID-19 business impact survey reported that 26% were about to collapse due to a revenue drop of over 80% (Al-Fadly, 2020). Businesses slowed down in one of the BRICS bloc countries, Russia, where most businesses were affected negatively by the COVID-19 pandemic that disturbed the global economy in February 2020. The Russian government imposed restrictions against the background of the spread of COVID-19, which did not allow businesses to operate normally, and the demand decreased (Razumovskaia *et al.*, 2020). At the end of 2019, there was a decline in sales in the SME sector, which was expected to increase in 2020. However, due to the COVID-19 pandemic that spread globally, it has decreased revenue by 78% in the SME sector, and 60% of entrepreneurs expect a further decline in revenue (Razumovskaia *et al.*, 2020).

Since the beginning of 2020, entrepreneurs have been experiencing difficulties in selling their products and services while facing challenges in important raw materials, particularly from China (also a member of the BRICS bloc), in which many entrepreneurs rely on their exports (Alessa *et al.*, 2021). Giones *et al.* (2020) state that the rise of the COVID-19 pandemic has caused a massive challenge for entrepreneurs because they could not continue with business as they were short of stock and product availability. Customers were unable to get serviced because of the COVID-19 pandemic disruption. Alessa *et al.* (2021) explain that the emergence from China and spread to the rest of the world, COVID-19 has caused a drastic variety of changes worldwide, and governments have been trying to find ways to slow its spread. Odusola and Mkhumane (2020) emphasise that COVID-19 has devastated the informal sector in South Africa.

DOI: 10.4324/9781003475606-6

No customers came to buy at the taxi ranks and train stations because of the lockdown restrictions, and few people went to work. Lightelm (2013) explains that the informal sector is collectively defined as small, unregistered businesses operating as street vendors and in-home businesses established on residential sites (often termed "Spaza shops" or "tuck shops" in South Africa). Lightelm (2013) continues to explain that, in contrast, small formal businesses are defined as businesses operating from fixed building structures located on business stands demarcated by local government (municipal) town planning regulations. Odusola and Mkhumane (2020) continue to explain that there was a huge loss for business owners who work in the beauty industry because hair and nail stylists were not allowed to work for months. Business owners only made a small portion of their pre-COVID-19 pandemic revenues. Many business owners failed to keep up with their monthly instalments for their business apartments or car instalments; they had no money left to buy new equipment due to the drop in customers. There was a ban on international travel; events were not allowed, and others were cancelled. The impact of the lockdown on these businesses was huge and direct (Odusola and Mkhumane, 2020).

The outbreak of COVID-19 has caused a major economic shock and has changed business operations. The South African government activated the Disaster Management Act with different alert levels that showed how the country is coping with the spread of the COVID-19 pandemic. The South African Government (2020a) has created a five-level COVID-19 alert system that has been introduced to manage the gradual easing of the lockdown. The Department of Health (2020) explains the criteria for determining alert levels: Alert levels determine the restrictions to be applied during the national state of disaster. These below-alerted levels also determine whether businesses should be operating.

a "Alert Level 1 indicates a low COVID-19 spread with a high health system readiness".
b "Alert Level 2 indicates a moderate COVID-19 spread with a high health system readiness".
c "Alert Level 3 indicates a moderate COVID-19 spread with a moderate health system readiness".
d "Alert Level 4 indicates a moderate to a high COVID-19 spread with a low to moderate health system readiness".
e "Alert Level 5 indicates a high COVID-19 spread with a low health system readiness".

As a result of these alert levels, this chapter looks at small and medium enterprises' dilemma by checking how SMEs survived under the lockdown restrictions. The changes that COVID-19 has brought towards SMEs and the way they operate on a normal basis. It will also look at how the government tried to intervene and help SMEs during the pandemic.

South African Economy during the COVID-19

South Africa is a developing country with a high unemployment rate; the COVID-19 pandemic made things worse for the country's economy because no exports and imports were happening there. The lockdown measures were felt economically in South Africa (Channing *et al.*, 2020). In 2019, the South African economy entered a technical recession in the fourth quarter, where economic growth had fallen to 1.5% compared to 3% in 2010. Unemployment was also rising at 27.3% in the first quarter, and by the third quarter it had reached 29.1% (Chitiga-Mabugu *et al.*, 2020). Statistics South Africa (2019) states that in 2019, poverty in South Africa registered at 49.2% compared with the 2015 stats, which were 55.5%. Poverty had decreased, but inequality was still high (Sulla and Zikhali, 2018).

According to the World Bank (2021) report, when the COVID-19 pandemic entered South Africa, they faced huge job scarcity and years of weak job creation. Even when the government finds solid solutions to the pandemic, employment has been negatively impacted far below the standards of upper-middle-class countries. The World Bank (2021) showed that the number of unemployed people decreased to 1.5 million by the end of 2020, and the salaries of people who still had jobs decreased by 10%–15% and 40%. As per the Reserve Bank of South Africa's report released in March 2020, the recovery of job losses clarifies the repo rate cut by 100 points basis from 6.25% to 5.25%. A further 100 basis points reduced the repo rate to 4.25% from 15 April 2020. The repo rate was reduced by a further 50 basis points from 22 May 2020 to 3.75% and by 25 basis points on 24 July 2020 to 3.50%. IOL (2021) explain that the South African Reserve Bank's decision to keep the repo rate unchanged at a record low of 3.5% and the prime lending rate at 7%, the decrease of all the interest rates was meant to put down the pressure to the customer from their debts and SMEs be able to manage paying loans. IOL (2021) explains that this would help support SMEs constantly having financial difficulties because of the COVID-19 pandemic and its impact. Keeping interest rates on hold was assisting many SMEs keep themselves afloat.

Small and Medium Enterprises (SMEs)

According to Fubah and Moos (2022:03), SMEs play a fundamental role in economic growth and development locally and globally. Al Buraiki and Khan (2018) concur that SMEs are the economic boosters of every country. SMEs create jobs, reduce unemployment and generate wealth. During the COVID-19 pandemic, SMEs were highly affected because of the lockdown restrictions that did not allow employees to work unless they were only essential workers. According to BusinessTech (2020b), the Department of Cooperative and

Government Affairs issued new rules stating the "essential services" accepted and processed to work for the 21-day COVID-19 lockdown. These rules made exceptions for the following sectors to work: "Medical, health (including mental health institutions), laboratory and medical services; disaster management, fire prevention, firefighting, and emergency services; financial services were needed so that they would be someone who is monitoring the banking and payments, including the Johannesburg Stock Exchange (JSE) and insurance services. Production and sales of the goods (related to food, cleaning and hygiene products, medical products, fuel, and basic goods such as airtime and electricity). Grocery stores, including spaza shops. Electricity, water, gas and fuel production, supply and maintenance critical jobs for essential government services as determined by the Head of National or Provincial Departments Birth and Death Certificates and replacement Identity Document ID documents, essential municipal services, care services and social relief of distress provided to older persons, mentally ill, persons with disabilities, the sick and children; funeral services, including mortuaries" (Gurría, 2020). Because of all these restrictions, SMEs have suffered from a shortage of workers and could not produce anything. The supply chain was affected, negatively affecting their sales and ability to fulfil financial obligations and pay employees' salaries. SMEs will always be the first sector affected by economic crises (Adam and Alarifi, 2021). The COVID-19 pandemic is a social and economic issue that affects people's lives. It hugely affects SMEs because the business has a good connection with people, whether they are customers or suppliers (Nugent and Yhee, 2002).

According to Oni and Omonona (2020), a Facebook survey has shown that 31% of SMEs have shut down during the spread of COVID-19 in 2020. Many business owners had to follow and obey the regulation by the government and health authorities to close businesses, which did not work for most of them because 52% of sole businesses were closed permanently. While hotels, cafes, and restaurants account for 43%, wellness, grooming, fitness, or other professional services account for 41%. A minority, 9%, claimed that the reason for shutting down was due to financial constraints, and 7% cited the absence of client demand. Therefore, many reasons resulted in SMEs shutting down permanently when the COVID-19 pandemic started. Baporikar (2021) also states that a lack of budgeting and a poor understanding of financial awareness are some of the most common problems faced by small businesses with the impact of COVID-19. More than 68% of SMEs have permanently collapsed. Rathore and Khanna (2020) also agree that the South Africa SME Finance Association (SASFA) did a survey. The result revealed that 70% of SMMEs could not work under the lockdown level 4 restriction, which has affected 75% of small and micro businesses and caused them to shut down. The survey included responses from 2,300 business owners.

COVID-19 Impact on SMEs during Lockdowns in South Africa

According to Statistics South Africa (2020), the second wave of the COVID-19 pandemic showed an update that South Africa is not coping under lockdown restrictions, and it indicated that businesses were suffering. The first survey was done from 30 March to 13 April 2020, and the results were released on 21 April 2020; the survey questions were about the survival of the businesses under the lockdown restrictions, whether firms were coping or not in terms of trading, and their turnover. And how is COVID-19 affecting them in terms of the supply chain?

Statistics South Africa (2020) followed up with another survey covering 15 days of fieldwork between 14 April and 30 April 2020. The survey results showed an improvement on the second round of the survey, and the number of participants was bigger, covering 2,182 SMEs compared with the first survey's total of 707 businesses.

- Turnover: the first survey revealed they had 85% of their business turnover. When we compare it with the second survey, the result showed that 90% of their business turnover was lower than their normal range. Other sectors are expected to report a lower turnover, such as electricity, gas, water supply, mining, transportation, trade, personal services, communication, and manufacturing, to name a few.
- Trading activity: the results from the first survey showed that 48% of businesses were put on hold and could not trade on 14 April 2020–30 April 2020. The second survey showed 46%. Other business owners reported that they needed to shut down their services, which recorded a 9% permanent closure. Other industries reported shutting down: the construction business had 14%, community, social, and personal services at 12%, and agriculture, hunting, forestry, and fishing at 12%. 56% of the business owners indicated they would still carry on and trade under lockdown level 4.
- Business survival without turnover: results revealed that only 7% of the business owners could survive for three months without any turnover, 55% showed that they would be able to sustain themselves for one to three months only, and 30% could only be able to sustain themselves for less than 30 days.

The spread of COVID-19 was the cause of closing off businesses globally and it was due to the policy mandate and the downward demand shifts, health concerns and other factors. Many of these closures were permanent because of the inability of owners to pay ongoing expenses and survive the shutdown (Fairlie, 2020). BusinessTech (2021) reports on the closer of the Ticketpro Dome. The management of the Ticketpro Dome has confirmed that the Ticketpro Dome at Northgate in Gauteng is closing down. Furthermore, BusinessTech (2021) explains that Ticketpro Dome tried to launch a hybrid event so that it could try to maintain the business and still proceed with events under the restrictions of lockdown; this hybrid held events online, which did not result in good numbers because it lacked the full experience. It still incurred many costs to maintain the online stream and pay for the physical building. The Ticketpro Dome managing director confirms that the sales were extremely disappointing and heartbreaking for the event industry (BusinessTech, 2021).

Small businesses trying to diversify their entrepreneurial endeavours are affected by these hard times of COVID-19 restrictions. Ngcobo (2021) reports that the lockdown restrictions at level 4 have caused the owner of a popular burger joint, Buns Out, to close down one of his Rosebank branches. Ngcobo (2021) further explains that the Bun Out management released a statement regarding the closure of their brunch: "It is with great sadness that we post to you this evening to confirm the closure of our Rosebank branch. We started our journey in Rosebank with an eye on the future and optimism for growth and life beyond the level 3 lockdown. Unfortunately, having been put back into level 4 lockdown and the restrictions that have been placed on us with regards to the sale of alcohol has made this journey ever tougher and insurmountable" (Ngcobo, 2021). In addition, BusinessTech (2020a) encored that closing the beauty industry because of the lockdown restrictions has created a massive impact on the industry and its employees because their income depends on the operation of the business. BusinessTech (2020c) further explains that the lockdown restrictions were due to change by 1 June 2020, where many businesses were hoping that the restriction would be lifted so they could be able to go back and operate because if it takes longer than that, many salons will not be able to maintain their properties. Sorbet Salon has reported that 40% of their branches may have to close should the restriction continue. Therefore, the impact of COVID-19 brought many changes for SMEs in South Africa. The economy was affected by the shutdown of businesses and job losses. This caused an increase in the unemployment rate in South Africa (BusinessTech, 2020c).

Salons and Nail Bars Sustainability during Lock-Down

Some SMEs were affected badly and could not even operate under the restrictions of the lockdown, especially salons and nail bars, because the nature of their business is physical touch with a human being to deliver a service; with the lockdown level 5, they could not operate at all. The salons and nail bars were closed in South Africa from 26 March 2020 onwards. Pikoos *et al.* (2020) explain that the COVID-19 pandemic and the lockdown restriction opened a big gap in South Africa's beauty industry because it had to shut down for over two months. Pikoos *et al.* (2020) continue to explain that only level 3 regulations gave the beauty industry time to breathe and come back to work. According to Nombembe (2020), salons can open under "advanced Level 3" of the COVID-19 lockdown. Nombembe (2020) continues to explain that many businesses were allowed to go back and trade, but some rules/regulations were followed by a consent to open businesses. These regulations were attached to safety. The beauty industry got the opportunity to go back and trade as well.

Tammy Taylor Nails (2020) explains that the lockdown has had a major impact on all industries in the economy, specifically the nail and beauty sector, as their services require direct contact with clients. Tammy Taylor Nails (2020) emphasised that the beauty and nail industry is female-dominated in South Africa. These businesses are very important to the economy's growth in South Africa because they promote skills development and job opportunities for women across the country (Tammy Taylor Nails, 2020). Lucero, Saba, and Kean (2020) argued that only 6% of owners could pay for their employees, and many small business owners could not afford or even have the means to pay their monthly rent for their properties and other business expenses, such as paying their workers. The survey illustrated that over a third of owners had no financial means. Other owners were able to sustain rent payments for two months only, and two-thirds of the owners had no money even to sustain their home expenses, such as food. Lucero, Saba, and Kean (2020) continue to explain that three-quarters of owners could apply for business loans, but not all were lucky enough to get them. Other owners needed help applying for the loan as they were not a technology survey. Other business owners could not get the loan because the forms were not filled out, and no one was there to clarify what they needed and how to fill them out (Lucero *et al.*, 2020).

Debts Relief Finance Scheme for SMEs in South Africa

Small Business Development (2021) took the initiative to release a scheme for small and medium businesses which are negatively affected, directly or indirectly, due to the COVID-19 pandemic. This scheme aimed to help and keep SMMEs in business by borrowing money; others called it a soft loan during the COVID-19 pandemic for six months from April 2020, whereas the Department of Small Business Development (DSBD) allocated R513 million towards the Debt Relief Fund and gave instructions to the Small Enterprise Finance Agency (SEFA) to administer the SMME Debt Relief Fund as a direct lending facility for Small Business Development (2021). From the 35,865 applications SEFA received, roughly 14,800 applications were fully complete of which 1,497 were approved. According to SME South Africa (2020), the Combat COVID SMME survey revealed that 68% of relief applications were unsuccessful. Most small businesses do not trust the government scheme, and others were wallowing in the COVID-19 pandemic, not seeking help. SME South Africa (2020) states that the result shows that less than half of the business owners surveyed have made the effort to apply for relief from the government, banks, or other financial institutions. Those who took the chance and applied the unsuccessful rate resulted in 68%.

Debts Relief Finance Scheme Requirements

The South African Government (2020b) states that there are qualifying criteria measures outlined for SMEs to get the funding; for instance, "SMEs must have been registered with Company and Intellectual Property Commission (CIPC) by the 28 February 2020"; "Company must be (100%) owned by South African Citizens"; "Employees must be (70%) South Africans"; Priority will be given to businesses owned by Women, Youth and People with Disabilities; be registered and compliant with SARS and UIF; SEDA assisted micro-enterprises to comply. Whereas SMEs must ensure their compliance and registration on the national SMME database. "Proof that the business is negatively affected by COVID-19 pandemic; complete the sampled online application platform; Company Statutory Documents; Federal Insurance Contributions Act (FICA) documents (e.g., Municipal accounts, letter from traditional authority); Certified Identity Documents (ID) copies of Directors; 3 months Bank Statements; Latest Annual Financial Statements or Latest Management Accounts not older than three months from date of application(where applicable); Business Profile; 6 months Cash Flow Projections(where applicable); Copy of Lease Agreement or Proof ownership if applying for rental relief; If applying for payroll relief, details of employees – as registered with UIF and including banking details – were required as payroll payments were made directly to employees; SMME employers who are not compliant with UIF must register before applying for relief; Facility Statements of Other Funders; Detail breakdown on application of funds including salaries, rent etc" (South African Government, 2020b).

The above requirements indicate that formal businesses that are registered have not included businesses that are not registered with the CIPC and do not have a six-month cash flow. The South African Government (2020b) supported the local Spaza shops doing business in the townships. There was a scheme dedicated to the Spaza shops to assist them through the tough time of COVID-19 because Spaza shops were the only convenient shops around that allowed people to buy goods at the time in the townships and offered buying in bulk. The South African Government (2020b) continues to explain which Spaza shop qualifies for the funding:

(1) Permit holders (2) owner-manager South African Spaza shops. Kalidas, Magwentshu, and Rajagopaul (2020) state that in a survey they conducted on the impact of COVID-19 on SMEs, the results showed that few people qualified for the funds and only a few entrepreneurs knew about this government assistance. They did not know where to find the information. They were not given proper communication and the qualifying criteria many could not meet it. The result was that 36% did not receive government loans or support, and a quarter were not using payment reliefs such as UIF and PAYE. Kalidas, Magwentshu, and Rajagopaul (2020) continue to explain that the low awareness of opportunities prevents SMEs from accessing public sector funding.

Kalidas et al. (2020) conducted a flash survey with 100 SMEs in the South African market to check if they were aware of any public sector funds that were available for SMEs or any opportunities or awareness that was given to SMEs so that it assists with the COVID-19 pandemic crises. These were the outcomes of the survey.

- Receiving government loan/support = 64% Yes
- Making use of the payment relief (e.g.) UIF/Pay = 75% Yes
- Top three reasons for not utilising support available
  1. I do not qualify for them
  2. I was not aware of them
  3. I am unaware of them but do not know where to find information

Examples from Salons and Nail Bars that Could Not Access the Public Sector Funding

According to Mbovane (2020), there has been a protest from salon owners from township salons who could not access the government debt relief fund. One of the salon owners explained that he had lost about R30,000 a month during the COVID-19 national lockdown. The owner continued to explain that he needed to close the salon because he could not afford the daily bills for the salon. He tried to contact the COVID-19 small business relief funds, but the criteria were difficult to meet. Other salon owners stipulated that even when they received the forms to claim the funds, they still could not qualify because, at the small business relief refund office, they needed the following documents: "annual financial statements, six months cash flow projections, a management account, plus you must be registered with the Unemployment Insurance Fund (UIF)" which they did not have (Mbovane, 2020).

Mbovane (2020) further explains that another salon owner was affected, Nkwame, a hairdresser from Ghana, who lost about R5 000 every month since the lockdown started. The owner explained that because no customers were coming to the salon because of the lockdown restrictions, he needed to let go of five of his employees because he did not have the funds to pay for their salaries. Other salon owners started to challenge the government, and they opened an online petition pleading with the government to allow them to work during lockdown because Cobus Grobler, an association national manager, had stated that many people had applied for the relief funds, but they were unsuccessful. So, the petition numbers grew very fast. Within a week, they received over 69,700 signatures. The Employers Organisation for Hairdressing, Cosmetology and Beauty were the one who assisted the business owners and helped them post the petition on the 25 April 2020. In May, it had already received 69,700 signatures, while they had a target of 75,000 signatures (Mbovane, 2020).

Entrepreneurs in the Pandemic

Haeffele, Hobson, and Storr (2020) state that entrepreneurs are a signal of hope, ensuring that communities recover and the rebound is on its way. The COVID-19 crises have clearly shown evidence that commercial and social entrepreneurs fill three important roles: (1) providing needed goods and services; (2) reconnecting or creating new social networks; and (3) indicating that recovery is likely to happen and is on the way. Amid the COVID-19 pandemic, commercial and social entrepreneurs already perform each key function. Haeffele, Hobson, and Storr (2020) continue and explain that other entrepreneurs need to be resilient in the COVID-19 pandemic; they need to provide goods and services for their community still, and they also learn new ways of doing things, which means creating new social networks. Chang and Wyszomirski (2015) also concur that entrepreneurs must think outside the box, be innovative, and come up with solutions for their businesses so that it does not collapse during the COVID-19 pandemic. Maritz *et al.* (2020) explain that entrepreneurs may or may not respond with more resilience to new economic forms and business models. Some entrepreneurs could not bounce back from the COVID-19 pandemic, leading to their businesses closing down. Maritz *et al.* (2020) continue to explain that in an ecosystem context, resilience has three forms:

1. Ability to recover
2. Ability to adapt to the new norms
3. Creating a radical change with an entirely new and different socioeconomic structure.

Other entrepreneurs could adapt to online services and continue running their businesses under the new circumstances.

Online Services

According to Kitomba (2020), online booking is booming, and clients are expected to adapt to the new system, which has become the norm. It also benefits clients to know what time they need to be at the salon, which prevents much misunderstanding. Kitomba (2020) continues to give five reasons why online bookings are important for salons: (1) Making online bookings reduces barriers between your clients. It allows your clients to make bookings at their own convenient time without miscommunication. (2) It has the potential to increase revenue. (3) It gives your clients convenience and flexibility; they do not have to come to the salon just to book/to place the date they wish to come and do their nails. (4) Avoid lost bookings that might have been forgotten to be recorded on the dairy. (5) Avoid cancellations and clients not attending appointments (Kitomba, 2020). This is great news as, on average, 10% of appointments are "lost" as cancellations or no-shows. Kitomba (2020) further argued that the benefits of operating in an e-commerce market for consumers include the following:

- Convenience – easy access to information.
- Prices – the ability to compare between retailers and
- Choice – the ability to compare products and benefits.

Deen-Swarray, Moyo, and Stork (2013) state the difference between informal and formal businesses, where the formal business will have a fixed business location and the informal does not. Deen-Swarray, Moyo, and Stork (2013) continue to explain that most informal businesses are not registered and usually operate on temporary buildings where they can be disassembled and reassembled. Hall, Hockey, and Robinson (2007) explain the difference between a home-based salon and a professional salon; a home salon may suit a client because the prices are typically lower. Some clients may prefer the more intimate nature of the appointment as there is often just one stylist working independently from home. Hall, Hockey, and Robinson (2007) explain that at a professional hair salon, a client will generally be looked after by more than one staff member, which can be an enjoyable experience. Kłopotek (2017) also discusses the advantages of a home hair salon (informal salon). It helps and saves many startup costs because they will be working from the comfort of their homes. There will be no need for insurance agents, and no one will need to pay or get a license to start operating or need a permit to start working; if equipment is available for one to work, that is enough. Kłopotek (2017) states that since your hair salon business is in your home, there will be no need for many things that contribute to wasting time, like being stuck in traffic and driving back and forth from your home to your workstation. Clients can make cancellations, and they will not affect much of the time spent being available at work. This will save money and time.

Commercial hair salons (formal salons), according to Kłopotek (2017), talk about the advantages of the commercial business because one can handle the business finances based on affordability. One has a choice of who to hire based on their skills and what they need. Kłopotek (2017) also mentions the disadvantages of a commercial business. Some costs are associated with starting the business and having money upfront for rent and equipment. If there is a need for one to get a working permit, they also need money or a license that shows that they are operating legally. Pikoos *et al.* (2020) also state that many barbers, stylists, and make-up artists have taken their services online during this period. Several businesses have now begun to incorporate tutorials into their service offering, teaching people some do-it-your-self (DIY) they are trying to make an income while they are at home, so clients who are comfortable getting online lessons are given a small fee. Many salons tried to use digital tools as their plan B since that was the only option that seemed to work then. Barber shops, beauty salons, and nail bars took to social media to do promotions and started live videos to explain more about their services (Pikoos *et al.*, 2020).

Some Examples of Salons and Nail Bars that Operated during Lockdown Restrictions

PayFast (2020) states that some salon owners needed to find a way to try to operate during the lockdown restriction and generate income for their salons and nail bars. One salon owner asked some of her clients if they would be interested in buying a complete root touch-up kit containing their regular treatment, which included tools they would need to apply safely at home. The salon owner would schedule a one-on-one Zoom or WhatsApp call to have a consultation to see what colour the client would be most likely to need. The Zoom call would proceed, and payment would be made via online payment, and the owner would arrange for the kits to be delivered to the client's home address once the payment had been cleared (PayFast, 2020). Thompson (2020) explains that other salon owners and business owners who could adapt to online services used all the opportunities to try operating and generate income while under lockdown restrictions. A barbershop owner in Cape Town's central business district (CBD) has also received feedback from desperate clients, some of whom have requested online assistance for virtual tutorials on cutting hair, which has helped his salon operate even under the lockdown restrictions (Thompson, 2020).

Thompson (2020) also states that Sorbet nail salons also took the chance to operate under the lockdown restrictions, and they ran a competition for their clients for the worst home haircuts; this competition was meant to equip their clients and engage with them online. They also guided how their clients could remove gel nail polish using home remedies (Thompson, 2020). According to Robertson (2021), since the pandemic started, many beauty professionals have been doing everything possible to keep the business going; data shows that 10% of beauty appointments were held online. Robertson (2021) continues to explain that there are many YouTube tutorials about markup and how to do your hair and nails at home. However, people are not confident about trying it on and prefer to get the treatment at a beauty salon. YouTube tutorials are not live; they are not made for the client's needs, and there is an opportunity for live question and answer (Q&A) or other interaction (Robertson, 2021).

Metrics of Running a Beauty Salon and Nail Bar

Boos (2017) explains that when it comes to running a business, knowing what is working and what is not helps prevent those random panic attacks where you question not just your business but your purpose in life. Boos (2017) continues to explain in the below metric table 4.1 that they have nine of the most important metrics that can help in tracking your business.

Table 4.1 Metrics for running a beauty salon and nail bar table

Number of new clients (per week and Month)	The purpose of this is it allows you, as an owner, to be able to check and trace how much you make monthly and how much you make in a week. One can compare and see if they are making a loss or profit in that month.
Number of referral clients (per week and monthly)	This also helps in terms of your marketing strategy, and it assists you to create more referral discounts for your clients, so it can boost new clients.
Repeats numbers (weekly and monthly)	You will be able to know when clients are not coming back for their repeats and treatments. It also assists in generating more promotion based on repeats to encourage clients to come back.
Number of your clients pre-booked	It will assist in checking if appointments work for your salon or not; do they prefer booking in or walk-ins without any appointments made. This will help your salon structure on what best works for your clients and you implement that.
The cost per service versus the amount charged	Is the time spent doing a certain service worth the amount being charged to a client? Example: If a treatment takes an hour or more, be able to measure and charge accordingly.
The average retail income per client	
Where did new clients come from?	It is important to know so that you can try and focus on that platform; if it is social media, you will advertise more on those platforms, or if it is referral marketing than you would know and nurture that site.
Most common services (per week and per month)	This assists in putting in training where it is needed the most, to boost other products or services so they can do well as well.

Moreover, Boos (2017) also states that by doing this, it helps to have a clear picture of what is happening towards the salon and can see how to change, what to implement, and where that change should be. Forbs (2007) also explains the three most important performance metrics and states that cash flow is king, and being able to utilise client retention, employee retention, and retail sales per client because when the business gets this right, it means it is doing something right, and clients and staff are happy. Having high returns on customers elevates the salon's name, and this means more business will be coming in because clients are recommending your salon. Forbs (2007) continues to explain that client retention is the most important metric for the salon. About 80% of the clients are returning customers, and this will help the staff to make sure that they keep a close eye on those clients looking for colour treatments because they tend to come in more often. Employee retention: Forbs (2007) states that it is normal for clients to build a relationship with their stylist, and that would be the reason why they come back to the salon because the stylist treats them well and does a good job. Employee retention is important because if your stylist leaves, the chances of losing a client are also very high (Forbs, 2007). Retail money per client is the most important metrics that measure the health of a beauty salon. Quiros-Alcala *et al.* (2019) further explain that salon income is to be generated by the salon's services and product sales. Selling your salon product also boosts the business as much as washing clients' heads. Making sure that both balances help the business. It is important to follow these metrics to produce a successful nail bar or hair salon (Caramela, 2022). In the lockdown restrictions, no salon could perform these metrics. Every salon and nail bar owner needed to figure out how to survive and run a salon during the COVID-19 pandemic.

Conclusion

COVID-19 and the lockdown restrictions have caused a massive impact on SMEs that operate in walk-in clients' salons and nail bars. The impact has caused SME owners to find new ways of generating income while they are not allowed to operate on-site so that they can pay rent, pay salaries, and sustain their households.

As a result, different business metrics are there for entrepreneurs so that they can help salons and nail bars trace and grow their businesses. However, they are not designed for digital transformations, which was one of the things that other SMEs were trying to adopt so that they could generate income for the month. There is a huge gap between formal and informal SMEs. The government tried to intervene and assist SMEs with debt relief funds, but not all SMEs could access the funds because of the qualification criteria that immediately excluded informal businesses.

One of the challenges encountered while compiling the chapter is that there was not enough data on informal businesses negatively affected by the COVID-19 pandemic; the focus was merely on formal businesses. SMEs and entrepreneurs can learn from this pandemic that being flexible to change and willing to adapt to new trends is necessary for a business. Building resilience for your business was proven to be the greatest skill, which worked for many SMEs. Resilience helps business owners and entrepreneurs overcome any storm or pandemic that may arise; it also helps businesses survive future emergencies. It prepares one to have ideas on responding to potential problems. This COVID-19 pandemic affected the majority of SMEs throughout the globe, and one thing made us realise the importance of one another and how crucial supply chains are from one country to another. We have learned how other BRICS countries and entrepreneurs solved their challenges while facing the COVID-19 pandemic.

References

Adam, N.A. and Alarifi, G. (2021) Innovation practices for the survival of small and medium enterprises (SMEs) in the COVID-19 times: The role of external support. *Journal of Innovation and Entrepreneurship* 10(1): 15.

Al-Fadly, A. (2020) Impact of COVID-19 on SMEs and employment. *Entrepreneurship and Sustainability Issues* 8(2): 629–648.

Al Buraiki, A. and Khan, F. (2018) Finance and technology: Key challenges faced by small and medium enterprises (SMEs) in Oman. *International Journal of Management, Innovation & Entrepreneurial Research* 4(2): 1–12.

Alessa, A.A., Alotaibie, T.M., Elmoez, Z. and Alhamad, H.E. (2021) Impact of COVID-19 on entrepreneurship and consumer behaviour – A case study in Saudi Arabia. *Asian Finance, Economics & Business* 8(5): 1–10.

Baporikar, N. (2021) *Handbook of research on sustaining SMEs and entrepreneurial innovation in the post-COVID-19 era*. IGI Global (Print).

Boos, N. (2017) *9 Salon Metrics You Need to Know 2017*. Available at: https://www.americansalon.com/business-career/9-metrics-you-need-to-know (Accessed 2 July 2023).

BusinessTech. (26 April 2020a) *Hair salons and nail bars will remain closed as South Africa enters curfew from 1 May* 2020. Available at: https://businesstech.co.za/news/business/392873/hair-salons-and-nail-bars-will-remain-closed-as-south-africa-enters-curfew-from-1-may/ (Accessed 2 July 2023).

BusinessTech. (25 March 2020b). *Here are all 28 jobs which are considered 'essential services' during South Africa's coronavirus lockdown* 2020. Available at: https://businesstech.co.za/news/business/384821/here-are-all-28-jobs-which-are-considered-essential-services-during-south-africas-coronavirus-lockdown/ (Accessed 2 July 2023).

BusinessTech. (14 May 2020c). *Sorbet wants salons, hairdressers and nail bars to reopen in South Africa – Under these conditions* 2020. Available at: https://businesstech.co.za/news/business/398003/sorbet-wants-salons-hairdressers-and-nail-bars-to-reopen-in-south-africa-under-these-conditions/ (Accessed 2 July 2023).

BusinessTech. (19 July 2021) *The Ticketpro Dome is closing down* 2021. Available at: https://businesstech.co.za/news/business/507206/the-ticketpro-dome-is-closing-down/ (Accessed 2 July 2023).

Caramela, S. (2022) *10 Things to Do Before Opening a Salon*. Available at: https://www.businessnewsdaily.com/8647-opening-salon-tips.html (Accessed 8 July 2023).

Chang, W.J. and Wyszomirski, M. (2015) What is arts entrepreneurship? Tracking the development of its definition in scholarly journals. *Artivate* 4(2): 33–31.

Channing, A., Davies, R., Gabriel, S., Harris, L., Makrelov, K., Sherman Robinson, B., Simbanegavi, W., van Seventer, D. and Anderson, L. (2020) Impact of Covid-19 on the South African economy. *Southern Africa-Towards Inclusive Economic Development Working Paper*, 111:1–37.

Chitiga-Mabugu, M., Henseler, M., Mabugu, R. and Maisonnave, H. (2020) Economic and distributional impact of COVID-19: Evidence from macro-micro modelling of the South African economy. *South African Journal of Economics* 85: 82–94.

Deen-Swarray, M., Moyo, M. and Stork, C. (2013) ICT access and usage among informal businesses in Africa. *Info Journal* 15(5): 52–68.

Department of Health. (2020). *Disaster Management Act, 2002* (Print).

Fairlie, R.W. (2020) The impact of COVID-19 on small business owners: The first three months after social distancing restrictions. *Journal of Economics & Management Strategy* 29(4): 727–740. https://doi.org/10.1111/jems.12400

Forbs. (2007) *How to Run A Beauty Salon: Metrics* 2007. Available at: https://www.forbes.com/2007/04/20/paul-mitchell-salon-ent-fin-cx_mc_0420fundsalonmetrics.html?sh=6a22e781878d (Accessed 2 July 2023).

Fubah, C.N. and Moos, M. (2022) Exploring COVID-19 challenges and coping mechanisms for SMEs in the South African entrepreneurial ecosystem. *Sustainability* 14(4): 1944. https://doi.org/10.3390/su14041944

Giones, F., Brem, A., Pollack, J.M., Michaelis, T.L., Klyver, K. and Brinckmann, J. (2020) Revising entrepreneurial action in response to exogenous shocks: Considering the COVID-19 pandemic. *Journal of Business Venturing Insights*, 14: e00186. https://doi.org/10.1016/j.jbvi.2020.e00186

Gurría, A. 2020. Tackling coronavirus (COVID-19) contributing to a global effort. *Organisation for Economic Co-operation and Development (OECD). https://www.oecd.org/dac/development-assistance-committee/daccovid19statement.htm* (Accessed 28 June 2023).

Haeffele, S., Hobson, A. and Storr, V.H. (2020) Coming back from COVID-19: Lessons in entrepreneurship from disaster recovery research. *Mercatus Special Edition Policy Brief* (Print).

Hall, A., Hockey, J. and Robinson, V. (2007) Occupational cultures and the embodiment of masculinity: Hairdressing, estate agency and firefighting. *Gender, Work & Organization* 14(6): 534–551.

IOL. (2021) *SARB rates announcement to benefit SMEs* 2021. https://www.iol.co.za/business-report/opinion/sarb-rates-announcement-to-benefit-smes-e4347a2a-6431-42ed-95ba-5531f7105d74.

Kalidas, S., Magwentshu, N. and Rajagopaul, A. (2020) *How South African SMEs can survive and thrive post Covid-19* (10). Available at: https://www.mckinsey.com/featured-insights/middle-east-and-africa/how-south-african-smes-can-survive-and-thrive-post-covid-19 (Accessed 28 June 2023).

Kitomba. (2020) *5 reasons why your salon needs online booking* 2020. Available at: https://www.kitomba.com/blog/5-reasons-you-need-online-booking/ (Accessed 28 June 2023).

Kłopotek, M. (2017) The advantages and disadvantages of remote working from the perspective of young employees. *Organizacja i Zarządzanie: kwartalnik naukowy*.

Kłopotek, M., 2017. The advantages and disadvantages of remote working from the perspective of young employees. *Organizacja i Zarządzanie: kwartalnik naukowy*, 4: 39–49.

Lightelm, A.A. (2013) Confusion about entrepreneurship? Formal versus informal small businesses. *Southern African Business Review*, *17*(3): 57–75.

Lucero, H., Waheed, S., Flowers, K., Fu, L., Nguyen, D., & Nguyen, C. (2020, June 12) A Survey of Nail Salon Workers and Owners in California During Covid-19. Escholarship.org. https://escholarship.org/uc/item/70b6t85q

Maritz, A., Perenyi, A., de Waal, G. and Buck, C. (2020) Entrepreneurship as the unsung hero during the current COVID-19 economic crisis: Australian perspectives. *Sustainability*, 12, 4612. https://doi.org/10.3390/su12114612

Mbovane, T. (2020) Uitenhage stylist uses his hair to protest against COVID-19 lockdown 2020. https://www.news24.com/news24/SouthAfrica/News/uitenhage-stylist-uses-his-hair-to-protest-against-covid-19-lockdown-20200615 (Accessed 14 June 2023).

Ngcobo, K. (2021) Buns out closes Rosebank branch due to ongoing level 4 restrictions https://www.sowetanlive.co.za/good-life/food/2021-07-14-buns-out-closes-rosebank-branch-due-to-ongoing-level-4-restrictions/ (Accessed 28 June 2023).

Nombembe, P. (2020) Beauty is back: Industry can reopen as Covid-19 regulations are unveiled. https://www.timeslive.co.za/news/south-africa/2020-06-19-beauty-is-back-industry-can-reopen-as-covid-19-regulations-are-unveiled/ (Accessed 28 June 2023).

Nugent, J.B. and Yhee, S.-J. (2002) Small and medium enterprises in Korea: Achievements, constraints and policy issues. *Small Business Economics* 18(1): 85–119.

Odusola, A. and Mkhumane, L. (2020) *Impact of COVID-19 on micro and Informal Business – South Africa*. UNDP South Africa. https://www.undp.org/south-africa/publications/impact-covid-19-micro-and-informal-businesses-south-africa (Accessed 28 June 2023).

Oni, O. and Omonona, S. (2020) The effect of COVID-19 on small retail. *The Retail and Marketing Review* 16(3): 48–57.

PayFast. (2020) *How Just Peachy Hair is surviving COVID-19 lockdown*. https://www.payfast.co.za/blog/how-just-peachy-hair-is-surviving-covid-19-lockdown/ (Accessed 28 June 2023).

Pikoos, T.D., Buzwell, S., Sharp, G. and Rossell, S.L. (2020) The COVID-19 pandemic: Psychological and behavioral responses to the shutdown of the beauty industry. *International Journal of Eating Disorders* 53(12): 1993–2002.

Quiros-Alcala, L., Pollack, A.Z., Tchangalova, N., DeSantiago, M. and Kavi, L.K.A. (2019) Occupational exposures among hair and nail salon workers: A scoping review. *Current Environmental Health Reports* 6(4):269–285. https://doi.org/10.1007/s40572-019-00247-3. PMID: 31541357.

Rathore, U. and Khanna, S. (2020) From slowdown to lockdown: Effects of the COVID-19 crisis on small firms in India. *Available at SSRN 3615339*.

Razumovskaia, E., Yuzvovich, L., Kniazeva, E., Klimenko, M. and Shelyakin, V. (2020) The effectiveness of Russian government policy to support SMEs in the COVID-19 pandemic. *Journal of Open Innovation: Technology, Market, and Complexity* 6(4): 1–21.

Robertson, N.L. (2021) *A qualitative study on business operational sustainability within the nail salon industry*. Trident University International (Print).

Ruch, W. (2020). National Poverty Lines. https://www.statssa.gov.za/publications/P03101/P031012019.pdf

Small Business Development. (2021) *SMMEs benefiting from COVID-19 Debts Relief Fund: Oversight*. https://pmg.org.za/committee-meeting/32611/ (Accessed 28 June 2023).

SME South Africa. (2020) *Covid-19 Small Business Relief Packages Updates + Reasons Applications Are Rejected*. https://smesouthafrica.co.za/covid-19-sme-packages-updates/ (Accessed 28 June 2023).

South African Government. (2020a) *About alert system* 2022. https://www.gov.za/covid-19/about/about-alert-system (Accessed 28 June 2023).

South African Government. (2020b) *Support to business* 2020. https://www.gov.za/covid-19/companies-and-employees/support-business (Accessed 20 March 2023).

Statistics South Africa. (2020, May 14). *COVID-19: Nine in ten businesses reported reduced turnover*. http://www.statssa.gov.za/?p=13313 (Accessed 20 March 2023)

Sulla, V. and Zikhali, P. (2018) *Overcoming poverty and inequality in South Africa: An assessment of drivers, constraints and opportunities*. The World Bank (Print).

Tammy Taylor Nails. (2020) Tammy tailor nails is excited to re-open their doors in accordance with the strict Covid-19 nail salon operations rules in South Africa. https://www.tammytaylornails.co.za/covid-19-nail-salon-operations/ (Accessed 10 May 2022).

The World Bank. (2021) South Africa Economic Update: South Africa's Labor Market Can Benefit from Young Entrepreneurs, Self-Employment 2021. https://www.worldbank.org/en/country/southafrica/publication/south-africa-economic-update-south-africa-s-labor-market-can-benefit-from-young-entrepreneurs-self-employment#:~:text=The%20report%20finds%20that%20South,most%20upper%20middle%2Dincome%20countries.&text=At%20the%20time%20of%20releasing,employment%20losses%20had%20been%20recovered (Accessed 20 March 2023).

Thompson, A. (2020) Salons expect to be flooded when lockdown eases. Here's how they plan to cope. 2020. https://www.businessinsider.co.za/the-rush-for-haircuts-after-lockdown-and-preparing-for-safe-salons-2020-4#:~:text=Hermanos%2C%20a%20barbershop%20in%20Cape,difficult%20to%20put%20into%20practice.%E2%80%9D (Accessed 20 March 2023).

5 China's SMEs in the Scope of COVID-19

Strategies and Prospects for Survival and Development

Xi Chen, Jai Kumar, and Chensi Li

Introduction

COVID-19 is a massive health crisis and a systemic shock with profound implications, both in the short- and medium- to long-term for every country worldwide. The significant economic downturn caused by this virus has resulted in the closure of numerous businesses, both large and small, and has had other effects on commercial operations.

Small- and medium-sized enterprises (SMEs) have been at the front lines of the economic shock caused by the COVID-19 pandemic. Lockdown measures have disrupted economic activity, plummeted demand, and disrupted supply chains worldwide. In early surveys, over 50% of SMEs indicated they could be out of business within the next few months. Since then, bankruptcies have piled up, and start-up rates are collapsing. From a global perspective, since the start of the pandemic in February 2020, the OECD has monitored more than 180 surveys among SMEs in 32 countries, and the results show that 70%–80% of SMEs experienced a serious drop in revenues/sales. Several surveys indicate this drop in revenue to be between 30% and 50%.

Due to the huge environmental changes, international organisations, research institutions, and scholars worldwide have paid great attention to the impact and risk faced by SMEs under the impact of the epidemic when studying how the global community is affected by COVID-19 and its response strategies. This chapter will use China as an example to introduce what happened to Chinese SMEs after the pandemic outbreak and why it happened. Furthermore, the present study focuses on the specific attributes of SMEs in China. This article's primary objective is to provide a comprehensive portrayal of Chinese SMEs in the context of the COVID-19 pandemic and present viable approaches SMEs in other BRICS countries can adopt.

DOI: 10.4324/9781003475606-7

An Overview of SMEs in China

Similar to other developing countries, Chinese SMEs play a crucial role in the prosperity of the national economy and society. SMEs are the foundation for China to practice its modern economic system and achieve high-quality economic development. Meanwhile, SMEs are a significant pillar for expanding employment and improving people's livelihoods in the country. Considering the huge amounts of SMEs nationwide, they are also an important source of entrepreneurship.

As for the definition of SMEs, the concept varies from country to country. Also, even in the same country, concepts can change with different stages of economic development and can be discrepant among different industries. Taking the dynamic change in the definition of SMEs and the object of study into consideration, this article will take the *Statistical Methods for the Division of Large, Medium, and Small Enterprises (2017),* published by China's National Bureau of Statistics as the only standard for the definition of SMEs that has been discussed below. Overall, Chinese SMEs refer to enterprises established according to the law within the territory of the People's Republic of China with relatively small operation scale and staff size, including medium-sized enterprises, small enterprises, and micro enterprises. Table 5.1 shows the concept of SMEs based on the 2017 statistical document in China.

Table 5.1 Statistical Methods for the Division of Chinese Large, Medium, and Small Enterprises (2017)

Sectors	Index	Unit of Measure	Medium	Small
Agriculture, forestry, husbandry and fishery	Operating income (Y, in RMB)	Ten thousand	$500 \leq Y < 20{,}000$	$50 \leq Y < 500$
Industry	Employee (X)	Person	$300 \leq X < 1{,}000$	$20 \leq X < 300$
	Operating income (Y, in RMB)	Ten thousand	$2{,}000 \leq Y < 4{,}000$	$300 \leq Y < 2{,}000$
Construction	Operating income (Y, in RMB)	Ten thousand	$6{,}000 \leq Y < 80{,}000$	$300 \leq Y < 6{,}000$
	Total assets (Z)	Ten thousand	$5{,}000 \leq Z < 80{,}000$	$300 \leq Z < 5{,}000$
Wholesale trade	Employee (X)	Person	$20 \leq X < 200$	$5 \leq X < 20$
	Operating income (Y, in RMB)	Ten thousand	$5{,}000 \leq Y < 40{,}000$	$1{,}000 \leq Y < 5{,}000$
Retail trade	Employee (X)	Person	$50 \leq X < 300$	$10 \leq X < 50$
	Operating income (Y, in RMB)	Ten thousand	$500 \leq Y < 20{,}000$	$100 \leq Y < 500$

(*Continued*)

Table 5.1 (Continued)

Sectors	Index	Unit of Measure	Medium	Small
Transportation	Employee (X)	Person	300≤X<1,000	20≤X<300
	Operating income (Y, in RMB)	Ten thousand	3,000≤Y<30,000	200≤Y<3,000
Warehousing industry	Employee (X)	Person	100≤X<200	20≤X<100
	Operating income (Y, in RMB)	Ten thousand	1,000≤Y<30,000	100≤Y<1,000
Post services	Employee (X)	Person	300≤X<1,000	20≤X<300
	Operating income (Y, in RMB)	Ten thousand	2,000≤Y<30,000	100≤Y<2,000
Accommodation	Employee (X)	Person	100≤X<300	10≤X<100
	Operating income (Y, in RMB)	Ten thousand	2,000≤Y<10,000	100≤Y<2,000
Catering	Employee (X)	Person	100≤X<300	10≤X<100
	Operating income (Y, in RMB)	Ten thousand	2,000≤Y<10,000	100≤Y<2,000
Information transmission industry	Employee (X)	Person	100≤X<2,000	10≤X<100
	Operating income (Y, in RMB)	Ten thousand	1,000≤Y<100,000	100≤Y<1,000
Software and information technology services	Employee (X)	Person	100≤X<300	10≤X<100
	Operating income (Y, in RMB)	Ten thousand	1,000≤Y<100,000	50≤Y<1,000
Real estate development and management	Operating income (Y, in RMB)	Ten thousand	1,000≤Y<200,000	100≤Y<1,000
	Total assets (Z)	Ten thousand	5,000≤Z<1,000	2,000≤Z<5,000
Property management	Employee (X)	Ten thousand	300≤X<1,000	100≤X<300
	Operating income (Y, in RMB)	Ten thousand	1,000≤Y<5,000	500≤Y<1,000
leasing and business service	Employee (X)	Person	100≤X<300	10≤X<100
	Total assets (Z)	Ten thousand	8,000≤Z<120,000	100≤Z<8,000
Others	Employee (X)	Person	100≤X<300	10≤X<100

Data Source: the *Statistical Methods for the Division of Large, Medium, and Small Enterprises (2017)* published by China's National Bureau of Statistics

According to the fourth National Economic Census, China's SMEs have developed rapidly. By the end of 2018, there were 18.07 million SMEs in the country, accounting for 99.8% of all legal enterprises of all sizes. Therefore, the impressive role that SMEs play in creating jobs is apparent. By the end of 2018, Chinese SMEs had employed 233.004 million people, accounting for 79.4% of the total employment of enterprises in China. Meanwhile, in the same year, the total assets owned by SMEs reached RMB 402.6 trillion (US$59.5315 trillion), accounting for 77.1% of the total enterprise assets. In contrast, the annual operating revenue of SMEs reached RMB 188.2 trillion (US$27.6641 trillion), accounting for 68.2% of all enterprises' annual operating revenue.

In 2019, the Small and Medium Enterprises Development Index (SMEDI) was generally stable, with a quarterly average of 92.9 out of 100, and the fluctuation was no more than 0.3 points. Chinese SMEs were on a stable and healthy growth trajectory in 2019, before the COVID-19 outbreak. They played a crucial role in stabilising employment, boosting economic activity, and safeguarding the people's livelihoods in China. At the beginning of 2020, SMEs in China contribute more than 50% of the tax revenue, more than 60% of GDP, more than 70% of technological innovation, more than 80% of urban labour employment, and more than 90% of the number of enterprises.

How Has the COVID-19 Epidemic Affected Chinese SMEs?

As in other countries, the outbreak of COVID-19 has profoundly affected the survival and long-term development of SMEs in China, owing to global and domestic changes. The impact caused by the epidemic on Chinese SMEs is mainly reflected in the following aspects.

Initially, the burst of COVID-19 forced the country to take comprehensive lockdown policies to avoid massive infection. From a production standpoint, SMEs could not conduct regular product production, sales, and services. Concurrently, they were also faced with the disruption of the supply chain and the shortage of raw materials for production, which led to the failure of delivery of orders or even the breach of contract. Also, due to logistics and transportation limitations, certain products could not be traded normally. On the demand side, the epidemic has not only affected the income of enterprises but also greatly affected the income of consumers. Many consumers experienced the burden of mortgages, car loans, and other loans coupled with a decreased income, leading to a reduced desire to spend. This created a significant amount of stress for them. The dual difficulties on both the production and demand sides create a vicious circle. A survey by the Chinese Association of SMEs titled *"Research Report on the Impact of COVID-19 on Small and Medium-sized Enterprises and Countermeasures"* revealed that due to a significant decline in consumption, most businesses in various sectors experienced a challenging situation. Specifically,

85.74% of cultural, sports, and entertainment enterprises, 78.02% of accommodation and catering industries, 63.47% of residential services, repair, and other services, 62.50% of transportation, storage, and postal services, 57.38% of manufacturing, and 56.82% of wholesale and retail trade were affected.

Secondly, the cash flow of SMEs shrank greatly while the cost of survival was huge. SMEs' capital chain is highly susceptible because a significant proportion of their fixed costs are attributed to employee salaries, social security contributions, loan repayments, and rent expenses. According to a joint survey of 995 SMEs conducted by Tsinghua University and Peking University, employees' salaries, social insurance, housing fund, rent, and loan repayment account for 90% of the total expenditure, and staff expenses accounted for 62.78%. Taking the catering industry as an example, Haidilao Hot Pot lost RMB 1.1 billion ($160 million) in the two weeks after it was shut down, including RMB 700 million ($102 million) in employee wages and the rent of stores. Jia Guolong, the chairman of Xibei Catering, a famous Chinese catering company with stores around the country, said that the company had suffered a major blow. Following the onset of the COVID-19 pandemic, Jia stated that the organisation was compelled to monthly disburse RMB 150 million (US$21.8401 million) to its personnel. However, despite securing a bank loan, the company's viability was limited to three months as the epidemic persisted. According to a survey conducted by the School of Economics and Management of Tsinghua University on 1,435 SMEs after the outbreak of the epidemic, 35.96% of interviewees could not survive for one month, 31.92% could only survive for two months, and 17.03% could survive for no more than three months. Such data means that a total of 85% could not survive three months, and only 9.27% of SMEs were able to survive six months. Conversely, SMEs frequently rely on bank loans and non-financial institutions to cover their interest expenses. The statement means that SMEs often face significant challenges when obtaining financing for their operations and growth. For example, a bank may require a certain collateral or credit score before approving a loan. If an SME does not meet these requirements, it may be unable to access the financing it needs to expand its operations or invest in new projects. Even when SMEs can obtain financing, the interest rates or other fees associated with the financing can be quite high. This can make it difficult for the SME to generate enough revenue to cover the cost of the financing, which can, in turn, limit the SME's ability to grow and succeed. Many SMEs rely more on private loans due to their small operating scale and large fluctuation in income, which is related to seasonal and special events. Such features make it difficult for SMEs to receive bank loans. Their interest expenditure cost is much higher than bank loans through formal channels, making the burden even heavier.

Thirdly, as a major manufacturing country in the world, the epidemic has significantly impacted the foreign exchange earnings of manufacturing exports by SMEs in China. Since the pandemic proliferated globally, countries' epidemic lockdown policies led to the stagnation of import and export trade, with some countries imposing trade restrictions on goods from China. Hence, China faced difficulties with production on schedule, insufficient consumer demand from major trading partners, and the cancellation of many foreign trade orders. The foreign exchange earnings of Chinese SMEs have been influenced by tightened regulations on cross-border logistics, inspection, and quarantine management, which have compounded the impact. According to statistics, from January to February 2020, China's textile export volume was RMB 96.23 billion (US$14.0112 billion), 18.7% lower than past year, and the exports of clothing and clothing accessories were 20.0% lower yearly. Until now, it has been more than two years since the outbreak of the epidemic, but Chinese SMEs engaged in manufacturing industries are still facing the loss of orders, especially those SMEs exporting to Japan, South Korea, and the United States. European countries are also facing unprecedented pressure to increase foreign exchange.

What Supportive Policies Has the Chinese Government Launched for SMEs?

The COVID-19 pandemic has severely impacted SMEs, prompting governments worldwide to adopt and implement policies to support these businesses during these challenging times. We have noted that governments worldwide have been taking effective actions to reduce and mitigate the negative impact of COVID-19 in the context of tremendous uncertainty and multiple economic, financial, and social pressures. Since the mid-2020s, many countries have seen new waves of infections and virus mutations, so governments must act on all fronts simultaneously and synchronously. This need for flexibility and adaptability leads governments to reconsider their multi-level governance systems and reassess their regional development priorities.

Two and a half years after the epidemic outbreak, both central and local Chinese governments have introduced supportive measures for SMEs to counter the difficulties. The following section mainly introduces the support for SMEs by taking the central level as an example.

1 Cut or defer the payment of taxes and fees
2 Strengthen and improve financial support
3 Provide labour support and promote the policy of stable employment
4 Other supportive policies

Cut or Defer the Payment of Taxes and Fees

The cut and deferment measures implemented by banks during the pandemic in China had different impacts on both banks and consumers. Cut measures, such as reduced interest rates and fees, were implemented by banks to support the economy and help consumers during the pandemic. This resulted in lower consumer borrowing costs, making it easier to access credit, invest in their businesses, or pay off existing debts. However, these cuts also affected banks' profitability, as they earned less interest income from loans and other financial products. Banks had to manage their margins carefully to maintain their financial health and avoid losses. On the other hand, deferment measures, such as delayed payments, loan restructuring, and extensions, were implemented to help consumers experiencing financial difficulties due to the pandemic. These measures allowed consumers to delay their payments or extend their loan terms, reducing their immediate financial burden. In February 2020, the Chinese government recognised stable enterprises as the foundation of stabilised employment. It took measures to reduce the contributions of pension, unemployment, and work-related injury insurance for businesses during the outbreak of the epidemic. They also reduced tax burdens on SMEs and exempted VAT for essential services. All provinces except Hubei exempted these fees for SMEs from February to June 2020, while Hubei received additional tax exemptions and VAT moratoriums for struggling enterprises. Enterprises were also allowed to defer payment of housing provident funds until the end of June.

In 2021, the Chinese government continued supporting SMEs in the epidemic's context. This year, based on preferential policies, the government levied only half of the income tax on the part of SMEs and individual industrial and commercial households whose annual taxable income did not exceed RMB 1 million (US$0.1456 million). The implementation period was planned to be two years. From 1 April to the end of 2021, for small-scale VAT taxpayers in Hubei Province, the taxable sales income with a levy rate of 3% was reduced to 1%.

According to the government work report on 5 March 2022, about RMB 2.5 trillion of tax rebates and cuts will be provided to enterprises throughout the year, all of which will go directly to enterprises. The government aims to increase the scope of exemptions from tax and fees and extend the policies' application this year. For SMEs in China whose annual taxable income is between RMB 1 million and three million (US$0.1456 and US$0.4368 million), the enterprise income tax will be levied by half again. Synchronously, the government stepped up implementing the policy of additional deductions for research and development expenses, raising the proportion of additional deductions for technology-based SMEs from 75% to 100%, with the extension of deferred payment of social insurance. In the early stage, the government will provide deferred payment policies for enterprises in the three extremely poor industries, including catering, retail, and tourism overseas for civil aviation, highway, waterway, and railway transportation industries, and extend the scope of deferred payment insurance to endowment insurance. Among the policies, the deferred payment period for endowment insurance premiums is three months. The deferred payment period for insurance premiums and work-related injury insurance premiums is a year, and no late payment fee will be charged during the deferred payment period.

Strengthen and Improve Financial Support

In January 2020, the China Banking and Insurance Regulatory Commission issued the *"Notice on Strengthening the Financial Services of the Banking and Insurance Industry to Cooperate with the Prevention and Control of the Epidemic"*, specifically proposing financial services for distressed enterprises. The central government also released several enhanced financial services. China Merchants Bank, China Construction Bank, Bank of Communications, and Agricultural Bank of China should actively support the development of SMEs affected by the epidemic and provide differentiated and preferential financial services. Afterwards, the *"Notice on Further Strengthening Financial Support for the Prevention and Control of the Epidemic"* and the *"Notice on Supporting Financial Strengthening Services to Do a Good Job in the Prevention and Control of the Epidemic"* were also issued. According to the above documents, if SMEs promise to keep employment stable while applying for an extension, the bank will extend the principal and interest of SMEs' loans. Loans that have previously enjoyed the extension policy launched by the government can also enjoy this policy. It is estimated that the extension policy can cover the principal of inclusive SMEs' loans of about RMB 7 trillion (US$1.0192 trillion).

On the other hand, the support programme for credit loans is mainly targeted at local corporate banks with better operating conditions. For the inclusive SMEs' credit loans newly issued by qualified local corporate banks at the end of 1 March 2020, with a term of not less than six months, it is expected to drive the local corporate bank to issue new inclusive SMEs' credit loans for about RMB 1 trillion (US$0.1456 trillion). The policy has been expected to alleviate the financing difficulties of SMEs effectively.

For SMEs in key sectors, the Chinese central government allocated no less than RMB 3 billion (US$0.4368 billion) before the end of 2021 to support about 1,300 or so "Little Giant" enterprises. The support aimed to bring high-quality development to the above enterprises by providing point-to-point services, guiding the local finance to increase investment for the "Little Giant" enterprises, improving the financing of SMEs' public service system, and enhancing innovation ability and professional skills.

At the same time, the Chinese central government also strengthened re-credit and re-discount policy tools to benefit SMEs specifically, making full use of RMB 300 billion (US$43.6802 billion) for re-lending. Correspondingly, the government increased credit loans and implemented inclusive credit loan support policies for SMEs under regulations. For SMEs seriously affected by the epidemic, flood disasters, and rising raw material prices, the government has been strengthening the supportive policy of liquidity loans and implementing the policy of deferred repayment of principal and interest for SMEs' loans following regulations.

The government encouraged active participation in the national 12366 tax payment service hotline for SMEs to enhance their service capabilities. They also proposed using big data to identify SME taxpayers meeting policy application standards. Timely, proactive, and targeted promotion of preferential policies can help enterprises fully enjoy the tax reduction and exemption dividends and further consolidate and expand "contactless" tax services. The development of online service platforms will provide SMEs with more convenient services. At the same time, local taxation departments across the country have accelerated the progress of tax rebates and further reduced the average time for processing normal tax rebates to within 7 working days in 2021.

In 2022, the government will further improve the quality and efficiency of financial services and expand their coverage by steadily increasing the supply of credit from the banking sector to SMEs, optimising the credit structure, and promoting a reasonable reduction in comprehensive financing costs. Also, as encouraged by the government, banks are committed to enriching inclusive insurance products and businesses to provide better financing, credit enhancement, and security services for SMEs. To fully implement the above policies, efforts will be made to increase the proportion of first-time lenders among SME loan households. The national government is also supporting the cooperation among banking financial institutions, the national financing guarantee fund, and its co-operative guarantee institutions to carry out the specific batch guarantee business in an orderly manner and encourage priorities for SMEs and individuals for the first loan accounts under the same conditions. This year, China encourages insurance institutions to steadily finance credit insurance businesses for SMEs by offering preferential rates to high-quality SMEs.

Provide Labour Support and Promote the Policy of Stable Employment

In 2022, the Chinese government relaxed the layoff rate standard of the unemployment insurance policy for SMEs to no more than 20% of the total number of employees for enterprises with less than 30 employees. The insurance for SMEs has also been refunded at a rate of no more than 60%, of which the return standard for SMEs can be raised to 100% of the unemployment insurance premiums paid by the enterprise and its employees in the previous year. The coordinating area that implements the return of stable employment of enterprises should have the ability to prepare for payment for more than 12 months in the previous year's unemployment insurance fund, and the area that implements the return of stable employment of enterprises in difficulty should have the ability to prepare for payment for more than 24 months. In coordinating regions, it is necessary to give full play to the role of provincial adjustment funds to help local enterprises implement the policy of stabilising their human resources so that eligible enterprises can enjoy policy support as much as possible.

At the same time, the government has provided special subsidy funds for expenditures such as work-for-work training and living allowances for employees. After the application of qualified enterprises is reviewed and approved by the local human resources and social security department, the subsidy funds will be paid to the basic account opened by the enterprise in the bank every month according to regulations.

In 2021, the Chinese government continued implementing the inclusive unemployment insurance policy for stable jobs. Enterprises participating in the insurance that had not laid off employees in the previous year or whose layoff rate was not higher than the unemployment rate control target of the national urban survey in the previous year could apply for unemployment insurance to stabilise their jobs and return. For SMEs that recruited people with employment difficulties and family members who had zero jobs and carried out work-for-work training, the enterprises would be given vocational training subsidies according to the number of recruits. In light of the actual situation, all provinces may include various types of enterprises in the industries of accommodation, catering, tourism, transportation, wholesale, and retail, which have been greatly affected by the epidemic, into the scope of subsidies.

The government would issue unemployment subsidies for unemployed persons who have received unemployment insurance benefits but remain unemployed and those who do not meet the conditions for receiving unemployment insurance benefits. Also, temporary living subsidies will be issued to unemployed migrant workers who have participated in the insurance for less than one year. For instance, Shanghai has launched a special insurance product for people who have resumed work and production in the flexible employment industry. This insurance protection plan is based on "protecting the basics, helping the disadvantaged, promoting public welfare with a non-profit, sharing and taking the main responsibility". It is creatively designed to meet the security needs of non-indigenous workers returning to work in Shanghai.

In 2022, China continued to implement the policy of returning unemployment insurance to stabilise jobs and support SMEs. The return ratio of unemployment insurance will be raised from 60% to a maximum of 90%; for SMEs that do not have public accounts, funds can be directly returned to the account that they registered with the local tax department to pay social insurance premiums. Additionally, two new-phased policies were added to provide a one-time training subsidy for SMEs that are temporarily unable to produce and operate normally due to the epidemic. The central government has allowed local governments with large funds remaining to withdraw about 4% of the unemployment insurance fund surplus to contribute to vocational training.

Other Supportive Policies

In 2020, the Chinese government vigorously reduced the operating costs of enterprises. For instance, in terms of rent, the central government encouraged technology business incubators and start-up spaces to reduce or exempt rents for incubating companies appropriately. Local governments were also asked to reduce or exempt rents for SMEs that lease state-owned properties according to the actual situation. At the same time, the government provided policy support to encourage other types of operating entities to reduce or exempt rents. Regarding reducing energy costs, the central government stipulated that except for high energy-consuming industries, from 1 February to 30 June 2020, the electricity price would be 5% less than the original price.

The Chinese government also encouraged reducing or exempting property fees for SMEs. For example, Guangzhou reduced or exempted the property rent for February and March 2020 for SMEs that lease the properties of municipal and district state-owned spaces for offline commercial store operations from February to March 2020. Depending on the situation of the epidemic, the property rent in April and May of the same year could be halved.

Meanwhile, China has actively guaranteed the payment of SMEs. Organs and institutions purchasing goods, projects, and services from SMEs have been requested to make payment within 30 days from the delivery date of the goods, projects, and services; if the contract otherwise stipulates, the payment period shall not exceed 60 days. Under industry norms and transaction habits, large enterprises purchasing goods, projects, and services from SMEs shall reasonably agree on payment terms and make timely payments. Organs, public institutions, and large enterprises that delay payment to SMEs shall pay overdue interest. On 31 March of each year, information such as the number and number of contracts overdue but not paid to SMEs will be disclosed through websites, newspapers, and other easy means for the public to know.

In the year 2021, the Chinese government further implemented the *Regulations on Guaranteeing the Payment of Small- and Medium-sized Enterprises*, formulated methods for handling complaints about guaranteeing the payment of SMEs, strengthened the management of accounts that were payable for large enterprises, and increased punishment for abuse of dominant market positions, overdue occupation, and malicious delinquency of accounts to SMEs. It has been strictly prohibited to evade the obligation of timely payment by not signing a contract or not agreeing on a specific timeline of payment in the contract.

Moreover, the Chinese government has stocking activities for supply and demand, supporting large enterprises to purchase more from SMEs. From a more comprehensive perspective, China has built a government-bank cooperation platform and carried out cross-border information docking and integration services for SMEs. Relying on new forms of foreign trade, such as cross-border e-commerce, relevant entities are working on providing services such as remote online communication and supply and demand information docking for SMEs. Accelerating the development of overseas warehouses and ensuring the smooth operation of the foreign trade industry chain and supply chain are also helpful for SMEs.

From the view of energy, China has strengthened the construction of the power generation, supply, storage, and sales system by using scientific and orderly electricity consumption. A stable energy supply to SMEs can be ensured by reasonably arranging off-peak electricity consumption.

Furthermore, to encourage innovation, the central government of China continues to implement the policy of additional deductions for research and development expenses. It increases the proportion of additional deductions to 100%. In addition to financial support, China is also improving intellectual property protection. The country has been continuously helping SMEs improve their innovation ability and professional level while cultivating "Little Giant" enterprises by providing strong support regarding funds, talents, and incubation platform construction. On 8 March 2022, the Minister of Industry and Information Technology issued a demonstration of the development of SMEs. This year, the country will further expand the scale and scope of "high-quality development of technologically advanced specialised SMEs" ("Little Giant"), further innovate the development pattern, and expand the number of SMEs at the national level by adding another 3,000 "Little Giant" enterprises across the country. The number of "Little Giant" enterprises is expected to increase by 50,000 at the provincial level.

The Impact of the Chinese Government Support on SMEs

With the support of a series of supportive policies from the central and local governments, China's SMEs have achieved remarkable development. The specific performance can be seen as follows.

In 2020, China's GDP exceeded RMB 101 trillion (US$14.7057 trillion), surpassing RMB 100 trillion (US$14.5601 trillion) for the first time. According to the data released by the Chinese Association of SMEs, in the fourth quarter of 2020, the development index of Chinese SMEs was 87, rising quarter by quarter since the outbreak of COVID-19 and reaching the highest point in 2020 in the fourth quarter. The decline and rise of the development index of Chinese SMEs are completely consistent with the curve of China's economic change.

China has demonstrated significant institutional advantages in supporting SMEs to deal with the impact of the COVID-19 pandemic. Various departments at the national level have introduced over 120 policies aimed at supporting SMEs, encompassing public finance, finance, examination and approval, and other related aspects. Electric power consumption data suggests that SMEs' electricity usage increased by 7.6% in 2021. Small and micro-loans also rose by 27.3% by the end of 2021 compared to the previous year. The government and large state-owned enterprises worked together to clear up accounts in arrears to private enterprises, particularly SMEs, amounting to over RMB 22 billion (US$3.2032 billion) in 2020. Additionally, the government reduced new taxes and fees for SMEs by over RMB 2.5 trillion (US$0.364 trillion) in 2020. By the end of the fourth quarter of 2020, the macroeconomic sentiment index, which reflects business confidence, had reached 101.4, an increase of 0.5 points from the previous quarter. The composite business index also rose by 0.4 points to 95.9, indicating overall optimism in the business environment. These measures demonstrate China's strong commitment to supporting its SMEs during the pandemic and highlight the country's proactive efforts to mitigate the negative economic impact of the pandemic.

Data from the Chinese Ministry of Industry and Information Technology showed that the production and operation of SMEs maintained a steady recovery in the country. In 2021, the operating revenue and total profits of SMEs in industries above the designated size increased by 19.9% and 25.6% year-on-year, respectively, with an average growth of 9.9% and 16.8% in the past two years, 5.8% and 15.4% points higher than the same period in 2019. The operation of state-level technologically advanced "Little Giant" enterprises has been in good condition and has realised effective enterprise transformation. In 2021, the operating income margin of "Little Giant" Enterprises was 10.6%, 4.4% points higher than that of industrial SMEs in industries above the designated size.

Based on a survey from the China Association of SMEs in June 2022, the SMEDI was 88.4, up 0.2 points month-on-month, and stopped falling and recovered after four consecutive months of decline (see figure 5.1).

According to an operating rate survey for sample enterprises, 25.90% were fully started, 42% had an operating rate of more than 75%, and 7.70% were not started. Compared with the previous month, the proportion of fully started enterprises increased by 5.85%, and the proportion of enterprises that did not

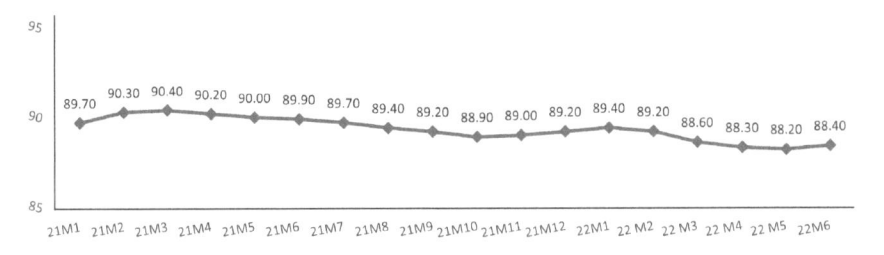

Figure 5.1 Chart of SMEDI trend of SMEs in China since the beginning of 2021

Data Source: *the SMEDI Index of China SMEs stopped falling and rebounded in June 2022 (2022)* published by the China Association of SMEs

start construction decreased by 5.70%. The index of industry, construction, transportation, postal and warehousing, real estate, wholesale and retail trade, social services, information transmission, computer software industry, and accommodation and catering industry rose by 0.2, 0.1, 0.1, 0.3, 0.1, 0.4, 0.5, and 0.6 points, respectively, compared with the previous month; among them, the accommodation and catering industry index rose the most. The construction, transportation, postal warehousing, wholesale, and retail trade indices have risen for two consecutive months.

An Outlook on the Future Development of SMEs in the Post-COVID Era

The report of the 19th National Congress of the Communist Party of China proposed that China should speed up building an innovation-oriented country, with special emphasis on State-level Technologically Advanced "Little Giant" Enterprises and promoting the transformation of scientific and technological achievements. According to the report, the Chinese government has paid special attention to the development vitality of SMEs' innovation capacity, which is related to the realisation of building an innovative country. COVID-19, as a worldwide epidemic and public crisis, is essentially a thorough inspection of the national government's vision, governance ability, and enterprise management mode. If a government can combine the need for epidemic prevention management and the positive guidance of the state for the development of SMEs. In that case, the country can turn the crisis into an opportunity, accelerating the successful transformation of SMEs in the long term. Supporting policies for SMEs to cope with the epidemic should follow the following value orientations.

Implement Scientific Recovery Support Strategies at the National Level

First of all, the government is supposed to consider the characteristics of SMEs to provide support policies needed by enterprises during the pandemic and gradually adopt more long-term and effective strategies for SMEs' recovery. The design, timing, and pace of the policy mentioned above symbolize the governing ability and sense of responsibility of a country's government. Withdrawing support measures too early may provoke massive failure for SMEs and weaken competition. However, prolonged support could result in distortions, reduce incentives to adapt and innovate, and trap resources in unproductive activities. The core aim of supporting SMEs is to eliminate the pandemic's impact as soon as possible and to guide SMEs to actively upgrade themselves and generate sustainable development capacity with potential from within. Therefore, China's central and local governments conduct field studies and investigations annually. By comprehensively considering the development of the epidemic and its impact on SMEs, the government can timely issue phased and appropriate supportive policies.

Guide SMEs to Develop Innovation and Better Digital Capabilities

Pay close attention to and support entrepreneurs and SMEs that could contribute to the economy and transform innovative production patterns in the post-pandemic era. The government can actively cultivate the entrepreneurial spirit of SMEs and focus on key areas conducive to society's future development. Also, policy formulation should be based on the direction of future development and promote innovation, entrepreneurship, and new business models. It will also be helpful to strengthen cooperation and communication among SMEs, guiding them to seize the benefits of digital transformation by accelerating the adoption of digital technology, the innovation of organisational patterns, and the upgrading of skills. The government should be responsible for summarising the trend of SMEs' digital transformation and improving SMEs' potential development and competitiveness.

Grasp the Full Advantages of Diversified Subjects

Governmental departments at all levels should involve all kinds of non-governmental entities in supporting the operation and development of SMEs during the epidemic. For example, during the pandemic, various industrial associations launched rent relief initiatives for SMEs; in response, real estate developers, including Wanda, Longhu, Huarun, and Baoli, have announced rent reduction policies for their commercial projects to help their merchants overcome difficulties together. Meanwhile, the banking industry and other financial institutions actively respond to the national policy by providing differentiated and preferential financial services for SMEs. In addition, diversified entities also provided more opportunities and platforms to connect the supply and demand chain for SMEs; Shanghai Zaitu Network Technology is a typical case. Zaitu is a technology-based SME established in 2015 to create an intelligent management platform for business and travel data. By developing a fully developed independent cloud system named SaaS for business travel and an online fee control system, Zaitu became the first domestic company with two online business travel solutions with two fully independent property rights. Accordingly, Harbin Pharmaceutical Group Co., Ltd., a representative pharmaceutical enterprise in China that has provided many medical products during the epidemic, built a cooperation relationship with Zaitu in 2021. Zaitu provides one-stop services from budget management, booking approval, consumption payment, account reconciliation, and expense reimbursement to data analysis for Harbin Pharmaceutical Group's business travel needs. The service offered by Zaitu has met the Harbin Pharmaceutical

Group's demand for the integration of industry and finance from front-end business consumption to back-end financial reimbursement, which not only helps large enterprises improve the efficiency of overall service during the pandemic but also expands the platform for more SMEs to get engaged in cooperation and development.

Give Full Play to SMEs' Entrepreneurship with Independent Development and an Innovative Spirit

SMEs should strengthen research and development based on the demand of the epidemic when seeking a future development path in the post-pandemic era. For example, Tongdun Technology Co., Ltd., an SME established in 2012 based on artificial intelligence technology, has helped customers prevent fraud and security risks and promoted intelligent decision-making through two platforms. The "AI-Based Decision Intelligence Platform" and the "Sharing Intelligent Platform Based on Privacy Computing" are the platforms. During the epidemic, Tongdun Technology has applied AI and other digital technologies to effectively solve problems such as decreasing credit risk and fraud risk and increasing the economic scale of SMEs in financial services. The model developed by Tongdun has been implemented in many provinces in China, such as Hebei, Zhejiang, and Shandong provinces. Furthermore, during the pandemic, the Tangshan Enterprise Comprehensive Financial Service Platform led by the Tangshan government, which received technical support from Tongdun, has helped many SMEs to recover operations. The Spring Rain Gold Service project launched by the platform, which benefited amounts of SMEs, was praised by the State Council.

On the other hand, from the government's perspective, the government should ensure more free entry and exit for enterprises and gradually revive the production mode of SMEs with a more inclusive attitude. Efforts should be made to reform the existing bankruptcy system, promote the closure of unproductive enterprises and the restructuring of promising SMEs, and improve the ability of entrepreneurs to start new ventures after failure. As bankruptcies are likely to rise sharply due to the pandemic, reforms should focus on limiting the negative impact and reducing the personal costs for entrepreneurs. However, these systems must be well-justified and rigorously standardised to assess qualified SMEs, which could be supported throughout the recovery and transition to new business models.

Conclusion

The COVID-19 pandemic has significantly impacted the survival and development of SMEs in China. However, the Chinese government has implemented various strategies to support SMEs during this challenging period, including fiscal and monetary policies, tax relief, and subsidies. These strategies have helped SMEs to adapt to the new normal and emerge stronger from the pandemic. Furthermore, China's experience supporting SMEs during COVID-19 can be a reference for other BRICS countries to develop effective policies and strategies to support SMEs. As the world grapples with the pandemic, SMEs remain vital to countries' economic growth and development. Therefore, governments must continue prioritising SMEs and providing the necessary support and resources to ensure their survival and success. By doing so, SMEs can continue to drive economic growth, create employment opportunities, and contribute to the overall prosperity of nations.

References

China Association of Small and Medium Enterprises Press Release (2021) China Association of Small and Medium Enterprises, Enable Harbin Pharmaceutical Co., LTD., "the leading pharmaceutical industry enterprise, to build intelligent travel and create a compliant and efficient travel platform on the way". https://ca-sme.org/content/Content/index/id/32874 (Accessed 30 July 2022).

China Association of Small and Medium Enterprises Press Release (2022) China Association of Small and Medium Enterprises, AI helps the development of small and medium-sized enterprises with the shield again praised by the authority. https://ca-sme.org/content/Content/index/id/33759 (Accessed 20 November 2022).

China Business Network (2022) The policy of stabilising employment and expanding employment has been further expanded, and small, medium and micro enterprises in difficulties can delay their social security payments. http://www.gov.cn/zhengce/2022-04/29/content_5687967.htm (Accessed 27 July 2022).

China Business News (29 April 2022) The policy of stabilising employment and expanding employment has been further expanded, and small, medium and micro enterprises in difficulties can delay their social security payments. http://www.gov.cn/zhengce/2022-04/29/content_5687967.htm (Accessed 30 May 2023).

China Government (2020) More than RMB 660 billion had been paid off in arrears to private enterprises and SMEs by 2020. http://www.gov.cn/xinwen/2020-01/16/content_5469855.htm (Accessed 10 July 2023).

China News (28 February 2022). The Ministry of Industry and Information Technology (MIIT): This year, it plans to cultivate another 3,000 national specialised and special new "little giant" enterprises. https://www.chinanews.com.cn/cj/2022/02-28/9687879.shtml (Accessed 3 August 2023).

China News (July 30, 2022), This year, it plans to cultivate another 3,000 national specialised and special new "little giant" enterprises, The Ministry of Industry and Information Technology (MIIT). https://www.chinanews.com.cn/cj/2022/02-28/9687879.shtml (Accessed 30 July 2022).

Economic Daily (15 April 2021) PSBC Small and Micro-sized Enterprise Operating Index Report of March 2021. https://www.psbc.com/en/products_and_services/corporate/samseoi/202104/t20210415_88641.html (Accessed 20 September 2023).

Economic Daily (14 June 2022) Advance to enjoy additional deduction preferential institutionalisation. http://www.gov.cn/zhengce/2022-06/14/content_5695541.htm (Accessed 30 July 2022).

Economic Daily (14 June 2022) Institutionalise the preferential treatment of super-deduction in advance. http://www.gov.cn/zhengce/2022-06/14/content_5695541.htm (Accessed 30 October 2023).

Economic Daily (14 June 2022) More than 2.5 trillion yuan was added to cut taxes and fees in 2020 (www.gov.cn, 2020). http://www.gov.cn/zhengce/2022-06/14/content_5695541.htm (Accessed 19 May 2023).

Guangzhou Daily (7 February 2020) People's Government of Guangdong Province, Guangzhou free rent, cut interest rates to support the stable operation of micro, small and medium-sized enterprises. https://www.gd.gov.cn/gdywdt/dsdt/content/post_2886519.html (Accessed 30 July 2022).

Ifeng.com Guangdong Comprehensive (2 February 2020) China Banking Regulatory Commission, Notice on Strengthening the Financial Services of the Banking Industry and Insurance Industry to coordinate well with the Coronavirus Prevention Work. http://gd.ifeng.com/a/20200202/8166466_0.shtml (Accessed 12 August 2022).

IMF (2014) People's Republic of China: 2014 article IV consultation-Staff Report; Press Release; and statement by the executive director for the People's Republic of China, IMF, IMF country report NO. 14/235 (Print).

Kamal-Chaoui L. (26 May 2020) Rescuing SMEs from the COVID storm: What's next? (The Forum Network. 2020). https://www.oecd-forum.org/posts/rescuing-smes-from-the-covid-storm-what-s-next (Accessed 30 July 2022).

Ling M. (2022) The balance of inclusive small and micro loans increased by 27.3% year on year. https://www.financialnews.com.cn/sj_142/jrsj/202202/t20220207_238774.html (Accessed 23 July 2023).

Ma Z, Liu Y, Gao Y. (2021) Research on the impact of COVID-19 on Chinese small and medium-sized enterprises: Evidence from Beijing. *PLoS ONE* 16(12): e0257036. https://doi.org/10.1371/journal.pone.0257036

Minyin Think Tank Research (2020) China Minsheng Banking Research Institute, Analysis and Policy Recommendations on the Impact of COVID-19 on the Global Industrial Chain and Major Import and Export Industries in China (No.14) (Print).

National Bureau of Statistics (2017) National Bureau of Statistics of People's Republic of China, Notice on the Statistical Methods for the Division of Large, Medium, and Small Enterprises. http://www.stats.gov.cn/zs/tjws/tjbz/202301/t20230101_1903367.html (Accessed 8 September 2023).

OECD (March 2020) "Italian regional SME policy responses", OECD tackling coronavirus, (COVID-19) contributing to global effort. https://www.oecd.org/cfe/leed/COVID-19-Italian-regions-SME-policy-responses.pdf (Accessed 30 July 2022).

OECD (2020), Coronavirus (COVID-19) SME Policy Responses, OECD tackling coronavirus, (Covid-19) contributing to global effort. https://www.oecd.org/coronavirus/policy-responses/coronavirus-covid-19-sme-policy-responses-04440101/ (Accessed 12 August 2022).

OECD (2021) The territorial impact of COVID-19: Managing the crisis and recovery across levels of government. https://read.oecd-ilibrary.org/view/?ref=1095_1095253-immbk05xb7&title=The-territorial-impact-of-COVID-19-Managing-the-crisis-and-recovery-across-levels-of-government (Accessed 20 July 2023).

OECD (2021) One year of SME and entrepreneurship policy responses to COVID-19: Lessons learned to "build back better", OECD tackling coronavirus (COVID-19), contributing to a global effort. https://www.oecd.org/coronavirus/policy-responses/one-year-of-sme-and-entrepreneurship-policy-responses-to-covid-19-lessons-learned-to-build-back-better-9a230220/ (Accessed 30 July 2022).

OECD (2021) One year of SME and entrepreneurship policy responses to COVID-19: Lessons learned to "build back better". https://www.oecd.org/coronavirus/

policy-responses/one-year-of-sme-and-entrepreneurship-policy-responses-to-covid-19-lessons-learned-to-build-back-better-9a230220/ (Accessed 2 September 2023).

People's Daily (19 January 2021) China's economic aggregate exceeded 100 trillion yuan for the first time. http://www.gov.cn/xinwen/2021-01/19/content_5580925.htm (Accessed 5 July 2023).

People's Daily (13 January 2021) SME development index continued to pick up in the fourth quarter of 2020 (www.gov.cn, 2021), http://www.gov.cn/xinwen/2021-01/13/content_5579336.htm (Accessed 15 July 2023).

Pedauga, L., Sáez, F. and Delgado-Márquez, B.L. (2022). Macroeconomic lockdown and SMEs: the impact of the COVID-19 pandemic in Spain. *Small Business Economics* 58: 665–688 https://doi.org/10.1007/s11187-021-00476-7.

Priyono, A., Moin, A., Putri, V.N.A.O. (2020), Identifying digital transformation paths in the business model of SMEs during the COVID-19 pandemic. *Journal of Open Innovation: Technology, Market, and Complexity*, 6(4):104. https://doi.org/10.3390/joitmc6040104

Reuters (31 January 2020) Reuters Staff, Wanke, Longhu and other department store tenants to waive rent to tide over the difficulties of pneumonia. https://www.reuters.com/article/vanke-longhu-real-estate-rent-virus-0131-idCNKBS1ZU0E5 (Accessed 30 July 2022).

Sina Technology (01 June 2020) Central bank: It is estimated that the extension policy will cover about 7 trillion yuan of loans to small and micro enterprises. https://tech.sina.com.cn/roll/2020-06-01/doc-iirczymk4713377.shtml (Accessed 30 May 2023).

Shao, Z. (2015) "Social Security Policy." In *The New Urban Area Development: A Case Study in China*, pp. 295–297. Berlin, Heidelberg: Springer Berlin Heidelberg. doi: 10.1007/978-3-662-44958-5_36

State Taxation Administration (2020), The State Taxation Administration of People's Republic of China, Notice on VAT Policy to support the resumption of work and employment of individual businesses. http://www.chinatax.gov.cn/chinatax/n810341/n810755/c5145325/content.html (Accessed 30 July 2022).

State Taxation Administration (2022) The State Taxation Administration of People's Republic of China, Interpretation of VAT exemption policy for small-scale taxpayers. http://www.chinatax.gov.cn/chinatax/n810351/n810906/c5174222/content.html (Accessed 30 July 2022).

The Beijing News (3 February 2020) "Xu Xiaonian on the impact of the epidemic: The Situation of small and medium-sized enterprises should not be taken lightly". http://www.stats.gov.cn/tjsj/tjbz/201801/t20180103_1569357.html (Accessed 17 October 2023).

The Ministry of Human Resources and Social Security of People's Republic of China (2022) Notice on unemployment insurance to stabilize jobs and improve skills to prevent unemployment. http://www.gov.cn/zhengce/zhengceku/2022-05/13/content_5690133.htm (Accessed 23 July 2023).

The Ministry of Human Resources and Social Security of People's Republic of China (2022) Notice on unemployment insurance to stabilise jobs and improve skills to prevent unemployment. http://www.gov.cn/zhengce/zhengceku/2022-05/13/content_5690133.htm (Accessed 28 July 2023).

The Ministry of Finance of People's Republic of China (2020) Notice on Supporting Financial Services in Strengthening Coronavirus Prevention Policies (Ministry of Industry and Information Technology of the People's Republic of China. https://www.miit.gov.cn/ztzl/rdzt/ydxgfyyqzcqyfgfccsjrzc/jrzc/zdkzc/art/2020/art_cd1b3b6e5faa43f38597ab5535b72cee.html (Accessed 6 April 2023).

The People's Bank of China (2020) Notice on Further Strengthening Financial Support for Preventing and Controlling Coronavirus Epidemic. http://www.gov.cn/zhengce/zhengceku/2020-02/01/content_5473639.htm (Accessed 18 March 2023).

The People's Bank of China (2022) The People's Bank of China implements two direct instruments for continuous conversion. http://www.gov.cn/xinwen/2022-01/02/content_5666092.htm (Accessed 15 June 2023).

T. H. E. S. Council (2023) China to continue with policies that help lessen business burden, keep jobs stable and expand employment, and further support flexible work (Print).

The State Council of People's Republic of China (2020) Notice of the National Development and Reform Commission on phasing down electricity costs for Enterprises to support their resumption of work and production. http://www.gov.cn/zhengce/zhengceku/2020-02/22/content_5482141.htm (Accessed 3 May 2022).

The State Council of People's Republic of China (2021) Routine State Council policy briefing. http://www.gov.cn/xinwen/2021zccfh/53/index.htm (Accessed 30 July 2022).

The State Council of People's Republic of China (2022a) The 2022 Report on the Work of the Government. http://www.gov.cn/gongbao/content/2022/content_5679681.htm (Accessed 30 July 2022).

The State Council of People's Republic of China (2020b) Regulations on Protection of Payments by Small and Medium-sized Enterprises. http://www.gov.cn/zhengce/content/2020-07/14/content_5526768.htm (Accessed 30 July 2022).

Wolters K, (2022), "Fiscal and Tax Information Database: Professional Chinese-English Bilingual Fiscal and Tax Information", *Ministry of Finance, State Administration of Taxation*. https://taa.wkinfo.com.cn/legislation/detail/MTAxMDAxMzcyNjk%3D (Accessed 25 June 2023).

Xinhua Finance (5 February 2022) Ministry of Industry and Information Technology (MIIT): The production and operation of small and medium-sized enterprises in China will maintain a stable recovery trend in 2021. https://www.cnfin.com/hg-lb/detail/20220205/3529213_1.html (Accessed 3 July 2023).

Xinhua Finance (2022) Ministry of Industry and Information Technology (MIIT): The production and operation of small and medium-sized enterprises in China will maintain a stable recovery trend in 2021. https://www.cnfin.com/hglb/detail/20220205/3529213_1.html (Accessed 30 July 2022).

Xu P. (2020) Vigorously support SMEs in coping with the impact of the pandemic (Print).

Zhejiang Daily (2023) Report on the Work of the Government 2023, The People's Government of Zhejiang Province. https://www.zj.gov.cn/art/2023/3/1/art_1229631731_60047201.html (Accessed 5 June 2023).

Zhu W. (2020) The Plight of Micro, Small and medium-sized Enterprises under the impact of COVID-19 and the Improvement of Policy efficiency (Print).

Zhu W.L.J. and Wei W, Ouyang L. (2020) The impact of the epidemic on SMEs and thoughts on response. http://mis.sem.tsinghua.edu.cn/ueditor/jsp/upload/file/20200206/15809602399130009300.pdf (Accessed 19 October 2023).

6 Emerging Trends among Indian Entrepreneurs

A Post COVID-19 Outlook

S. Yavana Rani and Ravinder Rena

Introduction

Entrepreneurship is the backbone of any economy in the world. The Micro Small and Medium-sized Enterprises (MSMEs) contribute almost 33% of India's GDP. The COVID-19 outbreak and nationwide lockdown have impacted all facets of society. The Indian Micro-Small and Medium Enterprises are under much stress due to the restrictions that have lasted for several months in 2020.

Entrepreneurs are renowned for their agility, which was also true during the COVID-19 pandemic. Ute et al. (2021), more than 50% of entrepreneurs worldwide adjusted their business strategies throughout the pandemic, and nearly 40% discovered new business prospects. Diverse opportunities connected to digitalisation, health and wellbeing, local *vs* global company focus, sustainability, and innovative business models were also available.

Before 2020, MSMEs were defined based on the initial plant, machinery, and equipment investment. Manufacturing and service industries have different investment thresholds. The Cabinet Committee of India authorised a revised definition of MSMEs on 1st June 2020, to combat the COVID-19 pandemic (Table 6.1). According to the new MSMED Act, 2006 definition, MSMEs will be classified into one group using a standardised norm that considers investment and turnover (no distinction between manufacturing and services enterprises).

MSMEs are important from a strategic and imperious standpoint in developing nations. MSMEs' importance in the Indian economy was excluded from the first five-year plan 1951. Vashisht et al. (2016). Over 5000 products, ranging from conventional to highly innovative ones, are produced by MSMEs in India. Compared to India's industrial sector, the MSMEs sector has recently seen a phenomenal growth rate. A 13% increase was recorded as the sector's average growth rate for MSMEs. Countries must enhance their MSMEs to advance and develop their economies (Sipahi, 2020).

The Udyam Registration platform registered 12,201,448 MSMEs as of 25 November 2022, according to data from the Ministry of Micro, Small, and Medium Businesses (MSME, 2022). Microbusinesses made up 11,735,117

DOI: 10.4324/9781003475606-8

Table 6.1 Existing and revised classification of MSME's

MSME Classification – Existing

Based on: Total amount invested in Plant/Machinery/Equipment

Classification	Micro enterprises	Small enterprises	Medium enterprises
Manufacturing enterprises	Total investment less than Rs 25 lakhs	Total investment less than Rs 5 crores	Total investment less than Rs 10 crores
Service Enterprises	Total investment less than Rs 10 lakhs	Total investment less than Rs 2 crores	Total investment less than Rs 5 crores

MSME Classification – Revised

Based on: Total amount invested and Annual Turnover

Classification	Micro enterprises	Small enterprises	Medium enterprises
Manufacturing and Services	Total investment less than Rs 1 crore & Turnover less than Rs 5 crores	Total investment less than Rs 10 crores & Turnover less than Rs 50 crores	Total investment less than Rs 20 crores & Turnover less than Rs 100 crores

Source: https://msme.gov.in

(96.17%) of all registered businesses, while small businesses made up 426,864 (3.49%) and mid-sized businesses made up 39,467 (0.32%) (Table 6.2). To ensure sufficient liquidity is maintained in business operations, domestic business needs a significant financial stimulus from the government and financial institutions in the form of favourable working capital loans.

Table 6.2 Contribution of MSMEs in India's GDP (in rupee crores)

Year	Total GVA	Share of MSMEs in GVA (%)	Total GDP	Share of MSMEs in GDP (%)
2011–2012	8106946	32.35	8736329	**30.0**
2012–2013	9202692	32.82	9944013	**30.4**
2013–2014	10363153	32.71	11233522	**30.20**
2014–2015	11504279	31.80	12467958	**29.34**
2015–2016	12574499	32.28	13771874	**29.48**
2016–2017	13965200	32.24	15391669	**29.25**
2017–2018	15513122	32.79	17098304	**29.75**
2018–2019	17139962	33.5	18971237	**30.27**

Source: Annual Report, Ministry of MSME (2020–2021).

Table 6.3 Private sectors/social entrepreneurs effort to uplift MSME industry after COVID-19

Beneficiaries	Supporting agencies	Support initiatives
Aerospace Engineers Private Limited, Tamil Nadu	Aerospace company – Boeing	To produce and supply critical aviation components
>2,500 MSMEs	Walmart and Flipkart	Vriddhi-training programme for the supplier development
MSMEs	Online retail company – Flipkart	"Flipkart Boost" will assist digital-first consumer companies and provide more power.to MSMEs
MSMEs	HDFC Bank team up with the National Small Industries Corporation (NSIC)	Supporting credit facilities
MSMEs	US Agency for International Development (USAID) and the US International Development Finance Corporation (DFC) collaborated with Kotak Mahindra Bank	Supporting credit facilities
Small and Medium Businesses (SMBs)	Facebook India, in collaboration with Indifi	Small business loans initiative
MSMEs in Odisha	Indian Bank, Odisha	"MSME Prerana"- credit support
MSME members	NSIC, through an MoU with Agricultural & Processed Food Products Export Development Authority (APEDA)	To explore their agriculture and processed food export possibilities

The Gross Value Added (GVA) of the MSMEs sector in the nation has been rising rapidly. The proportion of MSMEs in the total GVA and GDP of the nation has steadily increased over the last ten years. Micro, small and medium enterprises across India accounted for nearly 27% of India's GDP in the financial year 2021. This was a decrease in contribution to the country's GDP (during COVID-19) pandemic (Table 6.3).

As opposed to Rs. 7,572 crore (US$1.03 billion) in the financial year 2021, the budget allocation for MSMEs is doubled to Rs. 15,700 crore (US$2.14 billion) in the financial year 2022.

Problem Statement

The impact of the COVID-19 pandemic on the development of MSMEs has caused the economy of India to decline (Table 6.4). The sudden impact was very difficult for Indian Entrepreneurs to tolerate. This article portrays the condition of

Table 6.4 Schemes introduced by government of India to uplift MSME industry post COVID-19

Name of the scheme	Benefits
Prime Minister's Employment Generation Programme (PMEGP)	Government subsidy
Scheme of Fund for Regeneration of Traditional Industries (SFURTI)	To strengthen the traditional industries
Scheme for Promoting Innovation, Rural Industry and Entrepreneurship (ASPIRE)	To establish a network of technology hubs and incubators
Entrepreneurship and Skill Development Programme (ESDP)	To motivate youth for self-employment
The Credit Guarantee Fund Trust for Micro and Small Enterprises (CGTMSE)	To provide loans without a collateral
SAMBHAV – Awareness programme	To promote entrepreneurship and domestic manufacturing.
Pradhan Mantri Mudra Yojana (PMMY)	Pro-entrepreneurship and self-employment Scheme
Credit Linked Capital Subsidy – Technology Up-gradation Scheme (CLCS-TUS)	Technology Up-gradation
Micro & Small Enterprises – Cluster Development Programme (MSE-CDP)	Cluster Development Programme
National Scheduled Caste and Scheduled Tribe Hub (NSSH)	SC, ST development
Guarantee Emergency Credit Line' (GECL)	Credit facility
Amendment on Factoring Regulation	Increasing the speed payments ecosystem's
India Export Initiative and "IndiaXports 2021 Portal"	Increasing the exports

micro, small and medium-sized organisations, the economy, and the market climate of the nation generally impacted by the spread of COVID-19. Furthermore, it depicts the trends among Indian Entrepreneurs after the COVID-19 pandemic.

Study Objectives

1 To assess the situation of India's micro, small, and medium-sized businesses.
2 To evaluate the challenges and the trends of Indian Entrepreneurs after the COVID-19 pandemic.

Literature Review

This section provides some important reviews related to this study.

Williams et al. (2017) found that the execution of a business is under threat during a crisis. Khan and Al Mamari (2019), COVID-19 has now become a threat to business entrepreneurs across the globe. The training on various aspects and education becomes the basis of individuals' efforts to rebuild their lives to succeed in their business.

Khan, Mohammed Aref, and Farooque (2020) proposed that technology can help Small and Medium-sized Enterprises (SMEs) be more innovative in getting clients internationally and a chance to identify and develop businesses worldwide. After Covid-19, businesses are forced to reevaluate their plans of action, moving tasks on the web or carrying out the work with smartness to sustain in the industry (The Organization for Economic Cooperation and Development (OECD), 2020). Riom and Valero (2020) found that almost three-fourths of the business firms in the UK have moved to work from concept during the pandemic and have invested in new digital technologies.

Zdnet (2020) study revealed that more than half of the SMEs in Brazil accepted that there was a significant growth in customer relationships, process agility, and attracting new customers due to the adoption of digitalisation during the pandemic and almost 75% of online. Yet another study by Paypal (2020) alluded that SME entrepreneurs in Canada trust that technology transformation is now essential to succeed in the business.

SME adoption gaps are significant in many sectors. Diffusion rate, median OECD, based on national averages for the proportions of businesses utilising the technology between 2015 and 2018 (OECD, 2021).

The government initiatives are forcing the COVID-19 pandemic to get things in order. There is hope that it will bring back the same business scenario. Therefore, the upcoming time frame is more than just making up lost time and balancing requests with limits. Organisations need to prepare for a future unexpected period and the post-COVID-19 reality (Deloitte, 2022).

World Bank classification shows the SME assistance policies developed by groups of nations based on their income levels in response to the COVID-19 crisis (February 2020–February 2021). The number of nations per income group is displayed in the horizontal bars. The percentage label on the graph indicates the share of nations that use the metric in that income group. Data from the World Bank are used to classify countries depending on their revenue. 39 nations are categorised as high-income nations, 12 as upper middle-income groups, and 4 as lower middle-income groups. According to World Bank data, Brazil, China, and South Africa are upper-middle-income countries, Russia is a high-income country, and India is a lower-middle-income country. All four countries except Russia fall in the lower and upper middle countries.

Ullah, Ullah Khan, and Wijewickrama (2021) in their study found that the pandemic has impressively expanded dependence on nearby associations and neighbourhood staff, especially as movement limitations diminished worldwide admittance to networks. The more noteworthy struggle will be expected to formalise the change of key jobs and obligations to these nearby entertainers.

Ahmed, Kar, and Ahmed (2018) found that the characteristic of an individual is an essential trait that builds the confidence to make their business sustainable in any situation.

According to Bakhtiar et al. (2022), the government has aided the development of MSMEs by providing assistance through people's business loans, simplifying business permits, lowering the percentage of income taxes, and providing business assistance; however, during the pandemic rules such as social distancing, activity restrictions, and operating hour restrictions have resulted in a decrease in MSME income.

Impact of the COVID-19 Pandemic on MSMEs

The spread of the COVID-19 virus worldwide, starting in 2020, caused significant issues for trade and many other economic sectors. Suppose MSMEs are to maintain their place in the global and international markets. In that case, they must remain globally competitive and regularly update themselves to meet the challenges brought on by technological changes, shifting consumer needs, entering new markets, etc. (MSME, 21–22).

Estupinan et al. (2020), in April–July 2020–2021, the overall exports of both Merchandise and Services are expected to be 141.82 billion US dollars, performing a negative growth of 21.99% compared to the same time the previous year. The COVID-19 lockdown hurt the economy through shocks to the labour supply because it restricts people's movement and orders them to work from home. In many professions, particularly manufacturing and traditional services (travel, broker activities), employees needed help to work from home. Then, due to demand shocks, people lost their income, earnings, and salaries. As a result of losing their jobs, enterprises cannot pay employee salaries. A recent study found that Lockdowns 1.0 and 2.0 affected the lives of 116.18 million (25%) and 78.93 million (17%) workers in India.

MSMEs give business and occupation to 25% of India's total labour force and contribute around 30% to India's gross domestic product (GDP) MSME (2018–2019). The MSMEs contribute a considerable percentage to the exports of India and GDP (Table 6.5). Over the recent couple of years, their export stake has floated around 42–48%. The Worldwide slowdown in exports has seriously impacted the actual endurance of MSMEs. Most significant commodities have shown negative development during July 2020 versus July 2019.

Rathore and Khanna (2020) revealed that, on average, the loss incurred is 17% of their yearly sales, which means that two months' worth of revenue has already been lost. The losses were greatest for the smallest MSMEs. Those with fewer than eight employees lost 24% of their yearly sales, compared to companies with more than 45 employees, which saw a much lower loss of only 10%. The survey results also demonstrate that, before the shutdown, MSMEs typically function at 75% of capacity. MSMES

Table 6.5 Negative growth of commodities during July 2020 compared to July 2019

Commodities	Percentage growth in July 2020 compared to July 2019
Petroleum goods	−51.54
Gems and Jewellery	−49.61
Leather products	−26.96
Man-made fabrics	−23.33
Ready-Made Garments (RMG) of all textiles	−22.09
Cashew nuts	−21.25
Marine goods	−20.14
Tobacco	−19.49
Electronic gadgets	−17.42
Spices	−11.38
Mica/Coal ores and processed minerals	−8.21
Handicraft materials	6.12

Source: MSME (2018–2019).

only generated an average of 11% of their capacity after the lockdown, with 56% doing nothing.

According to the Asian Development Bank's prediction for the eight Asian nations' annual GDP growth as of September 2020, Bangladesh and Vietnam were expected to experience growth rates of 5.2% and 1.8%, respectively (Table 6.6). The other six countries had negative growth estimates, notwithstanding their significant commitment to pandemic relief policy packages. The Asian Development Bank (ADB) anticipated that the Indian economy would experience significant shrinkage due to the sharp decline in private consumption and investment brought on by local lockdowns and the ongoing COVID-19 epidemic. ADB (2020).

Table 6.6 Forecast for Asian countries' GDP growth (as of September 2020)

Countries	GDP
Bangladesh	5.20%
Vietnam	1.80%
Pakistan	−0.40%
Indonesia	−1.00%
Lao PDR	−2.50%
Mongolia	−2.60%
Malaysia	−5.00%
India	**−9.00%**

Source: ADB Asian Development Outlook, September 2020.

High-frequency (monthly) data on the index of industrial production (IIP), one of the most crucial metrics, is used to analyse the industrial sector's current and forecast output trends. IIP in April 2020 was significantly lower than in April 2019. A shocking 66.6% contraction was observed in output compared to the 2.5% positive growth rate in the same month last year. The following months saw a slight improvement in IIP growth, although the growth rate remained negative until September 2020.

The manufacturing industry suffered significant job losses during the lockdown, and the recovery of about 50% of the enterprises has been exceedingly slow since it ended, according to research published in Vyas (2021). Compared to the same months in the previous two years, the unemployment rate in April and May 2020 was above 20%. Importantly, the unemployment rate decreased and followed the same path as during the previous two years as economic activity increased in the later part of the post-lockdown era (i.e. in the months of October and November 2020).

In short, various studies and the examination of high-frequency IIP data indicate that the MSME sector suffered heavily during the lockdown. The study found a drastic drop in the sector's output, employment, revenue, and capital inflow. To address the unique issues the sector is experiencing, the government of India and industry organisations have announced significant policy actions for the survival and regeneration of the sector. Make in India 2.0 focuses on 27 sectors to make India a Manufacturing Hub.

Research Methodology

The research study is descriptive in nature and is based on secondary data. The information was gathered from reputable secondary sources published between 2017 and 2021 in journals such as Research Journal in Advanced Humanities, *Academy of Management Annals*, magazines, reports, and websites. Most data were retrieved from the Indian Government's Ministry of MSME website (http://msme.gov.in). The statistical information from various reports has been mentioned to emphasise the subject's significance.

Analysis and Discussion

From the literature studies, five major trends have been identified among Indian entrepreneurs during the COVID-19 pandemic.

Trends and Perspectives of Indian Entrepreneurs

Digital Transformation

Sahasranamam et al. (2021), the most prevailing trend is the digital transformation of the business activities supported by the consumer readiness and acceptance of online products and services. The digital transformation has impelled the use of digital financial trades, unfolded new markets and stimulated many digitally enabled startups. Digitally enabled hyper-local business models like Meesho and PayNearby are expanding rapidly. Customers in developing countries like South Africa and India who did not believe in online buying and transactions have now started to explore online businesses. Chinese entrepreneurs started their direct sales through the social media App TikTok.

The emergence of digitised education and healthcare tools has solved the challenges faced due to the COVID-10 pandemic. The entrepreneurs sensed the prospects directly associated with expanding healthcare services and telemedicine. As such, people in developing countries like India and South Africa generally accept using chatbots and artificial intelligence in healthcare. Digitisation makes it possible to operate remotely, shifting the labour force away from cosmopolitan cities and toward new process opportunities outside urban areas.

Inter-Professional Collaboration

Various professional sectors like start-ups, higher education institutes and civil society collaborated with the government to face the challenges posed by the COVID-19 pandemic. Startups in diagnostics, respiratory devices, medicines, and cold chain technology have received support from the government-funded C-CAMP COVID-19 Innovation Development Accelerator (C-CIDA). Collaborations of this nature assist business owners in commercialising their goods and services and complying with legal requirements (EY Global, 2020).

Mostly, governments across the globe have offered assistance to businesses to lessen the COVID-19 pandemic's economic effects. During the pandemic, 32.5% of Indian business owners requested government assistance for job retention programmes and postponed tax and rate payments.

Globalisation to Localisation

Even if digitalisation made it harder for enterprises to connect with clients abroad, many entrepreneurs saw how the pandemic disruption of global trade raised awareness of local markets and the desire for domestic production and supply. The Indian government launched the Atma-Nirbhar Bharat (self-reliant India) program to aid MSMEs. The government has increased its assistance by offering incentives and laws to aid in localising some industries, including manufacturing toys and electronics (IBEF, 2021).

International corporations are assisting MSMEs by establishing new manufacturing platforms and clusters. These fantastic programmes and resources could aid MSMEs in building trustworthy supply chains, increasing employment, and lowering the amount of electronic goods India buys. Electronic imports are about 13% of all of India's imports.

This further supports the National Policy on Electronics of the Indian Government to make India a $400 billion centre for Electronics System Design and Manufacturing (ESDM) by 2025 (IBEF, 2022).

Inclusive and Sustainability Models

Many entrepreneurs took advantage of the post-COVID-19 economy by committing to philanthropic endeavours through inclusive and sustainable business strategies. Giving social and environmental impact can be more easily sustained over the long term when integrated into the business and aligned with income development. Furthermore, studies show that business owners who positively impact society and the environment are more satisfied and fulfilled in their profession. Therefore, inclusive business models support the trends toward more focus on mental health and increased use of the circular economy models.

World Economic Forum (2021), most Indian entrepreneurs showed high societal commitment during the COVID-19 pandemic. Almost 75% of the Indian entrepreneurs volunteered their time and business services for social commitment. Most companies make an effort to raise money for COVID-19-related projects. Indian entrepreneurs have the highest societal commitment of any nation, whether developing or developed.

Mental Well-Being and Build Resilience

Indian entrepreneurs' mental and physical lifestyle choices appear crucial during the pandemic. Stress brought on by the pandemic has endangered business owners' productivity. Almost everywhere in the world is now aware of the importance of mental health. The life satisfaction and stress of Indian entrepreneurs were equivalent to pre-COVID-19 population estimates.

According to Sahasranamam et al. (2021), *many Indian Entrepreneurs engage in daily exercise 69% are committed to a 30-minute workout,* 58% to healthy sleep, 45% to yoga and meditation, and 58% to religious or spiritual beliefs. These patterns are significant because they show how resilient entrepreneurs are personally and how they pay attention to self-care to keep this resilience. According to World Economic Forum (2021) research, this is a crucial foundation for their enterprises' durability, long-term success, creativity and productivity. These demonstrate the entrepreneurship ecosystem in India's strength and resiliency throughout the COVID-19 pandemic. They will be essential in achieving India's goal of developing a 5 trillion-dollar inclusive and sustainable economy by 2025 (Ministry of Commerce and Industry, 2018).

Conclusion

Millions of Indians enjoy their livelihood because of the development of MSMEs. Almost all areas of economic activity, including raw materials supply, the demand for finished goods, and employment opportunities, are now unpredictable due to COVID-19. Due to chronic loss of revenue, many units, notably in the small and micro segments of the economy, were forced to go out of business.

MSMEs integrated with e-commerce platforms have profited for the last two years of the COVID-19 Pandemic; hiring, sales, turnover, and earnings have increased. The government's initiatives for the MSME sector under the "*Atma Nirbhar Bharat Abhiyan*" certainly came at the appropriate time with the noble goal of reviving the sector and transforming it from "local to global" within the general "Make in India" strategy.

Recommendations

The industry will be better able to compete and survive the coronavirus outbreak if MSMEs and startups work together effectively and form alliances The Entrepreneurs take advantage of the post-COVID-19 economy by committing to social responsibility through inclusive and sustainable business models. The new social initiatives among industries, including agriculture, healthcare, and sanitation, are progressing due to the societal involvement of entrepreneurs and the demand for sustainable goods and services. During the pandemic, societal support for newly established enterprises became more prominent. People are encouraged to participate in social enterprise by societal participation and government backing. Many foreign businesses have expressed a desire to move their manufacturing operations away from China, which provides India with a great opportunity to seize these chances and establish itself as a truly global manufacturing hub.

References

Ahmed, Y. A., Kar, B., & Ahmed, H. M. S. (2018) Critical factors of entrepreneurial competencies for successfully managing micro and small SME in Ethiopia. *IOSR Journal of Business and Management*, *20*(7):84–91. https://doi.org/10.9790/487X2007018491

Asian Development Bank (ADB). (2020) *Asian development outlook (September)*. Asian Development Bank, Manila.

Bakhtiar, S., Ramlan, P., Saleh, W., Andreani, A. R., & Herman, B. (2022) The role of governments in developing MSMEs in line with social changes due to the COVID-19 pandemic. *KnE Social Sciences*, *7*(5):289–295. https://doi.org/10.18502/kss.v7i5.10556

Deloitte. (2022) Embracing digital: From survival to thriving in the post-COVID-19 world. https://www2.deloitte.com/nl/nl/pages/consumer/articles/the-post-covid-19-world-is-digital.html (Accessed 20 September 2023).

Estupinan, X., Sharma, M., Gupta, S., & Birla, B. (2020) Impact of COVID-19 pandemic on labour supply and gross value added in India. http://www.igidr.ac.in/pdf/publication/WP-2020-022.pdf (Accessed 20 September 2023).

EY Global. (2020) COVID-19 and pandemic planning: How companies should respond. https://www.ey.com/en_gl/covid-19/covid-19-and-pandemic-planning–how-companies-should-respond (Accessed 20 September 2023).

IBEF (15 February 2021) National Action Plan to Accelerate India's Toy Sector, INDIA ADDA – Perspectives on India. https://www.ibef.org/blogs/national-action-plan-to-accelerate-india-s-toy-sector (2 November 2022).

Khan, M., & Al Mamari, S. (2019). Correlation between organisational learning and employee productivity in the Gulf Cooperation Council. *Opcion*, *35*(19), 1972–2007. Retrieved from https://produccioncientificaluz.org/index.php/opcion/article/view/24112/24556 (5 August 2022).

Khan, M. I., Mohammed, A., & Farooque, M. (2020) Entrepreneurial intention to adopt and use fin-tech financial services during pandemic: Case study of entrepreneurs in the Gulf Cooperation Council. *International Journal for Innovative Research in Multidisciplinary*, *6*(12):286–293.

Ministry of Micro, Small and Medium Enterprises, Government of India. (2018) *Annual report (2017-18) Periodic Labour Force Survey (PLFS)*. Ministry of Micro, Small and Medium Enterprises, Government of India, New Delhi.

Ministry of Micro, Small and Medium Enterprises, Government of India (2021) *Annual report (2020-21)*. Ministry of Micro, Small and Medium Enterprises, Government of India, New Delhi.

Ministry of Micro, Small and Medium Enterprises, Government of India (2022) *Annual report (2021-22)*. Ministry of Micro, Small and Medium Enterprises, Government of India, New Delhi.

OECD (2020). OECD Digital for SMEs Global Initiative, https://www.oecd.org/digital/sme/ (Accessed 20 November 2022)

OECD (2021) An in-depth analysis of one year of SME and entrepreneurship policy responses to COVID-19: lessons learned for the path to recovery, OECD SME and entrepreneurship papers, OECD Publishing, Paris (Print).

Paypal (2020) Pandemic Fast-Tracked Digital Transformation for Canadian Small Businesses, PayPal Canada Survey Finds. https://www.newswire.ca/news-releases/pandemic-fast-tracked-digital-transformation-for-canadian-smallbusinesses-paypal-canada-survey-finds-847168737.html (Accessed 24 November 2022).

Rathore, U., & Khanna, S. (2020) Covid-19 crisis and health of small businesses: Findings from a primary survey, Ideas for India https://www.ideasforindia.in/topics/macroeconomics/covid-19-crisis-and-health-of-small-businesses-findings-from-a-primary-survey.html (Accessed 17 June 2020).

Riom, C., & Valero, A. (2020) *The business response to Covid-19: The CEP-CBI survey on technology adoption*, London School of Economics, Centre for Economic Performance, Covid-19 analysis paper No.9. https://cep.lse.ac.uk/pubs/download/cep-covid-19-009.pdf (10 May 2023).

Sahasranamam, S. (2021). Innovation and entrepreneurship amidst coronavirus: a hybrid innovation network response. *South Asian Journal of Business Studies*, 10(2), 265–271.

Sipahi, E. (2020) COVID-19 and MSMEs: A revival framework. *Research Journal in Advanced Humanities*, *1*(2):7–21.

Ullah, Z., Ullah Khan, S., & Wijewickrama, E. (2021) *Covid-19: Implications for localisation. A case study of Afghanistan and Pakistan*. HPG working paper. ODI, London.

Vashisht A., Chaudhary A., & Priyanka. (2016). Role of SMEs in Indian economy. *International Journal of Management*, *3*(1):14–18.

Vyas, M. (2021) 'Jobs recovery eludes manufacturing sector', https://www.cmie.com/kommon/bin/sr.php?kall=warticle&dt=2021-01-19%2010:45:34&msec=233 (January 2023).

Williams, T. A., Gruber, D., Sutcliffe, A., Shepherd, K. M., & Zhao, A. (2017) Organisational response to adversity: Fusing crisis management and resilience research streams. *Academy of Management Annals*, *11*(2):733–769.

World Economic Forum (2021), https://www.weforum.org/agenda/2021/07/five-post-covid-trends-among-indias-entrepreneurs/ (20 January 2023).

Zdnet (2020) Brazilian SMBs accelerate tech adoption amid pandemic, https://www.zdnet.com/article/braziliansmbs-accelerate-tech-adoption-amid-pandemic/ (20 January 2023).

7 The Future of Entrepreneurship in a Post-COVID-19 Era in South Africa

Njabulo Ndlovu and Richard Shambare

Introduction

In South Africa, the Risk-Adjusted Strategy for dealing with COVID-19 introduced challenges for entrepreneurs (Javed, 2020). These challenges may make it difficult to navigate the post-COVID-19 economy. For instance, how does a business plan for a future that is largely unknown and unpredictable? This advent phenomenon has precariously threatened the existence of many entrepreneurs, with some already subjected to a total collapse. Businesses from a significant number of countries were affected by the advent coronavirus. For instance, evidence of that was the unprecedented decline in sales of their products (Bartik et al., 2020). In South Africa, as a result of lockdowns, many companies have suffered catastrophic disruptions in supply chains, and as a result, they were compelled to downsize with some completely shutting down (Hlatshwayo, 2020). This exacerbated the challenges businesses were already facing such as payment of salaries and other expenses related to funding the business. Ironically, disruptions did not negatively affect all businesses, as some were viewed as essential, and were not shut down, and such sectors included among others Health and Agriculture. For some, the teleworking model became the norm to maintain business activities. Interestingly, teleworking had its own challenging, businesses were compelled to suffer additional costs associated to data to support online working from home, internet connectivity equipment and electronic gadgets such as smart phones and laptops.

Regrettably, in South Africa, the coronavirus made landfall in an economy that was already suffering from low levels of investment and growth. The coronavirus therefore exacerbated the economic situation the country was already experiencing (Nsomba, Tshabalala, and Vilakazi, 2021). Notably, the coronavirus phenomenon not only did it affect established or large businesses but small to micro businesses as well. In response, just like all other countries, South Africa developed several initiatives meant to reduce the damage and build a sustainable and resilient economy. Such initiatives were meant to promote the economy during the pandemic, and these included re-industrialisation and export promotion

(Nsomba et al, 2021). It is against this background that this chapter seeks to provide a picture of the entrepreneurial landscape that includes entrepreneurial barriers and opportunities in the post-COVID-19 world (Gondwe, 2020). Above all else, the chapter wishes to inspire entrepreneurs that there is a future, albeit it being a tricky and precarious one.

In the next section, we provide a brief background to entrepreneurship. Following on, the government's balancing act of trying to save people's lives and their livelihoods including small businesses is discussed. Some COVID-19 entrepreneurship barriers are presented. Thereafter, the chapter concludes by providing some images of the future of entrepreneurship in the post-COVID-19 era in South Africa.

Towards Re-Defining Entrepreneurship

Entrepreneurship is generally understood as the emergence and growth of new businesses (Nieman and Nieuwenhuizen, 2009). Entrepreneurial ventures are extremely varied and their limitations can vary significantly according to the perception of entrepreneurs as well as the environment from which they operate in. Consequently, entrepreneurship may not be viewed as a single and homogenous phenomenon. Acknowledging that entrepreneurship is a multifaceted concept, creation of a typology provides criteria for classifying and understanding the different facets of entrepreneurship (Erikson, 2001). Illuminating entrepreneurship's variability through a typology is therefore important in building a taxonomy of entrepreneurial ventures. So, whenever a commercial enterprise is established or any action is directed towards sustaining a business, this, too, constitutes entrepreneurship. A business, for clarity's sake, is any organisation that is created for the express purpose of generating a profit for its owners. These profit-making organisations are the workplaces of entrepreneurs. Businesses can exist as either registered legal entities or unregistered informal structures.

In this chapter, all reference to business or businesses includes both registered and unregistered entities. Furthermore, the chapter considers the owners of these business or commercial entities to be entrepreneurs.

A Narrow Definition of Entrepreneurship

Entrepreneurship is a social function whose ultimate objective is value creation through opportunity recognition that involves the processes of: (1) innovation and creativity, (2) opportunity creation, (3) creating a market, and (4) creating an identity formation (Gwija, Eresia-Eke, and Iwu, 2014). What this means is that entrepreneurship does not exist in some island, it takes place within a social environment comprising of people. It is people who are entrepreneurs, employees, and customers of these businesses. To that end, Bruyat and Julien (2001) contend that entrepreneurship is a process of "new" value creation in which new products, new identities, new companies, and new entrepreneurs are collectively co-created by the entrepreneur and his interaction with society. Similarly, Shambare, Shambare, and Chakuzira (2020) explain that entrepreneurship is the total of social, psychological, commercial, and economic interactions. In addition, the latter authors decompose the entrepreneurial process into three major phases – the innovation, management, and leadership phases, as illustrated by Figure 7.1, in page 4.

From Figure 7.1, it is clear that the activities of the innovation and leadership phases are fully embedded within society and through people. Creativity and innovation are the building blocks of all entrepreneurial endeavours (Bartik et al., 2020). In other words, as explained by Shambare et al. (2020), perception is defined as the entrepreneurial mental pictures that emerge from the interaction of the social, economic, and physical aspects of the external world. Hence entrepreneurship is a social function. In the leadership phase, the entrepreneurs put all pieces of the business puzzle together to co-create value for themselves, customers, and society. Now, the question that begs an answer is, when society is under lockdown or restrictions of social distancing, can there be entrepreneurship?

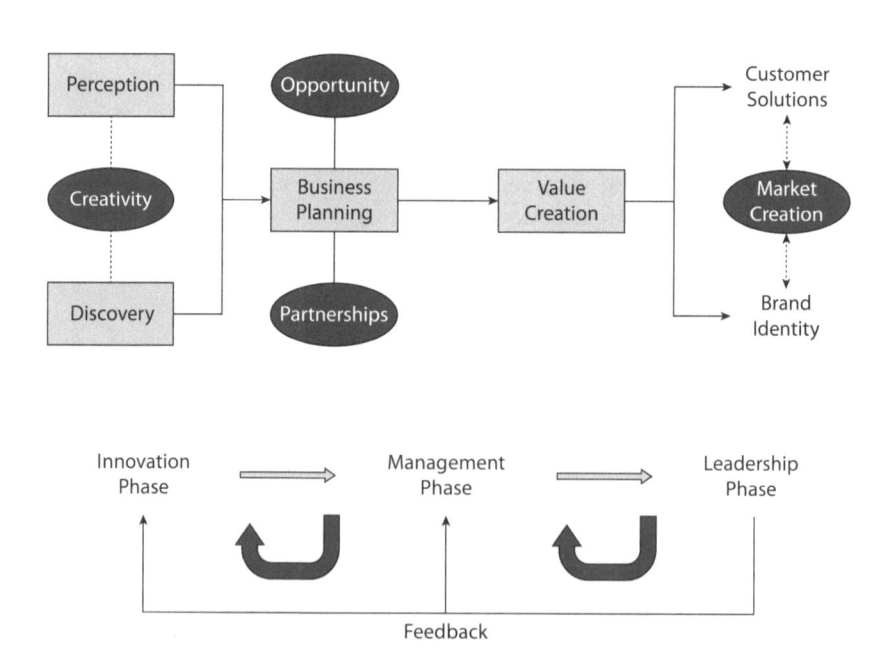

Figure 7.1 The entrepreneurial process

Source: Shambare et al. (2020).

The Future of Entrepreneurship in a Post-COVID-19 Era 111

Entrepreneurship and Various Typologies of Entrepreneurs in South Africa

An alternative way of defining entrepreneurship involves describing the roles and functions that are performed by entrepreneurs. Entrepreneurship, as we have seen in the previous sections tends to be a cyclical series of events that ultimately result in value (see Figure 7.2).

In their day-to-day activities, entrepreneurs perform at least one of the functions identified in Figure 7.2 (from innovating to creating value). Studying these functions provides insights into understanding both entrepreneurship and entrepreneurs. But, before going into detail what entrepreneurs do, it is important to highlight the different forms of entrepreneurship, as they are practiced in South Africa. However, the traditional nomenclature of entrepreneurial activities

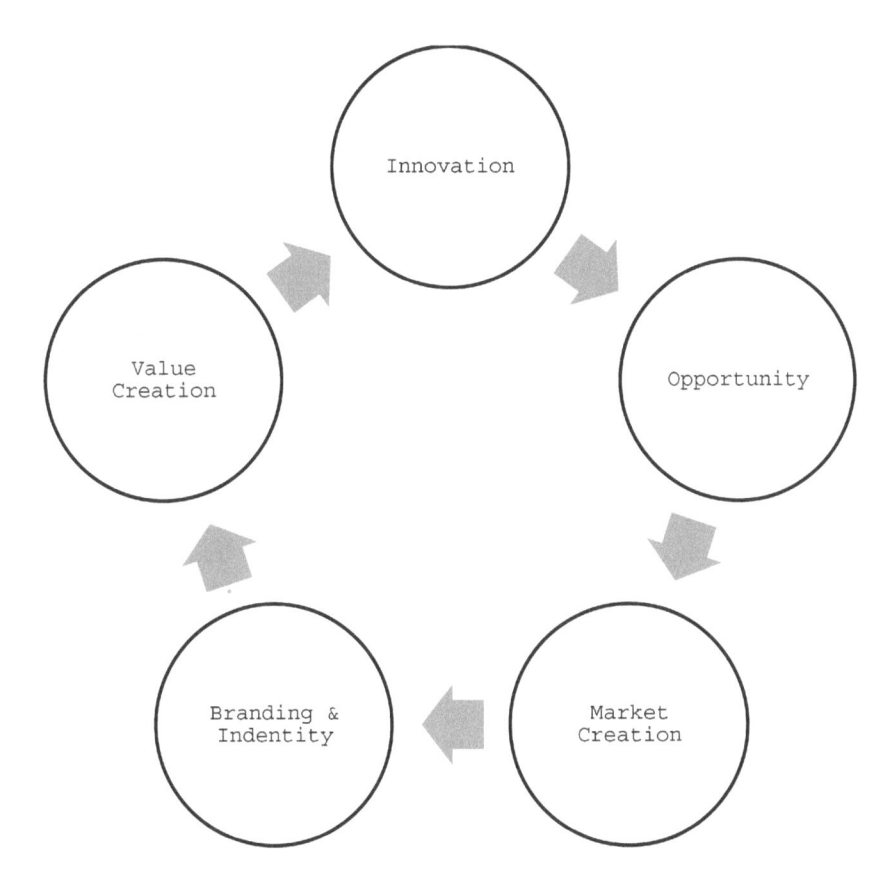

Figure 7.2 The entrepreneurial cycle
Source: Own source.

revolves around two forms of entrepreneurship – necessity (i.e., survivalist) and opportunity-driven entrepreneurship. Largely these are distinguished as follows:

> We define individuals who are initially unemployed before starting businesses as "necessity" entrepreneurs, and define individuals who are not unemployed (i.e. wage/salary workers, enrolled in school or college, or are not actively seeking a job) before starting businesses as "opportunity" entrepreneurs.
>
> (Fairlie and Fossen, 2018)

While the foregoing is a widely accepted practice in the literature, in this chapter, we adopt a slightly different and more comprehensive approach to classifying entrepreneurial activities. To do justice in surveying the South African landscape, this chapter adopts the C9 Typology of Small Medium Enterprise (SME) classification.

Given these realities, SME taxonomy consisting of nine variants is adopted in this chapter (Chakuzira, 2019). Chakuzira (2019) identified two variables associated with business formations: The level of investment and infrastructure required to start a business as the basis for developing the taxonomy. Accordingly, the 3 × 3 matrix yielded nine categories of SMEs.

- *Lifepreneurs*: Refers to people who venture into a business with a self-employment motive. Profit maximisation is not pursued by these individuals. Examples include artisans such as handymen, plumbers, and carpenters.
- *Part-timers*: Full-time employed individuals who seek to supplement their income, usually within the industry of their formal employment. A university lecturer operating a student boarding house is an example of a part-time entrepreneur. The profit is a clear for this type of business.
- *Hobbypreneurs (social entrepreneurs)*: Individuals who upgrade their hobbies into business ventures. Profit is a motive, but more so to cover operational costs as well as managing copyrights or trademarks, were applicable. *Hobbypreneurs are commonly known as* social entrepreneurs.
- *Entremployees*: Are most prevalent in developing countries. Whereas in developed countries, people often pursue one career at a time, either a full-time job or entrepreneurship; in developing countries, however, there is a growing phenomenon of hybrid entrepreneurs. These individuals, in addition to their full-time jobs, they also run their businesses. Like part-timers, *entremployees* pursue both a job and entrepreneurship simultaneously. The major difference between part-timers and *entremployees* is that the former generally hire someone to manage the business in their absence. But, the latter pursue their business interests even during the ordinary working hours at their place of employment. These entrepreneurs also have a proclivity to utilise their employers' resources (e.g., office space, telephones, or computers) for their private businesses. Professional services such as accounting services, language

editing, and consultancy services are examples of the *entremployee* sector. The majority of *entremployees* are employed in government departments or public sector organisations.
- **Empreneurs**: Are the entrepreneurs sitting right at the centre of the C9 matrix. *Empreneurs* have four distinguishing characteristics: (1) unlike entremployees, they are full-time entrepreneurs, who (2) started their business careers as entremployees. (3) Their businesses grew to levels requiring their full-time attention. (4) *Empreneurs* operate businesses within the same industry as their previous employment such as a mechanic opening an automotive repair shop.
- **Techpreneurs**: Technological and often family supported business enterprise. The entrepreneur in this classification has vast technical expertise and knowledge, but faces challenges in terms of capital acquisition.
- **Carte-blanche**: The SME indeed, requires a lot of capital in its set-up. The capital should be coupled with acquisition of physical infrastructure. This is a description of many franchise businesses, hence the classification name, Carte-blanche.
- **Profeneurs**: A grouping for all specialist entrepreneurs who are involved in a lot of legislative regulations as well as considerable amounts of capital for their SMEs. Entrepreneurs who fall in this classification are usually involved in huge capital tenders and classic service offering experts.
- **Smartpreneurs**: Form the typology of capital intensive businesses, usually in the hi-tech industries. These businesses almost always start-off as medium-scale ventures and have the capacity to grow into LSEs. Generally, smartpreneurs are not only ambitious, but very calculative personalities. Examples of smartpreneurs are Strive Masiyiwa's Econet, Aliko Dangote's Sephako. The individuals themselves are often highly intelligent and charismatic.

This typology is in line with the advice provided by Kunkel (2001) that a more viable way to understand entrepreneurship requires studying not only the form of business enterprises, but also their formation processes. To that end, the dichotomy of defining entrepreneurs as either necessity-driven or opportunistic is rendered inadequate in developing countries for numerous reasons: Firstly, because the rate of unemployed people in developing countries such as South Africa tends to be high, Fairlie and Fossen's (2018) definition that "individuals who are initially unemployed before starting businesses as 'necessity' entrepreneurs," would greatly overstate the incidence of necessity entrepreneurs. Secondly, unlike in developed countries, in South Africa and several other developing countries, it is fairly common for individuals to simultaneously pursue paid employment and entrepreneurial careers. Clearly, this form of entrepreneurs needs to be accounted for somehow. Lastly, the high-growth motive of entrepreneurship in non-Western contexts is not nearly as high as it is in the West. In collectivist societies such as South Africa, there are several other social and cultural imperatives to satisfy other than profit-maximisation and high-growth (Saffu, 2003; Tshikovhi and Mvula, 2014).

Although there are differences among entrepreneurs, it is equally important to emphasise that there too are commonalities among these small businesses. We examine some of the common structural features of SMEs.

The Size and Scope of Small to Medium Enterprises

As their name suggests, SMEs operate small-scale operations in terms of size, production, and capital requirements. Because of their size, SMEs are in a better position to specialise in niche markets in smaller geographic areas (Chivasa, 2014). Because of this, business functional areas including production, marketing, sales, and accounting are often not as clearly defined as in big businesses. More often than not, entrepreneurs perform most of the functional activities of their businesses. Most of these small business are family businesses. Because of this, sources of equity and managerial expertise for SMEs is often restricted to family and other social relations. Consequently, there is a tendency of family politics encroaching into business affairs and operate according to family traditions and values, even across generations.

Besides, unlike in big businesses, where the owners are not involved in the day-to-day operations of the business, small business owners play the dual role of owner-manager or owner-employee. Consequently, their presence significantly influences the daily operations of the enterprise. Further, SMEs rely on capital from their owners, whom we have identified are mostly individuals or individual families. As such, capital outlay is restricted to a bare minimum. As suggested by the C9 model, a third of all SMEs only by entrepreneurs investing their time and energy. At the same token, two-thirds rely on time, energy, and family support. Naturally, the resource bases for most SMEs is generally lean.

Particularly, by definition, SMEs emerge out of creativity and innovation. As such, creativity and innovation are embedded in virtually all aspects of SMEs. Creativity is also one key attribute exploited by SMEs such as empreneurs, profeneurs, techpreneus, and smartpreneurs who utilise innovative marketing strategies including social media marketing. Noteworthy, SMEs tend to be informal. While small and micro enterprises are mostly unregistered businesses, a majority of medium-scale enterprises are formally registered. However, whether registered or not, the management style and the general philosophy of SME management leans more towards informality than formality (Shambare et al., 2020). For instance, rather than having formally written down procedures and policies, owners' discretion is often exercised and this leads to informality.

Brief Entrepreneurs' Activities

Having noted the various forms of entrepreneurs in South Africa, it is important to underscore that regardless of the form or type of SME venture, the most important job to be performed by any entrepreneur is to keep his or her businesses going and making profit, albeit, and the varying persuasions towards the profit-maximisation motive. In pursuit of this goal, Tobak (2014) observes that entrepreneurs perform seven main functions. These are to: Formulate Vision for the business, sustain the business and keep it going, raise capital all the time, keep up with the market, devise a differentiating strategy, work 24 × 7 and wear lots of hats, and lead and motivate their employees. Nevertheless, having defined entrepreneurship as well as the entrepreneurial functional areas, the focus of the chapter now turns to describing COVID-19 and how it affects entrepreneurship.

COVID-19 vs SMEs: A Balancing Act of Saving People's Lives or Their Livelihood

COVID-19 is the scientific name for the Coronavirus disease that was first discovered in 2019 (World Health Organisation, 2020). The disease presents symptoms similar to those of the common flu and malaria – fatigue, fever, coughing, and respiratory illnesses. What makes COVID-19 a deadly disease are essentially three factors:

a *Highly infectious*: The COVID-19 virus spreads very fast among people. It is transmitted primarily through droplets of saliva or discharge from the nose when an infected person coughs or sneezes.
b *No cure and vaccines*: At the moment there is no cure for COVID-19 and neither are there any vaccines. Scientists and medical practitioners are still studying the behavioural patterns of the virus in an effort to discover a cure.
c *Low incubation period*: The time from which an individual contracts the Coronavirus to exhibiting symptoms (i.e., the incubation period) is about 7 to 14 days.

Given that the Coronavirus is highly contagious without a known cure and that the disease progresses very fast, this makes COVID-19 a very dangerous disease. Moreso, the COVID-19 virus attaches to various types of surfaces and body parts such as hands and fingers; because of this, it can easily be transmitted through human-to-human contact. It is against this background, that COVID-19 was declared a global pandemic by the World Health Organisation (WHO). However, to manage the spread of COVID-19, numerous countries opted for the national lockdown approach as means to enforce social distancing (Government Gazette, 2020). In South Africa's lockdown, the entire population except essential workers (e.g., medical practitioners, fuel and energy suppliers) was required to confine themselves to their homes. All other non-essential sectors including businesses, schools, and universities as a result closed down.

Managing COVID-19: A South African SME Perspective

As the Coronavirus pandemic ravages global health systems and taking lives, it is also destroying people's livelihoods with it. Since the virus spreads through human-to-human contact, a lockdown helps by limiting contact among people. This approach has been proven to be quite effective in China and Europe, where the numbers of Coronavirus infections and deaths have reduced significantly after initiating lockdowns. On the 26th of March, 2020, South Africa began its lockdown. All ports of entry into the country were closed, factories closed, government offices closed, schools and universities closed; in short the economy was also under lock and key.

While lockdown measures are quite successful in containing the spread of the Coronavirus, these unfortunately have a negative impact on the economy and businesses. For instance, Edcon and Comair – Kulula Airline's parent company, among others are in business rescue. Generally, the conclusion is that the lockdown was and still is bad for business. It, especially, was devastating for SMEs; small businesses rarely survive economic shocks. However, the converse might also be true. Crises are often a good source of creativity and innovation, which in turn stimulate entrepreneurial activity. Consequently, many believe that entrepreneurs will not let a good crisis go to waste, they will always extract opportunities from crises, and COVID-19 is no exception. While there is a big threat to small businesses, today, there is hope for entrepreneurship tomorrow. We will elaborate on this in later sections of the chapter. The more immediate concern is to look at how the South African government stepped in to help small businesses.

Attempts to Save SMEs

In South Africa, SMEs are among the most affected by the lockdown. IOL (2020) reports that almost 70% of Cape Town SMEs have closed and most likely gone out of business. Of the small businesses that continued operations in the lockdown, more than 85% of them reported a significant reduction in turnover. While these data are for the IOL (2020) survey in Cape Town, the trend across the country is similar. Small businesses are under serious threat.

In response, the South African government availed a R500 billion (approximately US$30 billion) rescue package to resuscitate the ailing South African economy. Of this, R200 billion was earmarked for SMEs under the COVID-19 loan scheme (Hlatshwayo, 2020). The COVID-19 loan scheme is a commercial arrangement and requires a credit application process, through which lenders and banks must evaluate if the business will likely be able to service all its commitments after the pandemic and lockdown. However, the lenders are under no obligation to extend COVID-19 loans and business owners may be required to sign surety (CNBC Africa, 2020). In total, as shown in Table 7.1, seven loan packages have been made available to small businesses. To qualify for the standardised COVID-19 loan, businesses, including sole proprietors, must among others meet the following requirements: (a) have a turnover under R300 million (approx. US$16 million) per annum, (b) be in good standing with their bank, (c)

Table 7.1 COVID-19 SME rescue packages

Rescue package	Type of support and requirements
The SMME Relief Finance Facility	A soft-loan funding for existing businesses which are distressed due to the effects of the COVID-19 pandemic. The aid will be available for six months from 1 April 2020.
The SEFA-Debt Restructuring Facility	For SMMEs that are already funded by the Small Enterprise Funding Agency (SEFA) and are negatively affected by the COVID-19 outbreak. SEFA will grant a payment holiday for up to six months.
The Industrial Development Corporation (IDC)	R3 billion for industrial funding to address vulnerable firms and to fast-track financing for companies critical to efforts to fight COVID-19 and its economic impact. R200-million in aid has been made available by the Department of Tourism to assist SMMEs in the tourism and hospitality sector who are under particular stress due to the travel restrictions.
UIF COVID-19 Temporary Relief Benefit:	Temporary UIF relief fund for businesses that suffer distress directly due to COVID-19 – claims for three months or less. • You need to be up-to-date with all UIF payments. • Employees will be paid in terms of the income replacement rate sliding scale (38%–60%) as provided in the UIF Act
SA Future Trust (SAFT)	Salary support for SMEs with less than R25 million annual revenue. Requirements are as follows: • Businesses must be under stress directly due to the COVID-19 outbreak and in a strong financial position prior to the crisis. • Interest-free loan with 5-year term, paid directly to employees from banks. • R750 per qualifying employee per week, over a max period of 15 weeks, or R11,250 per permanent employee.
Sukuma Relief Fund – Business Partners:	Available for all industries but must have evidence of financial viability prior to COVID-19 as well as be tax and regulatory compliant. • **Close corporations, companies and trusts**: Must be registered, unsecured interest-bearing loan of R250,000 – R1 million coupled with a non-repayable grant of R25,000. 60-month max loan term. No repayment obligations in Year 1, no interest for Year 1, interest at prime and repayment commence from Year 2. • **Sole proprietors**: Non-repayable grant of R25,000. Must be registered and compliant, and employing 2 or more people. Online application process only, pay-outs in 7 days.
NEF COVID-19 Fund:	Businesses will get funding for working capital, machinery and equipment to manufacture and supply a range of medical products. R500,000 to R10 million concessional loan for black-owned businesses with existing retail supplier relationships. Up to 60 months repayment, 0% interest in first year.

before the onset of the COVID-19 pandemic, (d) be registered with the South African Revenue Services (SARS), (e) have the insufficient normal borrowing capacity to fully fund its monthly operating expenses, and (f) be adversely impacted by the lockdown.

From the above, requirements "b" and "c," by default suggest that quite a significant number of SMEs, particularly the unregistered businesses and those in the informal sector will not be able to access the rescue package. It appears that three broad categories of businesses could have been excluded from accessing the rescue package. These are:

i *Businesses that were struggling prior to the onset of the Coronavirus*: Will find it difficult to prove that COVID-19 negatively impacted their businesses. Besides, there is a very high likelihood that their credit scores as well as their "good standing" with banks would not have not that "good."
ii *Unregistered businesses*: Because they are unregistered, they cannot be registered with SARS as business entities, as such, these operators would find it difficult to access funding on this basis.

Further discussion on SME challenges to access funding is continued in the section on New COVID-19 barriers. For now, the attention is on the SME rescue packages. Table 7.1 summarises these rescue packages.

COVID-19 Introduced New Barriers for Youth Entrepreneurs

Entrepreneurship is fraught with numerous pitfalls. Young entrepreneurs, especially, face numerous challenges and barriers as they try to set up and operate their businesses. As discussed in previous chapters, some of the more common barriers are lack of access to funding and cumbersome venture registration process and requirements. Over and above the health and medical challenges, COVID-19 has transformed the social and economic order. Invariably, this transformation introduces new barriers for young entrepreneurs. These new barriers include among others; the business opportunity barrier, the financial barrier, the informality barrier, and the psychological barrier.

The Business Opportunity Barrier

As the country went into lockdown, many SMEs closed their doors for the last time. Those that re-opened, did so in a post-COVID-19 era – a very different world from the one they knew when they closed shop to go into lockdown. Such, precisely is what the billionaire Johann Rupert warned when he cautioned that the lockdown is "not a pause; it's a reset" (Bloomberg, 2020). A pause is when entrepreneurs would simply resume their operations from whence they left; more like a shop reopening after the Christmas shutdown on the 2nd of

January of the following New Year. A reset, on the other hand, is starting afresh, from ground zero. In this new post-COVID-19 world, Rupert further hints of "grave economic consequences" that could last for more than three years after the lockdown, as there will be permanent changes in consumer spending and behaviour patterns.

Simply put, the lockdown eroded past opportunities and competitive advantages that SMEs once capitalised. Speculation and expert opinion in mainstream media, alike, seem to suggest that SMEs are dead (IPSOS, 2020). One real and present danger for young entrepreneurs is coming from Corporate South Africa. Big businesses such as Shoprite have already positioned themselves in township economies, the former domain of small informal traders. Now the young entrepreneurs that once tested their ideas in townships, are going to find the new Shoprite *spaza* shop model more of a hindrance; they cannot outcompete these retail giants. The sad reality is that the lockdown has also locked entrepreneurial opportunities.

The Financial Barrier

Basic business finances constitutes two elements: Revenues and costs. While the revenue side of the income statement stagnated to zero, during the lockdown, the cost side continued to grow. For each and every day that a business was closed, the costs for re-opening grew exponentially; expenses and financial obligations including insurance, rent, rates, and salaries still needed to be paid. Ordinarily, total costs[1] (TC) for businesses consist of fixed costs (FC) and variable costs (VC). FC are the costs that remain constant over time and do not change even when the level of production or sales change, for example, rent, insurance, and rates. On the other hand, VC items such as fuel, utilities, and wages change (or vary) in proportion to the changes in output. However, because of no revenue in the lockdown, there was no distinction in terms of VCs and FCs, as these began to behave in a similar pattern. In other words, since revenue was zero because there was no production, businesses continued to incur costs. For instance, inventory depreciated and this accounted for cost; electricity was needed to keep machinery running, to the businesses' costs; and the usual FCs still needed servicing. The mounting overheads and accruing debts are going to be too much for small businesses to sustain. Without sources of revenue, many businesses became insolvent; they had to borrow more just to service past debts. Those that reopened realised a bigger financial burden to deal with.

Ordinarily, a business starts making profit past the breakeven point (BEP). All the sales up until the breakeven point are absorbed by the total costs of the business.

Despite the net profit that is realised beyond the BEP, there is another important measure that entrepreneurs consider. This is the margin of safety (MOS).

For instance, it is not just important to sell, say one more unit beyond the BEP, a business budgets the amount of units it needs to sell within a given year. In this case, the budgeted sales is 150 units. The MOS is, therefore, calculated by deducting the total sales at BEP from the total budgeted sales. The time at which COVID-19 hit, at the beginning of the year, further exacerbates the financial challenges for SMEs. Most SMEs' financial years were just beginning when South Africa went into lockdown. Quite a number of businesses were still in the loss region of the BEP graph. But because of the mounting costs incurred during Coronavirus pandemic, the old breakeven point (BEP_1) no longer applies. There are new costs, as explained in the foregoing; this new cost regime results in the dual breakeven phenomenon illustrated in Figure 7.3.

Because of the new cost regime, in the post-COVID-19 environment, the revised fixed costs would be FC_2. Consequently, this results in TC_2, the revised costs, as a result. Because of this, a new breakeven point (BEP_2) needs to be surpassed if the business is to make profit in the post-COVID-19 world. Now, this is where things become tricky and difficult for SMEs. On the one hand, SMEs are now overburdened with both old and new debt and, on the other hand, they have to compete with new competition in the marketplace, such as Shoprite and Pick n Pay, as discussed earlier with respect to the *spaza* shop sector. Competition would mean reduced selling price and reduced profits. To illustrate the

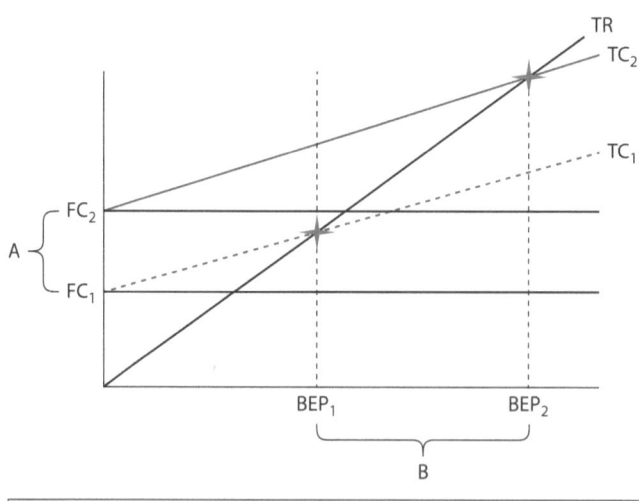

Key:
A: Increase in Fixed Costs due to accruing overheads
B: Shift in Breakeven Point due to Increased Fixed Costs from FC_1 to FC_2

Figure 7.3 Dual breakeven analysis in the post-COVID-19 era

Source: Own Source.

Table 7.2 Gumi Breakeven analysis in post-COVID-19

Breakeven Analysis: Pre-COVID-19			
Selling Price (per unit)	R 20.00	BEP (units)	2000
Fixed Costs	R 10,000.00	MOS (units)	500
Variable Costs	R 15.00		
Budgeted Units	2500		
Breakeven Analysis: Post-COVID-19			
Selling Price (per unit)	R 19.00	BEP (units)	3,125
Fixed Costs	R 10,000.00	MOS (units)	500
COVID-19 Costs	R 2,500.00		
Total Costs	R 12,500.00		
Variable Costs	R 15.00		
Budgeted Units	3625		

impact of big retailers in the market, let us consider an example of a hypothetical business, Gumi Spaza Shop that sells one product only, say bread.

Case Study: Gumi Spaza Shop (Own Source)

The owner of Gumi *Spaza* Shop calculates that to make profit a year, she needs to sell 2,500 loaves of bread per annum. Her fixed costs include rent and rates. If she buys a loaf of bread for R15 and sells it for R20, Table 7.2 demonstrates that the BEP is 2,000 units and the MOS is 500 loaves. This is in the ideal world.

Now, let's fast forward into the post-COVID environment. To survive the lockdown, Gumi continued paying rent to her landlord. But, to do so, she had to get a loan from the local loan shark because her business was not registered and could not qualify for government relief funding. This was her only option or close down. Closing down was not an option, as the local industries were also shutting down because of the COVID-19. Life was tough, business was tough, and so she continued to hang on to her business.

By the time she reopened, after the lockdown, there were now new entrants in the market, Gumi could no longer afford to sell bread at R20 and decides to reduce the selling price to R19 per loaf. Furthermore, the costs associated with sustaining her business in the lockdown amounted to R2,500. So, her new breakeven (BEP_2) is now 3,215 loaves of bread.

Points of Discussion:

- Is such a jump in the breakeven from 2,500 to 3,215 units sustainable?
- What strategies can Gumi implement to keep her business afloat?
- If you were Gumi, what could your state of mind be during and after the lockdown?

The Barrier of Informality: COVID-19 Rescue Package Barrier

In response to the Coronavirus threat to the economy, government introduced a R500 billion stimulus package. Some R200 billion was earmarked for SMEs. While the government intervention, on paper, is a progressive one; its practical implementation is somewhat burdensome, if at all possible. In South Africa, the majority of SMEs are not registered businesses. Accordingly, these are considered informal and sometimes survivalist businesses. Because they are not registered, these businesses will not qualify for the COVID-19 relief funding. This is one aspect of the barrier of informality – businesses that are too informal to receive financing assistance.

The other, slightly mild, form of the barrier of informality relates to registered businesses that seemingly do not have all their registration and compliance paperwork in order and up to date, for one reason or another. The business compliance processes (e.g., annual returns and VAT refunds) are quite involving and complex. The typical entrepreneur in South Africa operates his or her business on a semi-formal basis. This is largely true among the SMEs regardless of how big or how fancy the businesses look on the outside. From the inside, SMEs remain largely informal. Besides the requirements for the COVID-19 relief funding are too onerous and too rigid for small businesses. This appears to be one of those COVID-19 promises from politicians that are "not deliverable" given the realities of the South African economy.

The Psychological Barrier

During and after the COVID-19, the critical question was and still is: Can entrepreneurs and their businesses survive in the post-COVID-19 world? The answer is both yes and no. On the one hand, those that do not survive, will be permanently traumatised. On the other hand, those that survive will also experience trauma.

The COVID-19 scars are financial, emotional, and social. The financial scars are the easiest to address. Government, banks, and lenders can address these sorts of scars, as we have seen with the COVID-19 relief fund (Hlatshwayo, 2020). But the others are not as straightforward and even much more difficult to measure. Even if it is assumed that businesses received the financial bail-out, a business is not just money. A business consists of people – entrepreneurs, employees, and customers; all of who have feelings and emotions. COVID-19 has battered these feelings on numerous fronts and on numerous counts. Firstly, it is the fear of contracting the disease and just to stay healthy. Secondly, it's worrying about strategies to keep the business afloat. Thirdly, the rush to secure government funding. Fourthly, entrepreneurs have to solve the challenge of sourcing money to cover salaries when revenue is non-existent (Erero and Makananisa, 2021). These challenges continually corrode entrepreneurs' sprits, thereby leading to psychological barrier.

This section described the new entrepreneurial barriers, as introduced into the marketplace by the COVID-19 lockdown. While lockdown measures are quite successful in containing the spread of the Coronavirus, these unfortunately have a negative impact on the economy (Gilbert et al., 2020). In other words, the lockdown is bad for business. However, the converse is also true. Crises are often a source of creativity and innovation, which in turn stimulate entrepreneurial activity. Many believe that entrepreneurs will not let a crisis go to waste, they always find opportunities from crisis and that COVID-19 is no exception (Erero and Makananisa, 2021). While there is a big threat to small businesses, today, there is hope for entrepreneurship tomorrow. At this juncture, the chapter turns to discussing COVID-19 entrepreneurial opportunities.

A New Hope: Post-COVID-19 Entrepreneurship Opportunities

Wilson (1995) in his book *For Entrepreneurs Only* observed that: Entrepreneurship tends immediately after crises and wars. Harrell (1995) explains that the natural human instinct of self-preservation encourages heightened entrepreneurial activities in the period following human crises and wars. Indeed, COVID-19 is a dark cloud, but despite this, every dark cloud has its silver lining. While there is a big threat to small businesses, today, there is hope for entrepreneurs and entrepreneurship. To elaborate on this, let us consider the characteristics of SMEs, as summarised in Table 7.3, to help explain some of the COVID-19 opportunities.

Table 7.3 SME opportunities

SME characteristics	Business opportunities
Lean resource base	Low barriers of entry/exit:
	Given the limited resources available to SMEs, there are low barriers to exit from the current industry and low barriers to entry into new markets, therefore, SMEs are versatile.
	Example: A vegetable vendor can now venture into buying and selling face masks.
Creativity and innovation	New supply chains:
	Because of social distancing, SMEs can utilise technology to leverage their businesses and develop new supply chains.
	Example: Creches and pre-schools are now pre-recording lessons and using Zoom and Skype to connect to their students

(*Continued*)

Table 7.3 (Continued)

SME characteristics	Business opportunities
Small target markets SMEs are owner-operated SMEs provide customised service	SMEs are versatile: SMEs tend to have broad organisational structures. • The fact that the entrepreneurs interact with customers all the time (e.g., a *lifepreneur* who is a hairdresser gets immediate feedback from clients on without the need for large market research. • SMEs engage one-on-one with customers, and they become more versatile since decisions are made relatively quickly. • Micro and small enterprises, provide customised and bespoke services and products to customers, which promotes versatility.
Community businesses Flexible management style Small distance between owners and customers	Capitalise on local and community needs: SMEs are community businesses; they could concentrate on servicing the needs of the community. The business owner, being part of the community, they can gain an upper hand when venturing into new needs of the community.

Source: Own Source.

Conclusion

This chapter sought to advance the knowledge about how small to medium business may survive during post-COVID-19 era, particularly in the context of developing countries. Notably, just like in any other economy in the world, South Africa has different types of entrepreneurs, and none of them was precluded from COVID-19 battering. However, the chapter utilised South Africa as the case study to present alternative opportunities available to entrepreneurs during the post-COVID-19 era. Such opportunities include among others, a lean resource base, creativity and innovation, small target markets, and a flexible management style.

In essence, given the low barrier of exit and low barrier of entry, that may promote versatility amongst SMEs. The advent of the pandemic complicated many traditional business processes, as a result, SME just like any other business were compelled to adopt and utilise digital technologies. The use of digital technologies will enable SMEs to leverage their businesses and develop new supply chains.

The aforementioned opportunities can be a game changer for many SMEs towards their success particularly during the post-COVID-19 era. Particularly, these opportunities would promote internal sustainability and growth as compared to the reliance on traditional government grants which are out of reach for many SMEs due to lack of business formalisation. This chapter presented these opportunities to illustrate how SMEs can survive the post-COVID-19 era. Subsequently, the aforementioned SME's survival trajectories could be the basis for future research in exploring their effectiveness and suggesting other possible support policies for entrepreneurship.

Note

1 TC = FC + VC.

References

Bartik, A. W., Bertrand, M., Cullen, Z., Glaeser, E. L., Luca, M., and Stanton, C. (2020). The impact of COVID-19 on small business outcomes and expectations. Proceedings of the National Academy of Sciences, 117.30 (July 2020): 17656–17666.

Bloomberg. (2020). *'This is not a pause, it's a reset' – Johann Rupert*. [Online]. https://businesstech.co.za/news/business/398335/this-is-not-a-pause-its-a-reset-johann-rupert/ [Accessed: 15 May 2020].

Bruyat, C., and Julien, P.-A. (2001). Defining the field of research in entrepreneurship. Journal of Business Venturing, 16, 165–180. DOI: 10.1016/S0883-9026(99)00043-9

Chakuzira, W. (2019). A grounded theory approach to examine the taxonomy of entrepreneurial ventures in Limpopo province. University of Venda repository.

Chivasa, S. (2014). Entrepreneurship culture among SMEs in Zimbabwe: A case of Bulawayo SMEs. International Journal of Economics, Commerce and Management, 2 (9): 1–13.

CNBC Africa. (2020). *How SA's R200bn Covid-19 loan scheme for small businesses works*. [Online]. Available at: https://www.cnbcafrica.com/news/2020/04/29/how-sas-r200bn-covid-19-loan-scheme-for-small-businesses-works/ [Accessed: 19 May 2020].

Erero, J. L., and Makananisa, M. P. (2021). Impact of Covid-19 on the South African economy: A CGE, Holt-winter and SARIMA model's analysis. Turkish Economic Review, 7 (4): 193–213.

Erikson, T. (2001). Revisiting Shapero: A taxonomy of entrepreneurial typologies. New England Journal of Entrepreneurship, 4 (1): 9–20.

Fairlie, R. W., and Fossen, F. M. (2018). Opportunity versus necessity entrepreneurship: Two components of business creation. IZA DP No. 11258.

Gilbert, M., Pullano, G., Pinotti, F., Valdano, E., Poletto, C., Boëlle, P.-Y., D'Ortenzio, E., Yazdanpanah, Y., Eholie, S. P., Altmann, M., Gutierrez, B., Kraemer, M. U. G., and Colizza, V. (2020). Preparedness and vulnerability of African countries against importations of COVID-19: A modelling study. Lancet, 395(10227), 871–877. https://doi.org/10.1016/S0140-6736(20)30411-6

Gondwe, G. (2020). Assessing the impact of COVID-19 on Africa's economic development. United Nations, Trade and Development. Retrieved 21 March 2022, from https://unctad.org/system/files/official-document/aldcmisc2020d3_en.pdf

Government Gazette. (2020). Declaration of Disaster Management Act, No. 43096, 15 March. https://www.gov.za/issues/national-development-plan-2030 [Accessed 23 March 2022].

Gwija, S. A., Eresia-Eke, C., and Iwu, C. G. 2014. Assessing the impact of support structures and initiatives to youth entrepreneurship development in a selected Township in the Western Cape Province of South Africa.

Hlatshwayo, D. (2020). 7 COVID-19 Business Rescue Funds to Help SMMES. [Online]. TransformSA. Available at: https://transformsa.co.za/2020/04/7-covid-19-business-rescue-funds-to-help-smmes/ [Accessed: 19 May 2020].

IOL. (2020). Covid-19 Impact: How SMEs can access relief packages. [Online]. Available at: https://www.iol.co.za/business-report/economy/covid-19-impact-how-smes-can-access-relief-packages-46838507 [Accessed: 19 May 2020].

IPSOS. (2020). SMME's – Understanding the impact of Covid-19. [Online] Available at: https://www.ipsos.com/en-za/smmes-understanding-impact-covid-19 [Accessed 23 March 2022].

Javed, A. (2020). Impact of COVID-19 on Pakistan's services sector.

Kunkel, S. W. (2001). Toward a typology of entrepreneurial activities. Academy of Entrepreneurship Journal, 7 (1): 75–90.

Nieman, G., and Nieuwenhuizen, C. (2009) Entrepreneurship. A South African perspective. 2nd edition, Van Schaik, Pretoria.

Nsomba, G., Tshabalala, N., and Vilakazi, T. (2021). Global Initiative towards post-COVID-19 resurgence of the MSME sector: MSME surge project: Cluster "Access to Markets". UN DESA Development Account Project coordinated by UNCTAD.

Saffu, K. (2003). The role and impact of culture on South Pacific Island entrepreneurs April 2003. International Journal of Entrepreneurial Behaviour & Research, 9 (2): 55–73. DOI: 10.1108/13552550310461045

Shambare, R., Shambare, J., and Chakuzira, W. (2020). Revisiting entrepreneurship marketing research. Towards a framework of SMEs in developing countries. 2nd edition, published 2020 Routledge.

Tobak, S. (2014). 7 Things Successful Entrepreneurs Do. [Online]. Available at: https://www.entrepreneur.com/article/239999. The Entrepreneur South Africa. [Accessed: 12 May 2020].

Tshikovhi, N., and Mvula, A. (2014). Entrepreneurship education and its concerns in South African universities. International Journal of Higher Education Management, 1 (1): 77–85.

Wilson, H. (1995). For Entrepreneurs Only. Topics new business enterprises – management., Business planning., Entrepreneurship. Publisher Career Press Collection in Library; Internet Archive Books.

World Health Organisation. (2020). Coronavirus. [Online]. World Health Organisation https://www.who.int/health-topics/coronavirus#tab=tab_1 [Accessed: 13 May 2020].

8 Restaurants and COVID-19

A Focus on the Learning Experiences of Restaurant Entrepreneurs Amidst COVID-19 in South Africa

Knowledge Shumba, Wellington Chakuzira, Richard Shambare, and Ntswaki Petunia Matlala

Introduction

The advent of a worldwide COVID-19 pandemic in 2020 triggered an unprecedented crisis in the tourism and hospitality industry in South Africa. The years 2020 and 2021 will be remembered for the destruction caused COVID-19 pandemic. The virus's rapid spread caused widespread disruption, and its consequences were so severe that they eclipsed some social and economic activities. According to Liñán and Jaén (2022), the pandemic is the most severe economic crisis since the Second World War and has been substantially more destructive than the 2008–2012 financial crisis. Furthermore, it has been stated that the COVID-19 pandemic has worsened entrepreneurship and start-up activities. The COVID-19 pandemic significantly impacted the global hospitality market (Türkeş et al., 2021). The ban on international and domestic travel resulted in the decline of tourism activities. Tourism businesses such as hotels, restaurants, cafés, cruises, conferences, and festivals were severely affected (Sobaih et al., 2021). The UNWTO (2020) recorded a significant drop of 72% in international tourist movement between January and October of 2020, resulting in a loss of ten times more than the 2009 world financial crisis. In June 2021, COVID-19 was still highly prevalent throughout the world, with over 180 million cases documented globally and about 4 million deaths (Gössling et al., 2020).

By the end of 2021, several protective measures, also called lockdown restrictions, still existed in many parts of the world (Rogerson & Rogerson, 2020). Donga et al. (2021) note that the restrictions affected many small businesses across South Africa despite their major contribution to economic growth. In the hospitality sector, calls for lifting restrictions on operations were raised on several occasions, but saving lives was prioritized during the adjusted levels of lockdown (Aharon et al., 2021). The restrictions aimed at curbing the transmission of COVID-19 infections posed challenges for economic entities involved in the preparation, promotion, and consumption of food, as well as alcoholic and

DOI: 10.4324/9781003475606-10

non-alcoholic beverages. This included establishments like restaurants and cafes, which had to stop their indoor operations temporarily and in public areas or conduct their activities partially, ensuring they did not exceed 30–50% of their maximum spatial capacity (Zeb et al., 2021).

A research conducted on the consequences of the COVID-19 outbreak on the tourism industry in South Africa confirmed that 98% of the examined enterprises were impacted by the global health crisis. It was observed that Small and Midsize Enterprise (SMEs) endured larger decreases in their income (Department of Tourism South Africa in 2020). Small enterprises, particularly restaurants, encountered numerous economic and social challenges, including workforce reductions and struggles to meet financial obligations such as salaries, rent, and taxes (Sucheran, 2022). During the strict lockdown restrictions and even after the strict lockdown measures, entrepreneurs had to use survival tactics while complying with the adjusted levels of lockdown restrictions. Moreover, facing this distress forced some SMEs out of their operations while others downscaled and thrived.

COVID-19 has significantly impacted SMEs in South Africa, especially in the restaurant industry. The implementation of rigorous lockdown measures led to a steep decline in revenues for numerous restaurants. Most of these establishments reported that they had to significantly reduce business expenditures to endure the challenging circumstances (Kalidas et al., 2020). The effect of COVID-19 on restaurants has received little attention from academic scholars. Kuckertz and Brändle (2022) noted that the extensive research on the COVID-19 crisis primarily comprises editorials, commentaries, and conceptual write-ups. Research on this matter has generally been from Europe (Kuckertz & Brändle, 2022; Rashid & Ratten, 2021; Ratten, 2020; Stam & Van de Ven, 2021). Research in the developing countries such as South Africa, had also received little or no attention from scholars in this regard. In South Africa, research on COVID-19 is notably constrained, especially regarding the challenges posed by the pandemic and strategies to mitigate its impact on businesses (Fubah & Moos, 2022). This demonstrates a gap in empirical studies on the COVID-19 pandemic. The novelty of the pandemic and the absence of any prior reference case in living memory contribute to this situation in the COVID-19 crisis. The novelty of the pandemic and the absence of any prior reference case in living memory contribute to this situation in the COVID-19 crisis. Flu pandemics, Black Monday, the 2008 global financial crisis, and various other incidents, such as Chornobyl, the Iraqi invasion of Kuwait, 9/11, and Hurricane Katrina, have posed threats and disasters with implications at regional, national, and global levels. However, the complexity of the COVID-19 pandemic surpasses other crises experienced by entrepreneurs before because it was global in scope and had dire economic consequences. It transformed the routine life and the business world. In these challenging circumstances, the survival of all businesses was jeopardized, especially the restaurant industry in South Africa.

The chapter seeks to address the research void by examining the challenges posed by COVID-19 and the strategies restaurant entrepreneurs employ to overcome the devastating effects of COVID-19 in operating their businesses in South Africa. The research questions for this chapter are:

i What were the COVID-19 challenges that restaurant entrepreneurs in South Africa experienced?
ii What are some of the strategies that restaurant entrepreneurs use to fight the devastating effects of COVID-19?

Restaurant Industry Amidst COVID

Elshaer (2022, 720) mentioned that, "during that period, the food service industry appeared susceptible to significant shock, with the likelihood of failure escalating from 18% (1-month crisis) to 85% (6-month crisis) due to the impact of the Covid-19 pandemic". Dube et al. (2020) argue that the pandemic caused colossal job losses, forcing the restaurant sector to decide to continue or shut down in the face of a worsening restaurant market and financial constraints. The outbreak of the COVID-19 pandemic led to a decline in the demand for restaurant services in many countries (Abay et al., 2020). On the 5th March 2020, South Africa reported its first case of COVID-19, prompting President Ramaphosa to declare a state of national disaster in response to the rising infection rate and to contain the spread of the virus. President Cyril Ramaphosa announced fresh measures to combat the spread of COVID-19 in South Africa on 23 March 2020 (Rogerson, 2020). The implemented measures included a three-week nationwide lockdown and stringent restrictions on travel and movement starting from midnight on Thursday, the 26th of March 2020, to midnight on Thursday, the 16th of April 2021 (Adebiyi et al., 2021). People were only permitted to leave their residences in dire situations, such as purchasing basic commodities or obtaining medical assistance. Additionally, during this lockdown period, people had to abide by governmental guidelines that imposed limitations on public assemblies, travel from countries with high-risk factors, and the distribution of alcohol.

Before 2020, restaurants involved several conditions conducive to spreading contagious diseases (e.g., touching, putting objects in mouths, and proximity) (Shigihara, 2020). Thus, restaurants underwent significant limitations, no longer serving as retreat spaces for camaraderie and reconnection due to their potential as virus vectors. With the relaxation of restrictions, some regulations were lifted, marking the emergence of a new normal in both customers' and entrepreneurs' lifestyles. This shift led to a growing trend of avoiding in-person dining services (Shokhsanam & Ahn, 2021). Hence, Nagi (2020) contends that dine-in restaurants have achieved only 10–15% of their pre-pandemic rates, while fast-food establishments have reached 30–40% since the strict lockdown.

These projections indicate a major setback, suggesting that small restaurants are vulnerable to collapse under the impact of the pandemic (Kim et al., 2020; Zeb et al., 2021). Accordingly, restaurateurs needed to adapt their roles to embrace this new approach (Lakshmi & Shareena, 2020).

Existing literature indicates that larger organizations, particularly chain enterprises, handle pandemics like COVID-19 more effectively than smaller organizations. Larger, chain-affiliated restaurants possess significant advantages, including international recognition, robust systems, skilled staff, experienced management, and greater financial stability, which bolster their resilience during challenging times (Dube et al., 2021; Elshaer, 2022). Beyond safety measures like temperature checks, improved sanitation, modern layouts, and customized healthy menus, chain restaurants go further by offering smart technology services. These include electronic menus, convenient reservation systems, and mobile payment options, features typically unavailable to smaller establishments (Kim et al., 2021). Large companies also benefit from economies of scale and can maintain buffer staff costs, whereas small businesses are strained, primarily when no external support mechanisms exist (Cusmano & Raes, 2020).

Even though restrictions on indoor dining were lifted, most restaurant owners faced labour shortages and a severe cut in customer base due to concerns about employees spreading the virus and other people who might be present on the restaurant premises (Lippert et al., 2021). Many restaurants, upon reopening, reinforced their health and safety protocols to reduce the risk of coronavirus infection and encourage customers to feel safe returning (Chuah et al., 2022). These safety precautions involved monitoring the body temperature of both staff and customers, providing hand sanitizing stations, and consistently cleaning and disinfecting high-touch surfaces such as tables and menus. In addition, restaurants adopted payment baskets and implemented social distancing measures by spacing out tables and seating arrangements. As a precaution, all the staff members had always to wear gloves and masks and wash their hands regularly. Also, the workers had to sanitize their hands regularly, which increased the operations costs for restaurant owners as they had to incur sanitizer costs.

During COVID-19, numerous restaurants have embraced a paradigm shift, employing diverse and innovative techniques to attract customers. Many restaurants used their parking spaces to serve food, takeaway, and home delivery (Zeb et al., 2021). Some customers were directed to eat in their cars. South African businesses adopted drive-thru services to minimize customer interaction during the pandemic. Kim et al. (2020) observed that restaurants additionally offered compact table sets designed to fit easily in the cupholder between the two front seats of a car, allowing customers to dine out in a secure and protected environment. In this context, innovative ideas were required to enhance safety measures and minimize the spread of the disease.

Decision-Making for Entrepreneurs

Decision-making includes defining problems, gathering information, generating alternatives, and choosing a course of action. An organization's decision-making environment is shaped by uncontrollable external factors (developments and events) that can have future implications for the outcomes of those decisions. Therefore, decisions are influenced by a spectrum of factors, spanning from the introduction of new technologies or new market competitors to changes in laws, political unrest, and occurrences such as natural disasters and pandemics. In addition to identifying and quantifying these forces, entrepreneurs must gauge their potential impact. For instance, when entrepreneurs grappled with the realities of the COVID-19 pandemic and the necessity to transition many employees to remote work. For example, when entrepreneurs confronted the realities of the COVID-19 pandemic and the need to shift many employees to virtual working. COVID-19 has forced entrepreneurs to break through the technology barriers that prevented home working in the past, initiating a 'structural shift in where work takes place' and maintaining an online presence for business ventures. The impact of the pandemic was, therefore, a litmus test that assessed the decision-making for entrepreneurs in ensuring that their businesses are sustainable and protected against the impact of COVID-19 (Servest, 2020).

The impact of such events as COVID-19 was never experienced and felt before. Entrepreneurs and their managers who forecast and plan for their businesses were hard-pressed as they were unaware of the impact of COVID-19 as it emerged. Their decisions had to be grounded in limited information. This chapter broadly categorizes the circumstances under which decisions are made into three categories: Certainty, risk, and uncertainty.

Certainty

Entrepreneurs with comprehensive knowledge of a problem and a clear understanding of potential solutions and their likely outcomes can make informed decisions, even under conditions of uncertainty. Under these conditions, they can foresee events and probable outcomes that may affect their businesses. Certainty implies that both the problem and alternative solutions are known and well-defined for the purpose of decision-making (Hellriegel et al., 2012). Having multiple well-defined solutions with anticipated outcomes simplifies decision-making for entrepreneurs, allowing them to select the most advantageous option for their businesses.

Risk

Risk arises when entrepreneurs make decisions under conditions of uncertainty, which involves defining the problem, estimating the probability of various events, identifying and evaluating alternative solutions, and assessing the likelihood of each solution achieving the desired outcome (Hellriegel et al., 2012). Risk exists on a spectrum, where problems and solutions can range from well-defined and familiar to unusual and ambitious.

Uncertainty

Uncertainty is the condition under which entrepreneurs need the necessary information to assign probabilities to the outcomes of alternative solutions. Entrepreneurs require assistance in defining the problem and identifying alternative solutions and potential outcomes. Uncertainty highlights the potential need for clearer problem definitions and more innovative solutions (Griffin, 2014). The analysis, prediction, and incorporation of economic factors such as market prices, exchange rates, inflation, and interest rates into decision-making processes can be challenging due to their constantly changing nature. Managers often rely on assumptions to guide their choices in such an environment. Inaccurate assumptions can lead to poor decision-making, potentially causing harm to the business. The COVID-19 era presented entrepreneurs with unprecedented challenges in their decision-making due to a confluence of ongoing disruptions and global shifts, including digitalization, technological advancements, evolving geopolitical landscapes, innovative business models, shifting perspectives on globalization and trade, and the pandemic itself. While the post-COVID-19 future holds much uncertainty, entrepreneurs are crucial in rebuilding the South African economy (Meyer et al., 2020; Zahra, 2020).

The International Monetary Fund (IMF) (2021) pointed out that, "South Africa experienced the impact of the COVID-19 pandemic at a time when its economic vulnerabilities were already increased by an extended period of low investment, sluggish growth, and escalating levels of public debt". This confluence of pre-existing vulnerabilities further exacerbated the impact of the pandemic, causing South Africa to experience one of the most severe economic downturns among emerging market economies (EMEs) in 2020. The pandemic further exacerbated already challenging social conditions characterized by persistent high poverty, unemployment, and inequality. Educational systems suffered disruptions, and job losses disproportionately impacted the most vulnerable segments of society, which are the youth, women, and people experiencing poverty. In addition, job losses have been recorded, taking the unemployment rate to record-high levels. Despite the significant economic challenges, the IMF noted a relatively strong cyclical recovery in 2021. The IMF estimates suggested an output rebound of about 4.6% following the 2020 contraction of −6.4%, driven by the easing of lockdown restrictions (IMF, 2021). It further indicates that, "the rebound was further bolstered by external factors like favourable commodity prices and stable financial conditions, which are likely to be temporary. However, this economic rebound has not translated into a significant decrease in the unemployment rate. Deteriorating confidence, exacerbated by the July social unrest and sluggish private-sector investment and credit growth, poses further challenges". The COVID-19 pandemic has transformed our shared understanding of risk. There are many questions for which there are no answers. Some of the decisions that entrepreneurs across the globe and in South Africa have had to make due to the COVID-19 pandemic include (Hellriegel et al., 2012):

- Deciding on the number of employees working from home while others are working from the office premises
- Adjusting budgets and looking for finances to purchase PPE (personal protective equipment) and update technology
- Manufacturing companies deciding on whether to diversify into manufacturing PPE
- Changing advertising to include the impact of COVID-19
- Setting up COVID-19 task teams to ensure that the organization and its employees adhere to all COVID-19 protocols
- Retail supermarkets had to decide which products would be limited in quantities, especially during the Level 5 lockdown in South Africa

Methodology

This research adopted an interpretive paradigm to explore the socially constructed meanings restaurant owners attribute to their experiences. This research employed a secondary data collection method to investigate how restaurant owners in South Africa perceive the experience of opening their businesses during the COVID-19 pandemic. The study focused on the published articles from the 23rd of March 2020, when the state of national disaster was announced by the President of South Africa, Cyril Ramaphosa, to control the spread and alleviate the adverse effects of the coronavirus (South African Government, 2020a,b). All the articles published between the 23rd of March 2020 and the 15th of March 2022 and accessible through the internet were examined and chosen based on their relevance to the study's objectives. The articles were selected based on their relevance to the challenges and strategies faced by restaurant entrepreneurs during the COVID-19 pandemic. The qualitative data collected from the articles was analysed using the Atlas ti version 8 software. The software offers efficient and consistent data coding, creating clear, well-defined themes. Some reviewed articles have been provided as examples to support the study's findings.

Challenges Faced by Entrepreneurs Due to COVID-19

Financial challenges, lockdown restrictions, and lack of government support emerged as sub-themes of restaurant entrepreneurs' challenges due to the COVID-19 pandemic.

Financial Challenges

Financial challenges have been identified as one of the biggest challenges for restaurant entrepreneurs in South Africa due to the COVID-19 pandemic and the first five weeks of the level 5 lockdown of 2020, which severely affected the industry. Forced closures due to the pandemic severely impacted the restaurant industry, with many establishments, including iconic names like La Tête, Restaurant Mosaic, Café 1999, and The Stack (Mbonambi, 2021), permanently shutting their doors. This highlighted the urgent need for entrepreneurs to find alternative revenue streams. Besides being unable to generate revenue for their businesses, the businesses incurred salaries and rental expenses. The total lockdown made it difficult for restaurant owners operating from rented spaces, as they faced the dual challenge of paying rent and employee salaries despite revenue loss. In this regard, COVID-19 posed a significant financial challenge for some entrepreneurs who incurred rental expenses. At the same time, they did not have any income they generated during the level lockdown of 2020. Madubela (2021a,b) reported that, "at the peak of the lockdown in April 2020, 94% of the franchise industry halted trading with the restaurant chain franchisor Spur Corporation revenue declining by 40.2% from R525 million reported in the prior comparable period to R314.2 million for the six months to end the 31st of December 2020". According to Madubela (2021a,b), the South African franchise industry was severely impacted by the lockdown, with 94% of businesses closing down operations at its peak in April 2020. This translated to significant financial losses, as evidenced by Spur Corporation, a major restaurant chain, experiencing a 40.2% decline in revenue (from R525 million to R314.2 million) for the six months ending December 31st, 2020, compared to the previous comparable period (Madubela, 2021a,b). In addition, several restaurant brands experienced similar revenue decline, including Panarottis and Casa Bella (46.7%), John Dory's (49.8%), The Hussar Grill (41.5%), RocoMamas (23.8%), and Nikos (48.7%) (Madubela, 2021a,b). These examples show that restaurant entrepreneurs experienced financial challenges due to the COVID-19 pandemic.

Lockdown Restrictions

During the strict lockdown, the South African government restricted trade to essential goods such as food products (including non-alcoholic beverages), animal supplies, cleaning chemicals, hygiene products, personal protective equipment, fuel, and airtime. Similarly, only essential services like healthcare, disaster management, grocery stores, basic municipal services, funeral services, media infrastructure, and essential goods transport remained operational (Bruwer et al., 2020). On the 1st of May 2020, South Africa shifted into the 'Adjusted Strategy'. South Africa implemented a five-level alert system to manage COVID-19 restrictions, with Alert Level 5 being the strictest. At this highest level, only essential services were allowed to function (SA Government, 2020).

Due to their non-essential status, restaurants were not permitted to operate under Alert Level 5 restrictions. The Five Alert Level System (FALS) was introduced as a framework for progressively lifting lockdown restrictions. This adjusted risk approach was informed by various criteria, including the infection levels, transmission rate, healthcare facility capacity, the extent of implementing public health interventions for COVID-19, and the economic and social consequences of ongoing restrictions (SA Government, 2020).

Alert levels determine the restrictions to be applied during the national state of disaster, as shown in Table 8.1. The Ministerial Advisory Committee (MAC) guided the Minister of Health on the appropriate declaration of national or provincial Alert Levels based on epidemiological trends. This assessment considered factors such as the number of tests conducted, individuals screened, positive cases reported, recoveries, and the demographic profile of positive cases.

Due to stringent lockdown measures restricting the operation and sale of alcohol in restaurants, many restaurants experienced a sharp decline in revenue. Consequently, most restaurants were forced to reduce business spending to stay afloat (Kalidas et al., 2020). In this regard, restaurant entrepreneurs still struggle to recuperate from the losses incurred during this period. For restaurants, the easing of these restrictions came very late. The easing of these restrictions has been mixed with a re-ban on alcohol and limitations on sit-ins. For example, alcohol sales in restaurants were banned three times since the gradual easing of COVID-19 restrictions during the pandemic (Toyana, 2021).

Some online articles published during the pandemic revealed that the various lockdown restrictions implemented to curb the spread of COVID-19 negatively affected restaurant entrepreneurs. The Restaurant Association of South Africa (RASA) also feared that stricter lockdown restrictions would mark the end of many establishments (SABC News, 2021). In support, Caboz (2021) claimed that

Table 8.1 Criteria for determining alert levels (Disaster Management Act, 2020)

Criteria determining alert levels	Alert level	Description
(a) The epidemiological trends of COVID-19 infections. (b) The health system capacity in a specified area to respond to the disease burden (c) Any other factor that would influence the level of infection, hospitalization, and mortality.	Five (5) Four (4) Three (3) Two (2) One (1)	High COVID-19 spread with a low health system readiness Moderate to a high COVID-19 spread with a low to moderate health system readiness Moderate COVID-19 spread with a moderate health system readiness. Moderate COVID-19 spread with a high health system readiness Low COVID-19 spread with a high health system readiness

hundreds of restaurants closed for good in January 2021 due to strict lockdown restrictions. These included independent restaurants, fast food outlets, coffee shops, casual dining establishments, hospital canteens, mobile restaurants and franchise group outlets. Among some of the restaurants that closed down their operations were; V&A Waterfront, Balducci's (an award-winning steak and seafood restaurant) Belthazar, one of the Waterfront's oldest tenants, The Kitchen in Cape Town, popular Pablo Eggs Go Bar, Myoga restaurant, launched in 2007 in the grounds of The Vineyard hotel in Cape Town, The Kalk Bay Theatre & Restaurant, Cape Town CBD based Brownies and Downies, a ground-breaking coffee place which employed the intellectually disabled, The Restaurant at Waterkloof, Somerset West, Upper Bloem Restaurant, Green Point, SMAK Delicatessen and Eatery, Cape Town CBD, Farro's in Illovo, Johannesburg, Two and Sixpence Tavern, Simon's Town, after 21 years, Fork, in Franschhoek, Calexico in Milpark, The Countess, and La Petite Maison in Melville, Urbanologi, 33 High Street Restaurant, Epicure by Chef Coco, Coobs, and Douglas + Hale in Johannesburg, Café 1999 in Durban, Two Olives and Tilting Heads Taco Cafe, and Margarita Bar in Port Elizabeth.

Lack of Government Support

Lack of government support towards the restaurant industry is another challenge that restaurant owners experienced during the COVID-19 pandemic. Palm (2021) also noted that the RASA has repeatedly emphasized the struggles faced by restaurant owners throughout the pandemic, urging the government to provide support. Their plea illustrates that restaurant entrepreneurs desperately needed government support during the COVID-19 pandemic, given that the lockdown restrictions had severely affected the industry. Example 2 *Bars and Restaurants Hit Hard in South Africa* shows that entrepreneurs desperately needed to lift lockdown restrictions.

Strategies to Overcome the Devastating Effects of COVID-19

The study results from the reviewed articles showed that the strategies used to overcome the devastating effects of COVID-19 are adopting digital technologies, using deliveries, good hygiene and sanitizing, retrenching employees, kerbside pickup, and innovative practices.

Adoption of Digital Technologies

The closure of dine-in restaurants and the subsequent growth, and in some cases, the inclusion of take-out services, compelled numerous restaurant entrepreneurs to exhibit their innovativeness and explore alternative approaches, not only in terms of their menus and physical spaces, but also in terms of delivering a unique experience to their patrons and offering exceptional value. As emerging businesses struggled to recover from the impact of COVID-19, many entrepreneurs recognized that investing in smart ICT solutions was essential for survival. South African entrepreneurs with physical storefronts were severely impacted by the strict lockdown measures of the pandemic (Nhamo et al., 2020). Faced with regulations that shuttered locations and restricted operations, businesses rapidly pivoted to online platforms to ensure survival. As Kendall Shaw of Maybach Media (cited by Rios, 2020) states, "If you cannot go to your store or your location to do business, you have to find another outlet to stay afloat."

The move to online platforms meant businesses had to adapt to meet customer demands in new ways. This was evident in the surge of social media use during the coronavirus outbreak, with increased usage, engagement, and overall time spent on these platforms (Chan et al., 2020). The entrepreneurs adopted online food ordering and delivery platforms to increase their sales and efficiency, attracting potential customers, especially among millennials and Generation Z (Gen Z), and gaining a competitive advantage during the pandemic. The necessity for restaurants to adopt online food ordering due to the COVID-19 pandemic led to a significant boost in sales and alleviated financial burdens. A United States of America study by Brewer and Sebby (2021) found that customers were more likely to order when presented with detailed visual information on platforms, such as menus with photos and descriptions of dishes. This example shows an article that reveals restaurant owners adopted digital technology and used deliveries to overcome the devastating effects of COVID-19.

Use of Deliveries

Government restrictions on dine-in service and the need to generate revenue pushed restaurants to offer delivery, making it the only option in some cases. They had to offer their deliveries or sign up for delivery partners to feed the community and continue employing restaurant workers (Elliott, 2020). Delivery services, whether through third-party applications or directly managed by the restaurant, were crucial for survival during the COVID-19 pandemic.

Good Hygiene and Sanitization

The COVID-19 pandemic has instilled a fear of exposure in many people, prompting them to avoid dining out or even ordering restaurant food for home delivery. The COVID-19 pandemic severely impacted the restaurant industry, highlighting the need for restaurants to prioritize reassuring customers about their safety and hygiene practices (Pasiya, 2021). Survival and customer trust hinged on restaurants prioritizing food safety and significantly enhancing hygiene protocols during the pandemic. The owners needed to ensure they kept sanitizing their restaurants and all the essential utensils they used. Government regulations mandate the widespread availability of sanitizers and disposable gloves within the restaurant industry. Staff members must wear gloves and masks at all times and wash their hands regularly, even though it increases operational costs. Companies like Starbucks and McDonald's prioritized frequent handwashing among their staff to mitigate the spread of the disease (Zeb et al., 2021). Restaurants also sought to reassure customers by highlighting the frequent handwashing practices of their employees and the regular sanitization of surfaces like door handles and tables to prevent the spread of the contagious disease.

Retrenchment of Employees

COVID-19 made it impossible for restaurants to generate profits, especially during the first two months of lockdown. Due to the strict lockdown, businesses operating on a monthly salary schedule could not meet their payroll obligations. As a result, some entrepreneurs had to retrench some of their employees to save expenses. As a result of the pandemic that followed government lockdown measures that included restrictions on how restaurants would operate, especially on the sale of alcohol and the number of customers allowed in the restaurant while considering social distancing, many restaurant entrepreneurs believed they needed to reduce the number of service staff. This was the most dangerous outcome of the pandemic as entrepreneurs resorted to retrenching some of their employees and even cutting down their compensation. While entrepreneurs had to retrench their employees as a strategy to survive during the pandemic, this impacted the livelihoods of many employees, as the restaurant subsector provided thousands of jobs that "put food on the table for many South African families, especially those in rural communities" (Western Cape Government, 2020). The economic devastation of COVID-19 within the restaurant industry fuelled protests, with employees pleading for government support to address widespread unemployment. In another demonstration, restaurant managers, owners, and employees united under the slogan "#jobssaveslives" to advocate for the full resumption of restaurant operations, aiming to preserve jobs (Maxwell et al., 2020, 1). Restaurants had retrenched their workforce by over 70% when the pandemic started (Botha, 2020).

Kerbside Pickup

Restaurant businesses also utilized the kerbside service to ensure their operations ran smoothly and overcome the lockdown restrictions. The service allows customers to collect their orders from specially designated parking bays made through online platforms.

Innovative Practices

The innovative practices employed by the restaurant entrepreneurs include establishing ghost restaurants. COVID-19 has forced businesses to innovate their models urgently in order to preserve customer relationships. Many entrepreneurs accepted the paradigm shift and started attracting customers using innovative techniques due to the pandemic. Restaurant entrepreneurs adopted innovative approaches to maintain operations and cater to customer needs during the pandemic. These included utilizing parking spaces for dine-in services within customers' cars and, in some cases, introducing drive-thru options, previously uncommon in the industry. They also offer compact table arrangements, which conveniently fit within the cup holder situated between the two front seats of an automobile. This imparted a sense of dining outside the confines of one's vehicle, within a secure and sheltered environment for the diners.

The above shows that due to COVID-19, restaurant entrepreneurs had to be innovative for their businesses to survive. COVID-19 challenges spurred restaurants to seek innovative survival strategies, including rebranding, altering offerings, establishing dark kitchens for delivery, or entering temporary hibernation.

Conclusions and Recommendations

Restaurants require a well-defined and comprehensive re-entry strategy. This strategy should balance interventions that address both demand and supply side factors alongside considerations for economic restructuring in the post-pandemic landscape. Figure 8.1 below shows some strategic recommendations that will guide the conclusions of this chapter.

The COVID-19 lockdowns, stay-at-home orders, and border restrictions severely disrupted the restaurant industry, forcing a shift in focus to the devastating consequences of the pandemic. It is now important to comprehend how to survive in the marketplace. The COVID-19 pandemic has dramatically reshaped consumer demands in the restaurant industry, leading to a global crisis and disrupting established value chains and business models. In the advent of such quantitative findings as presented in the preceding narrative, scholars and policymakers alike have overlooked the qualitative aspects of the effects of COVID-19 experienced by restaurants. In the quest to resuscitate the restaurants, as narrated above, the chapter unravelled the experiences of restaurant businesspersons. It provided much-needed insight into directing the refurbishment efforts of the industry in general. This has led scholars and this chapter to broach issues around the revival of restaurants amidst the new normalcy. More specifically, the current chapter describes contemporary South Africa's restaurant business dynamics and the responses undertaken by the governments during the COVID-19 pandemic.

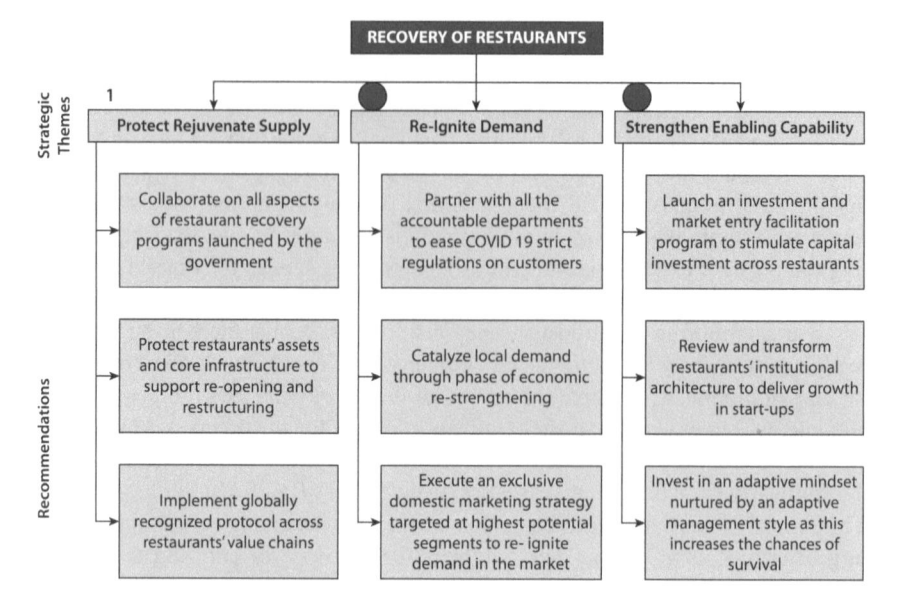

Figure 8.1 Strategic recommendations

Strategic Themes / Recommendations

RECOVERY OF RESTAURANTS

1. Protect Rejuvenate Supply
- Collaborate on all aspects of restaurant recovery programs launched by the government
- Protect restaurants' assets and core infrastructure to support re-opening and restructuring
- Implement globally recognized protocol across restaurants' value chains

Re-Ignite Demand
- Partner with all the accountable departments to ease COVID 19 strict regulations on customers
- Catalyze local demand through phase of economic re-strengthening
- Execute an exclusive domestic marketing strategy targeted at highest potential segments to re-ignite demand in the market

Strengthen Enabling Capability
- Launch an investment and market entry facilitation program to stimulate capital investment across restaurants
- Review and transform restaurants' institutional architecture to deliver growth in start-ups
- Invest in an adaptive mindset nurtured by an adaptive management style as this increases the chances of survival

Figure 8.1 Strategic recommendations

The chapter contributes to the growing knowledge of the impacts of pandemics on restaurants in South Africa and Africa. Further research is needed to explore the full impact of COVID-19 on restaurant operations and customer behaviour. This research could include aspects such as the effectiveness of government measures, the evolution of consumer preferences, and the long-term consequences for the industry. The pandemic underscores the importance of strengthening the relationship between the government and fast-food industry stakeholders. This includes ensuring clear, consistent, and reliable communication and fostering trust and collaboration as they navigate the challenges and opportunities the evolving landscape presents. Academics and policymakers should see this as an opportunity to further engage with all stakeholders within the industry and seek to strengthen relationships and collaboration efforts, which may result in more trust in the government's support systems.

This chapter has provided insights into the implications of the COVID-19 pandemic on South African restaurant operators. Though the pandemic exposed the restaurant industry's vulnerabilities, it highlighted the sector's potential to play a key role in recovery and drive long-term transformation within the fast-food industry towards greater resilience. In light of the pandemic's impact, restaurant operators and stakeholders should comprehensively re-evaluate the domestic fast-food industry. A holistic and innovative approach is needed to develop recovery strategies, protocols, and policies that balance public safety concerns with consumer demand for restaurant services, ultimately driving the industry's revitalization.

The economic recovery from the pandemic presents a critical opportunity for research. Studies should investigate the multifaceted impacts of digital transformation on the support networks underpinning restaurant businesses' success. The need to constantly evolve as a business is of immense value and cannot be over-emphasized. Stagnation coupled with failing to be adaptive is a means to business failure. Digitalization has proved to be pivotal in improving businesses' survival chances. Empowerment of entrepreneurs and staff through the upskilling of key skills will aid with the preparation for the unknown future 'tussles' such as those caused by COVID-19. Therefore, investing in an adaptive mindset nurtured by an adaptive management style IS recommended because this increases the chances of survival. Subsequently, restaurant businesspersons may easily invest resources towards digitalizing their services.

References

Abay, K.A., Ibrahim, H., Breisinger, C. and Bayasgalanbat, N. (2020). *Food policies and their implications on overweight and obesity: Trends in selected countries in the near East and North Africa Region.* Cairo, Egypt (Print).

Adebiyi, B.O., Donga, G.T., Omukunyi, B. and Roman, N.V. (2021) How South African families protected themselves during the COVID-19 pandemic: A qualitative study. *Sustainability*, 14: 1236. https://doi.org/10.3390 (Accessed the 25th of March 2022).

Aharon, D.Y., Jacobi, A., Cohen, E., Tzur, J. and Qadan, M. (2021). COVID-19, government measures and hospitality industry performance. *PLoS ONE*, 16(8):e0255819.

Botha, R. (2020). COVID-19 lessons for SA's restaurant industry. City Press. https://www.news24.com/citypress/voices/COVID-19-lessons-for-sas-restaurant-industry-20200929 (Accessed the 26th of May 2021).

Brewer, P. and Sebby, A.G. (2021). The effect of online restaurant menus on consumers' purchase intentions during the COVID-19 pandemic. *International Journal of Hospitality Management*, 94:102777.

Bruwer, J.P., Hattingh, C. and Perold, I. (2020). Probable Measures to Aid South African Small Medium and Micro Enterprises. *Sustainability, Post-COVID-19: a Literature Review', SSRN Electronic Journal*.

Caboz, J. (2021). These popular SA restaurants did not survive COVID. https://www.businessinsider.co.za/almost-4000-restaurants-forced-to-close-during-level-3-adjusted-says-rasa-some-local-favourites-didnt-make-it-2021-2 (Accessed the 22nd of March 2022)

Chan, A.K., Nickson, C.P., Rudolph, J.W., Lee, A. and Joynt, G.M.. (2020). Social media for rapid knowledge dissemination: Early experience from the COVID-19 pandemic. *Anaesthesia*, 75(12):1579–1582. DOI: 10.1111/anae.15057

Chuah, S.H.W., Aw, E. and Cheng, C.F. (2022). A silver lining in the COVID-19 cloud: Examining customers' value perceptions, willingness to use and pay more for robotic restaurants. *Journal of Hospitality Marketing & Management*, 31(1):49–76.

Cusmano, L. and Raes, S. (2020). OECD policy responses to coronavirus (COVID-19); Coronavirus (COVID-19): SME policy responses. *Retrieved from OECD Better Policies for Better Lives*. https://www.oecd.org/coronavirus/policy-responses/coronavirus-covid-19-sme-policy-responses-04440101/#%20section-d1e160%20%20 (Accessed the 10th of June 2022).

Disaster Management Act (2020), Republic of South Africa https://www.gov.za/documents/disaster-management-act

Donga, G., Ngirande, H. and Chinyakata, R. (2021). Business as unusual: Carving out the South African small, medium and micro-sized Enterprises' path for navigating past COVID-19 pandemic. *Himalayan Journals Economics and Business Management*, 2(6):48–56.

Dube, K., Nhamo, G. and Chikodzi, D. (2021). COVID-19 cripples global restaurant and hospitality industry. *Current Issues in Tourism*, 24(11):1487–1490.

Elliott, F. (2020). LA's famous apple pan does delivery for first time in 73-year history, Eater LA. https://la.eater.com/2020/3/17/21183842/apple-pan-burger-restaurant-los-angelesdelivery-75-years-news (Accessed the 26th of March 2022)

Elshaer, A.M. (2022). Restaurants' response to Covid-19 pandemic: The realm of Egyptian independent restaurants. *Journal of Quality Assurance in Hospitality & Tourism*, 23(3):716–747.

Fubah, C.N. and Moos, M. (2022). Exploring COVID-19 challenges and coping mechanisms for SMEs in the South African entrepreneurial ecosystem. *Sustainability*, 14(4):1944.

Griffin, R.W. (2014) *Fundamentals of management* (7th ed.). Australia: South-Western Cengage Learning.

Hellriegel, D., Slocum, J., Jackson, S.E., Louw, L., Staude, G., Amos, T., Klopper, H.B., Louw, M., Oosthuizen, T., Perks, S. and Zindiye, S. (2012). *Management*. 4th South African ed. Cape Town: Oxford University Press.

IMF (2021). *South Africa: Staff concluding statement of the 2021 Article IV mission*. IMF Communications Department. https://www.imf.org/en/News/Articles/2021/12/07/south-africa-staff-concluding-statement-of-the-2021-article-iv-mission (Accessed the 10th of December 2021).

Kalidas, S., Magwentshu, N. and Rajagopal, A. (2020). How South African SMEs can survive and thrive post-COVID-19. https://www.mckinsey.com/featured-insights/middle-east-and-africa/how-southafrican-smes-can-survive-and-thrive-post-covid-19 (Accessed the 10th of March 2022).

Kim, D., Lee, J.Y., Yang, J.S., Kim, J.W., Kim, V.N. and Chang, H., 2020. The architecture of SARS-CoV-2 transcriptome. Cell, 181(4), pp.914-921.

Kim, J., Kim, J. and Wang, Y. (2021). Uncertainty risks and strategic reaction of restaurant firms amid COVID-19: Evidence from China. *International Journal of Hospitality Management*, 92:102752.

Kuckertz, A. and Brändle, L. (2022). Creative reconstruction: A structured literature review of the early empirical research on the COVID-19 crisis and entrepreneurship. *Management Review Quarterly*, 72(2):281–307.

Lakshmi, B.M. and Shareena, P. (2020). Impact of COVID-19 on restaurants. *Journal of Interdisciplinary Cycle Research*, 13(8):1327–1334.

Liñán, F. and Jaén, I. (2022). The Covid-19 pandemic and entrepreneurship: Some reflections. *International Journal of Emerging Markets*, 17(5):1165–1174.

Lippert, J.F., Furnari, M.B. and Kriebel, C.W. (2021). The impact of the COVID-19 pandemic on occupational stress in restaurant work: A qualitative study. *International Journal of Environmental Research and Public Health*, 18(19):10378.

Madubela, A. (2021a). Little reprieve for franchise sector as restaurants brace for level 4 impact. https://www.news24.com/fin24/Economy/South-Africa/little-reprieve-for-franchise-sector-as-restaurants-brace-for-level-4-impact-20210701 (Accessed the 20th of July 2022).

Madubela, A. (2021b). Ocean Basket uses a unique roadhouse-style dining option, saving jobs in the process. *Fin24*. https://www.news24.com/fin24/Companies/TravelAndLeisure/ocean-basket-uses-unique-roadhouse-style-dining-option-saving-jobs-in-the-process-20210705 (Accessed the 25th of March 2022).

Maxwell, K., Hennig, W. and Emond, M. (2020). Tables laid bare around South Africa as the industry fights back. #jobssaveslives. https://www.dailymaverick.co.za/

article/2020-07-24-tableslaid-bare-around-south-africa-as-industry-fights-back/ (Accessed the 20th of June 2022).

Mbonambi, B. (2021). Level 4: Restaurants impacted by lockdown regulations. https://www.iol.co.za/lifestyle/food-drink/restaurants/level-4-restaurants-impacted-by-lockdown-regulations-54406620-0b66-437b-95ea-33054e7c65e7 (Accessed the 10th of March 2022).

Meyer, S., Gounden, P. and Barden, C. (2020). More bark and bite: Competition law as an additional means of post-pandemic support. *Without Prejudice*, *20*(5):29–30.

Nagi, I. (2020, April 29). The food and beverage industry in the time of curfew. *Egypt Tomorrow*. https://cipe-arabia.org/wp-content/uploads/2020/05/ETEF_Interviews_Ibrahim_Nagi.pdf (Accessed the 11th of March 2022).

Nhamo, G., Dube, K. and Chikodzi, D., 2020. Counting the cost of COVID-19 on the global tourism industry (pp. 109-133). Cham: Springer International Publishing.

Palm, K. (2021). Eased lockdown restrictions came a bit too late for some business owners. https://ewn.co.za/2021/09/14/eased-lockdown-came-a-bit-too-late-for-some-business-owners (Accessed the 22nd of March 2022).

Pasiya, L. (2021). Innovations and technology used by the restaurant industry are exciting and should help secure its future, even with lockdowns.https://www.iol.co.za/lifestyle/food-drink/restaurants/innovations-and-technology-used-by-restaurant-industry-is-exciting-and-should-help-secure-its-future-even-with-lockdowns-fe060fad-c8b9-4018-aec0-95c2e103aa6d (Accessed the 22nd of March 2022).

Rashid, S. and Ratten, V. (2021). Entrepreneurial ecosystems during COVID-19: The survival of small businesses using dynamic capabilities. *World Journal of Entrepreneurship, Management and Sustainable Development*, *17*(3):457–476.

Ratten, V. (2020). Coronavirus and international business: An entrepreneurial ecosystem perspective. *Thunderbird International Business Review*, *62*(5):629–634.

Rogerson, C.M. and Rogerson, J.M. (2020) COVID-19 and tourism spaces of vulnerability in South Africa. *African Journal of Hospitality, Tourism and Leisure*, *9*(4): 382–401. [Online]. Available at: https://doi.org/10.46222/ajhtl.19770720-26 (Accessed the 26th of March 2022).

SABC News. (2021). Stricter lockdown restrictions may mark the end to many restaurants. *RASA*. https://www.sabcnews.com/stricter-lockdown-restrictions-may-mark-end-to-many-restaurants-rasa/ (Accessed the 20th of March 2022).

Shigihara, A.M. (2020). Postmodern life, restaurants, and COVID-19. *Contexts*, *19*(4):26–31.

Shokhsanam, Z. and Ahn, Y.J. (2021). Employee service quality at Uzbekistani halal restaurants amid the COVID-19 pandemic. *Sustainability*, *13*(10):5712.

Sobaih, A.E.E., Elshaer, I., Hasanein, A.M. and Abdelaziz, A.S. (2021). Responses to COVID-19: The role of performance in the relationship between small hospitality enterprises' resilience and sustainable tourism development. *International Journal of Hospitality Management*, *94*:102824.

South African Government. (2020a). Disaster management act: Regulations to address, prevent and combat the spread of coronavirus COVID-19: Amendment. 2020. https://www.gov.za/documents/d (Accessed the 2nd of April 2020).

South African Government. (2020b). President Cyril Ramaphosa: Measures to combat Coronavirus COVID-19 epidemic. https://www.gov.za/speeches/statement-president-cyril-ramaphosa-measurescombat-covid-19-epidemic-15-mar-2020-0000 (Accessed the 20th of March 2022).

Stam, E. and Van de Ven, A. (2021). Entrepreneurial ecosystem elements. *Small Business Economics*, *56*(2):809–832.

Sucheran, R. (2022). The COVID-19 pandemic and guesthouses in South Africa: Economic impacts and recovery measures. *Development Southern Africa*, *39*(1):35–50.

Toyana, M. (2021). South Africa's renewed booze ban may deal the final blow to crippled restaurants. https://www.dailymaverick.co.za/article/2021-07-12-south-africas-renewed-booze-ban-may-deal-the-final-blow-to-crippled-restaurants/ (Accessed the 22nd of March 2022).

Türkeş, M.C., Stăncioiu, A.F., Băltescu, C.A. and Marinescu, R.C. (2021). Resilience innovations and the use of food order and delivery platforms by Romanian restaurants during the COVID-19 pandemic. *Journal of Theoretical and Applied Electronic Commerce Research, 16*(7):3218–3247.

UNWTO. (2020). *UNWTO World Tourism Barometer, 18*(2) https://www.e-unwto.org/toc/wtobarometereng/18/2 (Accessed the 28th of March 2022).

Western Cape Government. (2020) Provincial economic review & outlook. Western Cape Government, Provincial Treasury. https://www.westerncape.gov.za/provincialtreasury/files/atoms/files/2020%20PERO%20Publication.pdf (Accessed the 10th of June 2022).

Zeb, S., Hussain, S.S. and Javed, A. (2021). COVID-19 and a way forward for restaurants and street food vendors. *Cogent Business & Management, 8*(1):1923359.

Part II
Challenges and Opportunities in BRICS Countries

9 Importance of Governance in Entrepreneurship

Namrata Dhasmana

Introduction

The pandemic has given an economic shift to the global economy. The starvation in the global economy since 2020 still has been an exciting trajectory for economists worldwide. The layoffs, the great resignation, and the Change of intent in life that people are going through are some factors that have created a vacuum in economic growth and development. Where there is a sharp increase in quitting jobs, 33% is attrition in the Western Countries. (Brazil, Russia, India, China, and South Africa) BRICS countries' people cannot even afford to retire and sit idle because of low socioeconomic status and per capita income. Hence, the people continue in unsatisfactory low-paid jobs and risk their happiness index life. The pandemic created deflation in BRICS with the increase in the number of the poor segment and also shifting the middle class to the poor. The economists feared deflation. The author here being a scholar, and an industry expert, has integrated some practical aspects of the industry and academics to uproar the trajectory of economies. She has researched the essence of wealth creation and how to use the available resources to improve the trajectory of Gross Domestic Production (GDP).

Wealth creation is pivotal to continuing the flow and circulation of wealth and creating equality in the distribution of resources to suppliers and buyers to mitigate the risk of deflation and further damage. According to the Organisation for Economic Co-operation and Development (OECD), global demand declined due to various factors even after analysing significant reductions in the cost price of goods and services (Perelm, 2015). One of the determinants was the low economic power to purchase. The signs of deflation begin with this scarcity and a misbalance in demand and supply. The phenomenon is economically incorrect for the global economy. So, even when the taxes are reduced, and the best policies are at the government level if entrepreneurs do not follow governance, the socioeconomic status of common people does not improve.

Background

The author is an Industry Expert and has integrated some practical aspects of the industry and academics. The research has been done to give an essence of Wealth Creation and reduce the poverty gap. The reasons for misbalance are also seen when we witness the dissimilar economy of BRICS with Western economies. To mitigate economic misbalance and have an early recovery, the growth of BRICS Economies needs a boost in their economies and per capita income. BRICS represents 40% of the global population, 24% of the global gross domestic product, and 16% of worldwide trade. Entrepreneurship is the key for BRICS countries to boost economic development globally. India is the 7th largest economy, 65% of its population below 35. This world population has immense potential to drive the economic condition of the global economy. With a population of 1.4 billion, according to the World Population Review, India is expected to surpass many other developing economies in terms of population. As per the report of Fortune 500 companies, 30% of Indians as their Chief Executive Officers (CEOs). One-third of all Silicon Valley (United States) engineers are from India, and 10% of the world's high-tech company CEOs are Indians (Gulf Today, 2021). These Indian CEOs also give a deeper insight into the country's talent and indicate the potential and capability of people as resources to take on challenges as Entrepreneurs. There is also a thought associated with Entrepreneurship. When economies have to begin with Entrepreneurship for wealth creation, it reflects inequality and lagging economies. The phenomenon is a result of the insanity of many misadventures. This paper uses survey data to examine the nature and determinants of entrepreneurship in India. The first part assesses the basic characteristics of entrepreneurship in India. At the same time, the following sections analyse the main determinants of BRICS entrepreneurship based on the literature and test their significance at the state level in BRICS with the support of regressions on panel data. It also examines existing policies relating to economic crises caused by COVID-19 and one of the BRICS national conflicts (Russia-Ukrainian War) with a big impact of this crisis in the world economic dynamic system. The author makes recommendations for new policies in this area. The author advocates that entrepreneurship can provide new economic opportunities for people and contribute to overall growth and the exit from poverty.

The Policy for the Promotion of Employment Creation Programmes (PPECP) activities reinforce, support the implementation, and complement existing policies and strategies that entrepreneurship will increase business and job creation in the world economic agenda. Strategies for private sector development and employment of youth entrepreneurs and business development policy of employment reinforce the goals of major countries, including India, committed to sustainable world economic development. Although the Small and Medium Enterprises Development Policy has reached many fold, but it did not create the necessary infrastructure for entrepreneurship and innovation in micro, small and medium enterprises. This requires building people's capacity at the national and local levels and the power to provide appropriate means to support the implementation of the planned activities in social-economic politics. This policy aims to address these broad-based challenges that have characterised the operations of BRICS States.

At present, the five economies of the group contribute to more than half of world growth. According to Sergei Karatayev, "BRICS occupy a central place in the search for solutions to reform the international financial system" (IMF, 2022). The deputy director of the Economic Research Centre of the Russian Institute for Strategic Studies cited the example of strengthening voting rights from China and India to the International Monetary Fund (IMF) and the World Bank. The BRICS leaders strive to expand partnerships with emerging markets and developing countries, However, the dialogue and cooperation with non-BRICS countries would be "on full foot" of equality. At the behest of the BRICS, many global governance structures are undertaking gradual reform. He added that BRICS have gained momentum in international relations, noting that the group is increasingly united in international affairs. Indeed, it "advocates dialogue and the peaceful settlement of disputes, in addition to lifting all restrictions on trade and investment" and "tries to protect the interests of developing countries."

History of Entrepreneurship

The term Entrepreneur was first coined by Richard Cantillon as early as the 18th century. Early19th century French economist Jean-Baptiste Say defined entrepreneurship broadly, saying it "shifts economic resources out of an area of lower and into an area of higher productivity and greater yield" (Entrepreneurship – Wikipedia, 2021). The tribes were exchanging goods even 20,000 years ago. The bartering system was a practice being followed as Entrepreneurship. Entrepreneurship has evolved in all these eras. Earlier also, the exchange was as per the need of the customer. The goods were exchanged as per the requirement. Hence the needs of the customer were of utmost necessity. Today, the entrepreneurship journey is about satisfying customer and stakeholder demands and creating a balance of supply and demand. Let's look back at how our industries have evolved and revolutionised. The first Industrial Revolution began in the mid-18th century with the advent of Factories (Jooris, 2021). There was a paradigm shift from the agriculture sector to the primary factories in an organised way. The second and third revolutions were about mass production and computing. These revolutions started in the middle of the 19th century. The era of automobiles also began during this time. The third revolution was about Mainframe Computing. This era brought about Bill Gates and Steve Jobs. The fourth Industrial Revolution concerns the Internet of Things (IoT) and Cyber-Physical

Systems. It will not be doing justice if the essence of Information Technology (IT) and Artificial Intelligence (AI) is left unattended in the Research. IT and AI are the critical drivers of Governance with minimal effort. AI is not only to mitigate risks but also to improve efficiency for long-term sustainability. Use of Artificial Intelligence by BRICS enables them to globalise in business and expand their entrepreneurship. AI also creates a compelling Governance and improves checks and controls through innovations. This era comes with opportunity entrepreneurship, which is business-driven and AI-based. As per the definition mentioned earlier, Entrepreneurship is all about creating higher productivity of the resources, which is the determining force of entrepreneurship. In BRICS, the resources are there and have significant potential to improve the economic power of their respective countries and give a powerful shift to the Global Economy in the GDP.

Potential of India in Entrepreneurship to Strive Global Economy

The GDP of a country gives a snapshot of its economy. GDP ranking by country 2022 ranked India as the 7th with a GDP of $2.72 trillion, following the United States (GDP: $20.49 T), China (13.4 T), Japan (4.97 T), Germany (4.00 T), the United Kingdom (2.83 T), and France (2.78 T). After a continuous fall of 7.5% to 5% for three straight years in GDP growth, India lost its fifth position as the Highest GDP in the world in 2019 (IMF, 2022). The nation, being diverse and robust with the modern infrastructure, can combat poverty with reformation in education. A stable political government strengthening laws against Governance violations will be significant and more profound for the implementation. The central government steering the policies will have a solid foundation because of the stability. The central government driving the policies will have a solid foundation because of the stability. The advent of Entrepreneurship at a grassroots level in India is a key lever to boost Wealth Creation. The scope of Entrepreneurship in India is recognised by the initiative of the Indian government's "Start-up India." A 10% increase in the registration of new firms per district year yields a 1.8% increase in the Gross Domestic District Product (GDDP). The results concluded that entrepreneurship is the Torch-Bearer of the growth of the Indian economy in future years. Entrepreneurship is also an alternative employment option and will significantly impact the global economy. The labour migration from unproductive sectors into entrepreneurship has a high potential to reduce the productivity gap in India (The BRICS Report, 2012).

The Indian Context

In many views, India is a benchmark for values and change makers as an economic development model. The political stability and the long-term planning for economic development with a boost to exports and Foreign Direct Investment

(FDI) invite other economies to invest and progress. The research emphasises the governance of emerging economies due to volatility in the market after the Pandemic and continuous geopolitical conflicts. India has integrated political and economic institutions with social science to remove paradoxes in the theories. The continuity, collaboration, and consensus model advocated by Honourable Prime Minister of India Mr Narender Modi at the 13th BRICS 2021 Conference was deemed fit for the economic development of BRICS.

After analysing the continuance of inflation worldwide, people's support is essential to economic recovery. No matter of choice, good governance is impeccable for the stakeholders. To get the circular economy back in action and create a happy balance for all the stakeholders Indian Companies Act 2013. Governance has been an integral part of the ecosystem in India right from the early days of Kautilya to Gandhi and now with the new India. The Pandemic has reset the world, and with the Geopolitical crisis and inflation, all the emerging countries are looking into their geographic strengths and boosting their respective economies to boost the global economy.

In India, the teachings of Kautilya and considering the Customer as the business's centricity remain prevalent. Yet, good governance is now all the more important as industries play a pivotal role in Nation-Building and taking the Nation towards development. The economic unrest in emerging economies leads to significant social unrest. Emerging economies also move on the human sentiments and their socioeconomic status. This further jolted the country's political stability, yet in India, the stability of the government has solidified its strategy and theologies. Thus, the Continuity, Collaboration, and Consensus model not only opens opportunities for BRICS but also a step ahead to build bilateral relations and unite with each other's strengths. India has a foundation of Global Governance, and now, when humanity is in crisis, the model of *4Cs* by PM Modi plays a more significant role.

Nowadays, we are living in a global village. The term village has its history that means Self-Sufficient entity, which has all kinds of resources like geography, animals, and humans. The Western country's very definition of the State includes Territories, People, Government, and sovereignties, which are self-explanatory. But the world of the West always put statecraft in a different sphere. The ancient Indian works of literature like "Ramayana" in their definition of Ramrajya and *"The Saptanga Theory"* of Indian scholar Vishnu Gupta, also known as Kautilya or Chanakya, spoke contrary. Kautilya states, *"State and Statecraft are not divorced from each other."* Statehood is a blend of both. The *Saptanga Theory* includes:

1 The King: Kautilya puts the king in the centre of statehood.
2 Ministers: He speaks about the expert council, which is none other than the cabinet or the council of ministers.
3 Allies: He talks about allies that reflect *International Relations* today.

4 Treasure: The economic wealth of the country. Kautilya emphasised wealth and the creation of wealth. And depict it as the *"Wheels of the chariot of the State."*
5 Fort: The state's infrastructure gives idealism and faith in the *state* and the king. The government institutions and buildings are the ones and the same.
6 Army: Defence system for securing the state from internal and external threats. Kautilya also mentioned the non-conventional threats, which were unseen in those days.
7 Territories: The geolocation and area of a state.

Shiv Shankar Menon, the former Foreign Secretary of India, and National Security Adviser (NSA) during a seminar by Institute of Indian Defence Studies and Analysis (IDSA), speaks about the relevance of "Arthashastra" in today's global world (Menon, 2013). He emphasised international alliances and internal threats. The author contemplates Arthashastra's Saptanga and Mandala Theory in the global sphere as traditional Gunboat diplomacy (Mandel, 1986). is out of context today. The honourable Finance Minister, Mrs Nirmala Sitharaman, said, *"Those who create wealth are India's wealth!"* She emphasised ethical wealth creation and pointed it out as a noble human pursuit. The greatness of a nation is not in history but in its industries. The United States is great because of its great companies like Apple, Microsoft, Google, etc. These companies, by providing employment and products and paying valuable taxes to the government, create a fortune for their employees and the nation where they are established and even worked. The idea of a free market, i.e., *"minimum government engagements,"* is the base of the strategic disinvestment in enterprises of sectors where competitive markets have come to an age. Better technology and management expertise would create wealth and, thus, economic growth for the nation (Ministry of Finance, 2020). An increase of INR 33,000 crore is seen due to strategic disinvestment in Bharat Petroleum Corporation Limited (BPCL) compared to Hindustan Petroleum Corporation Limited (HPCL), which is under government control. Analogous to the same gain, there are almost 11 more Central Public Sector Enterprises (CPSEs) examples in the economic survey 2019–2020 (Mandel, 1986; Gulf Today 2021). The country has already begun by building new institutional policies and capabilities. These steps have merit with the system-based high growth and creation of an entrepreneurial ecosystem. With the "Make in India" boom, entrepreneurship will also enable India to reach its Make in India Goals. As Asia's third-largest economy, India's FDI has steadily increased since 1991. The World Investment Report, 2020 by the UN Conference on Trade and Development (UNCTAD) said that India was the 9th largest recipient of FDI in 2019, with $51 billion of inflow during the year, an increase from $42 billion of FDI received in 2018 when India ranked 12 among the top 20 host economies in the world.

The political stability and make in India also boost many entrepreneurs' confidence. India is one of the choicest countries in the West to drive their business because of the finest education, intellect, and visionary will to work and thrive in the industry. It shows the quantum of the task force and creative talent. Hence, India's prospects are more promising because of demographic development and political stability. After assessing the industry and present scenario, the author has given certain factors *"why has India considered a good hub for start-ups?"*

- Political Stability
- Government Will and support
- Technical Development and advancement
- The boom in Digital Marketing for marketing their products
- Low Infrastructural costs
- Change in Perception about Entrepreneurship

Higher Wealth Creation for Developing Economies

Higher Wealth is just not the only determinant of a healthy economy. Additionally, higher income does call for higher savings and higher taxes. The higher savings enable banks to invest further and circulate wealth to boost economic development. Let's see the studies of Chanakya's Arthashastra. The main objective was to create an ecosystem to create and gain wealth. In "Arthashastra," the role of a king (or government in today's time) is defined as a facilitator (Menon, 2013). The western scholars has rephrased the Kautilya long before as, "The root of wealth creation is economic activities and lack of it brings material distress. In the non-economic activities, both current and future growth is in danger of destruction."

Banks or financial intermediaries are the pillars or the backbone of present-time economies. They do not control the market demand and supply. But they provide strength to the invisible hands of the economy (Smith, 2002), which are the capital market, which helps in wealth creation, and the hand of trust, which supports the first hand. Therefore, macroeconomics is the domain of the banks. Banks with colossal capital and coverage can give loans to enterprises to produce goods and services, providing wages and boosting economic activities and transactions. The failure of a bank shows the collapse of an economy and government policies. In developing countries, higher wealth creation is so essential to the potential to attract FDI. Studies show that many low enterprises and a stringent entrepreneurship environment have caused Nigeria's poor human development index (HDI) for continuous years (Igwe, Adebayo, Olakanmi, Ogbonna, & Aina, 2013). The recent case of the giant Chinese real estate company "Evergrande" missing its debt premium has significantly affected the market in China and even globally. The default made a question on the Chinese banks and the market. The price was paid by the international markets, too.

In globalisation, wealth creation is not limited to the boundaries of a nation and the banking system. In 2001, the chairman Jim O'Neil of Goldman Sachs gave a report named "Building Better Global Economic BRICS."

BRICS constituting 40% of the world population and 22% of the world GDP; Jim stated that BRICS nations will be the global leaders by 2050. Even after many setbacks in the past, political conflicts, disputes between the nations, and pandemic crises, the chairman still has faith in the BRICs, now BRICS. These nations are developing in the context and have huge potential. They first created a bank to finance the member nations' Foreign Reserves and Development Work. They are Contingent Reserve Arrangements and New Development Bank, respectively. Here, governance plays an essential role in the success of these institutions. A better entrepreneurship environment with transparent and robust MoUs between the nations will increase the ranges for new enterprises, and economic activities will flourish exponentially. Such development will increase the number of new enterprises. Legalising dual income sources and part-time and full-time jobs should also be permitted.

The Pandemic has given a maximum jolt to developing economies and people. The people who were laid off in their prime age were lost and had no source of income. With five days a week and 9 hours a day working, it is high time that developing countries allow their people to generate sources of income as freelancers during their non-office time. The BRICS cannot afford to make their people survive in one job and then make them wait for a three-month notice period to switch over to a new job. An aggressive approach towards wealth creation at the individual level will get them material gains and more taxes to the government, increased purchasing power, and robustness to the economy. There is a need for policy advocacy at the government level to permit people to generate wealth with their skills. This will enable a gap in wealth inequality, a significant concern in developing economies. It has been clearly remarked in the 13th BRICS Summit that took place on 9 September 2021 in New Delhi, India, that even when we have achieved a lot, we cannot be satisfied and increase the rate of development.

Prime Minister Mr Modi also emphasised integrating the BRICS to strengthen the ties and cooperation. The 4Cs of Cooperation, Continuity, Consolidation, and Consensus will be the governing principles of BRICS as a stepping step towards growth.

Governance in BRICS Entrepreneurship Has an Ethical and Sustainable Impact on the Economy

Reaching a point where no return should be the last an entrepreneur should do. Creating an ecosystem of compliance and governance in BRICS Countries is vital for the sustainable economic growth of the global economy. Compliance brings Trust, long-term sustainability, and goodwill. It also enforces discipline and accountability of the entrepreneurs towards various stakeholders. Start-ups can be transactional; hence, in developing countries and incubation centres, the importance of governance for sustainable positive growth cannot be ignored. The emphasis should not be only on the governance but also on the strict implementation and audit. The selection of countries in BRICS is based on population and demography. The rate of the increased number of people in families enables the potential and scope of success of entrepreneurship in these countries. The awareness of being in the framework of compliance will create confidence in the Global Economy in developing nations. These are the proxies that will make entrepreneurship sustainable once the framework of governance follows:

- Reduced Corruption
- The rule of law
- Regulatory framework
- Government effectiveness
- Political stability

The above indicators in the countries of BRICS play a pivotal role. Along with economic growth, Entrepreneurship also improves the socio-economic status of the BRICS countries. Along with development, it also develops and improves the socio-economic status and the well-being of the society (Mandel, 1986; Käkönen, 2014).

BRICS's economy was among the most affected economies in the post-pandemic time, which was due to BRICS's low economic strength. The economies also must thrive back with their available financial resources. The critical determinant is the multiple income sources and a wealth multiplier. Let us evaluate what is best in these economies for the global shift to the Global Economy.

According to Statista (2022), in 2021, BRICS countries, Russia and China, had the highest GDP per capita, 11,000 USD and 12,000 USD, respectively. Then followed by Brazil and South Africa and later by India with $2000 per person. This gap between China and India is unfair even though smaller economies like Brazil and South Africa are higher than India. The sense of the results is very unclear seeing the data. Analysing the governance of the BRICS, the author has come to the consensus that the political and social stability of the countries also needs to be intrigued to give the requisite shift. There must be a thought of creating transparency in the regulations and governance. We have spoken a lot about creating wealth, and we cannot underestimate the innate skills of our human capital. Governance is required in SMEs and MSMEs also for sustainability. With governance practices, we attract better visionaries, reduce costs, quick decision-making, trust in people, and higher investment from the market. The goodwill the SMEs gain in practicing good governance enables them to expand in the market and scale up to the next level. Bad governance creates legalities and legal costs and further business expenses.

According to the United Nations, these are the characteristics of *Good Governance-*

- Participation
- Rule of Law
- Transparency
- Responsiveness
- Consensus Oriented
- Equity and Inclusiveness
- Effectiveness
- Efficiency and Accountability

These factors are theoretical and are used and required in any company. The author will highlight each aspect that adds to its value propositions.

Governance also creates income equality. The disparity of income also brings a lagging economy. To sustain the recession after the Pandemic, we need a good understanding of the basic principles of mutuality and interdependence. The author recommends that the OECD corporate governance model covers most diversified industries. The regulations further build the robustness of any entrepreneurship. It is not to create challenges but to ease the functioning and create equality and inclusivity for all stakeholders, along with a decent income, clean environment, and access to knowledge and skills. It covers the challenges of Youth Empowerment, quality education, climate change, and automation, which fall in the gambit of successful Entrepreneurship across BRICS. The elements are:

- Ensuring the basis for a practical corporate governance framework
- Fundamental rights of shareholders and essential ownership functions
- Equitable treatment of shareholders
- Role of stakeholders in corporate governance
- Disclosure and transparency
- Board Responsibilities

Entrepreneurship also comes with responsibility, and that's why an entrepreneurial mindset has to be wealth creation in the right way while considering their reputation. To avoid future scams and failures in business and to run a loss and closure of business, the framework of governance is framed for their sustainability and to take their business closer to the goals of United Nations-Sustainable Development Goals (UN-SDGs).

Social Change and Creating Some Benchmarks

Any research is done to create benchmarks with knowledge and practical experience. Being close to industry, the author has explored and counted unparalleled potential in BRICS to emphasise social change. Good governance nurtures entrepreneurship development. Governance will bring Social Change by being ethical in business. The ethics being followed, in turn, will create Trust among the stakeholders. As mentioned earlier, it is all about creating resources for the customers, and keeping in the interest of the stakeholders creates the sustainability of entrepreneurship. There is a social change when Entrepreneurs follow ethics in business. The reputation is acknowledged, and there will also be a shift in importance to the values of Integrity, Trust, and Compliance. By having these values systems, entrepreneurship in the BRICS will be a model in the world.

The study examines how the Akshaya Patra Foundation business model has created some benchmarks after following all governance policies and creating global social change- An entrepreneurial model of Non-Government Organisations (NGO) Public-Private Partnership of 60% government-funded and 40% funded by corporates and private companies. This unique Public-Private Partnership (PPP) has created social reformation by providing a Government Midday Meal Program. This business model aligns closely with the UN-SDGs Zero Hunger and Quality Education goals. While researching the business model, we also learned about the supply chain model of the Akshaya Patra and providing rations to prepare 20,000 meals a day during the Ukraine-Russia War. During the pandemic, when most entrepreneurs were struggling with funds, they could feed 22.9 crores of meals from March 2020 to 28th February 2022. These were not charity but a collective duty that they did and created some significant benchmarks. Providing one-day mid-day meals offers economic support to families and encourages them to send their children to school. These children are not deprived of education because of food and are preparing for the future. Today this trust is running because of the untiring and relentless work done by its founders and entrepreneurs who begin this entrepreneurship. The sustainability model of their entrepreneurship enabled them to globalise and expand in countries like the United States, the United Kingdom, and many other countries. To create benchmarks, it is also essential to use all the knowledge management for policy reformation.

New World Order and Governance

Today, even a small country like North Korea is capable of bringing the United States on its terms. The nuclear powers are no more direct threats today, as the consequences are fatal on both sides. Second, globalisation has blurred the territories. Third, the democratic governments have changed the character of the King. He is an institution instead being a person. Fourth, the LPG policies have made MNCs a symbol of Infrastructure. Therefore, only three components are relevant in the global sphere (Figure 9.1). No single power, state, or organisation is present which has whole and authority over the world's nations. Thus, globalisation has created anarchy in the world (IMF, 2022).

```
Lack of Governance
    ↓
  Anarchy / Chaos
        ↓
    Self-Centric Policies
            ↓
        Threats to Global
        Prosperities
```

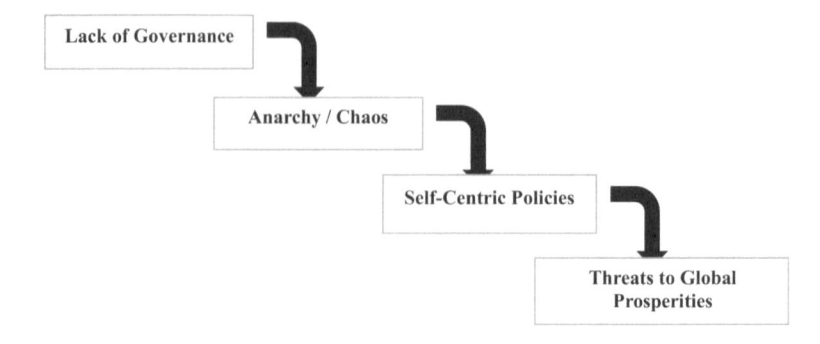

Figure 9.1 Anarchy and prosperity in the global sphere

The author suggests the solutions as the state of anarchy creates self-centric policies, which will generate worldwide national security and global prosperity. That directly points towards the economy of nations. Globalisation creates these threats. The nature of this threat is global and non-traditional. As cyber-attacks, cutting economic chords, Bankruptcy in countries, civil war, lack of happiness index, inflation, etc. The experience of the COVID pandemic also increased the fatality of these threats and added global health threats to the list. Therefore, the solutions should be global. The most affected countries are the emerging economies. These developing countries' concerns are unavoidable, as are the concerns of BRICS nations. BRICS nations are the most powerful group in globalisation and International Relations (Käkönen, 2014). The geolocations, the populations, and the common goals of economic boost gave them high importance. All of the BRICS nations are seen to have expanding economies. The traditional Western hubs of the international economy have endured weak economic growth or stagnation since the global financial crisis in 2008. As a result, the conversation surrounding BRICS has primarily been economic. The BRICS itself has provided further justifications for focusing on economic factors. The experts' inaugural report mainly focuses on the global economy and the economies of the BRICS nations. BRICS nations comprised 40% of the global population and almost 27% of the global GPD in 2010. Further, according to an estimate by the famous financial institute Goldman Sachs Group, in 2020 BRICS will have surpassed the G7 in the form of GPD. But the pandemic has changed these estimates, one of the most significant factors to come together.

With this global change, the major takeaways are that the regulatory forces must be strengthened and user-friendly based on the people and economy. The model of (Cooperation, Continuity, consolidation, and Consensus) 4-Cs, as discussed earlier, not only improves geopolitical relations but also trade among each other. There should be treaties to ensure Good Governance is followed at an international level. The tech giants across the globe should take on to boost the global economy at a strategic level.

Conclusion

The author has brought the importance of Governance and Compliance in Entrepreneurship which will further boost the Global Economy. The findings of this research have meaningful implications for understanding the importance of Governance and the long-term sustainability of economic growth. Undoubtedly, Post Pandemic Wealth Creation is a key driver to boosting the Global Economy; yet, parallelly, the importance and awareness of Governance should be kept in mind. The business start-up cost, Property Registration expenses manufacturing cost, and all other expenses entrepreneurs tend to face are challenging to tempt the governance aspect. Yet, the research has given perspectives on creating sustainable entrepreneurship and sticking to the social norms to gain the trust of Stakeholders. This is because governance plays diversely in specific industries. The external stakeholders' interest can never be ignored in the manufacturing and mining industry as it directly affects Climate Change. Governance is non-importable across the border and affects all aspects of our lives. It could be a daunting task and a constraint to business, yet the winnings are ethical and long-term sustainable. A framework to have a stable economy is the only way to stay away from deflation or inflation and the volatility of developing economies.

The author's work also strongly advocates the distrust of IT giant Facebook. Even if its business is booming, its reputation is sinking. It has dropped three points down from 2019. The change of name is not enough to fix the reputation. The high-profile battles are one of the biggest challenges. It is one of the most distrusted social websites when it comes to sharing personal information. That is where complying and winning over the confidence of our customers is the key to driving the economy and providing a positive global impact. Therefore, where Entrepreneurship is one of the major driving forces for an economic boost, this research has proven for long-term sustainability, it should be well-governed with regulatory practices to create a robust and scalable business. Framework based on good governance will always be a sustainable economic boost and shift the economic wellness of BRICS, and subsequently to the global economy.

Acknowledgement

The scholar acknowledges the assistance given by Mr. Manish, a PhD candidate at School of Computational and Integrative Sciences, from Jawaharlal Nehru University, New Delhi, India.

References

Entrepreneurship – Wikipedia (2021, August 1). *Entrepreneurship – Wikipedia*; en.wikipedia.org. https://en.wikipedia.org/wiki/Entrepreneurship (Accessed 30 March 2022)

Gulf Today (09 December 2021) Indian CEOS making it to the top league. https://www.gulftoday.ae/opinion/2021/12/09/indian-ceos-making-it-to-the-top-league (Accessed 30 March 2022).

Igwe, C.N., Adebayo, M.S., Olakanmi, O.A., Ogbonna, I.G., and Aina, O.S. (2013). Promoting Wealth and Job Creation in Nigeria-Review of the Role of Entrepreneurship. *Journal of Sustainable Development Studies*, 3(1):80–100.

IMF. (2022, April 22). *GDP Ranked by Country 2022*. GDP Ranked by Country 2022. https://worldpopulationreview.com/countries/countries-by-gdp (Accessed 30 March 2022).

Jooris, L. (October 2021). A brief history of entrepreneurship. https://gulfbusiness.com/a-brief-history-of-entrepreneurship/ (Accessed 30 March 2022).

Käkönen, J. (2014). BRICS as a New Power in International Relations? *Geopolitics, History, and International Relations*, 6(2):85–104.

Mandel, R. (1986). The effectiveness of Gunboat diplomacy. *International Studies Quarterly*, 30(1), 59–76. https://doi.org/10.2307/2600437

Menon, S.S. (2013, October 8). *Study of Arthashastra Important to Understand Our Strategic Culture: Shiv Shankar Menon | Manohar Parrikar Institute for Defence Studies and Analyses*. Study of Arthashastra Important to Understand Our Strategic Culture: Shiv Shankar Menon | Manohar Parrikar Institute for Defence Studies and Analyses. https://www.idsa.in/pressrelease/StudyofArthashastraImportantShivShankarMenon

Ministry of Finance. (2020). *Economic Survey*. New Delhi: Department of Economic Affairs (Print).

Perelm, M. (2015). The anarchy of globalization: Local and global, intended and unintended consequences. *World Review of Political Economy*, 6(3):352–374. https://doi.org/10.13169/worlrevipoliecon.6.3.0352

Smith, A. (2002). *The Wealth of Nations*. Oxford, England: Bibliomania Ltd.

Statista. (2022) BRICS: Gross Domestic Product (GDP) Per Capita 2026 | Statista. Statista. https://www.statista.com/statistics/741745/gross-domestic-product-gdp-per-capita-in-the-bric-countries/ (Accessed 30 March 2022).

The BRICS Report. (2012). *The BRICS Report. A Study of Brazil, Russia, India, China and South Africa With Special Focus on Synergies and Complementarities*. New Delhi: Oxford University Press.

10 The Impact of Entrepreneurship on Economic Growth in Emerging Economies

Evidence from BRICS Countries

Frank Ranganai Matenda and Mabutho Sibanda

Introduction

Discussions regarding entrepreneurship's impact on economic growth have been an issue among different parties in the world for a long time (Doran, McCarthy and O'Connor, 2018; Gaba and Gaba, 2022; Garcia-Rodriguez *et al.*, 2017; Gomes *et al.*, 2022; Matenda and Sibanda, 2022; Nwagu and Enofe, 2021; Savrul, 2017; Stoica, Roman and Rusu, 2020). These discussions started in the 19th century (Schumpeter, 1911). Since then, multiple studies have examined the connection between economic growth and entrepreneurship, employing diverse techniques and variables. Against a background of the 2007–2009 universal crisis, amplified research efforts have been directed to assess entrepreneurship's influence on economic growth. Since the emergence of the 2007–2009 global recession, national economies have been experiencing a multiplicity of challenges, including a swift decline in economic growth. Therefore, one of the fundamental challenges of policymakers is examining economic growth determinants and then designing and adopting measures that promote economic growth. In support of this, Stoica, Roman and Rusu (2020) proposed that the 2007–2009 crisis has motivated policymakers and researchers to tackle the fundamental challenge of analysing the drivers of economic growth. Fundamentally, economic growth is vital for enhancing living standards and fiscal stabilisation. It is also a precondition for amplifying productive employment (Gaba and Gaba, 2022).

Economic growth is not self-dependent; it depends on several external variables (Schumpeter, 1947), which include entrepreneurship, capital, and labour, among other factors (Schumpeter, 1947; Stoica *et al.*, 2020). In practice, the consensus is that entrepreneurship stimulates economic growth in both emerging and developed economies (Acs, Autio and Szerb, 2014; Bosma *et al.*, 2018; Coulibaly, Erbao and Mekongcho, 2017; Galindo and Mendez, 2014; Savrul, 2017; Stoica *et al.*, 2020). Matenda and Sibanda (2022) opined that entrepreneurship is an engine for economic growth, and Vatavu *et al.* (2021) articulated that entrepreneurship is the heart of several nations and upholds economies' development. Promoting entrepreneurship has become a top priority in all

DOI: 10.4324/9781003475606-13

economies since the 2007–2009 crisis. In support of this, Urbano and Aparicio (2016) discovered that the positive effect of total early-stage entrepreneurial activity (TEA) on economic growth has been more significant after the crisis than before the crisis.

Nevertheless, numerous investigations on the connection between economic growth and entrepreneurship divulge conflicting results. Almodovar-Gonzalez, Sanchez-Escobedo and Fernandez-Portillo (2019) postulated that the common mistake in the analysis of entrepreneurship is the acknowledgement that its influences in economic terms are encouraging at all times. These conflicting results are due to the diverse entrepreneurial attitudes and behaviour and entrepreneurial framework conditions of each country and the presence of dissimilar sorts of entrepreneurship (Acs *et al.*, 2018; Gomes *et al.*, 2022; Stam and Van Stel, 2011, 2009; Stoica *et al.*, 2020; Vatavu *et al.*, 2021). Gaba and Gaba (2022) propounded that contradicting results may be due to the different nature of each nation's economy. Entrepreneurship's influence on economic growth differs between advanced and undeveloped countries (Avnimelech, Zelekha and Sharabi, 2014; Marcotte, 2014; Van Stel, Carree and Thurik, 2005). Savrul (2017) promulgated that since entrepreneurship's influence on economic growth at the country level depends on the country's climate, it can be questioned in several dimensions. Interestingly, Gaba and Gaba (2022) proffered that, despite the mixed results, entrepreneurship is an essential driver of economic growth, especially nowadays due to the social media and digital technology revolution. Moreover, Naude (2010) postulated that, in developing economies, the discipline of economic growth and entrepreneurship is under-researched in entrepreneurship. Gaba and Gaba (2022) proffered that a restricted number of studies are devoted to emerging markets and, particularly, BRICS economies (i.e., Brazil, Russia, India, China, and South Africa).

Most studies are devoted to investigating entrepreneurship's effect on economic performance at the corporate, industry, or regional level (Aparicio, Urbano and Audretsch, 2016; Carree and Thurik, 2003; Miller, 1983; Savrul, 2017; Stel, Thurik and Carree, 2005). Savrul (2017) and Acs, Autio and Szerb (2014) opined that literature examining entrepreneurship's influence on economic growth at the nation's level is limited. Therefore, there is a need for more clarity regarding the association between economic growth and entrepreneurship at the country level. Farinha *et al.* (2020) and Stoica *et al.* (2020) articulated that more research efforts are needed to assess the influence of entrepreneurship on economic growth at the national level.

In the existing literature, entrepreneurship is defined in many dimensions, and there is no generally accepted entrepreneurship definition (Gomes and Ferreira, 2022; Pittaway, 2005; Wennekers *et al.*, 2005; Zaki and Rashid, 2016). Gomes and Ferreira (2022) indicated that entrepreneurship is generally defined as the action or aim to create value through new methods, products, or new businesses. Due to many entrepreneurship definitions, there are diverse ways of measuring entrepreneurship (Pittaway, 2005; Wennekers *et al.*, 2005). Therefore, finding a reasonable entrepreneurship measure that permits comparisons among economies is challenging (Gomes and Ferreira, 2022). Entrepreneurship has been measured quantitatively using metrics such as the number of new corporates designed and the self-employment rate for a long time. However, the extant literature has propounded that quantitative measures of entrepreneurship are not adequate to fully describe entrepreneurship's influence on economic growth (Acs and Szerb, 2010; Baliamoune-Lutz, 2015; Doran, McCarthy and O'Connor, 2018; Pita, Costa and Moreira, 2021). Hence, Doran, McCarthy and O'Connor (2016) postulated that other measures of entrepreneurship need to be adopted to examine entrepreneurship's influence on economic growth effectively. Under the same line of reasoning, Doran *et al.* (2018) and Marcotte (2013) opined that there is a requirement to examine entrepreneurship at country-level by implementing other measures besides new corporate creations or a solitary entrepreneurial activity index to permit more specific measures of entrepreneurship to be applied.

This chapter employs a fixed effects model to assess the connection between entrepreneurial attitudes, behaviour, and economic growth in BRICS countries. Our main aim is to assess the significance of the adopted entrepreneurial measures representing entrepreneurial activity, aspirations, and attitudes in describing economic growth. Entrepreneurial attitudes refer to the overall attitudes regarding entrepreneurship in an economy, entrepreneurial aspirations embrace aspirations concerning business growth and innovation, and entrepreneurial activity denotes new venture formation (Bosma *et al.*, 2009). Interestingly, Acs and Szerb (2010) suggested that entrepreneurship is a dynamic interaction of activities, aspirations, and attitudes. Our investigation addresses the following research question: *How do entrepreneurial activity, aspirations, and attitudes affect economic growth in BRICS economies?*

BRICS countries are the major emerging economies in the world (Chatterjee and Naka, 2022; Gaba and Gaba, 2022; Kondratov, 2021). They play a crucial role in the global economy, considering their fast-rising economic growth rates, financial and industrial power, huge populations, and booming markets for capital, services, and goods (Chatterjee and Naka, 2022). Over the years, BRICS economies have mainly contributed to global economic growth (Gaba and Gaba, 2022). Garcia and Bond (2019) promulgated that, in 2017, BRICS economies were responsible for 19% of global investment inflows. Further, BRICS economies contain 41% of the global population, contribute 24% of the global gross domestic product (GDP), occupy 29.3% of the world land surface, and are associated with over 16% of the world trade share.

The contribution of this article is that we adopt 15 different entrepreneurial attitudes and behaviour indicators from the Global Entrepreneurship Monitor (GEM) to analyse the influence of entrepreneurship on economic growth in BRICS countries over an extended observation period. The implemented indicators allow different entrepreneurship components, i.e., entrepreneurial attitudes, activity, and aspirations, to be considered. This is the first time such an investigation has been done for the scholars.

The rest of the article is organised as follows. Section 2 presents the literature review, and Section 3 looks at data and methodology. In Section 4, study results are outlined. Section 5 concludes the study and outlines the implications and opportunities for further research.

Literature Review

The use of quantitative measures of entrepreneurship has a long history. The number of new corporates formed and the self-employment rate are some of the quantitative metrics used to measure entrepreneurship (Acs and Szerb, 2010). In the extant literature (Hessels and Van Stel, 2011; Mariet Ocasio and Mariet Ocasio, 2016), the number of new corporates designed is widely implemented as a surrogate for entrepreneurial activity. Nevertheless, the number of new firms created has shortcomings (Baliamoune-Lutz, 2015). Doran et al. (2018) proffered that

 i Entrepreneurship is not narrowed to new start-ups and can happen inside the current organisations
 ii There is a multiplicity of motives for beginning a novel business and not all of these motives are a result of the craving to harness a novel notion
 iii The implementation of corporate births is an excessively unsophisticated elucidation of entrepreneurship.

Reviewed literature indicated that quantitative measures of entrepreneurship need to be improved to embrace entrepreneurship's effects on economic growth because entrepreneurship is complicated and multifaceted (Baliamoune-Lutz, 2015; Doran et al., 2018; Pita, Costa and Moreira, 2021).

In addition, it is challenging to design robust entrepreneurship measures that permit comparisons among countries in practice because entrepreneurship is defined in a multiplicity of ways (Gomes and Ferreira, 2022).

There is a dire need to implement measures that consider total entrepreneurship's influence on economic growth. Doran, McCarthy and O'Connor (2016) articulated that to perform a more comprehensive examination of the effect of entrepreneurship on economic growth, more specific measures of entrepreneurship need to be adopted instead of the number of novel corporates developed. Therefore, several novel entrepreneurship measures have been introduced by the GEM. These measures embrace entrepreneurial framework conditions and entrepreneurial attitudes and behaviour indicators (Acs and Szerb, 2010; Bosma et al., 2009). Implementing a Dynamic Ordinary Least Squares model, Gaba and Gaba (2022) assessed the association between economic growth and entrepreneurial indicators (i.e., TEA, entrepreneurial intention, established business ownership rate, and high job creation expectation rate) in BRICS economies. Data for entrepreneurial indicators was gathered from the GEM. The authors collected their sample panel data for the BRICS countries from 2014 to 2018, and they discovered that entrepreneurial intention is a significant driver of economic growth. Using an Ordinary Least Squares regression model, Vatavu *et al.* (2021) assessed the connection between economic growth, entrepreneurial attitudes, behaviour, and entrepreneurial framework conditions indicators in Group of eight countries. Data for entrepreneurial indicators was collected from the GEM over the sample period 2001–2018. The authors (Vatavu *et al.*, 2021) exposed that entrepreneurial attitudes and behaviour are adversely associated with economic growth, and entrepreneurial framework conditions are positively related to economic growth. Doran *et al.* (2018) analysed the association between economic growth and entrepreneurial aspirations, activity, and attitudes indicators using sample panel data for 55 high-income and low/middle-income economies collected from the GEM over the observation period 2004–2011. The authors propounded that entrepreneurial attitudes arouse economic growth in high-income economies, whereas entrepreneurial activity adversely impacts middle/low-income countries. Nonetheless, it should be noted that regardless of the GEM efforts to collate data concerning entrepreneurial attitudes and behaviour and entrepreneurial framework conditions, Marcotte (2014) indicated that researchers have been regularly implementing the TEA ratio at the expense of other GEM indicators.

Numerous studies have discovered a positive correlation between economic growth and entrepreneurship (Audretsch, 2007; Bosma *et al.*, 2018; Galindo and Mendez, 2014; Gomes *et al.*, 2022; Gu *et al.*, 2021; Gungah and Jaunky, 2017; Stoica *et al.*, 2020; Vazquez, Gomes and Vieira, 2010). In an economy, entrepreneurship impacts economic growth in several dimensions. These dimensions embrace augmented competition, knowledge spillovers, and amplified diversity concerning existing service and product offerings (Audretsch, 2007; Audretsch and Keilbach, 2004; Nwagu and Enofe, 2021; Stoica *et al.*, 2020; Stel, Carree and Thurik, 2005), and establishment of innovations, job creation, and productivity improvements (Acs, 2006; Decker *et al.*, 2014; Nwagu and Enofe, 2021; Savrul, 2017; Stoica *et al.*, 2020; Van Praag and Versloot, 2007; Van Stel, Carree and Thurik, 2005; Wong, Ho and Autio, 2005). Xu, Yu and Li (2021) propounded that entrepreneurship influences economic growth through the following four conduits: competition, innovation, industrial agglomeration, and increasing employment. Also, Karlan and Valdivia (2011) and Hermes and Lensink (2007) proffered that entrepreneurship can improve the stabilisation, income flows, and profits for risky, weak economies. Moreover, Fritsch (2008) opined that entrepreneurs could quicken the swiftness of creative destruction (i.e., a situation where new corporates push for industrial transformation by substituting the existing ones); promote efficiency in current businesses since they compete with them in the overall markets; offer a wider assortment of novel services, processes, and processes that could be obtainable from current corporates; and encourage innovation in sectors leading to the creation of new markets.

Even though several authors have examined entrepreneurship's effect on economic growth, there is yet to be an accord on entrepreneurship's influence on economic growth (Dvoulety, Gordievskaya and Prochazka, 2018; Xu, Yu and Li, 2021). Some sources (see, for instance, Zaki and Rashid, 2016) exposed an adverse association between economic growth and entrepreneurship. This indicates that not all entrepreneurship may lead to economic growth (Xu *et al.*, 2021) since entrepreneurship can be prolific, unproductive, and destructive (Baumgartner, Schulz and Seidl, 2013; Sautet, 2013). The likes of Urbano and Aparicio (2016), Wennekers *et al.* (2005), and Van Stel *et al.* (2005) indicated that entrepreneurship has an undefined influence on economic growth in a country except if particular circumstances exist. Wong, Ho and Autio (2005) discovered that only high-growth prospect entrepreneurship substantially influences economic growth. Further, some authors indicated that the association between economic growth and entrepreneurship is direct, while others articulated that the relationship is indirect (Nwagu and Enofe, 2021). This lack of scientific consensus indicates that the correlation between economic growth and entrepreneurship still needs to be clarified (Carree and Thurik, 2008; Valliere and Peterson, 2009) and noted an exciting picture that causes numerous academic problems.

Reviewed evidence indicated that the influence of entrepreneurship on the economy's growth is contingent on the economic development phase of that economy (Amoros, Fernandez and Tapia, 2012; Bosma *et al.*, 2009; Ferreira *et al.*, 2017; Gries and Naude, 2010; Urbano and Aparicio, 2016; Valliere and Peterson, 2009; Van Stel *et al.*, 2005). Almodovar-Gonzalez, Fernandez-Portillo and Diaz-Casero (2020) postulated that entrepreneurial activity performs diverse roles contingent on the economic stage of an economy of interest. Even though it is widely accepted in the extant literature that entrepreneurship's influence on economic growth hinges on the economic development phase of an economy, the results are heterogeneous.

Valliere and Peterson (2009) exposed that entrepreneurship is vital to economic growth in developed and developing countries. In 2016, Adusei (2016) opined that entrepreneurship positively influences economic growth in developing economies, Africa specifically. Gungah and Jaunky (2017) discovered a significant positive connection between economic growth and entrepreneurship by analysing the association between established business ownership and economic growth in the BRICS economies. Lepojevic, Djukic and Mladenovic (2016) postulated that the positive influence of entrepreneurial activity on economic growth is more significant in developed than in developing economies. Some sources showed that the influence of entrepreneurship on economic growth in developed and developing economies is different (Sternberg and Wennekers, 2005; Valliere and Peterson, 2009). Zaki and Rashid (2016), Stam and

Van Stel (2011), Sternberg and Wennekers (2005), Van Stel *et al.* (2005), and Wennekers *et al.* (2005) concluded that entrepreneurship has a positive influence on economic growth in highly advanced economies (rich economies) and an adverse influence in developing economies (poor countries). Boudreaux and Caudill (2019) proffered that entrepreneurship stimulates economic growth but not in developing economies. Stam *et al.* (2011) resolved that entrepreneurship does not straightforwardly impact economic growth in high-income economies but does in poor economies. Stam and Van Stel (2009) discovered that entrepreneurship does not influence economic growth in low-income countries, while entrepreneurship considerably influences economic growth in high-income and transition economies.

Even though a multiplicity of articles investigated the connection between economic growth and entrepreneurship, studies that examined the influence of entrepreneurial attitudes and behaviour on economic growth are generally restricted and are even more restricted in emerging economies, especially in BRICS countries. The degree to which entrepreneurial attitudes and behaviour contribute to economic growth in BRICS countries is still being determined. This indicates that the association between economic growth and entrepreneurship is yet to be examined convincingly. More comprehensive examinations of the influence of entrepreneurship on economic growth are required. To contribute to this continuous discourse, the study strives to assess the effect of entrepreneurial activity, aspirations, and attitudes on economic growth in BRICS economies over a lengthened observation period.

Data and Methodology

Panel data for entrepreneurial indicators and economic growth for the BRICS countries is gathered from the GEM and Penn World Table, respectively, over the sample period 2001–2021. This observation period was selected because BRICS economies have no entrepreneurship data before the year 2001 and after the year 2021. The GEM collects entrepreneurship data at a country level for developing and developed economies, offering a comparable entrepreneurship measure (Doran *et al.*, 2018). The scholars also postulated that the GEM data is defined reliably and consistently throughout all the GEM-covered countries, which promotes comparability. Moreover, the authors promulgated that data from the GEM offers a more comprehensive measure of entrepreneurship than merely the number of self-employed people or new corporate formed, some of the most generally implemented proxies for entrepreneurial activity. The gathered data has yearly data values. In the existing literature, the GDP per capita is widely implemented as a measure of economic growth (Gomes and Ferreira, 2022). Likewise, in this analysis, we implement the GDP per capita as a surrogate for economic growth. The researchers assume the adopted data accurately represents the general condition of BRICS economies.

Table 10.1 presents the 15 entrepreneurial indicators (with abbreviations in brackets) adopted in this current study. The entrepreneurial indicators are classified into three, i.e., entrepreneurial attitudes, entrepreneurial aspirations, and entrepreneurial activity.

Table 10.1 Entrepreneurial indicators

Indicator	Definition
Entrepreneurial activity	
Established business ownership rate (EBOR)	% of the population aged 18–64 years who are presently an owner-manager of an established business for more than 3.5 years
Total early-stage entrepreneurial activity (TEA)	% of the population aged 18–64 years who are a budding entrepreneur or owner-manager of a new business
Entrepreneurial employee activity rate (EEAR)	Rate of employee participation in entrepreneurial undertakings
Female/male TEA ratio (FTR)	% of the female population aged 18–64 years who are a budding entrepreneur or owner-manager of a new business, divided by the equivalent % for their male fellows
Business services sector rate (BSSR)	% of those implicated in TEA in the business services sector
Entrepreneurial aspirations	
Motivational index (MI)	% of those implicated in improvement-driven chance-motivated TEA, divided by the % of necessity-motivated TEA
Female/male opportunity-driven TEA ratio (FOTR)	% of females implicated in TEA who (i) assert to be motivated by opportunity, instead of failure, to look for other work, and (ii) who demonstrate the primary motive for being incriminated in this opportunity is being autonomous or growing their income, not just preserving their income, divided by the comparable % for their male fellows
High job creation expectation rate (HJCER)	% of those incremented in TEA who anticipate generating at least 6 jobs in 5 years
Innovation rate (IR)	% of those implicated in TEA who show that their service or product is novel to at least some clients and that few or no businesses provide the similar product

(*Continued*)

Table 10.1 (Continued)

Indicator	Definition
Entrepreneurial attitudes	
Entrepreneurship as a good career choice rate (EGCCR)	% of the population aged 18–64 years who believe that several individuals consider starting a business as an essential occupation alternative in their economy
High status to successful entrepreneurs rate (HSSER)	% of the population aged 18–64 years who believe that flourishing entrepreneurs obtain high status in their economy
Entrepreneurial intentions rate (EIR)	% of the population aged 18–64 years who are dormant entrepreneurs and who plan to commence a business in 3 years
Fear of failure rate (FFR)	% of the population aged 18–64 years who shows that fear of failure would impede them from establishing a business
Perceived capabilities rate (PCR)	% of the population aged 18–64 years who believe they have the essential skills and knowledge to commence a business
Perceived opportunities rate (POR)	% of the population aged 18–64 years who observe good prospects to commence a corporation in the area where they live

Source: Global Entrepreneurship Monitor (2022).

Since entrepreneurship is closely associated with the external environment, in this investigation, we incorporate three control variables whose data is collected from the Penn World Tables (PWT), i.e., human capital index (HCI) (premised on schooling years and returns to education), capital stock per capita (CSC), and employment per capita (EMP) (Doran *et al.*, 2018).

Some variables have missing values for some years. Since the dataset is restricted, we cannot drop observations with missing data. To diminish bias and augment accuracy, we impute the missing values. In this experiment, we adopt mean imputation. Each indicator means the non-missing and missing values (s) are determined for each country. Then, each missing value is substituted with the respective determined mean. Mean imputation is simple to apply and swift to perform. In this study, the logarithm of the GDP per capita is applied as the dependent variable to ensure that the GDP per capita scores match the entrepreneurial variables, which are less than 100.

We conduct our analysis in three phases. First, we present descriptive statistics for the adopted variables and correlations between the GDP per capita and the variables. Second, we create indexes using principal component analysis (PCA) with direct Oblimin rotation. PCA is a variable reduction technique that eradicates multicollinearity between variables. We opt for PCA since eliminating some of the variables would eliminate variables associated with essential information that can describe economic growth. PCA retains considerable original predictive power of the data (Doran et al., 2018). Third, we implement the fixed effects model to analyse entrepreneurship's influence on economic growth. Factor scores for the generated PCA indexes are used in regression analysis. We implement the Hausman test to select the best model to apply between the fixed and random effects models. Since the p-value of the Hausman test is below 0.05, we implement the fixed effects model.

The fixed effects model adopted in this analysis is given by:

$$GDP_{it} = a_i + \beta_1 PC_{1it} + \beta_2 PC_{2it} + \cdots + \beta_k PC_{kit} + aHCI_{it} + bCSC_{it} + cEMP_{it} + e_{it},$$

where GDP_{it} is the GDP per capita (logarithm) for economy i at time t, a_i is the intercept, $\beta_1 \ldots \beta_k$ are regression coefficients for PCA indexes, $PC_1 \ldots PC_k$ represent PCA indexes, HCI denotes the human capital index (logarithm), CSC represents the capital stock per capita (logarithm), EMP denotes the employment per capita (logarithm), $a \ldots c$ denote the regression coefficients for control variables, and e_{it} represents the error term.

Results

Table 10.2 outlines descriptive statistics for the adopted dependent, independent, and control variables. The descriptive statistics show essential features of the indicators.

Table 10.3 indicates the Pearson correlation coefficients between the GDP per capita and entrepreneurial indicators. The entrepreneurial intentions rate,

Table 10.2 Descriptive statistics

	Min.	Max.	Mean	Std. Dev.
GDP	2.65	4.20	3.65	0.39
POR	10.57	83.41	38.86	14.43
PCR	8.65	85.99	42.92	15.07
FFR	13.91	62.37	38.24	7.90
EIR	2.12	53.00	18.63	11.63
TEA	2.47	24.01	10.87	4.94
EBOR	0.83	20.25	7.34	5.00
EEAR	0.05	7.90	1.03	1.05
MI	0.55	2.01	1.19	0.25
FTR	0.30	1.07	0.73	0.15
FOTR	0.51	1.18	0.90	0.09
HJCER	3.05	43.30	18.57	9.01
IR	0.76	51.08	23.08	12.02
BSSR	0.70	32.25	9.07	4.44
HSSER	31.47	92.42	71.72	9.13
EGCCR	29.45	89.54	69.13	9.46
HCI	0.25	0.54	0.40	0.08
CSC	3.99	5.12	4.64	0.33
EMP	−0.54	−0.24	−0.37	0.09

Source: Authors' computations (2022).

Table 10.3 Correlation matrix for entrepreneurial indicators

	GDP	POR	PCR	FFR	EIR	TEA	EBOR	EEAR	MI	FTR	FOTR	HJCER	IR	BSSR	HSSER	EGCCR
GDP	1															
POR	−0.286**	1														
PCR	−0.269**	0.917**	1													
FFR	0.010	0.330**	0.221*	1												
EIR	−0.321**	0.568**	0.624**	−0.138	1											
TEA	−0.037	0.445**	0.542**	−0.136	0.768**	1										
EBOR	−0.092	0.353**	0.457**	−0.099	0.653**	0.811**	1									
EEAR	0.090	0.238*	0.350**	−0.028	0.596**	0.537**	0.281**	1								
MI	0.263**	0.100	0.187	−0.174	0.163	0.206*	0.174	0.378**	1							
FTR	0.432**	0.114	0.208*	−0.226*	0.269**	0.526**	0.460**	0.265**	0.336**	1						
FOTR	−0.346**	0.069	−0.081	−0.072	0.067	−0.064	−0.097	−0.210*	−0.222*	−0.220*	1					
HJCER	0.446**	−0.328**	−0.407**	0.002	−0.235*	−0.206*	−0.460**	0.063	−0.097	−0.019	0.036	1				
IR	−0.498**	0.287**	0.158	−0.025	−0.052	−0.182	−0.300**	−0.361**	−0.324**	−0.334**	0.544**	−0.135	1			
BSSR	0.435**	−0.264**	−0.222*	−0.138	−0.169	−0.250*	−0.374**	0.137	0.250*	0.046	−0.175	0.482**	−0.182	1		
HSSER	0.031	0.597**	0.637**	0.036	0.527**	0.540**	0.501**	0.233*	0.170	0.361**	−0.003	−0.042	−0.100	−0.063	1	
EGCCR	0.186	0.496**	0.581**	−0.018	0.466**	0.523**	0.441**	0.301**	0.260**	0.427**	−0.202*	0.028	−0.255**	0.053	0.904**	1

** Correlation is significant at the 0.01 level (two-tailed).
* Correlation is significant at the 0.05 level (two-tailed).

Source: Authors' computations (2022).

female/male opportunity-driven TEA ratio, innovation rate, perceived capabilities rate, and perceived opportunities rate are significantly negatively related to the GDP per capita. Alternatively, the motivational index, high job creation expectation rate, business services sector rate, and female/male TEA ratio positively correlated to the GDP per capita. Premised on the computed correlations, we conclude that entrepreneurial activity, aspirations, and attitudes influence economic growth in BRICS countries. Some entrepreneurial variables show a strong correlation between one another, i.e., perceived capabilities rate and opportunities rate, established business ownership rate and total early-stage entrepreneurial activity, and entrepreneurship as a good career choice rate and high status to successful entrepreneurs' rate. To eliminate multicollinearity issues (that can be caused by incorporating all entrepreneurial variables into the model) and reduce the number of independent variables, we implement PCA. The PCA indexes are then implemented when designing the model of interest.

We generate the PCA components within each class of entrepreneurial attitudes and behaviour indicators outlined in Table 10.1, i.e., entrepreneurial aspirations, entrepreneurial activity, and entrepreneurial attitudes. The PCA indexes reveal the significant features of entrepreneurial indicators and diverse facades of entrepreneurship. As expected, the use of PCA solved the problem of multicollinearity. Table 10.4 outlines PCA results. The analysis extracts two PCA

Table 10.4 Principal component analysis indexes

Panel A: Entrepreneurial activity				Factor loadings	
Component	Eigenvalue	Cumulative proportion	Indicator	PC1	PC2
1	2.538	50.769	EBOR	0.877	−0.266
2	1.213	75.032	TEA	0.944	−0.006
3	0.731	89.655	EEAR	0.580	0.541
4	0.381	97.275	FTR	0.676	0.273
5	0.136	100.000	BSSR	−0.295	0.880
Panel B: Entrepreneurial aspirations				PC3	PC4
1	1.746	43.641	MI	−0.606	−0.356
2	1.066	70.289	FOTR	0.803	−0.002
3	0.779	89.768	HJCER	−0.037	0.947
4	0.409	100.000	IR	0.856	−0.209
Panel C: Entrepreneurial attitudes				PC5	PC6
1	3.557	59.289	EGCCR	0.814	−0.277
2	1.203	79.338	HSSER	0.870	−0.207
3	0.743	91.719	EIR	0.733	−0.278
4	0.333	97.275	FFR	0.157	0.927
5	0.102	98.975	PCR	0.906	0.196
6	0.061	100.000	POR	0.869	0.329

Source: Authors' computations (2022).

indexes from each of the three classes of entrepreneurial indicators. These two indexes from each category have eigenvalues bigger than 1. As is the norm in the existing literature, we ignore principal components with eigenvalues less than one (Srholec, 2010).

Factor loadings in Table 10.4 are the correlation coefficients between the indicators and indexes. We extract PC1 and PC2 from the entrepreneurial activity category. These indexes describe 75.03% of the variance, as the cumulative proportion indicates. PCI indicates that economies associated with high levels of established business ownership rate, TEA, female/male TEA ratio and entrepreneurial employee activity rate, which contribute positively to the entrepreneurial activity score, and a low value of business services sector rate, which contribute negatively to the entrepreneurial activity score, are associated with a higher entrepreneurial activity value. PC2 shows that countries with high values for female/male TEA ratio, entrepreneurial employee activity rate and business services sector rate, and low levels for TEA and established business ownership rates are connected to a high entrepreneurial activity value. The cumulative proportion shows that PC3 and PC4 are retained in the entrepreneurial aspirations category, explaining 70.29% of the variance. PC3 specifies that high values for female/male opportunity-driven TEA ratio and innovation rate, and low values for high job creation expectation rate and motivational index result in a higher entrepreneurial aspirations score. PC4 highlights that a higher value for high job creation expectation rate, and low values for female/male opportunity-driven TEA ratio, innovation rate, and motivational index lead to a high value for entrepreneurial aspirations score. Finally, two indexes were retained from the entrepreneurial attitudes class, i.e., PC5 and PC6. These two indexes explain 79.34% of the variance, as the cumulative proportion indicates. PC6 indicates that economies get high scores for entrepreneurial attitudes when the values for entrepreneurship as a good career choice rate, high status to successful entrepreneurs' rate, entrepreneurial intentions rate, fear of failure rate, perceived capabilities rate, and perceived opportunities rate are high. Alternatively, PC6 shows that economies get high scores for entrepreneurial attitudes when the scores for entrepreneurship as a good career choice rate, high status to successful entrepreneurs and entrepreneurial intentions rate are low, and scores for fear of failure rate, perceived capabilities rate and perceived opportunities rate are high.

The entrepreneurial activity, aspirations attitudes indexes and control variables on the GDP per capita were regressed. Table 10.5 outlines regression analysis results with 95% confidence.

The results indicate that there are only three significant indicators, i.e., PC1, PC3, and CSC. PC1 represents entrepreneurial activity and PC3 denotes entrepreneurial aspirations. Therefore, entrepreneurial activity and aspirations substantially influence economic growth as measured by the GDP per capita. To understand these results, we look at the composition of PC1 and PC3. First, entrepreneurial activity is connected to the established business ownership rate, TEA, entrepreneurial employee activity rate, female/male TEA ratio, and

Table 10.5 Regression results

Factor	Coefficient	Sig.
PC1	0.131389	0.0001
PC2	0.024184	0.3859
PC3	0.120021	0.0004
PC4	−0.033005	0.2743
PC5	0.041644	0.1591
PC6	−0.034761	0.0919
HCI	1.207105	0.0821
CSC	1.061040	0.0000
EMP	−0.355789	0.2073
Constant	−1.889210	0.0039
Adjusted R-squared	77.16%	

Source: Authors' computations (2022).

business services sector rate. On PC1, the most significant impact comes from TEA (0.944), followed by the established business ownership rate (0.877), female/male TEA ratio (0.676), entrepreneurial employee activity rate (0.580), and then finally, by business services sector rate (−0.295). Only the business services sector rate has an unexpected negative impact on PC1. Second, entrepreneurial aspirations relate to the motivational index, female/male opportunity-driven TEA ratio, high job creation expectation rate, and innovation rate. Considering PC3, the most substantial influence originates from the innovation rate (0.856), followed by female/male opportunity-driven TEA ratio (0.803), motivational index (−0.606), and then finally, by high job creation expectation rate (−0.037). Innovation rate and female/male opportunity-driven TEA ratio positively affect PC3, and the motivational index and high job creation expectation rate adversely influence PC3. Promoting innovation and improving the female/male opportunity-driven TEA ratio is vital for economic growth. These results indicate that entrepreneurs' goals are essential (Van Stel *et al.*, 2005). The implication here is that intangible components of entrepreneurship are indispensable. Unexpectedly, the motivational index and high job creation expectation rate are associated with a negative influence. The unexpected effects of some indicators on economic growth may be attributed to the fact that, in BRICS economies, numerous entrepreneurs are marginal entrepreneurs who need to be better and there are no sufficient big businesses which are productive to promote economic growth.

The study results show that entrepreneurial attitudes do not significantly influence economic growth. This may be due to the following reasons: intentions to begin businesses might be nascent; ineffective, low quality and inadequate governmental programmes, policies and support initiatives; corruption; prejudicial distribution of grants to companies; learners are trained to be job seekers; qualified people are risk averse; and lack of trust by entrepreneurs on governments and their programmes (see, for instance, Matenda and Sibanda, 2022). Unlike in developed countries where people have positive attitudes towards entrepreneurship (Doran *et al.*, 2018), people in BRICS economies have negative attitudes towards entrepreneurship and entrepreneurship support given by governments. Further, in developing countries, the necessity of entrepreneurship resulting from a lack of alternative employment opportunities is increasing compared to advanced countries (Acs, Desai and Hessels, 2008). Usually, necessity entrepreneurship is not good enough to promote economic growth.

Doran *et al.* (2018) discovered that entrepreneurial activity hurts economic growth in low/middle-income economies and that entrepreneurial attitudes positively influence economic growth in high-income countries. On the other hand, the authors (Doran *et al.*, 2018) discovered that entrepreneurial activity and entrepreneurial aspirations have no significant influence on economic growth in high-income economies, and entrepreneurial attitudes and entrepreneurial aspirations do not significantly influence economic growth in low/middle-income countries. Arenius and Minniti (2005) discovered that perceptual indicators are essential in describing the decisions of individuals to become entrepreneurs. In BRICS economies, Gaba and Gaba (2022) exposed that entrepreneurial intention has a substantial positive influence on economic growth, while TEA, established business ownership rate, and high job creation expectation rate have no substantial influence on economic growth. Vatavu *et al.* (2021) opined that entrepreneurial attitudes and behaviour of individuals adversely affect economic growth, whereas entrepreneurial framework conditions are positively connected to economic growth. Gomes and Ferreira (2022) discovered that perceived opportunities are positively associated economic growth, while perceived capabilities and TEA are negatively connected to economic growth.

In essence, this study supports the proposition that entrepreneurship stimulates economic growth. This is in line with (Doran *et al.*, 2018; Gaba and Gaba, 2022; Gungah and Jaunky, 2017; Pita *et al.*, 2021; Stoica *et al.*, 2020). Nonetheless, we move further than this by examining the influence of various entrepreneurial indicators on economic growth. The study shows that the influence of these variables on economic growth is different. Entrepreneurial indicators representing entrepreneurial activity and aspirations directly impact the GDP per capita, whereas entrepreneurial variables representing entrepreneurial attitudes do not. Regarding control variables, CSC has a significant positive impact on economic growth. Employment per capita and HCI do not significantly influence economic growth. Doran *et al.* (2018) discovered that CSC and EMP significantly positively affect economic growth in high-income and middle/low-income countries. Also, the authors propounded that the HCI is associated with a significant positive influence on economic growth in middle/low income. The adjusted R-squared, a goodness of fit measure, for the designed model is 0.771584. This indicates that the included entrepreneurial indicators can describe 77.16% of the total variation in real GDP. Therefore, the designed model can be considered as a good model.

Conclusions

In this article, we employed the fixed effects model to evaluate the connection between entrepreneurial attitudes and behaviour and economic growth in BRICS countries at the national level. Our main aim was to assess the significance of entrepreneurial activity, aspirations, and attitudes in describing economic growth. PCA was applied to reduce the number of the embraced entrepreneurial measures. Panel datasets from the PWT and GEM were gathered over the observation period 2001–2021 for effectiveness purposes we employed. The study results reveal that entrepreneurial activity and aspirations are positively related to economic growth, while entrepreneurial attitudes do not substantially influence economic growth in BRICS economies. The study results have extensive policy implications concerning the imperativeness of entrepreneurship in inspiring economic growth in BRICS countries. They provide insights that help governments design and evaluate general and explicit policies and make decisions that encourage and support entrepreneurship in BRICS economies. When generating policies related to entrepreneurship, policymakers should consider and promote entrepreneurial activity and aspirations. Further, as indicated in Doran *et al.* (2018), policymakers should educate entrepreneurs about the importance of entrepreneurship, expose entrepreneurs to role models, reduce corporate failure, cultivate positive entrepreneurial attitudes to promote economic growth and design entrepreneurship policies to stimulate entrepreneurship to be more than just subsistence or necessity entrepreneurship. Entrepreneurship should be opportunity-driven entrepreneurship that would substantially affect BRICS economies in terms of economic growth.

The current study can be extended in several dimensions. Some variables have missing data. To overcome this challenge, we imputed missing data with mean values of the variables with missing data for each country. Other techniques for data imputation can be implemented. The influence of the combination of entrepreneurial framework conditions and entrepreneurial attitudes and behaviour on economic growth needs to be analysed. The assessment of entrepreneurship's influence on economic growth under distressed economic and financial conditions or during the COVID-19 crisis period could be performed. A comprehensive dataset can be adopted by incorporating more developing economies. Since BRICS countries are heterogeneous, each may need to be examined separately. In addition, comprehensive datasets can be implemented to evaluate the effect of entrepreneurial framework conditions and entrepreneurial attitudes and behaviour on economic growth in developed and developing economies.

References

Acs, Z. J. (2006) How is entrepreneurship good for economic growth? *Innovations* 1: 97–107.
Acs, Z. J., and Szerb, L. (2010) Global entrepreneurship and the United States. DTIC Document (Print).
Acs, Z. J., Autio, E., and Szerb, L. (2014) National systems of entrepreneurship: Measurement issues and policy implications. *Research Policy* 43: 476–494.
Acs, Z. J., Desai, S., and Hessels, J. (2008) Entrepreneurship, economic development and institutions. *Small Business Economics* 31: 219–234.
Acs, Z. J., Estrin, S., Mickiewicz, T., and Szerb, L. (2018) Entrepreneurship, institutional economics, And economic growth: An ecosystem perspective. *Small Business Economics* 51: 501–514.
Adusei, M. (2016) Does entrepreneurship promote economic growth in Africa? *African Development Review* 28(2): 201–214.
Almodovar-Gonzalez, M., Fernandez-Portillo, A., and Diaz-Casero, J. C. (2020) Entrepreneurial activity and economic growth. A multi-country analysis. *European Research on Management and Business Economics* 26: 9–17.
Almodovar-Gonzalez, M., Sanchez-Escobedo, M. C., and Fernandez-Portillo, A. (2019) Linking demographics, entrepreneurial activity, and economic growth. *Revista ESPACIOS* 40(28), 24.
Amoros, J. E., Fernandez, C., and Tapia, J. (2012) Quantifying the relationship between entrepreneurship and competitiveness development stages in Latin America. *International Entrepreneurship and Management Journal* 8: 249–270.
Aparicio, S., Urbano, D., and Audretsch, D. (2016) Institutional factors, opportunity entrepreneurship and economic growth: Panel data evidence. *Technological Forecasting and Social Change* 102: 45–61.
Arenius, P., and Minniti, M. (2005) Perceptual variables and nascent entrepreneurship. *Small Business Economics* 24(3): 233–247.
Audretsch, D. B. (2007) Entrepreneurship capital and economic growth. *Oxford Review of Economic Policy* 23: 63–78.
Audretsch, D., and Keilbach, M. (2004) Entrepreneurship capital and economic performance. *Regional Studies* 38: 949–959.
Avnimelech, G., Zelekha, Y., and Sharabi, E. (2014) The effect of corruption on entrepreneurship in developed vs non-developed countries. *International Journal of Entrepreneurial Behavior and Research* 20: 237–262.
Baliamoune-Lutz, M. (2015) Taxes and entrepreneurship in OECD countries. *Contemporary Economic Policy* 33: 369–380.
Baumgartner, D., Schulz, T., and Seidl, I. (2013) Quantifying entrepreneurship and its impact on local economic performance: A spatial assessment in rural Switzerland. *Entrepreneurship and Regional Development* 25(3–4): 222–250.
Bosma, N., Acs, Z., Autio, E., Coduras, A., and Levie, J. (2009) GEM Executive Report 2008. Babson College, Universidad del Desarrollo, and Global Entrepreneurship Research Consortium Babson Park, MA.
Bosma, N., Content, J., Sanders, M., and Stam, E. (2018) Institutions, Entrepreneurship, and economic growth in Europe. *Small Business Economics* 51: 483–499.
Boudreaux, C., and Caudill, S. (2019) Entrepreneurship, institutions and economic growth: Does the level of development matter? MPRA Paper 94244, University Library of Munich, Germany.
Carree, M. A., and Thurik, A. R. (2008) The lag structure of the impact of business ownership on economic performance in OECD countries. *Small Business Economics* 30: 101–110.

Carree, M. A., and Thurik, A. R. (2003) The impact of entrepreneurship on economic growth. In: Acs, Z. J., Audretsch, D. B. (Eds.) Handbook of Entrepreneurship Research. International Handbook Series on Entrepreneurship, vol 1. Springer, Boston, MA.

Chatterjee, M., and Naka, I. (2022) Twenty years of BRICS: Political and economic transformations through the Lens of land. *Oxford Development Studies* 50(1): 2–13.

Coulibaly, S. K., Erbao, C., and Mekongcho, T. M. (2017) Economic globalization, entrepreneurship, and development. *Technological Forecasting and Social Change* 127: 271–280.

Decker, R., Haltiwanger, J., Jarmin, R., and Miranda, J. (2014) The role of entrepreneurship in US job creation and economic dynamism. *The Journal of Economic Perspectives* 28(3): 3–24.

Doran, J., McCarthy, N., and O'Connor, M. (2018) The role of entrepreneurship in stimulating economic growth in developed and developing countries. *Cogent Economics and Finance* 6(1): 1442093.

Doran, J., McCarthy, N., and O'Connor, M. (2016) Entrepreneurship and employment growth across European regions. *Regional Studies, Regional Science* 3: 121–128.

Dvoulety, O., Gordievskaya, A., and Prochazka, D. A. (2018) Investigating the relationship between entrepreneurship and regional development: Case of developing countries. *Journal of Global Entrepreneurship Research* 8: 16.

Farinha, L., Lopes, J., Bagchi-Sen, S., Sebastiao, J. R., and Oliveira, J. (2020) Entrepreneurial dynamics and government policies to boost entrepreneurship performance. *Socio-Economic Planning Sciences* 72: 100950.

Ferreira, J. J., Fayolle, A., Fernandes, C., and Raposo, M. (2017) Effects of Schumpeterian and Kirznerian entrepreneurship on economic growth: Panel data evidence. *Entrepreneurship and Regional Development* 29: 27–50.

Fritsch, M. (2008) How does new business formation affect regional development? Introduction to the special issue. *Small Business Economics* 30: 1–14.

Gaba, A. K., and Gaba, N. (2022) Entrepreneurial activity and economic growth of BRICS countries: Retrospect and prospects. *The Journal of Entrepreneurship* 31(2): 402–424.

Galindo, M. A., and Mendez, M. T. (2014) Entrepreneurship, economic growth, and innovation: Are feedback effects at work? *Journal of Business Research* 67(5): 825–829.

Garcia, A., and Bond, P. (2019) Amplifying The contradictions: The centrifugal BRICS. *Social Register* 55: 223–246.

Garcia-Rodriguez, F., Gil-Soto, E., Ruiz-Rosa, I., and Gutiérrez-Tano, D. (2017) Entrepreneurial potential in less innovative regions: The impact of social and cultural environment. *European Journal of Management and Business Economics* 26(2): 163–179.

Global Entrepreneurship Monitor. (2022). Global Entrepreneurship Monitor. https://www.gemconsortium.org/data.

Gomes, S., and Ferreira, P. (2022) Entrepreneurial activity and economic growth: A dynamic data panel analysis of European countries. *Entrepreneurial Business and Economics Review* 10(2): 7–20.

Gomes, S., Ferreira, J., Lopes, J. M., and Farinha, L. (2022) The impacts of the entrepreneurial conditions on economic growth: Evidence from OECD countries. *Economies* 10: 163.

Gries, T., and Naude, W. (2010) Entrepreneurship and structural economic transformation. *Small Business Economics* 34: 13–29.

Gu, W., Wang, J., Huan, X., and Liu, Z. (2021) Entrepreneurship and high-quality economic development: Based on the triple Bottom line of sustainable development. *International Entrepreneurship and Management Journal* 17: 1–27.

Gungah, V., and Jaunky, V. C. (2017) Does entrepreneurship drive economic growth? Evidence from the BRICS. *International Journal of Conceptions on Management and Social Sciences* 5(1): 17–22.

Hermes, N., and Lensink, R. (2007) The empirics of microfinance: What do we know? *The Economic Journal* 117: F1–F10.

Hessels, J., and Van Stel, A. (2011) Entrepreneurship, export orientation, and economic growth. *Small Business Economics* 37: 255–268.

Karlan, D., and Valdivia, M. (2011) Teaching entrepreneurship: Impact of business training on microfinance clients and Institutions. *Review of Economics and Statistics* 93: 510–527.

Kondratov, D. I. (2021) Internationalisation of the currencies of BRICS countries. *Herald of the Russian Academy of Sciences* 91: 37–50.

Lepojevic, V., Djukic, M. I., and Mladenovic, J. (2016) Entrepreneurship and economic development: A comparative analysis of developed and developing countries. *Facta Universitatis, Series: Economics and Organisation* 13(1): 17–29.

Marcotte, C. (2014) Entrepreneurship and innovation in emerging economies: Conceptual, methodological and contextual issues. *International Journal of Entrepreneurial Behavior and Research* 20: 42–65.

Marcotte, C. (2013) Measuring entrepreneurship at the country level: A review and research agenda. *Entrepreneurship and Regional Development* 25: 174–194.

Mariet Ocasio, V., and Mariet Ocasio, V. (2016) Financing village enterprises in rural Bangladesh: What determines nonfarm revenue growth. *International Journal of Development Issues* 15: 76–94.

Matenda, F. R., and Sibanda, M. (2022) The influence of entrepreneurial framework conditions (EFCs) on economic growth in South Africa. *Interdisciplinary Journal of Economics and Business Law* 11(4): 57–74.

Miller, D. (1983) The correlates of entrepreneurship in three types of firms. *Management Science* 7(7): 770–791.

Naude, W. (2010) Entrepreneurship, developing countries, and development economics: New approaches and insights. *Small Business Economics* 34: 1–12.

Nwagu, N. B., and Enofe, E. E. (2021) The impact of entrepreneurship on the economic growth of An economy: An overview. *Journal of Emerging Trends in Economics and Management Sciences* 12(4): 143–149.

Pita, M., Costa, J., and Moreira, A. C. (2021) Entrepreneurial ecosystems and entrepreneurial initiative: Building a multi-country taxonomy. *Sustainability* 13: 4065.

Pittaway, L. (2005) Philosophies in entrepreneurship: A focus on economic theories. *International Journal of Entrepreneurial Behavior and Research* 11: 201–221.

Sautet, F. (2013) Local and systemic entrepreneurship: Solving the puzzle of entrepreneurship and economic development. *Entrepreneurship Theory and Practice* 37(2): 387–402.

Savrul, M. (2017) The impact of entrepreneurship on economic growth: GEM data analysis. *Journal of Management, Marketing and Logistics* 4(3): 320–326.

Schumpeter, J. A. (1947) Theoretical problems of economic growth. *Journal of Economic History Supplement* 7(1): 1–9.

Schumpeter, J. A. (1911) *The Theory of Economic Development*. Harvard University Press Havard.

Srholec, M. (2010) A multilevel approach to geography of innovation. *Regional Studies* 44: 1207–1220.

Stam, E., and Van Stel, A. (2011) Types of entrepreneurship and economic growth. In A. Szirmai & M. Wim Naudé (Eds.) *Entrepreneurship, Innovation, and Economic Development*. Oxford: Oxford University Press.

Stam, E., and Van Stel, A. (2009) *Types of entrepreneurship and economic growth. Working Paper Series*. Maastricht: UNU-WIDER.

Stam, E., Hartog, C., Van Stel, A., and Thurik, R. (2011) Ambitious entrepreneurship, high-growth firms and macroeconomic growth. In M. Minniti (Ed.), *The Dynamics of Entrepreneurship: Evidence from Global Entrepreneurship Monitor Data* (pp. 231–249). Oxford: Oxford University Press.

Stel, A. V., Carree, M., and Thurik, R. (2005). The effect of entrepreneurial activity on national economic growth. *Small business economics*, 24: 311–321.

Sternberg, R., and Wennekers, S. (2005) Determinants and effects of new business creation using global entrepreneurship monitor data. *Small Business Economics* 24: 193–203.

Stoica, O., Roman, A., and Rusu, V. D. (2020) The nexus between entrepreneurship and economic growth: A comparative analysis of groups of countries. *Sustainability* 12: 1186.

Urbano, D., and Aparicio, S. (2016) Entrepreneurship capital types and economic growth: International evidence. *Technological Forecasting and Social Change* 102(C): 34–44.

Valliere, D., and Peterson, R. (2009) Entrepreneurship and economic growth: Evidence from emerging and developed countries. *Entrepreneurship and Regional Development* 21: 459–480.

Van Praag, C. M., and Versloot, P. H. (2007) What is the value of entrepreneurship? A review of recent research. *Small Business Economics* 29: 351–382.

Van Stel, A., Carree, M., and Thurik, R. (2005) The effect of entrepreneurial activity on national economic growth. *Small Business Economics* 24: 311–321.

Vatavu, S., Dogaru, M., Moldovan, N.-C., and Lobont, O. R. (2021) The impact of entrepreneurship on economic development through government policies and citizens' attitudes. *Economic Research-Ekonomska Istrazivanja* 35(1): 1604–1617.

Vazquez, E., Gomes, S., and Vieira, E. (2010) Entrepreneurship and economic growth in Spanish and Portuguese regions. *Regional and Sectoral Economics Studies* 10(2): 110–126.

Wennekers, S., Van Wennekers, A., Thurik, R., and Reynolds, P. (2005) Nascent entrepreneurship and the level of economic development. *Small Business Economics* 24: 293–309.

Wong, P. K., Ho, Y. P., and Autio, E. (2005) Entrepreneurship, innovation and economic growth: Evidence from GEM data. *Small Business Economics* 24: 335–350.

Xu, B., Yu, H., and Li, L. (2021) The impact of entrepreneurship on regional economic growth: A perspective of spatial heterogeneity. *Entrepreneurship and Regional Development* 33: 309–331.

Zaki, I. M., and Rashid, N. H. (2016) Entrepreneurship impact on economic growth in emerging countries. *The Business and Management Review* 7(2): 31–39.

11 Does the Mixed Ownership Reform Promote the Innovation Level of State-Owned Enterprises?

A Dual Analysis of Equity Balance and Top Management Governance

Zhe Sun, Zhe Wang, Xiaoming Wang, and Liang Zhao

Introduction

It has become important for China to enhance its capacity for independent innovation and drive high-quality development of the Chinese economy through innovation. According to the "Guidance on Deepening the Reform of State-owned Enterprises", as a power in carrying out innovation-driven development strategy, it is important for China to cultivate many state-owned enterprises (SOEs) with creative ability and international competitiveness. Notably, developing a mixed ownership economy is an effective way and inevitable choice of improving the efficiency of the state-owned capital allocation. Therefore, developing a mixed ownership economy has become the reform focus of SOEs to achieve innovative development.

The academia recently discussed whether mixed ownership reform promotes SOEs' innovation. Most research believes that the mixed ownership reform positively impacts SOEs' innovation. The participation of non-state-owned capital changes the ownership structure and participates in internal governance, thus affecting the innovation decisions of SOEs. Yet, there are still some deficiencies. The research on the impact of mixed ownership reform on SOEs' innovation mainly focuses on the ownership structure. It mostly discusses the impact of reform on SOEs from the perspective of ownership diversity and change of control rights while ignoring the significant impact of the change in terms of SOEs' governance structure. It is worth noting that, compared to the change of ownership structure by non-state-owned capital participation, the change in SOEs' governance structure through non-state-owned shareholders appointing directors, supervisors and senior managers is a complementary factor affecting the innovation decisions of SOEs. In addition, prior research mainly focused on the direct impact of mixed ownership reform on enterprise innovation; little attention has been paid to the heterogeneity of SOEs and the divergent impact of the external environment on the relationship between the two.

DOI: 10.4324/9781003475606-14

Given the above deficiencies, this chapter intends to comprehensively consider how the changes brought by non-state-owned shareholders' participation in SOEs' governance affect the innovation level of SOEs. Meanwhile, the study also explored whether the impact of mixed ownership reform on SOEs' innovation differs due to the heterogeneity of SOEs and varying external environments. To answer these questions, this paper discusses the impact of mixed ownership reform on the innovation level of SOEs from two dimensions of governance structure: non-state-owned equity balance and top management governance, based on the political view and manager view, respectively. Specifically, this paper takes A-share listed SOEs from 2008 to 2019 as research samples. It uses the China Stock Market & Accounting Research (CSMAR) database, Wind database, and annual reports of listed enterprises to measure the relevant data. Regarding innovation data, used data from patent applications and grants in the Chinese Research Data Services (CNRDS) database. In addition, the samples are divided into groups by the industry competition degree (i.e. monopoly and competitive SOEs), regional marketisation development level and industrial technology level (technological and non-technological SOEs). In this way, the heterogeneous impact of mixed ownership reform on SOEs' innovation is investigated.

The theoretical contribution of this paper is mainly manifested in extending the existing research in the mixed ownership reform and SOEs' innovation. Specifically, this paper shifts the research focus from the ownership structure to the governance structure of SOEs with the mixed ownership reform. It pays more attention to the positive impact of the checks and balances of non-state shareholders and top management's participation in SOEs' innovation. In addition, this paper explores the influence of enterprise and environmental heterogeneity on the relationship between mixed ownership reform and SOEs' innovation. This research enriches relevant research and provides a theoretical reference to develop the mixed ownership reform of SOEs further.

Literature Review and Research Hypotheses

The Impact of Mixed Ownership Reform on SOEs' Innovation

The innovation of SOEs has always been the focus of research discussion. SOEs are widely believed to have low innovation capacity (Wu, 2012; Wu, 2014; Kong, Dai, and Li, 2014). The cause of this problem is attributed to the political and managerial views.

The political view holds that the lack of interest in innovation and innovation motivation of SOEs are mainly caused by the policy burden borne by SOEs (Lin and Liu, 2001). The natural connection between SOEs and the government enhances the motivation for government intervention (Shleifer and Vishny, 1994), and the pressure of political performance assessment makes local governments rely more on local SOEs (Zhong, Zhang, and Chen, 2016). As a result, SOEs' production and business operations are burdened by the goal of diversification, and SOEs bear more social responsibilities and excessive non-economic burdens. To solve the political goals of local employment, tax stabilisation, and improvement of social infrastructure, SOEs usually employ redundant employees (Jiang, 2016), invest more in tangible assets, and participate in investment projects such as infrastructure construction or merger and acquisition (Chen, Xia, and Yu, 2008). Under the policy burdens, this investment behaviour will ultimately crowd out the innovation investment funds, so the normal production of SOEs is distorted (Boubakri, Cosset, and Saffar, 2013). Specifically, SOEs often choose a more conservative investment strategy and tend to give up the high-risk, uncertain innovation decision (Zhu, Chen, and Wang, 2019), resulting in a lack of interest in innovation (Yuan, Hou, and Chen, 2015; Wang and Lan, 2019). Therefore, the primary problem of the reform of SOEs is to reduce the non-economic tasks and to strip the policy burden of SOEs.

By diversifying ownership structure to a certain extent, introducing different forms of non-state-owned shareholders, reducing government intervention, and strengthening the decision-making autonomy of SOEs, mixed ownership reform can ease the policy burden of SOEs and devote resources to innovation activities. At the same time, by improving the governance structure of SOEs, mixed checks and balances, and integrated development of enterprise subjects, mixed ownership reform can help to avoid the over-investment problem (Yang and Yin, 2018), achieve the long-term interests of all parties, enhance the competitive advantages of SOEs (Liu and Li, 2012), and generate more incentives to invest superior resources in innovation. Thus, the crowding-out effect of research and development (R&D) expenditure on SOEs can be reduced, and the innovation level of SOEs can be improved.

The manager's view holds that the principal-agent problem is prevalent in SOEs. Top managers in SOEs have difficulty receiving effective incentives and supervision (Zhang, 1996; Li and Yu, 2015), and the principal-agent problem is relatively serious (Liu, Zheng, and Cai, 2016). Due to the special relationship between SOEs and the government, as "quasi officials", managers in SOEs tend to consider more personal interests and have a stronger incentive to choose robust investment activities and undertake more political tasks that are more advantageous for their promotion (Bai, Lu, and Tao, 2006; Zhou, 2007). Regarding R&D activities with high risk and long-term investment, SOE managers have less motivation to participate (Tang and Wu, 2015). Therefore, the focus of SOE's reform is to improve the internal governance of SOEs (Lin and Liu, 2001).

The mixed ownership reform can adjust the ownership structure by introducing non-state-owned capital into SOEs. Through participating in the governance of SOEs, the non-state-owned shareholders compensate for the absence of controllers in SOEs and ease the principal-agent problem between owners and managers. To maximise their benefit, the non-state-owned shareholders will appoint suitable executives in SOEs, strengthen supervision over senior managers, and urge them to perform their management duties. In so doing, non-state-owned shareholders can be able to improve the incentive and supervision mechanism of SOEs.

Ultimately, managers will pay more attention to R&D and innovation in their careers (Hu, Song, and Zhang, 2005). In addition, after the reform of mixed ownership, non-state-owned shareholders can bring various resources, such as entrepreneurship, institutional investment and shareholders with management experience, into SOEs, which generates some advantages for SOEs' innovation activities (Wang and Lan, 2019). To sum up, this paper proposes:

> **Hypothesis 1**: The introduction of non-state-owned capital in SOEs improves the innovation level of SOEs.

Monopolistic Versus Competitive SOEs

SOEs undertake important tasks related to China's national economy and people's livelihood. Most of the monopolistic SOEs are dominant in the key industries of the national economy. To a large extent, it is difficult for non-state-owned capital to enter these key industries directly controlled by the government. Even if mixed-ownership reform is carried out, it is still difficult for non-state-owned capital to interfere in enterprise operations (Xia and Chen, 2007), including R&D and innovation activities. Therefore, the innovation level of monopolistic SOEs cannot be effectively affected. At the same time, SOEs have rich monopoly rents and easily enjoy excess profits. SOE managers tend to be content with the *status quo* and lack motivation to conduct R&D and innovation activities, resulting in low innovation levels of monopolistic SOEs (Liu, Zhang, and Lan, 2016).

Compared with monopolistic SOEs, non-state-owned shareholders have a certain right in competitive SOEs. Non-state-owned shareholders can supervise managers, alleviate principal-agent problems, improve the innovation willingness of competitive SOEs, and increase investment in R&D and innovation activities. In addition, competitive SOEs face higher survival pressure, and the participation of non-state-owned capital in business strategy formulation greatly affects the innovation strategy of SOEs. Based on the above analysis, this paper proposes:

> **Hypothesis 2**: Compared with monopolistic SOEs, competitive SOEs have a more significant role in promoting enterprise innovation by introducing non-state-owned capital.

Regional Marketisation Development

There are obvious differences in the marketisation development among different regions in China. An unbalanced pattern is formed in which the eastern region is superior to the central region, and the central region is superior to the western region (Zhao and Liu, 2016). In areas with higher marketisation development, the government needs more intervention in the production and operation of enterprises. At the same time, the non-state-owned economy develops better in these regions and can provide more jobs. In this case, local governments need more incentive to increase employment and obtain fiscal revenue from SOEs. In addition, in regions with higher-level marketisation development, enterprises' intellectual property rights can be better protected, and enterprises' R&D and innovation achievements can be guaranteed to a large extent. To survive in the fierce market competition (Jiao, Koo, and Cui, 2015), SOEs are strongly willing to introduce non-state-owned capital to conduct their innovation strategies and improve their innovation level. This is simply because the non-state-owned capital participation can better optimise ownership structure, improve supervision and incentive for managers in SOEs, and alleviate principal-agent problems. In regions with higher marketisation development, SOEs tend to have more modern governance mechanisms, such as open and transparent internal governance (Chen and Liu, 2013), and the rights of non-state-owned shareholders can be better protected. Therefore, non-state-owned shareholders are more willing to participate in the innovation activities of SOEs to obtain rich returns.

On the contrary, intellectual property protection could be much better in areas with low marketisation development. After the reform of mixed ownership of SOEs, non-state-owned shareholders are motivated to hollow out SOEs. Some non-state-owned shareholders enter SOEs only to participate in the operation of SOEs and share dividends. They are less willing to participate in high-risk investments such as innovation, which has a negative impact on the innovation of SOEs. Based on the above analysis, this paper proposes:

> **Hypothesis 3**: In regions with higher marketisation development, introducing non-state-owned capital by SOEs significantly promotes enterprise innovation.

Technological Versus Non-Technological SOEs

Compared with other types of enterprises, R&D and innovation activities have a more obvious supporting effect on the development of high-tech enterprises. Therefore, high-tech enterprises' innovation willingness and innovation ability are significantly stronger than other types of enterprises. Therefore, SOEs in the high-tech industry have always maintained a high innovation level. At the same time, mixed ownership reform has not significantly improved the innovation level of enterprises in the high-tech industry. However, non-state-owned capital will enter SOEs after the mixed ownership reform for non-technological enterprises, and non-state-owned shareholders will have a stronger desire for innovative R&D activities for enterprise operations. Based on the above analysis, this paper proposes:

> **Hypothesis 4**: Compared with technological SOEs, non-technological SOEs have a more significant promotion effect on enterprise innovation through introducing non-state-owned capital.

Research Design

Sample Selection and Data Sources

This chapter takes A-share listed SOEs in Shanghai and Shenzhen stock markets from 2008 to 2019 as the research sample (Liu, Zheng, and Cai, 2016; Wei, Cai, and Liu, 2017; Cai, Liu, and Ma, 2018) The reasons for selecting listed enterprises as samples are as follows. First, compared with listed enterprises, non-listed SOEs are generally wholly controlled by the government, and the barriers for non-state-owned capital to enter the non-listed SOEs are higher. Moreover, it is difficult to obtain relevant data on non-listed SOEs. Second, the internal governance information of listed enterprises is more open and transparent (Huang, 2014), and their equity data and senior management governance data can be obtained through the CSMAR database, Wind database and annual reports of listed enterprises. Therefore, taking listed SOEs as research samples is convenient for a more comprehensive study.

The sample data were selected from 2008 mainly because non-state-owned capital generally entered SOEs after the completion of the reform of non-state-owned shares in SOEs in 2007. Some may doubt that there are rare innovation cases by SOEs in the early days, such as in 2008. However, the state-owned economy in China, in our empirical context, is arguably the most active state-owned economy among emerging markets. Chinese President Xi Jinping has encouraged "state-owned enterprises (SOEs) to improve their innovation systems and develop sources of original technologies". Given their significance, it is necessary to have a nuanced understanding of the role of SOEs and their reform in shaping China's innovation landscape since the early days. Listed SOEs are screened according to the properties of actual controllers of listed enterprises in the CSMAR database to populate the sample. To ensure the accuracy of the results, the initial samples were processed as follows. First, according to the classification of listed enterprises by the China Securities Regulatory Commission in 2012, the financial data of listed financial and insurance enterprises were not comparable with those of other types of enterprises due to the particularity of their business, so the samples of financial and insurance enterprises were

Does the Mixed Ownership Reform Promote Innovation Level of SOEs 187

removed; Second, listed enterprises marked special treatment (ST), ST with delisting warning (*ST), and particular transfer (PT) were excluded due to the unstable business conditions and strong uncertainties; Third, the samples that have abnormal or missing financial data were eliminated.

In addition to the number of patent applications of enterprises from the CNRDS database, other data such as equity checks and balances, senior management, board size, corporate asset-liability ratio, corporate growth, equity concentration, etc., are from the CSMAR or Wind database. Some data were manually sorted out from the annual reports of listed enterprises. For more reliable research results, a 1%winsorisation reduction for all continuous variables was carried out in this paper to eliminate the influence of extreme values on the research results. Finally, 7215 observations were obtained.

Variable Selection and Measurement

Variable selection mainly includes dependent variables (innovation output), independent variables (equity checks and balances top management governance), and control variables.

Dependent Variable

Considering that there are many missing values of R&D expenditure in annual reports of listed enterprises and great differences in enterprise expenditure data under different accounting standards, this paper measures the innovation output using the number of patent applications (Lnpatent) (Feng, Zhang, and Duan, 2021). The number of patents granted by enterprises has a certain time lag, and enterprises may choose to keep some patents private due to their business considerations, thus reducing the number of patents disclosed. Therefore, there are some deviations in both the number of patents granted and the number of patents disclosed by enterprises. Based on this, this paper chooses the number of patent applications as the dependent variable to measure the innovation output of enterprises. The total number of patent applications is obtained from the total number of inventions, utility models and design patents applied by enterprises in the CNRDS database. The paper takes the natural logarithm of the total number of patent applications applied by enterprises in the current year plus 1.

Independent Variables

This paper measures the mixed ownership reform of SOEs from two dimensions: equity balance and top management governance. Liu *et al*. (2016), Ma, Tang, and Zheng (2021) noted that, based on the former top ten shareholders of an enterprise disclosed in the annual report, CSMAR database and Wind database, this paper divides the top ten shareholders into state-owned and non-state-owned shareholders. In terms of the degree of equity balance, it is measured by the sum of the percentage of the former ten non-state-owned shareholders (SHD_NONSOE) as well as the dummy variable (SHD_DUM) that whether the former ten non-state-owned shareholders are greater than 10%. This chapter measures top management governance by taking the proportion of the number of directors appointed by non-state-owned shareholders to the number of directors in the board of directors (D_NONSOE) and the dummy variable (D_DUM) that whether non-state-owned shareholders appoint directors to SOEs (Cai, Liu, and Ma, 2018; Ma, Tang, and Zheng, 2021). According to Chen and Wei (2013), to conclude whether non-state-owned shareholders appoint directors to SOEs is as follows: if the director comes from a legal person shareholder, and the legal person shareholder is non-state-owned, then the director is identified as being appointed by a non-state-owned shareholder; and if a natural person shareholder appoints the director, then it is also identified as being appointed by a non-state-owned shareholder.

Control Variables

Considering existing literature (Tang *et al.*, 2020; Ma *et al.*, 2021 and Cai *et al.*, 2018), this study selects the following control variables: enterprise size, leverage, return on assets, enterprise growth, years of going listed, Tobin Q, and a dummy variable in terms of whether the Chairman and the CEO is the same person. According to the existing literature, these factors may impact enterprise innovation and governance of non-state-owned shareholders. In addition, year and industry dummy variables are added to control time and industry effect. Table 11.1 presents the variable definitions.

Model Specification

Considering the study constructs the following regression model to the impact of mixed-ownership reform on SOEs' innovation:

$$Inn_{i,t} = \alpha_0 + \alpha_1 NONSOE_{i,t} + \sum Control_{i,t} + dummies + \varepsilon_{i,t} \qquad (11.1)$$

where $Inn_{i,t}$ is the dependent variable – innovation output, which is represented by the total number of patent applications of SOEs (Lnpatent) (Cai *et al.*, 2018 and Ma *et al.*, 2021). The more patents an enterprise applies for, the higher its innovation output will be. The variables in this study are mixed-ownership reform of SOEs. This study explores the degree of non-state-owned shareholders' participation in SOEs' governance under mixed ownership reform from equity structure and top management governance. Equity structure is measured by the proportion of non-state-owned shareholders in the top ten shareholders (SHD_NONSOE), and the dummy variable of whether the proportion of

Table 11.1 Variable definitions

Variable type	Variable name	Variable symbol	Definition of a variable
Dependent variable	Enterprise innovation	Lnpatent	Ln (Total number of patent applications from SOEs +1)
Independent variables	Proportion of non-state-owned shareholders	SHD_NONSOE	The total proportion of non-state-owned shareholders in the top ten shareholders of an enterprise
	Whether non-state-owned shareholders hold a higher proportion	SHD_DUM	The total proportion of non-state-owned shareholders in the top ten shareholders of an enterprise If the value is not less than 10%, the value is 1 if yes, otherwise, 0
	Proportion of directors appointed by non-state-owned shareholders	D_NONSOE	The proportion of directors appointed by non-state-owned shareholders to the total number of directors
	Whether non-state shareholders appoint directors	D_DUM	When non-state-owned shareholders appoint directors to SOEs, the value is 1 if yes, otherwise 0
Control variables	The company size	Size	Ln (total assets at the end of the year)
	Asset-liability ratio	Lev	Total liabilities/assets at the end of the year
	Return on total assets	ROA	Net profit/average balance of total assets
	Growth rate of operating income	Growth	Current year's operating income/last year's operating income
	Fixed number of year of the listed	Age	Ln(Current year - listing year +1)
	Tobin Q	Tobin Q	Market value/book value of total assets
	The two functions were consolidated	Dual	Whether the Chairman and the CEO are the same person, it is 1 if yes, otherwise, 0
	industry	industry	Industry dummy variables are classified according to the industry code published by China Securities Regulatory Commission (CSRC) in 2012
	year	year	Year dummy variable

non-state-owned shareholders is greater than 10% (SHD_DUM). Top management governance is measured by the proportion of directors appointed by non-state-owned shareholders (D_NONSOE) and the dummy variable of whether non-state-owned shareholders appoint directors to SOEs (DSubscript_DUM). $Control_{i,t}$ represents all the control variables listed in Table 11.1. Dummies represent the year and industry dummy variables. $\varepsilon_{i,t}$ is the random error term. This paper uses the fixed effect model to conduct regression test on the samples.

Empirical Results

Descriptive Statistics and Correlation Coefficient Matrix

Table 11.2 reports descriptive statistics of the main variables. The average number of patent applications of the sample enterprises was 162.542, the maximum value and minimum value were 32747 and 0, respectively, the standard deviation was 898.428, and the median was 16. The results of innovation output show a significant gap in innovation output among different sample enterprises, and the innovation output of most SOEs could be a lot higher. In terms of the variables representing SOEs' mixed ownership reform, the average ratio of non-state-owned shareholders (SHD_NONSOE) in the top ten shareholders in the sample period is 6.9%, and the average proportion of directors appointed by non-state-owned shareholders (D_NONSOE) is 3.5%. These results indicate that after the mixed-ownership reform, the proportion of non-state-owned shareholders and appointed directors in SOEs is relatively low, and non-state-owned shareholders may not fully participate in SOEs' governance. In addition, the standard deviation of D_NONSOE is 2.4 times

Table 11.2 Descriptive statistics

The variable name	Obs	Mean	SD	Min	Median	Max
Patent	7215	162.542	898.428	0	16	32747
Lnpatent	7215	2.714	2.228	0	2.83	10.4
SHD_NONSOE	7215	0.069	0.085	0	0.03	0.4
SHD_DUM	7215	0.223	0.416	0	0	1
D_NONSOE	7215	0.035	0.084	0	0	1
D_DUM	7215	0.2	0.4	0	0	1
Size	7215	22.554	1.316	19.35	22.41	26.4
Age	7215	2.639	0.453	1.39	2.77	3.33
Lev	7215	0.516	0.197	0.03	0.53	0.92
ROA	7215	0.029	0.052	-0.41	0.03	0.24
Growth	7213	0.143	0.43	-0.65	0.08	4.81
Tobin Q	7215	1.796	1.168	0.82	1.42	17.68
Board	7215	2.203	0.191	1.61	2.2	2.71
Dual	7215	0.098	0.297	0	0	1

Table 11.3 Correlation matrix

	Lnpatent	SHD_NONSOE	SHD_DUM	D_NONSOE	D_DUM	Size	Age
Lnpatent	1						
SHD_NONSOE	0.036***	1					
SHD_DUM	0.034***	0.855***	1				
D_NONSOE	0.067***	0.436***	0.401***	1			
D_DUM	0.051***	0.429***	0.410***	0.837***	1		
Size	0.384***	−0.032***	−0.0110	0	−0.019*	1	
Age	−0.00800	−0.068***	−0.062***	−0.208***	−0.195***	0.094***	1
Lev	0.055***	−0.076***	−0.069***	−0.068***	−0.059***	0.384***	0.082***
ROA	0.054***	0.049***	0.058***	0.112***	0.100***	0.075***	−0.080***
Growth	0.0170	0.049***	0.050***	0.029**	0.029**	0.071***	−0.035***
Tobin Q	−0.100***	0.056***	0.046***	0.053***	0.056***	−0.498***	−0.056***
Board	0.064***	0.032***	0.041***	0.052***	0.092***	0.180***	−0.126***
Dual	0.00100	0.026**	0.0160	0.033***	0.0150	−0.031***	0.00800
	Lev	ROA	Growth	Tobin Q	Board	Dual	
Lev	1						
ROA	−0.346***	1					
Growth	0.069***	0.199***	1				
Tobin Q	−0.299***	0.075***	−0.037***	1			
Board	0.072***	0.032***	−0.00100	−0.109***	1		
Dual	0.00700	−0.00600	−0.020*	0.0110	−0.075***	1	

Note: ***, ** and * are significant at the level of 1%, 5% and 10%, respectively.

the mean value, indicating that the proportion of directors appointed by non-state-owned shareholders varies greatly among different SOEs, and the governance level of non-state-owned shareholders varies among different SOEs.

Table 11.3 reports the correlations between the main variables. The correlation between Lnpatent and equity balance (SHD_NONSOE, SHD_DUM) and between Lnpatent and top management governance (D_NONSOE, SHD_DUM) are significantly positive. The results preliminarily verify Hypothesis 1 in this paper. Correlations between other variables were as expected. In addition, to eliminate serious collinearity among the model variables, the variance inflation factor (VIF) test was also carried out in this paper. The results show that the mean value of VIF was 2.05, which was significantly less than 10. Therefore, the existence of serious collinearity among variables can be excluded.

The Regression Results of Mixed Ownership Reform of SOEs and Enterprise Innovation

The regression results of the impact of SOEs' mixed ownership reform on enterprise innovation are shown in Table 11.4. The results show that SHD_NONSOE

Table 11.4 Mixed ownership reform and enterprise innovation

	Lnpatent			
	(1)	(2)	(3)	(4)
SHD_NONSOE	0.541**			
	(2.23)			
SHD_DUM		0.077*		
		(1.81)		
D_NONSOE			1.057***	
			(4.165)	
D_DUM				0.136***
				(2.763)
Size	0.557***	0.557***	0.553***	0.5555***
	(15.340)	(15.362)	(15.249)	(15.300)
Age	0.704***	0.696***	0.747***	0.715***
	(5.470)	(5.412)	(5.787)	(5.554)
Lev	−0.235	−0.242*	−0.245*	−0.251*
	(−1.635)	(−1.679)	(−1.709)	(−1.751)
ROA	0.064	0.049	0.033	0.056
	(0.196)	(0.156)	(0.122)	(0.175)
Growth	0.029	0.030	0.032	0.032
	(1.004)	(1.047)	(1.108)	(1.117)
Tobin Q	−0.015	−0.015	−0.013	−0.014
	(−0.860)	(−0.859)	(−0.747)	(−0.821)
Board	0.079	0.086	0.083	0.073
	(0.637)	(0.692)	(0.674)	(0.587)
Dual	−0.010	−0.011	−0.012	−0.012
	(−0.195)	(−0.212)	(−0.244)	(−0.238)
Industry	Control	Control	Control	Control
Year	Control	Control	Control	Control
_cons	−11.567***	−11.548***	−11.617***	−11.518***
	(−11.791)	(−11.763)	(−11.858)	(−11.739)
N	7213	7213	7213	7213
adj. R^2	0.195	0.195	0.195	0.195

Note: t-statistics in parentheses, ***, **, and * are significant at the level of 1%, 5%, and 10% respectively.

and SHD_DUM are significantly positive at a 5% level in the dimension of equity balance. In the dimension of top management governance, D_NONSOE and D_DUM are significantly positive at a 1% level. Top management governance is more significant in promoting enterprise innovation than equity checks and balances. The results indicate that in the context of SOEs' mixed ownership reform, appointing directors to participate in the corporate governance of SOEs has a more significant effect on the innovation level of SOEs than non-state-owned shareholders holding the shares of SOEs. Hypothesis 1 in this paper is verified. Given the growth of SOEs' mixed ownership reform, non-state-owned shareholders have been deeply involved in SOEs' governance, thus easing the principal-agent problem of SOEs, strengthening the supervision and incentives for managers, and effectively improving the innovation level of SOEs.

In addition, from the regression results of control variables, listed years and size of SOEs significantly impact enterprise innovation. This means that the size of an enterprise promotes its R&D and innovation activities of an enterprise, and the larger the size of an enterprise, the more resources it can invest in R&D and innovation activities. Moreover, leverage has a significantly negative impact on R&D and innovation because innovation activities need a large amount of long-term investment in enterprises, and the financial status of enterprises has a significant impact on enterprise innovation. Since innovation activities are characterised by high risk, high uncertainty and long investment cycles, enterprises with larger scales and more abundant capital will have higher innovation output. The results in Table 11.4 are generally consistent with the existing research findings.

Robustness Test

To enhance the robustness of the research, the robustness test of the benchmark regression model was carried out. First, according to Jiang (2016)and Feng, Zhang, and Duan (2021), the dependent variable for measuring the innovation output of enterprises was replaced by the number of invention patents applied by enterprises. The regression results are shown in Columns (1)–(4) of Table 11.5, and the results remain robust. Second, because some SOEs did not apply for patents during the sample period, this paper eliminated the sample with the number of patents being 0. The results are shown in Columns (4)–(8) of Table 11.5. The coefficients of the independent variables are significant at 10%, 5%, and 1%, respectively. The empirical results of this paper remain robust. Third, the crossed influence of non-state-owned shareholders' shareholding and top management appointment is considered regarding the independent variables. Samples were divided into four groups according to whether the shareholding ratio of the top ten non-state-owned shareholders (SHD_NONSOE) was greater than 5% and whether the non-state-owned shareholders appointed directors in SOEs (D_DUM). The dummy variable TREAT was constructed (Cai et al., 2018; Ma et al., 2021). If the sum of non-state-owned shareholders' shares of the top ten shareholders is less than 5% but non-state-owned shareholders appoint directors, it is assigned a value of 1; if the sum of non-state-owned shareholders' shares of the top ten shareholders is more than 5% but non-state-owned shareholders do not appoint directors, it is assigned a value of 0.

The regression results are shown in Column (9) of Table 11.5. The conclusions remain robust.

Table 11.5 Robustness test

	Replacing the dependent variable				OLS regression: Excluding the samples with no patent applications				Replacing the independent variable
	(1)	(2)	(3)	(4)	(5)	(6)	(7)	(8)	(9)
	LnInv	LnInv	LnInv	LnInv	Lnpatent	Lnpatent	Lnpatent	Lnpatent	Lnpatent
SHD_NONSOE	0.451**				0.653***				
	(2.081)				(2.758)				
SHD_DUM		0.1033**				0.089*			
		(2.125)				(1.821)			
D_NONSOE			0.8774***				0.457*		
			(3.875)				(1.938)		
D_DUM				0.1254***				0.107**	
				(2.846)				(2.113)	
TREAT									0.103**
									(2.102)
Size	0.532***	0.534***	0.528***	0.531***	0.518***	0.518***	0.518***	0.519***	0.565***
	(17.509)	(17.572)	(17.412)	(17.467)	(30.126)	(30.091)	(30.092)	(30.187)	(16.675)
Age	0.323***	0.314***	0.353***	0.335***	0.002	−0.004	0.010	0.010	0.686***
	(2.808)	(2.728)	(3.092)	(2.893)	(0.004)	(−0.096)	(0.205)	(0.212)	(5.354)
Lev	−0.166	−0.179	−0.174	−0.179	−0.663***	−0.674***	−0.685***	−0.693***	−0.168
	(−1.288)	(−1.388)	(−1.357)	(−1.407)	(−5.192)	(−5.275)	(−5.375)	(−5.421)	(−1.178)
ROA	0.164	0.153	0.133	0.155	1.175**	1.173**	1.122**	1.112**	0.097
	(0.529)	(0.492)	(0.434)	(0.501)	(2.462)	(2.457)	(2.346)	(2.323)	(0.289)
Growth	0.0305	0.0323	0.0331	0.0336	0.023	0.024	0.029	0.029	0.036
	(1.008)	(1.061)	(1.097)	(1.107)	(0.380)	(0.411)	(0.485)	(0.486)	(1.075)
Dual	−0.061	−0.063	−0.064	−0.063	−0.057	−0.053	−0.056	−0.053	−0.039
	(−1.303)	(−1.338)	(−1.361)	(−1.345)	(−0.849)	(−0.788)	(−0.828)	(−0.791)	(−0.646)

(Continued)

Table 11.5 (Continued)

	Replacing the dependent variable				OLS regression: Excluding the samples with no patent applications				Replacing the independent variable
	(1)	(2)	(3)	(4)	(5)	(6)	(7)	(8)	(9)
	LnInv	LnInv	LnInv	LnInv	Lnpatent	Lnpatent	Lnpatent	Lnpatent	Lnpatent
industry	control	control	control	control	control	control	control	control	control
year	control	control	control	control	control	control	control	control	control
_cons	−10.951***	−10.962***	−10.973***	−10.969***	−7.659***	−7.614***	−7.640***	−7.676***	−12.051***
	(−14.546)	(−14.553)	(−14.594)	(−14.582)	(−20.6156)	(−20.5173)	(−20.5563)	(−20.5852)	(−14.355)
N	7212	7212	7212	7212	5058	5058	5058	5058	7212
adj. R^2	0.167	0.167	0.168	0.168	0.174	0.173	0.173	0.173	0.181

Note: t-statistics in parentheses, ***, **, and * are significant at the level of 1%, 5%, and 10%, respectively.

Heterogeneous Analysis

Empirical Results: Monopolistic Versus Competitive SOEs

This study employed the Herfindahl-Hirschman Index (HHI) to measure industrial competition (Yang and Yin, 2015). The closer the value equals 1, the lower the industry competition degree is, and the lower the value, the industry is closer to the monopoly industry. In this paper, sample enterprises are divided into monopolistic and competitive industry groups for grouping regression according to the median value of HHI, and the results are shown in Table 11.6. In the competitive industry group, the coefficients of the independent variables are significantly positive, while in the monopolistic industry group, the coefficients of the independent variables are insignificant. The results show that non-state-owned shareholder governance significantly improves the innovation level of competitive SOEs from two dimensions: equity structure and top management governance. Still, non-state-owned shareholder governance has no significant impact on the innovation of monopolistic SOEs. The possible reason is that monopolistic SOEs are more controlled by the government, and it is difficult for non-state-owned capital to appoint directors to govern SOEs effectively and to influence the innovation behaviour of SOEs in monopolistic industries. Thus, hypothesis 2 is verified.

Table 11.6 The empirical analysis of monopolistic versus competitive SOEs

	Lnpatent							
	Monopolistic SOEs				Competitive SOEs			
	(1)	(2)	(3)	(4)	(1)	(2)	(3)	(4)
SHD_NONSOE	0.479				0.937***			
	(1.248)				(2.600)			
SHD_DUM		0.026				0.149**		
		(0.408)				(2.409)		
D_NONSOE			0.990***				1.011***	
			(2.601)				(2.7533)	
D_DUM				0.104				0.162**
				(1.423)				(2.239)
Control	yes	yes	yes	yes	yes	yes	yes	yes
_cons	−7.463***	−7.465***	−7.557***	−7.477***	−12.454***	−12.276***	−12.149***	−12.134***
	(−5.527)	(−5.527)	(−5.601)	(−5.538)	(−8.157)	(−8.047)	(−7.963)	(−7.947)
N	3753	3753	3753	3753	3460	3460	3460	3460
adj. R^2	0.106	0.106	0.106	0.106	0.141	0.141	0.141	0.141

Note: *t*-statistics in parentheses, ***, **, and * are significant at the level of 1%, 5%, and 10% respectively.

Empirical Results: Regional Marketisation Development

In this paper, the sample enterprises are divided by the marketisation development. According to the marketisation index of the province where the sample enterprises are located, the samples are divided into two groups according to the median value: the groups with higher-level marketisation development and lower-level marketisation development.

Table 11.7 reports the innovation impact of the mixed-ownership reform on enterprises in different marketisation regions. The results show that the coefficients of the independent variables are significantly positive at the 1% level in the sample groups of SOEs in regions with higher marketisation development. In areas with high-level marketisation development, non-state-owned shareholder governance under mixed-ownership reform significantly promotes enterprise innovation. However, in the sample groups of regions with lower-level marketisation development, the coefficients of the independent variables in Columns (1) and (2) are insignificant. In contrast, the coefficients of the independent variables in Columns (3) and (4) are significantly positive at 1% and 5% levels, respectively. This means that in areas with low marketisation, equity checks and balances are difficult to govern SOEs effectively because non-state-owned shareholders hold SOEs' shares, and the promotion of SOEs' innovation behaviour is not obvious. Non-state-owned shareholders' appointment of directors to participate in the

Table 11.7 The empirical analysis of regional marketisation development

	Lnpatent							
	Higher marketisation development				Lower marketisation development			
	(1)	(2)	(3)	(4)	(1)	(2)	(3)	(4)
SHD_NONSOE	0.899***				−0.016			
	(3.093)				(−0.032)			
SHD_DUM		0.109**				0.020		
		(2.170)				(0.234)		
D_NONSOE			0.999***				1.704***	
			(3.490)				(2.879)	
D_DUM				0.149***				0.192*
				(2.586)				(1.848)
Control	Yes	Yes	Yes	Yes	Yes	Yes	Yes	Yes
_cons	12.74***	12.64**	12.66***	12.61***	9.09***	9.06***	8.87***	8.99***
	(−10.72)	(−10.62)	(−10.64)	(−10.59)	(−4.915)	(−4.892)	(−4.814)	(−4.870)
N	5463	5463	5463	5463	1750	1750	1750	1750
adj. R^2	0.186	0.186	0.186	0.186	0.127	0.127	0.127	0.127

Note: *t*-statistics in parentheses, ***, **,and * are significant at the level of 1%, 5%, and 10%, respectively.

decision-making of SOEs has a more significant impact on enterprise innovation. This result basically verified hypothesis 3.

Empirical Results: Technological Versus Non-Technological SOEs

According to Luo and Qin (2019) and the industry classification guidelines for listed enterprises in the CSRC's 2012 edition, the pharmaceutical manufacturing industry (C27), general equipment manufacturing industry (C34), special equipment manufacturing industry (C35), electrical machinery manufacturing industry (C38), automobile manufacturing industry (C36), railway, shipbuilding, aerospace and other transportation equipment manufacturing industry (C37), computers, communications and other electronic equipment manufacturing (C39), instrument and meter manufacturing (C40), information transmission, software and information technology services (I) are defined as a high-tech industry. Therefore, the sample enterprises belonging to the above industries are defined as technological enterprises.

As shown in Table 11.8, for technological and non-technological SOEs, the coefficients of the independent variables in columns (1) and (2) of the two groups are insignificant, but the coefficients of the independent variables in columns (3) and (4) of the non-technological group are significantly positive at 1% level. The results show that after the mixed ownership reform of SOEs, the appointment of directors by non-state-owned shareholders to participate in

Table 11.8 The empirical analysis of technological versus non-technological SOEs

	Lnpatent							
	Technological SOEs				Non-technological SOEs			
	(1)	(2)	(3)	(4)	(1)	(2)	(3)	(4)
SHD_NONSOE	0.656 (1.581)				0.477 (1.644)			
SHD_DUM		0.081 (1.110)				0.063 (1.238)		
D_NONSOE			0.646 (1.463)				1.162*** (3.832)	
D_DUM				0.092 (1.004)				0.159*** (2.757)
Control	Yes	Yes	Yes	Yes	Yes	Yes	Yes	Yes
_cons	13.92*** (−10.05)	13.93*** (−9.92)	14.01*** (−10.07)	14.03*** (−10.08)	10.69*** (−10.16)	10.67*** (−10.13)	10.65*** (−10.14)	10.58*** (−10.05)
N	1755	1755	1755	1755	5458	5458	5458	5458
adj. R^2	0.323	0.323	0.323	0.323	0.177	0.177	0.177	0.177

Note: *t*-statistics in parentheses, ***, **, and * are significant at the level of 1%, 5%, and 10% respectively.

the high-level governance of SOEs can significantly improve the innovation level of non-technological SOEs. In summary, hypothesis 4 in this paper has been verified. When the non-state-owned capital enters SOEs, the non-state-owned shareholders will increase the innovation efforts to improve the profits of the enterprises. This has a significant impact on the innovation strategy of enterprises, and thus improves the innovation level of the non-technological SOEs.

Conclusion

Innovation is an important way to enhance enterprise competitiveness and promote sustainable development. As an important pillar of China's economy, SOEs are the key to shifting China from factor-driven development to innovation-driven development and achieving high-quality development. Understanding the impact of mixed ownership reform on SOEs' innovation is significant for further growth reform and developing innovation-driven strategy. Based on the background of mixed ownership reform of SOEs, this paper uses the A-share listed SOEs from 2008 to 2019 as research samples to construct a panel data fixed effect model and explore the impact of equity checks and balances and top management governance on the innovation of SOEs. On this basis, this paper introduces SOE and environmental heterogeneity to study the divergent effect on the relationship between non-state-owned shareholder governance and SOEs' innovation. The results show that non-state-owned shareholders' equity checks and balances and top management governance significantly promote SOEs' innovation. However, compared with non-state-owned shareholders' shareholding, non-state-owned shareholders' appointment of directors to participate in the internal decision-making of SOEs plays a more significant role in promoting the innovation of SOEs. This research confirms that the mixed ownership reform can promote the innovation level of SOEs by improving the internal governance of SOEs. According to the group analysis of enterprise heterogeneity and environmental heterogeneity, the mixed ownership reform has a more significant effect on the innovation promotion of competitive SOEs, non-technological SOEs, and SOEs in areas with higher-level marketisation development.

The empirical results of this study show that the focus of mixed ownership reform of SOEs lies in the improvement of the governance of SOEs by non-state-owned shareholders, and the reform of SOEs can only focus on the mix with reform. The main advantage of SOEs' mixed ownership reform lies in introducing non-state-owned shareholders to participate in SOEs' governance. Therefore, we should continue to deepen the reform and relax the entry threshold of the non-state-owned capital to alleviate the widespread principal-agent problem of SOEs. To further deepen SOEs' reform, emphasis should be placed on ensuring the effective participation of non-state-owned shareholders in SOEs' internal governance. The governance decisions within SOEs should be optimised, a modern governance system for SOEs should be established and improved, and their level of governance should be raised. The results of the grouping test show that there is a significant difference in terms of the impact of mixed ownership reform on SOEs' innovation in different industries and different regions. Therefore, the mixed ownership reform of SOEs should be promoted and implemented based on the classification of SOEs, better to play the role of the mixed ownership reform. Specifically, the mixed ownership reform should be carried out based on the operating conditions, industry classification and regional environmental differences of SOEs. At the same time, the government should strive to improve the market and institutional environment, provide healthy external conditions for the innovation and development of SOEs, and add strong impetus to the high-quality development of China's economy.

The research findings in this paper shed great light on the mega entrepreneurship of SOEs and non-state-owned shareholders in China's innovation landscape. This is particularly true in the context of a new development paradigm in China. First, it is of great importance to create and develop original key technologies with collaborative and open innovation as the focus, and enhance the innovation capacity of China. Therefore, it is necessary to break the boundaries of enterprises and allow SOEs, privately owned enterprises (POEs), and foreign enterprises of all types of ownership to participate in innovation through equity investment and cooperative funds, among others. In so doing, it is conducive to gathering advantageous innovation resources, and creating a new innovation ecological pattern in which SOEs and POEs coordinate their growth and development. Second, SOEs can participate in non-state-owned shareholders by mixed ownership reform, which can be seen as a joint entrepreneurship between SOEs and POEs. This is particularly important during the critical time such as the epidemic. For example, SOEs can help POEs solve capital needs and other difficulties and build a healthy supply chain ecosystem.

It is necessary to combine the perspectives of top management governance and equity balance to study the influence of mixed ownership reform on innovation for future research. In this way, it may provide a full picture regarding the innovation implications of the mixed ownership reform. Meanwhile, a comprehensive analysis of the influence of the mixed ownership reform on Chinese entrepreneurship, particularly the promotion of entrepreneurship in POEs, is of great value to examine the real entrepreneurship implications of the mixed ownership reform.

Acknowledgement

This research was funded by the National Social Science Fund of China (Grant number: 2020CJY032).

References

Bai, C N, Lu, J Y and Tao, Z G 2006, 'An empirical study on the effects of ownership reform in China', *Economic Research Journal*, vol. 41, no. 8, pp. 4–13+69, DOI: CNKI:SUN:JJYJ.0.2006-08-001

Boubakri, N, Cosset, J C and Saffar, W 2013, 'The role of state and foreign owners in corporate risk-taking: Evidence from privatization', *Journal of Financial Economics*, vol. 108, no. 3, pp. 641–658. DOI: 10.1016/j.jfineco.2012.12.007

Cai, G L, Liu, J H and Ma, X X 2018, 'Non-state shareholders' governance and executive compensation incentives of SOEs', *Management World*, vol. 34, no. 5, pp. 137–149. DOI: 10.3969/j.issn.1002-5502.2018.05.011

Chen, M Y and Wei, M H 2013, 'The excessive authority of related shareholders', *China Industrial Economics*, vol. 2013, no. 10, pp. 108–120. DOI: 10.19581/j.cnki.ciejournal.2013.10.009

Chen, X X and Liu, X 2013, 'Decentralization reform, salary regulation and corporate executive corruption', *Management World*, vol. 2013, no. 3, pp. 119–132+134–136, DOI: 10.19744/j.cnki.11-1235/f.2013.03.011

Chen, Z M, Xia, X P and Yu, M G 2008, 'Government intervention, pyramid structure and investment of local state-owned listed companies', *Management World*, vol. 2008, no. 9, pp. 37–47. DOI: 10.19744/j.cnki.11-1235/f.2008.09.004

Feng, L, Zhang, L R and Duan, Z M 2021, 'The governance of non-state-owned shareholders and enterprise innovation under the reform of mixed-ownership', *China Soft Science*, vol. 2021, no. 3, pp. 124–140.

Hu, Y F, Song, M and Zhang, J X 2005, 'Competition, ownership, corporate governance: Their importance and interactions', *Economic Research Journal*, vol. 2005, no. 9, pp. 44–57.

Huang, S J 2014, 'On the mixed ownership reform of Chinese state owned enterprises', *Economic Management Journal*, vol. 36, no. 7, pp. 1–10. DOI: 10.19616/j.cnki.bmj.2014.07.003

Jiang, X Y 2016, 'Government decentralisation and innovation of state-owned enterprises: A study based on the pyramid structure of local state-owned enterprises', *Management World*, vol. 2016, no. 9, pp. 120–135. DOI: 10.19744/j.cnki.11-1235/f.2016.09.010

Jiao, H, Koo, C K and Cui, Y 2015, 'Legal environment, government effectiveness and firms' innovation in China: Examining the moderating influence of government ownership', *Technological Forecasting & Social Change*, vol. 96, no. 2015, pp. 15–24. DOI: 10.1016/j.techfore.2015.01.008

Kong, D M, Dai, Y H and Li, Y 2014, 'The policy shock, the market environment and the productivity of state-owned enterprises: The status quo, the trend, and the development', *Management World*, vol. 2014, no. 8, pp. 4–17. DOI: 10.19744/j.cnki.11-1235/f.2014.08.002

Li, W G and Yu, M G 2015, 'Ownership structure and enterprise innovation of privatized enterprises', *Management World*, vol. 2015, no. 4, pp. 112–125. DOI: 10.19744/j.cnki.11-1235/f.2015.04.011

Lin, Y F and Liu, P L 2001, 'Indigenous capacity and state-owned enterprises reform', *Economic Research Journal*, vol. 2001, no. 9, pp. 60–70, DOI: CNKI:SUN:JJYJ.0.2001-09-007

Liu, X and Li, X R 2012, 'Pyramid structure, tax burden and enterprise value: Evidence based on local state-owned enterprises', *Management World*, vol. 2012, no. 8, pp. 91–105. DOI: 10.19744/j.cnki.11-1235/f.2012.08.009

Liu, Y G, Zheng, Q and Cai, G L 2016, 'Do non-state-owned shareholders improve the internal control quality in SOEs?', *Accounting Research*, vol. 2016, no. 11, pp. 61–68. DOI: +96, DOI: 10.3969/j.issn.1003-2886.2016.11.009

Liu, Y, Zhang, X C and Lan, X Y 2016, 'The influence of the mixed ownership reform on total factor productivity of the state owned enterprise: An empirical study based on PSM-DID method', *Public Finance Research*, vol. 2016, no. 10, pp. 63–75. DOI: 10.19477/j.cnki.11-1077/f.2016.10.007

Luo, H and Qin, J D 2019, 'Research on the influence of state-owned equity participation on family firms' innovation investment', *China Industrial Economics*, vol. 2019, no. 7, pp. 174–192. DOI: 10.19581/j.cnki.ciejournal.2019.07.010

Ma, X X, Tang, T J and Zheng, G J 2021, 'Can mixed ownership reform resolve the overcapacity of SOEs?', *Economic Management Journal*, vol. 43, no. 2, pp. 38–55. DOI: 10.19616/j.cnki.bmj.2021.2.003

Shleifer, A and Vishny, R W 1994, 'Politicians and firms', *Quarterly Journal of Economics*, vol. 109, no. 4, pp. 995–1025. DOI: 10.2307/2118354

Tang, Q Q and Wu, C 2015, 'Banking Structure and financing constraint of R&D investment', *Journal of Financial Research*, vol. 2015, no. 7, pp. 116–134.

Tang, T J, Wu, J Y, Ma, X X and Song, X Z 2020, 'Non-state shareholders' governance and audit fees—Empirical evidence from mixed ownership reform of SOEs', *Auditing Research*, vol. 2020, no. 1, pp. 68–77. DOI: CNKI:SUN:SJYZ.0.2020-01-010

Wang, J and Lan, M 2019, 'Reform of mixed ownership and innovation efficiency of state-owned enterprises—An SNA-based analysis', *Statistical Research*, vol. 36, no. 11, pp. 90–103. DOI: 10.19343/j.cnki.11-1302/c.2019.11.008

Wei, M H, Cai, G L and Liu, J H 2017, 'Research on classified governance of state-owned listed companies in China', *Journal of Sun Yat-Sen University (Social Science Edition)*, vol. 57, no. 4, pp. 175–192. DOI: 10.13471/j.cnki.jsysusse.2017.04.019

Wu, Y B 2014, 'Innovative capacities of different ownership enterprises', *Industrial Economics Research*, vol. 2014, no. 2, pp. 53–64. DOI: 10.13269/j.cnki.ier.2014.02.006

Wu, Y B 2012, 'The dual efficiency losses in Chinese state-owned enterprises', *Economic Research Journal*, vol. 47, no. 3, pp. 15–27, DOI: CNKI:SUN:JJYJ.0.2012-03-004

Xia, L J and Chen, X Y 2007, 'Marketization, SOE reform strategy, and endogenously determined corporate governance structure', *Economic Research Journal*, vol. 2007, no. 7, pp. 82–95+136, DOI: CNKI:SUN:JJYJ.0.2007-07-010

Yang, X Q and Yin, X Q 2018, 'How does the mixed ownership reform of state-owned enterprises affect the cash holdings?', *Management World*, vol. 34, no. 11, pp. 93–107. DOI: 10.19744/j.cnki.11-1235/f.2018.0008

Yang, X Q and Yin, X Q 2015, 'Industry concentration, competitive position of enterprises and competitive effect of cash holdings', *Economic Science*, vol. 2015, no. 6, pp. 78–91. DOI: 10.19523/j.jjkx.2015.06.008

Yuan, J G, Hou, Q C and Chen, C 2015, 'Curse effect of enterprise political resources: An investigation based on political connection and enterprise technological innovation', *Management World*, vol. 2015, no. 1, pp. 139–155. DOI: 10.19744/j.cnki.11-1235/f.2015.01.014

Zhang, W Y 1996, 'Problems in the capital structure of state-owned enterprises in China', *Journal of Financial Research*, vol. 1996, no. 10, pp. 27–29, DOI: CNKI:SUN:JRYJ.0.1996-10-005

Zhao F and Liu Y J 2016, 'A policy analysis of the impact of mixed ownership reform on the innovation efficiency of state-owned enterprises—An empirical study based on difference-in-difference method', *Journal of Shandong University (Philosophy and Social Sciences)*, vol. 2016, no. 6, pp. 67–73, DOI: CNKI:SUN:SDZS.0.2016-06-009

Zhong, Y J, Zhang, C Y and Chen, D Q 2016, 'Privatization and innovation efficiency: Promotion or suppression?', *Journal of Finance and Economics*, vol. 42, no. 7, pp. 4–15. DOI: 10.16538/j.cnki.jfe.2016.07.001

Zhou, L A 2007, 'Governing China's local officials: An analysis of promotion tournament model', *Economic Research Journal*, vol. 2007, no. 7, pp. 36–50, DOI: CNKI:SUN:JJYJ.0.2007-07-006

Zhu, L, Chen, X and Wang, C Y 2019, 'Research on the influence of mixed reform of state-owned enterprises on corporate innovation', *Economic Management Journal*, vol. 41, no. 11, pp. 72–91. DOI: 10.19616/j.cnki.bmj.2019.11.005

12 Strategic Development Opportunities through BRICS Innovation Cooperation Action Plans

Innovative Exchange as a Path to Integration

Arthur Chagas dos Santos

Introduction

When conceptualising the BRICS, it is imperative to bring forth the Global South concept. Although the term in question varies among scholars, it is possible to affirm that the Global South consists of 'an attempt by emerging powers to channel their interests through the collective vocalisation of demands for changes in the international system in the post-Cold War period' (Rinaldi, 2021:81). In this sense, the BRICS comprises countries of the Global South, and its integration and mutual cooperation evidence the 'rise of the rest' (Zakaria, 2011). The 'rise of the rest' is a term that:

> [...] implied that American/Western predominance was giving way to a more diverse world in which certain traditionally less-powerful countries, those countries lucky enough to have substantial and well-managed natural or human resources and/or had reached a relatively high stage of technological advancement, were emerging as worthy competitors—economically if not militarily—to the USA and the European 'great powers.'
>
> (Braveboy-Wagner, 2016:1)

Therefore, this increasing multipolarity of the world balance of power is the background for the emergence of the BRICS as a group and its main *raison d'être* can also be understood as an effort towards consolidating a multipolar world. However, in pursuit of consolidating this multipolar world, the BRICS member nations face considerable obstacles in achieving meaningful integration due to disparities in their economic, social and geographic dimensions (Radulescu *et al.*, 2014). Notably, this integration challenge is evident without a formalised international organisation for the BRICS, complete with a dedicated headquarters and a definitive statute. Consequently, the group is compelled to seek alternative paths for integration that can mutually benefit all its constituent members. In this context, Science, Technology and Innovation (STI) emerges as a compelling and undeniable solution to foster cooperation among the BRICS nations.

The development of STI by the BRICS members is also crucial because it can be used as a 'soft balancing' instrument, which is the 'use (of) nonmilitary tools to delay, frustrate, and undermine aggressive unilateral U.S. military policies' (Pape, 2005:10). Even though this concept is applied towards the United States in its original meaning, in this context it is possible to understand the concept as referring to the Global North as a whole. The main hypothesis is that BRICS are consolidating their STI sectors through integration among members to soft-balance global power in the 21st century.

In this sense, the present study examines the trajectory of the STI sector's significance within the BRICS nations. Focused on unravelling the motivations behind initiating the Innovation Cooperation Action Plans, this research seeks to understand the forces that propelled such strategic collaboration. Delving into the historical context and evolution of the STI sector's importance for BRICS countries, the study seeks to shed light on the implications of the first Action Plan and its potential ramifications for the group's future trajectory.

Methodology

The methodology in the first and second sections consists of a documental analysis of the joint declarations resulting from presidential summits and ministerial meetings held within the BRICS. This aims to evaluate the development of STI as an increasingly present and significant agenda for the group and analyse the Innovation and Cooperation Action Plans.

In the third part, an analysis will be made based on factual evidence on STI from each member country of the group supported by Process Tracing as a methodology. Beach and Pedersen (2013) indicate that there are three main variants in the use of Process Tracing as a methodology. The first two are oriented towards 'Theory Testing' and 'Theory Building' and, therefore, converge in the fact that they are 'Theory-centric'. That is, they seek to use existing theories or to form new theories that can be used in other cases. The third and final way of Process-Tracing is the 'Explaining-outcome', which aims to identify sufficient mechanisms that explain the outcomes of a specific case; therefore, it is a 'Case-centric' approach in which the purpose is to find sufficient mechanisms that explain a specific case.

The Case-centric approach will be used in the present work due to the specificity of the BRICS group, which will be detailed in the following sections. With this, it should be noted that the Explaining-outcome process tracing can be worked deductively and inductively. The deductive approach is used when using existing mechanisms and theories to provide sufficient explanations for the case.

The inductive approach is used when 'working backwards from the outcome by sifting through the evidence in an attempt to uncover a plausible sufficient causal mechanism that produced the outcome' (Beach and Pedersen, 2013:20). Therefore, using the inductive approach for the proposed research is considered more appropriate.

To reach the objective of finding sufficient causal mechanisms that explain the reasons for the BRICS to launch its Innovation Cooperation Action Plans, the historical development of the STI sector will be traced, and the documental analysis of both plans will be done. Finally, to complement the documental analysis, each group member's external and domestic realities regarding competitiveness and innovation ranking indexes will be taken into analytical account.

STI Development within the BRICS

This section does not pretend to be an extensive list of all the actions made by the BRICS. However, its objective is to provide a panoramic view of the sector's growing importance for the group throughout the first years of summits until the first proposed Innovation Cooperation Action Plan.

Hence, the intention of cooperation in STI among the BRICS countries, although present since the first summit held in 2009 in the Russian city of Yekaterinburg, did not prove to be a promising objective. The 11th point of the Yekaterinburg Declaration states that the group 'reaffirmed to advance cooperation among our countries in science and education with the aim, inter alia, to engage in fundamental research and development of advanced technologies' (BRICS, 2009). In this sense, the cooperation intention was vague and without a well-defined action plan.

With this, it is possible to identify the first solid effort from the Sanya Declaration in 2011, when five new proposals were included in the group's Action Plan. The fourth point of the aforementioned Action Plan indicates that it is among its objectives: 'Hold a meeting of Senior Officials for discussing ways of promoting scientific, technological and innovation cooperation in BRICS format, including by establishing a working group on cooperation in the pharmaceutical industry' (BRICS, 2011).

Thus, members who occupy significant positions in the ministries of their respective countries met in September of that same year, and the success of this meeting proved to be a key point which accelerated cooperation in STI among the BRICS member countries. This fact can be evidenced by the group's summit in New Delhi, held the following year, according to point 43:

> We have taken note of the meeting of S&T Senior Officials in Dalian, China in September 2011, particularly the growing capacities for research and development and innovation in our countries. We encourage this process in priority areas of food, pharma, health and energy as well as basic

research in the emerging inter-disciplinary fields of nanotechnology, biotechnology, advanced materials science, etc. We encourage the flow of knowledge amongst our research institutions through joint projects, workshops and exchanges of young scientists.

(BRICS, 2012)

This marked the beginning of state integration among members within the scope of STI, as meetings began to cover other sectors of the state apparatus in addition to presidential meetings and, in this way, promote joint action debates for joint development in the area. Therefore, for the first time, the areas involving the scope of STI in which the group shows intention of cooperation are specifically mentioned. Consequently, the second meeting of senior officials from their respective ministries was included in the seventh point of the action plan that arose from the Delhi Declaration.

The fifth BRICS summit and the eThekwini Declaration proved key for the STI sector. This is because it marked the entry of the role of entrepreneurship in innovation at the 19th declaration that resulted from the summit. In it, the group admits the fundamental role of small- and medium-sized enterprises (SMEs) in the country's economy and, therefore, cooperation in this area would be indispensable since entrepreneurship has a direct relationship with Innovation. In addition, the inclusion of the meeting not only of senior officials of the ministries of science and technology but also the meeting between the ministers of each country from BRICS proved to be an unprecedented move from the group in the sector (BRICS, 2013).

The first ministerial meeting, which took place on 10 February 2014, in Cape Town, was extremely successful, given that the first statement among the 15 points that the ministers agreed upon shows that the purpose of the meeting was 'to discuss and coordinate positions of mutual interest and identify future directions of institutionalising cooperation in science, technology and innovation within the framework of BRICS' (BRICS, 2014:1). In this sense, the importance of institutionalising STI is amplified because the BRICS itself does not yet constitute an institutionalised international organisation.

Therefore, STI demonstrates broad mutual support and is a solid path towards integrating its member countries. It should be noted that the broad support for innovation is a direct result of the shared vision that STI are means of achieving the public good sustainably while supporting equitable growth. The first ministerial meeting also allowed for the creation of a Memorandum of Understanding (MoU) on cooperation in STI between the member countries, which states that:

To support this common vision, we agreed to enter into a BRICS Memorandum of Understanding on Cooperation in Science, Technology and Innovation which shall serve as the strategic intergovernmental framework: (i) to strengthen cooperation in science, technology and innovation;

(ii) to address common global and regional socio-economic challenges utilising shared experiences and complementarities; (iii) to co-generate new knowledge and innovative products, services and processes utilising appropriate funding and investment instruments; (iv) to promote, where appropriate, joint BRICS partnerships with other strategic actors in the developing world.

(BRICS, 2014:2)

The MoU covered 19 areas of cooperation and defined that the ministerial meeting between senior officials and ministers would occur annually. In addition, the MoU demonstrated a joint commitment to invest in the sector. The MoU´s validity was intended to last 5 years but would be automatically renewed unless a member is against its renewal for any reason.

The summit in the Russian city of Ufa in 2015 marks an extremely important year for the advancement of cooperation in the field of STI. Evidence of this fact is point 62 of the Ufa Declaration, which says that:

The development of a BRICS Research and Innovation Initiative, which shall cover actions including: -cooperation within large research infrastructures, including possible consideration of Mega science projects, to achieve scientific and technological breakthroughs in the key areas of cooperation outlined in the Memorandum; - coordination of the existing large-scale national programs of the BRICS countries; - development and implementation of a BRICS Framework Programme for funding multilateral joint research projects for research, technology commercialisation and innovation involving science and technology ministries and centres, development institutes and national, as well as, if necessary, regional foundations that sponsor research projects; - establishment of a joint Research and Innovation Platform. **These activities will be carried out as per the BRICS STI Work Plan to be endorsed at the next BRICS Meeting of Ministers for Science, Technology and Innovation.**

(BRICS, 2015, highlights are ours)

With this, a much higher commitment is perceived about past summits. This is because, by dedicating well-defined Work Plans with an expiry date, it assumes responsibility for the members to reach the expected result at the end of their term.

The last interesting point for the present research is creating the Science, Technology and Innovation Entrepreneurship Partnership Work Group (STIEP WG), which emerged from the fourth ministerial meeting in 2016, held in Jaipur. Science Technology Innovation and Entrepreneurship Partnership (STIEP) is dedicated to studying possible areas of activity for the sector and proposing development actions for the STI ministers of each country. This group will

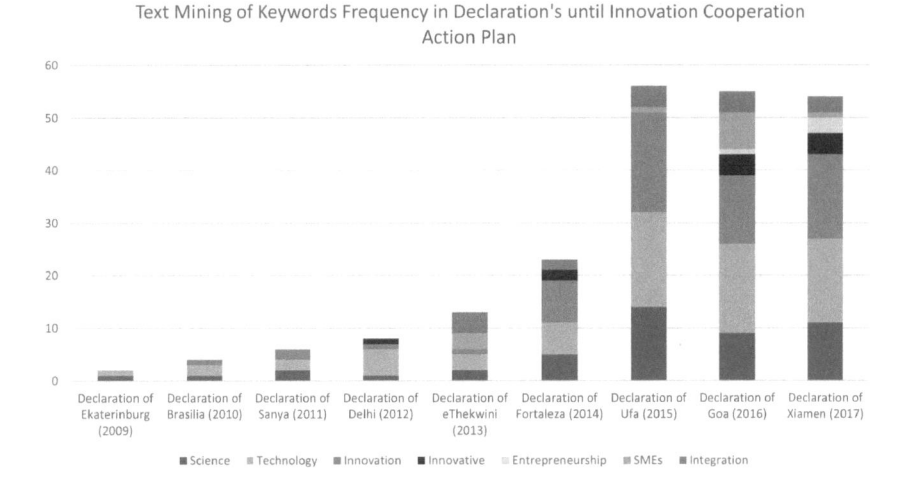

Figure 12.1 Text mining of keyword frequency in presidential declarations until innovation cooperation action plan.

Source: Author's creation.

formulate the Innovation Cooperation Action Plans, which will be discussed in the next section.

Finally, the technique of data mining keyword frequency will be used to demonstrate the evident growth of the STI sector for BRICS integration over the years through data. It analysed each presidential summit, from the first meeting held in 2009 until 2017, when the Innovation Cooperation Action Plan was launched. The words chosen to evaluate its appearances were 'Science', 'Technology', 'Innovation', 'Innovative', 'Entrepreneurship', 'SMEs' and 'Integration' (see Table 12.1 and Figure 12.1).

The result of text mining keyword frequency showed a clear trend in the behaviour and interests of the BRICS, especially about the 2015 summit, in which a noticeable increase was observed relating to STI integration. Having exposed a brief history of the summit's growing interest in the sector, the next sector will address the Innovation Cooperation Action Plans.

Documental Analysis of the Cooperation in Innovation Cooperation Action Plans

The first Innovation Cooperation Action Plan (2017–2020) involved 14 statements, divided into 3 sections, including the Foreword (with 4 statements), Action Plan (with 8 statements) and Implementation (2 statements).

In the first section, the BRICS nations explicitly assert their belief in fostering cooperation in innovation as a pivotal means to achieve sustainable

Table 12.1 keyword frequency table.

	Science	Technology	Innovation	Innovative	Entrepreneurship	SMEs	Integration	TOTAL
Declaration of Ekaterinburg. – (BRICS, 2009)	1	1	0	0	0	0	0	2
Declaration of Brasilia – (BRICS, 2010)	1	2	1	0	0	0	0	4
Declaration of Sanya – (BRICS, 2011)	2	2	2	0	0	0	0	6
Declaration of Delhi – (BRICS, 2012)	1	5	1	1	0	0	0	8
Declaration of eThekwini – (BRICS, 2013)	2	3	1	0	0	3	4	13
Declaration of Fortaleza – (BRICS, 2014)	5	6	8	2	0	0	2	23
Declaration of Ufa – (BRICS, 2015)	14	18	19	0	0	1	4	56
Declaration of Goa – (BRICS, 2016)	9	17	13	4	1	7	4	55
Declaration of Xiamen – (BRICS, 2017a)	11	16	16	4	3	1	3	54

Source: Author's creation.

development within their respective territories and for the global economy's sustainable progress. In addition, within the same section, the document defines innovation as related to technological, methodological and creative progress in the scope of STI, but closely interconnected with entrepreneurship as a guiding thread and incentive for innovation. Finally, it is clarified that this document will be dealt with by the MoU cited in the Jaipur Declaration which was the subject of the fifth ministerial meeting of the BRICS.

The Action Plan, which comprises the second section, was written based on the understanding that there are new challenges for the development of member countries. As it could not be otherwise, the document intends to promote and strengthen the practice of exchanging information in the area. Hence, cooperation needs to involve private companies and those in the public domain together with universities. To achieve this, financing infrastructure and research programmes are fundamental for integrating the axes of private industry, public companies and universities. With this, the creation of technology parks is fundamental for this exchange of information, not only between the axes of society in the domestic scope of a country but also for the transfer of technology between the members of the BRICS.

The third and seventh statements of the second section deserve to be analysed in a little more detail. The third point states, 'Organising joint activities on identifying priorities for STI cooperation of BRICS countries based on foresight and monitoring of global STI development' (BRICS, 2017b:3). This implies a more assertive group position facing global geopolitical stimuli regarding STI. With that, this point demonstrates that the group does not intend to be far behind international organisations regarding this scope of STI. While the seventh statement of the second section reads:

> Acknowledging the importance of supporting STI investment and the need to establish inter-BRICS investment instruments, we support exploring the possibilities of driving BRICS cooperation on innovation and entrepreneurship through the National Development Banks, New Development Bank and other existing financing institutions.
>
> (BRICS, 2017b:3)

The point that draws the most attention is the use of the New Development Bank (NDB) to finance and promote STI actions since it is a financial institution belonging to the group, promoting research and development can be quite significant.

Finally, the third and final section covers the issue of the actual implementation of STI efforts. The STIEP working group will create science parks and incubators for small and medium-sized companies and create an intercultural talent bank to deal with vital issues for developing emerging countries.

The second Innovation Cooperation Action Plan (2021–2024) was proposed by STIEP and endorsed at the 9th Ministerial Meeting of STI. Among its key elements, this plan aims at sharing good practices among member countries and 'Networking among BRICS Innovation ecosystem (Incubator-to-incubator, startup-to-startup, innovator-to-innovator)' (STIEP, 2021:6). It is noticeable that the second plan possesses a much greater focus than the first on the support that is intended to be provided to startups among the member countries, and this objective will seek to be achieved through innovation competitions for young entrepreneurs, greater integration between incubators, entrepreneurs and investors from the group member countries.

The second action plan also defines a timeline with nine well-defined activities according to the year to be carried out. Among these activities, two are intended to be carried out annually, which are the 'BRICS Young Innovators Prize Competition' and the 'BRICS Startup Knowledge Hub/BRICS Innovation Launchpad (Online View)'. Although the other activities are not yet expected to be carried out annually, they represent a significant advance. Other activities include the 'MSME Consultation', 'BRICS Unicorn Roundtable', 'BRICS Startup Forum', 'BRICS Innovation Forum', 'BRICS Open Innovation Challenge', 'BRICS Technology Transfer Training Program' and 'BRICS Incubation Training and Network' (STIEP, 2021:5).

At the end of the second plan, the group attached the proposed Framework called 'BRICS Tech transfer', which intends 'To be a mechanism for dialogue and cooperation of the BRICS countries, which will promote the exchange of actions and good practices, by stimulating the transfer of technology aiming at increasing the competitiveness and innovation outputs of the BRICS countries' (STIEP, 2021:6). The structure of this mechanism will be managed by a Steering Committee with two representatives from each country nominated by BRICS officials present in the STIEP, with a rotation of 3 years for each mandate. Finally, it is interesting to analyse the four main objectives of this mechanism, including: 'Fostering Intellectual Property protection', 'Expanding opportunities for technology transfer', 'Capacity building' and 'Metrics'.

Before moving on to the next section, where an effort will be made to trace the causal mechanisms of the Innovation Cooperation Action Plan, it is necessary to define the plans and compare their ontological characteristics with previous efforts in Innovation. Firstly, both plans are more committed and act as a 'call to action'. Therefore, the study infers that if the BRICS countries deemed the need for a document that allows for greater action, it is due to the lack of a more concrete action plan in the STI area. Furthermore, the temporal space of action (2017–2020 and 2021–2024) implies a deadline for achieving goals, making such a document possess a clear answer as to whether each plan was a success or failure by the end of its validity. Last but not least, these action plans clearly show a tendency to be ever more specific on which aspect of STI will be

Strategic Development Opportunities Through BRICS 213

targeted; for example, instead of simply stating that an effort will be made, the Innovation Cooperation Action Plans explain how it will be done.

Identifying Causal Factors for Launching Cooperation in Innovation Cooperation Action Plans

For analytical purposes, the situation of the countries in 2016 will be exposed since the mentioned year precedes the proposal of the first Innovation Cooperation Action Plan. For this, indicators that rank the levels of Innovation and competitiveness will be considered, such as the Global Innovation Index (GII), produced by Cornell University, the World Intellectual Property Organization and the *Institut Européen d'Administration des Affaires* (INSEAD) Business School. The World Economic Forum produces the Global Competitiveness Report (GCR). In addition to the reports produced by the Organization for Economic Co-operation and Development (OECD) to evaluate the development of STI in each country.

Regarding the position of the BRICS member countries in the GII in 2016, starting with Brazil was in 69th position in the general ranking and 7th in the regional ranking, Russia in 43rd in the general ranking and 29th in the regional ranking, India in 66th in the ranking overall but at 1 in Central and South Asia, China at 25th in the world ranking and 7th in the regional ranking and finally, South Africa at 54 in the overall ranking and 2nd in the regional ranking (WIPO, INSEAD, CORNELL, 2016). To the GCR ranking in 2016, Brazil was at 75th, Russia at 45th, India at 55th, China at 28th and South Africa at 49th (WEF, 2015).

The previous indicators will help us understand how these countries found themselves in the STI sector from a global or external perspective. However, to identify the internal situation of the member countries, the individual internal reports of the member countries will be used from the OECD STI Outlook 2016 since this document proved to be complete and robust in identifying the strengths and weaknesses of the countries in the STI area.

Starting with the report from Brazil, it is necessary to understand that in 2016, Brazil sought significant internal efforts to improve rates of STI. This is evidence that Brazil introduced the National Strategy for STI to develop the country's competitiveness *vis-à-vis* the international system. Furthermore, the 'Innovation Law' was introduced in that same year, facilitating knowledge transfer and encouraging exchanges between universities and the private sector. Among the main internal weaknesses for the development of STIs identified by the report are the low level of international scientific cooperation, the low level of Research and Development investing firms and the lack of trained human capital (OECD, 2016e).

The report from Russia indicates that the country's patenting index is below the average of OECD member countries. In addition to that, although a large part of the population has higher education, it is an ageing population.

This, coupled with the fact that young Russians score below the OECD average, is a cause for concern, so the Russian government is demonstrating efforts to make scientific careers more attractive for these young people. Another weakness that Russia faces is the bureaucratic barriers getting in the way of international scientific cooperation (OECD, 2016d).

Regarding the Indian report, despite demonstrating increasing advances in STI, the country still has low levels of investors in research and development and the levels of co-authored publications at the international level. In addition, many entrepreneurs in the country are informal, which generates a loss of opportunities for innovation since informality creates barriers to business development. Finally, the report also demonstrates India's concern with sustainability, given its high degree of impact on development in the country (OECD, 2016c).

The Chinese report addresses that after decades of abrupt growth, a new phase begins in which the State needs to find a constant path of growth while being sustainable. Another challenge is that despite China having the largest population in the world in 2016, the percentage of the population with tertiary education is quite low. Finally, international co-invention and co-authorship rates were still considered low because universities have relatively few links with global cooperation networks (OECD, 2016b).

The case of South Africa is quite worrying regarding the percentage of the adult population with Higher Education, a relatively low base of Research and Development infrastructure and Internet Infrastructure. Despite this, South Africa has shown to seek significant efforts to develop innovation rates by attracting business (OECD, 2016a).

Conclusions

Having presented the members' domestic and external situation before the Innovation Cooperation Action Plans, it is possible to understand the reasons behind the push for cooperation in the sector. Especially because, apart from India, no other member was yet leading their regional ranking, the situation was quite alarming for these emerging countries in particular because to lead a direction towards a multipolar world, there needs to be a movement towards cooperation in STI to develop and improve the life quality of citizens from the within the BRICS as well as the rest of the emerging countries.

It is also possible to infer from the facts previously exposed on the BRICS members' situation in 2016 that there was a profound need to develop the STI sector through international cooperation and concrete actions to support it. Therefore, the Innovation Cooperation Action Plan directly reflects this demand. The matching agendas from each country were aligned with the goals of the Innovation Cooperation Action Plans themselves. It is safe to say that the sector has a solid path to consolidation within the BRICS framework, not only due to its historical development but also because studies such as Tahir and Burki (2023) are just now emerging and confirming the positive impact that recent innovation and entrepreneurship had in BRICS countries.

As was shown from the first Innovation Cooperation Action Plan, there was a clear message that STI integration between BRICS countries had to be 'on foresight and monitoring of global STI development'. This refers to the Global North and its leading innovation and technology industry. If the global structure needs to be reformed it has to be done through soft power as a legitimising factor, and in this case, the STI leadership is the path towards achieving its geopolitical goals. STI and its development permits not only the integration between each member's goal but also pushes the objectives of the Global South as a whole, and that is because innovation is a powerful 'soft power' mechanism that decreases dependency on the Global North.

Finally, the development of the STI sector within BRICS proves to be an agenda mutually beneficial to its members' individual goals as emerging countries. It can also be used as a geopolitical mechanism of 'soft balancing' the global power structure. Therefore, the Innovation Cooperation Action Plans embody the mutual commitment among BRICS countries to achieve their goals in the sector through south-south collaboration.

Recommendations and Future Research Directions

The innovation cooperation within the BRICS countries seems to be a mutual consensus of a clear direction towards development as evidenced through this paper. However, the main constraint identified for the sector's development is in regard to internal factors, evidenced by the 'Domestic Level' section of Table 12.2. This is expected of developing countries, and the deficiencies in

Table 12.2 Diagnosis of BRICS members in the area of ST&I in 2016

	Brazil	Russia	India	China	South Africa
Domestic Level	Need for Human Capital. Low international scientific cooperation. Low Research and Development-investing firms.	Low patenting index. Youth science performance under the OECD median. Inefficient International Scientific cooperation.	High level of informality entrepreneurship. Low level of publications on international ST&I journals. Need for Sustainable development.	Need for Sustainable development. Low level of international co-authorship and co-invention (Weak links to global networks).	Need for Human Capital. Relatively low Research and Development Infrastructure. Improving, but still low in Business Research and Development Investment.

(Continued)

Table 12.2 (Continued)

	Brazil	Russia	India	China	South Africa
External Level	GII: 69th – general ranking 7th – regional ranking GCR: 75th – general ranking	GII: 43rd – general ranking 29th – regional ranking GCR: 45th – general ranking	GII: 66th – general ranking 1st – regional ranking GCR: 55th – general ranking	GII: 25th – general ranking 7th – regional ranking GCR: 28th – general ranking	GII: 54th – general ranking 2nd – regional ranking GCR: 49th – general ranking

Source: Author's creation.

the STI sector vary from each member due to enormous domestic differences. Therefore, future research directions should focus on each member's domestic challenges in developing its STI sector and how the BRICS could develop specific working groups to research and propose mechanisms to mature each other's internal STI sector.

Final Remarks

This study sought to identify possible mechanisms that caused the BRICS countries to seek integration through cooperation through the Innovation Cooperation Action Plans. Through documental analysis and identification of the members' situation in the STI sector in 2016, it was possible to infer that the low rankings in competitiveness and innovation rankings, as well as low international scientific cooperation, had a direct impact on the proposition and implementation of the Innovation Cooperation Action Plans.

References

Beach D., and Pedersen R.B. (2013). *Process-Tracing Methods: Foundations and Guidelines*. Michigan: The University of Michigan Press.
Braveboy-Wanger, J. (ed.). (2016). *Diplomatic Strategies of Nations in the Global South: The search for leadership*. New York: Palgrave Macmillan.
BRICS. (2009). Joint Statement of the BRIC Leaders. http://brics2022.mfa.gov.cn/eng/hywj/ODS/202203/t20220308_10649520.html (Accessed 14 July 2023).
BRICS. (2010). II BRIC Summit of Heads of State/Government Joint Statement. http://brics2022.mfa.gov.cn/eng/hywj/ODS/202203/t20220308_10649518.html (Accessed 14 July 2023).
BRICS. (2011). III BRICS Summit Sanya Declaration. http://brics2022.mfa.gov.cn/eng/hywj/ODS/202203/t20220308_10649517.html (Accessed 14 July 2023).
BRICS. (2012). IV BRICS Summit Delhi Declaration. <http://brics2022.mfa.gov.cn/eng/hywj/ODS/202203/t20220308_10649515.html (Accessed 14 July 2023).
BRICS. (2013). V BRICS Summit Ethekwini Declaration BRICS and Africa: Partnership for Development, Integration and Industrialisation. http://brics2022.mfa.gov.cn/eng/hywj/ODS/202203/t20220308_10649513.html (Accessed 15 July 2023).

BRICS. (2014). VI BRICS Summit Fortaleza Declaration. http://brics2022.mfa.gov.cn/eng/gyjzgj/ljldrhwcgwj/202202/t20220222_10644323.html (Accessed 20 July 2023).
BRICS. (2015). VII BRICS Summit Ufa Declaration. http://brics2022.mfa.gov.cn/eng/hywj/ODS/202203/t20220308_10649509.html (Accessed 16 July 2023).
BRICS. (2016). VIII BRICS Summit Goa Declaration. http://brics2022.mfa.gov.cn/eng/hywj/ODS/202203/t20220308_10649507.html (Accessed 16 July 2023).
BRICS. (2017a). VIIII BRICS Summit Xiamen Declaration. http://brics2022.mfa.gov.cn/eng/hywj/ODS/202203/t20220308_10649505.html (5 September 2017).
BRICS. (2017b). BRICS Action Plan for Innovation Cooperation (2017–2020). https://www.iri.edu.ar/wp-content/uploads/2017/10/BO_Documentos_BRICS_ActionPlanforInnovationCooperation.pdf (Accessed 21 Jul. 2023).
OECD. (2016a). OECD Science, Technology and Innovation Outlook 2016 Country Profile – South Africa. https://read.oecd-ilibrary.org/science-and-technology/oecd-science-technology-and-innovation-outlook-2016/south-africa_sti_in_outlook-2016-86-en (Accessed 20 July 2023b).
OECD. (2016b). OECD Science, Technology and Innovation Outlook 2016 Country Profile – China (People's Republic of China). https://read.oecd-ilibrary.org/science-and-technology/oecd-science-technology-and-innovation-outlook-2016/china_sti_in_outlook-2016-52-en#page1 (Accessed 20 July 2023b).
OECD. (2016c). OECD Science, Technology and Innovation Outlook 2016 Country Profile – India. https://read.oecd-ilibrary.org/science-and-technology/oecd-science-technology-and-innovation-outlook-2016/india_sti_in_outlook-2016-65-en#page1 (Accessed 19 July 2023).
OECD. (2016d). OECD Science, Technology and Innovation Outlook 2016 Country Profile – Russian Federation. https://read.oecd-ilibrary.org/science-and-technology/oecd-science-technology-and-innovation-outlook-2016/russian-federation_sti_in_outlook-2016-83-en (Accessed 19 July 2023).
OECD. (2016e). OECD Science, Technology and Innovation Outlook 2016 Country Profile – Brazil. https://read.oecd-ilibrary.org/science-and-technology/oecd-science-technology-and-innovation-outlook-2016/brazil_sti_in_outlook-2016-49-en#page1 (Accessed: 19 July 2023).
Pape, R.A. (2005). Soft balancing against the United States. *International Security*, 30(1): 7–45.
Radulescu I.G., Panait, M., and Voica C. (2014). BRICS countries challenge to the World Economy New Trends. *Procedia Economics and Finance*, 8:605–613. http://dx.doi.org/10.1016/s2212-5671(14)00135-x.
Rinaldi A.L. (2021). O BRICS nas Relações Internacionais Contemporâneas: alinhamento estratégico e balanceamento global. São Paulo: April, 2021.
STIEP. (2021). BRICS Working Group on Science, Technology, Innovation and Entrepreneurship Partnership (STIEP WG): Proposed Action Plan 2021–24. Disponível em: https://brics2021.gov.in/brics/public/uploads/docpdf/getdocu-67.pdf (Accessed 21 July 2023).
Tahir, M., and Burki, U. (2023). Entrepreneurship and economic growth: Evidence from the emerging BRICS economies. *Journal of Open Innovation: Technology, Market, and Complexity*, 9(2):1–21 (1 June 2023).
WEF. (2015). The Global Competitiveness Report 2015–2016. Geneva. https://www3.weforum.org/docs/gcr/2015-2016/Global_Competitiveness_Report_2015-2016.pdf (Accessed 23 July 2023).
WIPO, INSEAD, JOHNSON CORNELL UNIVERSITY. (2016). The Global Innovation Index 2016. https://www.wipo.int/edocs/pubdocs/en/wipo_pub_gii_2016.pdf (Accessed 19 July 2023).
Zakaria, F. (2011). *The Post-American World*. New York: Penguin.

13 Industry, Innovation, and Infrastructure

Contribution of SMEs in the Developing Economies

Zakia Tasmin Rahman, Ruhi Lal, and Ravinder Rena

Introduction

According to Chandra, Paul, and Chavan (2020), small- and medium-sized enterprises (SMEs) develop their standards, frequently grounded on assets, headcount or sales. Vietnam defines SMEs as having between 10 and 300 employees, while Egypt defines SMEs as having more than 5 but fewer than 50 employees (El Tarabishy, 2020). According to the World Bank, SMEs are businesses with annual revenue of $15 million, less than 300 employees, and assets valued at $15 million (OECD, 2017). Conversely, SMEs are businesses with up to $3 million of annual sales with 100 employees, per the Inter-American Development Bank (United Nations Department of Economic and Social Affairs (UNDESA) – Report on micro, small, and medium-sized enterprises. The operation definition of SMEs is that they can be business organizations with employees between 10 and 300 based on assets, headcounts, and sales. Every SME runs different ideologies as per the requirements.

"Micro, small, and medium-sized businesses are companies with less than 250 employees, an annual revenue of up to 50 million euros, and/or an annual balance sheet value of up to 43 million euros", the EU's definition of this term reads (Kota, 2018). Businesses between 10 and 250 employees are considered SMEs, and a balance sheet total or turnover of at least 10 million euros. SMEs are indispensable for fostering development, innovation, and prosperity in developing countries. Access to financing is cited by nearly half of SMEs in developing nations as a major barrier, which is unfortunate because it severely restricts their ability to grow and expand (UN Environment Programme, 2022). They might not be able to get financing from local banks at all because of the recent financial crisis, or they might only get it on extremely unfavourable terms (Bekeris, 2012). Lack of lender information and regulatory support for SME lending are additional obstacles for banks in developing nations to overcome (Kota, 2018). As a result, there is a lack of a robust SME lending market, which restricts the expansion of SMEs and has a detrimental effect on macroeconomic resilience.

DOI: 10.4324/9781003475606-16

Specific International Financial Institutions (IFIs) assistance, such as guarantees or technical support, aids in developing intermediaries' knowledge and expertise regarding SME lending, thereby assisting in the emergence of a self-sustaining SME lending market (Keskin et al., 2010). The advantages must outweigh the drawbacks, possible disincentives, and unintended consequences, just like with any form of government intervention in the market for goods and services (Pandey, 2022). IFIs, on the other hand, are frequently better suited to help SMEs than local governments, whose support programmes are frequently less economical and more prone to political entanglements. IFIs work with local middlemen to cut costs, which has the added benefit of promoting the development of a local lending sector. The economy's and society's sustainability are further improved by carefully assessing intermediaries, adhering to strict lending standards, and modifying controls and incentives.

Literature Review

SMEs' Contribution to Job Creation

Along with input and output, the employment situation in the global economy is significantly influenced by SMEs (Chandra, Paul, and Chavan, 2020). Here, it's important to comprehend a few things (Adam and Alarifi, 2021). Over the next 15 years, 600 million jobs will be required globally (Pasnicu, 2018). Most of the current formal employments within emerging markets were primarily developed by SMEs (Helmy, Adawiyah, and Banani, 2019). That equates to almost four out of every five available jobs. It is noted that although SMEs are essential to the expansion of the economy, about 50% of them lack access to financing or capital investments (Kota, 2018). The numbers increase even further when informal SMEs are included.

Size of Business in SMEs

SMEs can be categorised based on capital employed, annual sales, and number of employees. On the other hand, the asset value and number of personnel are what constitutes an SME. Nations have different classification standards. For instance, businesses classified as SMEs in Canada must have fewer than 500 employees. The maximum number of employees is, there are 250 for medium-sized businesses in Germany, 19 in New Zealand, and 50 for small businesses in the EU (Ackah and Vuvor, 2011). An SME in the UK is defined by the Companies Act of 1985 as having less than £5.6 million in revenue and no more than 50 employees (Keskin et al., 2010). On the other hand, initiatives are being made to use a definition of SMEs that is widely acknowledged (OECD, 2017).

SMEs generate jobs and boost the economy (Rena, 2009; Bhuyan, 2016). As a result, many government organisations, researchers, academics, and scholars frequently discuss them. SMEs frequently experience problems. However, different countries have different levels of awareness of how SMEs support economic development. SMEs support economic expansion in various ways.

Small- and Medium-Sized Enterprises

To some extent, SMEs are similar to MSMEs and are crucial to the expansion of any economy because they promote the growth of employment and exports. Although SMEs and MSMEs are similar in concept, we have tried to highlight the differences by comparing Indian MSMEs with global SMEs and comparing their meanings, objectives, contributions, and financing sources. Every nation defines a small business differently (AlQershi, 2021). Under the MSMED Act of 2006, MSMEs are also called SMEs in India (Chandra et al., 2020). SMEs are a fundamental concept, and MSME is its Indian definition (Adam and Alarifi, 2021). According to the number of employees, these SMEs are small and medium-sized businesses in European nations (Manikandan, n.d.). As a result, a business is small if it employs fewer than 50 people. As a result, while classification in Europe is based on workforce size, it is based on investment level in India (please see Table 13.1).

ORGANISATIONS THAT MAKE LOANS

The International Finance Cooperation created the Global SME Finance Facility to assist SMEs in developing countries with their financial needs. Through funding, risk management, and consulting services, this facility aids SMEs (Organisation for Economic Co-operation and Development (OECD), 2017). Lending to MSMEs is permitted in India by several Non-Banking Financial Companies (NBFCs), Regional Rural Banks (RRBs), commercial banks, small

Table 13.1 Difference of objectives between medium-sized and small businesses (SMBs) and micro, little, and medium-sized businesses (MSMEs) (SMEs)

S/No.	Objectives of SME	Objectives of MSME
1.	Creating new job opportunities.	Encourage entrepreneurs among small- and medium-sized business owners.
2.	Encouragement of entrepreneurial endeavours.	Boost the share of the MSME sector in Indian exports.
3.	Improving the living conditions of the impoverished.	Administrative processes are improving.
4.	Increasing the nation's SME sector's GDP contribution.	Giving most vulnerable members of society employment opportunities.

Source: Authors' Own Compilation.

industry development bank of India (SIDBI), North-Eastern Development Finance Corporation (NEDFi), National Smaill Industries Corporation (NSIC), and Small Finance Banks (SFBs) (Mpofu, 2022). SMEs can borrow irrespective of whether they are recently established (Singh and Wasdani, 2016). Some loan options available to MSMEs include the Micro Units Development and Refinance Agency (MUDRA) loan, Credit Guarantee Fund Trust for Micro and Small Enterprises (CGTMSE) loan, and Prime Minister Employment Generation Programme (PMEGP) loan. A minimum loan amount of 50 crores of Indian rupees and a maximum loan amount of Rs 200 lakhs or 2 crores are available under these programmes. As a result, depending on national SME laws, the distinction between SMEs and MSMEs varies. Regarding their contributions, one can see the differences between MSMEs in India and SMEs in other countries (OECD, 2017).

SMEs ARE WIDELY DISTRIBUTED IN OTHER NATIONS

1 **Africa:** Most businesses are SMEs, which make up the majority of business share on the continent and contribute to its Gross Domestic Product (GDP).
2 **Japan:** It contributes more than half of GDP in terms of value added. 70% of all employment in the nation comes from SME employment.
3 **Pakistan:** In 2018, 30% of Pakistan's GDP came from SMEs. Employment overall was 78% at the national level, while employment from exports comprised 25% of total employment.
4 **China:** Greater than 90% of businesses are SMEs. They generate 60% of the country's GDP and 80% of all jobs.
5 **United States of America:** About 27 million SMEs in the United States are responsible for 66.6% of all jobs. They contribute somewhere to the neighbourhood of 50% of the nation's GDP.
6 **Europe:** In European countries, SMEs create 70% of all new jobs.
7 **Australia:** Nearly 98% of Australian businesses are SMEs, contributing 33.5% of the nation's GDP (El Tarabishy, 2020).

THE PERCENTAGE OF MSMEs IN INDIA IS SIGNIFICANT

MSMEs, which produce 40% of all exports and 45% of manufacturing output, constitute the basis of the Indian economy, significantly boosting the creation of jobs in the nation (Ackah and Vuvor, 2011). From 3.87 lakh jobs in 2017 to 5.875 lakh in 2018, microbusinesses increased the number of jobs they produced by 51.6% (Fakieh, 2018). According to the Ministry of MSMEs head, this sector contributes 30% to the country's GDP (Sivasree and Vasavi, 2020).

India's 63.4 million small and medium-sized businesses employ about 460 million people (SMEs), contributing to 30% of the nation's GDP (Manikandan, n.d.). About 120 million Indians are employed in the sector, which generates 33.4% of India's industrial output, according to the Confederation of Indian Industry (CII). When exports are factored in, SMEs contribute about 45% (Adian et al., 2020).

Despite accounting for a significant portion of the GDP of India, SMEs have found it difficult to reach their full potential due to antiquated, inefficient business practices, and slow uptake of new technologies (Milutinović, Stošić, and Mihić, 2015).

Google research shows that 68% of the 51 million SMEs lack an internet connection (SME effects in 2020). The SMEs in India still have a long way to go before reaching their potential and moving on to the next step in the growth process. Technology adoption is the only obstacle to the finance ministry's goal of building India into a $5 trillion economy. As a result, these digital companies are rising to the occasion and offering solutions to help SMEs thrive (Keskin et al., 2010).

DISTINCTION OF SMEs FROM START-UPS

Initially, start-ups and small businesses had modest budgets (Keskin et al., 2010). However, a small business has less risk than a start-up because the latter can be considered an experiment that may or may not be successful (Fakieh, 2018). Since their primary objective is to develop into a business that can significantly impact society, start-ups are regarded as visionary (Adian et al., 2020). On the other hand, small businesses are created to produce steady and long-term income (Ramarao, 2012). Their primary objective is to generate profits and maintain their business, not to become very large. A start-up requires an innovative concept, but SMEs don't require that (Mpofu, 2022). SMEs require small investments and less manpower, but the innovation concept cannot be ignored.

A Sole Proprietorship May Register as an MSME

Comparable to other processes finished by Limited Liability Partnership (LLPs), partnership firms, etc., registration procedures and fees are the same (Sivasree and Vasavi, 2020).

BENEFITS OF MSMEs

- As interest rates are comparatively lower, loans become more affordable.
- Tax refunds.
- MSMEs are eligible for many government contracts (Hannan et al., 2021).

Issues Affecting MSMEs

1. The use of antiquated technology.
2. Non-professional management and entrepreneurship.

3   Abundant competition from big businesses and importing goods and services.
4   Inadequate infrastructural facilities, especially in rural areas.
5   Scale financial prudence is more difficult to achieve.
6   Difficulty in product marketing (Mathai, 2015).

THIS RESEARCH STUDY IS BASED ON THE FOLLOWING OBJECTIVES

1   To evaluate the contribution of the SMEs in developing nations.
2   To determine the achievements of SMEs in developing nations.
3   To analyse the responsibilities of SMEs in achieving Sustainable Development Goal No. 9, "Industry, Innovation and Infrastructure" of the United Nations in Developing economies.
4   To compare the roles of SMEs in India and China.
5   To explore the futuristic approach of the SMEs in developing economies.

Need of the Study

The study will help comprehend the concepts of SME and MSME. It is used in the developing economies. SMEs have significance in all the economies of the world. SMEs and MSMEs help in boosting economies by enhancing employment, capital formation, income, and other economic benefits. Emerging and developing economies can be developed to a great extent with the help of SMEs and MSMEs.

Research Methodology

Based on the contributions that have been recorded, the research is qualitative, and the achievements and futuristic developments of SMEs in developing economies are taken into consideration. Content analysis is done based on secondary data like government records and reports, published research papers, websites, and other relevant documents.

The study is qualitative to understand the perception and the contributions, achievements, and futuristics developments of SMEs in developing economies. The research approach is qualitative, exploratory-descriptive, and contextual as the researchers aim to understand the behaviour, perceptions, experiences, and feelings of various stakeholders of developing countries emphasising the understanding of these elements in this study.

Research Phase

The study was completed in three phases: Conceptual, narrative, and interpretative (Morse and Field, 1996).

Conceptual Phase: At this stage of the conceptual phase, formulation of research questions and objectives and the review of the literature were done to familiarise with the concept, content, and preconceived ideas about the research to understand the perception of SMEs in developing countries about its contributions, achievements, and futuristic developments.

Narrative Phase: The research design planning was based on the plans and strategies implemented by SMEs in developing nations. Stakeholders of SMEs in developing nations accepted various policies, plans, and strategies as part of the narrative phase. The stakeholders stated their views in the mass media and also through mails and messages.

Interpretative phase: The data collection phase was qualitative information gathering, analysis, and interpretation.

Context: The study focused on SMEs based in developing countries, and the context is significant in qualitative research. The participants comprise various stakeholders from developing countries – Ministries of developing countries working with SMEs and other related members. Newspapers, magazines, research papers, government documents, reports, and records published about environmental and global economic issues from the developing nations' perspective were considered. Social media also helped in gathering requisite information for the study.

Reflexivity of the research: In the research study, the researchers self-monitored the preconceived values, notions, feelings, assumptions, and conflicts to increase objectivity and prevent biases while selecting the Environmental and Economic Issues and Information for Research Credibility stakeholders.

Intuiting of the Study

In this study, the researchers tried to understand the concerned stakeholders by totally immersed in the study. The researcher's main attention was only on the phenomenon described from the view of the developing countries' stakeholders using SMEs. The challenge was to collect the correct information from various sources. The contents were reviewed and analysed.

The secondary data for the research study was sourced from the research papers, websites, Magazines, articles, and information published by the Government of India related to SMEs and MSMEs.

Findings and Analysis

The Research Study's Findings are Stated as Per the Study's Objectives

Contributions of SMEs in Developing Nations

The growth and development landscape changed when governments created small business or SME support organisations and implemented targeted policies in the late 1940s (see Table 13.2). Due to the idea of SME and free enterprise,

Table 13.2 Contribution of SMEs in developing nations

S/No.	Various contributions of SMEs in developing economies
1.	Effective antipoverty programme.
2.	Innovation and sustainable growth.
3.	Stable economic environment.
4.	Aids in overcoming obstacles that arise during the economies' start-up phase.
5.	Extremes in the distribution of labour and capital income can be prevented.
6.	SMEs support the creation of jobs and income.
7.	Increasing export earnings in developing nations.
8.	Take advantage of innovation.
9.	Increase the tax base.
10.	SMEs heat up the market environment and increase competition among peers.
11.	Because of SMEs, both the provider and the customer benefit.
12.	The innovations, concepts, and skills of new business owners are introduced.
13.	SMEs have potential to create jobs with little capital outlay.
14.	SMEs are crucial to the fast-paced industrialisation and development.
15.	SMEs produce more than approximately half of the internal production of goods and services.
16.	By adjusting and innovating in response to shifting conditions, SMEs serve as a safety net against recession.
17.	Even as major industries contract and lose jobs, SMEs keep growing and adding new jobs.
18.	By embracing online shopping and other forms of e-commerce, one can buy and sell goods and services almost anywhere, SMEs can quickly adapt to the fast-paced business world.
19.	Technology advancements have simplified buying and selling, but SMEs have also helped business owners cut the cost of advertising and marketing.
20.	SME traders and service providers are crucial to the primary industry.
21.	SMEs not only produce services but also finished goods.
22.	Many industries, including manufacturing, agriculture, and ICT services, depend on the development of SME.
23.	An SME and the economy cooperate for the benefit of both parties. As the economy expands, more SMEs are produced, and vice versa.

Source: Authors' own Compilation.

expansion initially surfaced (grants, subsidised credits, and special tax treatment). For instance, government-financed SME agencies were founded in Japan in 1948, in the United States in 1953, in India in 1954, in Tanzania in 1966, and Turkey in 1976(OECD, 2017).

The magnitude and significance of the SME segment vary from nation to nation, just like any other aspect of the economy; during recent decades, industrial countries have begun to recognise its importance, whereas developing countries have done so since the 1970s or so ("Small and Medium Enterprises", 2022).

Almost every economy in the world, particularly those in developing nations, depends on SMEs (Rena, 2009). SMEs in developing nations are highly sought after (Adian *et al.*, 2020). There are likely two primary causes for this (Mathai, 2015). One is the belief that encouraging the growth of SMEs could prove to be a fruitful anti-poverty initiative (Pasnicu, 2018). The second idea is that the growth of SMEs is one of the pillars of innovation and long-term development (Helmy, Adawiyah, and Banani, 2019). Naturally, there is a connection between these two factors because most of the research conducted globally shows that true poverty reduction and growth go hand in hand (AlQershi, 2021). The development of SMEs significantly contributes to economic growth and a stable business climate, and it almost certainly also lowers poverty (UN Environment Programme, 2022). For stable economic growth, SMEs must be supported in their operations (Keskin *et al.*, 2010). To specifically aid them in overcoming challenges when the company is just starting up, during regular business operations, they specifically need financial and consulting services.

The "labour elite" in developing countries' insignificant SME industries – in their firm size structure – often referred to as having a "missing middle" – tends to be able to negotiate for wages that are significantly higher than those paid elsewhere in the economy (Helmy *et al.*, 2019). The economy's capital stock has almost entirely been consumed by large firms, leaving little money to be shared among the numerous employees who are not employed by large companies (typically due to capital market imperfections). This results in a large micro-enterprise sector due to a lack of capital, which squeezes out the SME sector (Keskin *et al.*, 2010). The microbusiness sector's equilibrium wage and capital incomes are very low (AlQershi, 2021). In conclusion, income is distributed inequitably (Pasnicu, 2018). These extremes in capital and labour income distribution are avoided when the SME sector is large (Rena, 2009).

Additionally, SMEs support developing nations in job creation, revenue creation, and export revenue growth (Valenza, Caputo, and Calabrò, 2021). To fully realise Governments of transitional and developing countries, SMEs themselves, as well as their development partners, must deal with several issues if SMEs are to realise their potential for development and poverty reduction fully (OECD, 2017):

- The nationwide private sector, including SMEs, must grow through:
  - The establishment of fresh, creative businesses.
  - The transition of the greatest number of informal businesses into the formal sector.
- SMEs must raise their level of productivity and competition in their home markets (El Tarabishy, 2020).
- These globally competitive SMEs, at least a portion of which must reach a competitiveness level that will allow them to engage in trade and investment-based global value chains with connections to FDI (exports and internationalisation).

ACHIEVEMENTS OF SMEs IN DEVELOPING ECONOMIES

Small businesses impact different levels of the economy (UN Environment Programme, 2022). Small businesses in less populous regions contribute to national economic growth by generating jobs (Mpofu, 2022). It intensifies rivalry in the market. For example, local farmers are not responsible for payment of shipping (Table 13.3). They might be able to offer less expensive goods (Milutinović, Stošić, and Mihić, 2015).

Table 13.3 SMEs are crucial for fostering globalisation and growth that is more inclusive

S/No.	Various achievements of SMEs in developing economies
1.	SMEs are significant contributors to the economy and the larger business ecosphere.
2.	SMEs make up about 90% of companies worldwide.
3.	About 50% of all employment worldwide is held by SMEs.
4.	Formal SMEs in emerging nations can pay up to 40% of the country's income.
5.	The majority of formal jobs in emerging markets are produced by SMEs, which account for seven out of ten jobs.
6.	The $30 million Small and Medium Enterprises which are innovative (iSME) project in Lebanon provides equity co-investments in cutting-edge young businesses.
7.	The co-investment fund of iSME had made 22 investments totalling $10.23 million as of August 2019 and was able to leverage another $25.47 million in co-financing.
8.	India's Small Industry Development Bank was given access to a credit line of $500 million (SIDBI).
9.	New and existing businesses were encouraged to grow and expand by a 70-million-dollar credit line.
10.	79% of 7,682 jobs created by the project – which received funding for 8,149 MSMEs – were held by young people, and 42% by women.
11.	As of May 2019, the Development Bank of Nigeria's credit line to PFIs for on-lending to MSMEs had disbursed US$243.7 million, reaching nearly 50,000 end borrowers through seven banks and 10 microfinance banks, with 70% of them being women.
12.	Moroccan MSME Project for Development supported the provision of credit guarantees to increase MSMEs' accessibility to capital.
13.	Since the ending of 2011, quantity and number of MSME loans have increased by 88% and 18%, correspondingly, as a result of the MSME Development project.
14.	An IDA programme called the Entrepreneurship Development Project for Women (WEDP) in Ethiopia provides growth-oriented Ethiopian women business owners with loans and business training.
15.	More than 14,000 female entrepreneurs had accessed loans as of October 2019, and more than 20,000 had benefited from WEDP's business training programmes.
16.	It began lending $30.2 million of their own money through the WEDP.

(Continued)

Table 13.3 (Continued)

S/No.	Various achievements of SMEs in developing economies
17.	For Ethiopian women business owners, the average WEDP loan has increased annual profits by over 40% and net employment by almost 56%.
18.	A crucial component of raising SME financing is the Project on Bangladeshi Women's SMEs' Access to Finance.
19.	In September 2019, the nation's first comprehensive SME Finance Policy was released.
20.	The local governments in Ethiopia and Guinea are receiving help from the World Bank Group in creating a setting that is favourable for beginning and expanding leasing operations.
21.	Securing investors to broaden Ethiopian and Guinean SMEs' access to financing.
22.	The project led to the creation of a $200 million credit facility for Ethiopia, enabling the launch of four new leasing products and the support of seven leasing institutions.
23.	7,186 MSMEs had access to loans worth more than $147 million as of June 2019.

Source: Authors' own Compilation.

Most economies, especially those in developing nations, depend heavily on SMEs (World Economic Forum, 2021). SMEs make up most businesses globally, and they significantly contribute to the expansion of the global economy and the creation of jobs (Abdulsaleh and Worthington, 2013). Over 50% of all jobs and about 90% of all businesses are supported by them globally. Newly established SMEs, up to 40% of the GDP is accounted for in emerging economies (OECD, 2017). These figures significantly rise when informal SMEs are considered (Valenza, Caputo, and Calabr, 2021). According to our predictions, 600 million additional jobs must be created by 2030 to keep up with the growing global labour force, making the growth of SMEs an international government priority in many nations (Hannan *et al.*, 2021). Most formal jobs in emerging markets are produced by SMEs, which account for seven out of ten jobs there (Mpofu, 2022). Despite being the second most frequently cited obstacle to SMEs' ability to expand their businesses in emerging markets and developing countries, access to financing is a significant barrier to SME growth (OECD, 2017).

The SIDBI received a credit line of $500 million to give underserved MSMEs a more affordable, long-term source of funding (Milutinovi, Stoi, and Mihi, 2015). The lending component now includes approximately $3.7 million technical assistance, focusing on SIDBI and the PFIs' capacity building (Abdulsaleh and Worthington, 2013). The project advanced MSME financing by developing novel lending techniques that sped up turnaround times, reached additional untapped MSMEs, and attracted more private sector funding in addition to directly lending $265 million to MSMEs. Additionally, it connected with new clients, MSMEs owned by women, and MSMEs in states with low income (Adian *et al.*, 2020).

With the aid of the project, the fund of funds for start-ups, which plans to give start-ups indirect access to $1.5 billion by 2025, was scaled up (Valenza, Caputo, and Calabr, 2021). A digital matchmaker and aggregator of MSME loans, SIDBI's "contactless lending" platform has $1.9 billion in private sector funding for MSMEs and has grown to become India's largest online lender (Hannan *et al.*, 2021).

Credit Lines Two lines of credit from the Group of the World Bank in Jordan seek to enhance MSMEs' accessibility to capital as well as finally aid in job creation (World Economic Forum, 2021). Start-ups received 22% of the total funds from the line of credit (AlQershi, 2021). The project provided funding to 8,149 MSMEs, which resulted in the creation of 7,682 jobs (42% for women and 79% for youth), and funding 8,149 MSMEs (UNDESA – Report on MSMEs and SDGs, 2020). The $50 million in additional funding is moving in the right direction to fulfil its intended purpose. Nine participating banks have provided loans totalling $45.2 million to 3,345 MSMEs (Hannan *et al.*, 2021). The project's beneficiaries are primarily women and young people – 77% and 48%, respectively – and it is expanding its geographic scope because outside of Amman, governorates contain 65% of MSMEs (World Economic Forum, 2021).

Goal 9 of the SDGs Is "Infrastructure, Business, and Innovation" of the United Nations

Goal 9 of the SDG Agenda includes developing strong infrastructure, inclusiveness, maintainable industrialisation and encouraging novelty (Fakieh, 2018). Infrastructure, industrialisation, and innovation are three crucial aspects of sustainable development that the SDG addresses (Mondejar *et al.*, 2021). Infrastructure provides a society with the fundamental physical systems and structures it needs to function or business to develop (Hannan *et al.*, 2021). Industrialisation encourages economic growth, generates workplace possibilities, and lowers the income-poverty ratio (Kota, 2018). Innovation improves the industrial sectors' technological capabilities, which also encourages the creation of new skills (Goyal, Agrawal, and Sergi, 2020). For the benefit of the nations, inclusive and sustainable industrial development is necessary, as it also provides the technological tools necessary for environmentally friendly industrialisation so that all people's living standards can rise quickly and steadily (Hannan *et al.*, 2021).

Space technologies are crucial to (Di Pippo, 2019):

1 Infrastructure mapping and monitoring, including upkeep of roads in rural areas, where satellite-based technology is the most reliable.
2 Automated machine surveying for construction.
3 Smarter planning and driving behaviour monitoring can reduce fuel consumption.

Increase Innovation, Promote Inclusive and Sustainable Industrialisation, and Create Resilient Infrastructure

Successful communities are built on a strong and reliable infrastructure. Our industries and infrastructure must be upgraded to handle upcoming challenges (Mathai, 2015). To accomplish this, we must encourage and ensure everyone has access to information and financial markets and uses cutting-edge, environmentally friendly technologies (Mpofu, 2022). As a result, the world will experience prosperity, the creation of jobs, and the emergence of stable, prosperous societies (Hannan *et al.*, 2021).

The key forces behind economic growth and development are sustained investment in infrastructure and innovation (Dar and Ahmad, 2022). As more than half of the world's population now resides in cities, mass transit, renewable energy, the development of new industries, and information and communication technologies are all gaining importance (Di Pippo, 2019).

Technological advancement is essential for the long-term fixation of issues with the economy and the environment, including new job creation and promotion of energy efficiency (Goyal, Agrawal, and Sergi, 2020). Promoting sustainable businesses, funding scientific research, and supporting innovation are all crucial steps toward enabling sustainable development (Mondejar *et al.*, 2021).

Over four billion people live in the developing world, and 90% of those are without access to the Internet (Dar and Ahmad, 2022). Close the digital divide to guarantee equal access to knowledge and information, fostering entrepreneurship, and innovation (Mpofu, 2022).

One of the 17 Global Goals that make up the 2030 Agenda for Sustainable Development is to invest in infrastructure and innovation. For the multiple goals to be achieved, progress requires an integrated strategy (Goyal *et al.*, 2020).

Using the potential of smart technologies, creating new, environmentally friendly infrastructures, and modifying or upgrading existing infrastructure systems can all help reduce environmental impacts and disaster risks, build resilience, and increase the efficiency of using natural resources (Mondejar *et al.*, 2021).

The UN claims that infrastructure spending is essential in many countries to empower communities and achieve sustainable development. Infrastructure is thought to include things like transportation, irrigation, energy, and information and communication technology (Di Pippo, 2019). It is well known that infrastructure investment is necessary for increased income and productivity and better health and educational outcomes (Hannan *et al.*, 2021).

The UN has established 12 Indicators and 8 Targets for SDG 9. Targets define goals, and metrics and indicators determine whether these targets have been attained (Mavuri, Chavali, and Kumar, 2019). The original text of each Target, along with details on the agreed-upon Indicators, are cited below (Mpofu, 2022).

Targets

Everyone can help the world's citizens achieve global goals (Goyal *et al.*, 2020). These eight objectives can be used as motivation to encourage action in support of inclusive and sustainable industrialisation, create resilient infrastructure, and develop creative solutions (Mavuri, Chavali, and Kumar, 2019) (Figure 13.1).

The above figure states the various targets of SDG No. 9. There are eight targets need to be achieved. All the eight targets are systematically mentioned in the above figure (see Table 13.4).

9.1 Build dependable, sustainable, and resilient regional and global infrastructure focusing on open access and reasonable costs to support economic growth and societal well-being.
9.2 Promote inclusive and long-term industrialisation, boost the sector's contribution to GDP and employment by a sizable amount by 2030, while doubling that contribution to the world's least developed nations.
9.3 SMEs in the industrial and other sectors, especially those in emerging nations, should have access to more affordable credit to help them join value chains and markets.
9.4 By 2030, every country should take steps to modernise their infrastructure, make their industries more sustainable, and adopt newer, more eco-friendly technologies and industrial practices, depending on their capacities to do so.
9.5 Improve technical research, modernise the industrial sectors' scientific prowess in all nations, particularly developing nations, and, by 2030, promote innovation and greatly raise both public and private spending.
9.6 To encourage the development of dependable and durable infrastructure in emerging countries, increasing financial and technological assistance to African countries, less developed countries, landlocked emerging nations, and small islands with fewer developing states.
9.7 To aid emerging nations' internal technological enhancement, innovation, and research, ensure the controlling environment favours, among other things, the diversification of industries and the increase in commodity value.
9.8 Technology access to information and communications should be expanded significantly by 2020, and work toward providing affordable Internet access to everyone on the planet.

Table 13.4 Goal 9 of the UN's sustainable development agenda, "Industry, Innovation, and Infrastructure", outlines its objectives

S/No.	Various targets of goal nine is "Industry, Innovation, and Infrastructure"
9.1	Create infrastructures that are inclusive, resilient, and sustainable.
9.2	Encourage sustainable and inclusive industrialisation
9.3	Increasing Market and Financial Service Access
9.4	Upgrade all sectors' infrastructures and industries to be more sustainable
9.5	Improve Industrial Technologies and Research
9.6	Encourage the development of sustainable infrastructure in developing nations
9.7	Encourage domestic industrial diversification and technology development
9.8	Information and communication technologies are available to everyone

Source: Authors' own Compilation.

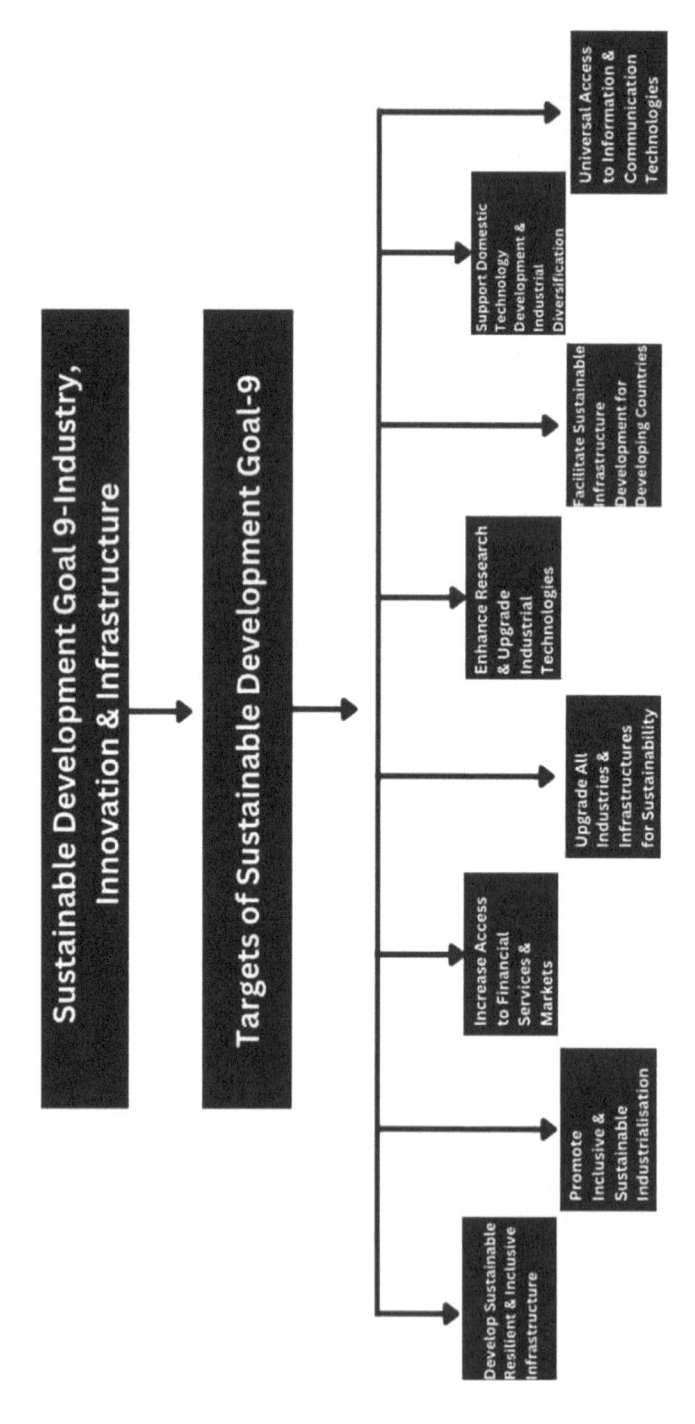

Figure 13.1 Model for goals of sustainable development and objectives
Source: Authors' own Compilation

Role of SMEs in Achieving Sustainable Development Goal No. 9 "Industry, Innovation and Infrastructure" of United Nations in Developing Economies

This goal has nine targets, the majority of which can be divided into three groups: Industrialisation, including the expansion of small industrial businesses, development of resilient infrastructure, and fostering research and innovation (Adam and Alarifi, 2021) (see Table 13.5).

The Goal Is Directly Related to Small Industrial Companies

Enhancing the performance and potential of small industrial businesses is the focus of SDG Target 9.3 (World Bank Group, 2022). United Nations Industrial

Table 13.5 SME's contribution to SDG No. 9

S/No.	Various roles of SMEs in achieving SDG No. 9
1.	Small-scale industries are directly related to the objectives
2.	Small-scale industrial enterprises (MSME) financing will help achieve the objectives.
3.	MSMEs encourage invention.
4.	Individual MSMEs may decide to change their business practises in order to further the objectives.
5.	New MSMEs business models and solutions that will aid in achieving the SDGs.
6.	It has pushed for more widespread use of environmentally friendly industrial procedures and efficient resource use.
7.	MSMEs driving innovation.
8.	It has taken advantage of technological or business opportunities that more established businesses have missed.
9.	Opening up business opportunities.
10.	Employment generation.
11.	Income generation.
12.	Small contribution to total industrial output.
13.	SMEs helping in the distributing new or niche products.
14.	SMEs make sure that initiatives and projects are managed sustainably.
15.	It gives all stakeholders the chance to propose original answers to sustainability-related problems.
16.	MSMEs are well suited for technology replication and commercialisation.
17.	Numerous fields, including software, nanotechnology, biotechnology, and clean technologies, benefit from its additions.
18.	Food stays fresher for a longer period of time due to a durable anti-fog coating developed by Palsgaard for industrial food packaging.
19.	A digital platform being developed by RGS Nordic which will enable carriers to make the most of the many trucks currently on the road.
20.	EON is developing a model for replacing fossil fuels in apartment buildings, townhouses, and schools with more affordable, environmental friendly heat pumps.

Source: Authors' own Compilation.

Development Organisation (UNIDO) claims a lack of country data on this target (Adian *et al.*, 2020). Data shows that developing countries' manufacturing value-added products and services from small-scale businesses vary significantly by region (UNDESA – Report on MSMEs and SDGs, 2020). While small businesses produced 21% of Albania's manufacturing, and other sectors represented 0.4% (Tonis, 2015). The report does, however, point out that small businesses, particularly in developing nations, significantly contribute to the creation of jobs, due to their high rate of labour absorption from traditional sectors, like agriculture or fishery, despite their modest contribution to overall industrial output (Bhoganadam, Rao, and Dasaraju, 2017). MSMEs produce, on average, between 50% and 60% of the value added in OECD nations, making up about 60% of manufacturing jobs and 75% of service jobs (Adam and Alarifi, 2021).

Small-Scale Industrial Enterprises (MSME) Financing Will Help Achieve the Objectives

Although it contributes significantly to industrial growth in developing countries, access to financial services is one of the biggest issues small businesses faces (Dar and Ahmad, 2022). Because it gives entrepreneurs the freedom to innovate, increase efficiency, enter new markets, and create new employment opportunities, small-scale industries need financial access to grow (Adian *et al.*, 2020). According to the World Bank Enterprise Surveys for the years 2015–2017, the highest percentages of small-scale manufacturing businesses with loans or lines of credit are found in the Solomon Islands (64%), Nicaragua (59%), and Benin (52%) (Ahmad and Dar, 2022). Contrarily, some countries had incredibly low shares, such as Laos (6.7%), Zimbabwe (5.7%), and Egypt (4.3%) (Bhoganadam, Rao, and Dasaraju, 2017).

MSMEs encourage invention. Even though not all MSMEs are creative, new, and small businesses frequently act as the engine for the innovations necessary for economic growth because they can overturn accepted wisdom, seize commercial or technological opportunities passed, enabling the commercialisation of knowledge that would otherwise go untapped by larger companies (Helmy *et al.*, 2019). For instance, MSMEs represent about 20% of patents in Europe's biotechnology-related fields, one indicator of innovation ("SMEs vs MSMEs", 2021). MSMEs also contribute to value creation by marketing new or specialised products, adopting innovations made by others, and modifying them slightly to fit different contexts (Adian *et al.*, 2020). Many MSMEs face significant challenges in finding the appropriate knowledge partners, establishing local, national, and international networks and enhancing management abilities and practices required to integrate knowledge produced by external partners with internal practices and innovation processes (Tonis, 2015).

Individual MSMEs May Change Their Business Practices to Further the Objective

They can set guidelines and advance laws to ensure that initiatives and projects are managed sustainably (Dar and Ahmad, 2022). They could also encourage innovation by allowing all participants to submit innovative responses to sustainability-related problems (Pandey, 2022).

New MSME business models and solutions that will aid in achieving the SDGs ("SMEs vs MSMEs", 2021). The SDGs promote resource-use efficiency and increased use of environmentally friendly industrial processes. MSMEs are well-suited to replicate and commercialise technology and add worth in various fields, such as nanotechnology, biotechnology, software, and clean technologies; this change in the business environment and economy will produce business opportunities (Tonis, 2015). To help MSMEs adopt these new technologies and business fields, knowledge and technology transfer, capacity building, financial resources, and an enabling policy framework supportive of the ease of doing business will be required (Bekeris, 2012).

Examples of Businesses from the MSMEs SDG Accelerator Programme of the United Nations Development Programme (UNDP) Show How MSMEs Are Driving Innovation

The following lists a few ground-breaking SDG remedies created with assistance from the UNDP programme, SDG Accelerator for MSMEs (Manikandan, n.d.).

A successful anti-fog coating developed by **Palsgaard** for commercial food packaging reduces food waste and keeps food fresher for longer (Tonis, 2015). Palsgaard will market the product internationally through its presence, focusing particularly on the major packaging manufacturers in Asia and the United States (World Bank Group, 2022).

The business's more than 35 receiving and handling facilities are located throughout Scandinavia to make the most of the numerous trucks that visit daily. RGS **Nordic** is creating a digital platform for them (Helmy *et al.*, 2019). The fix will result in fewer empty trucks, which will reduce emissions of CO_2 and particles (Pandey, 2022). In the long run, the consequences will act as an example of best practices for how cooperation between different industry actors and the sharing of transport data can significantly reduce the amount of road freight in Europe to protect the environment, businesses, and individuals.

Energy Company **E.ON** aims to promote affordable and clean energy while improving energy efficiency. This Company is developing a model for replacing fossil fuels in apartment buildings, townhouses, and schools with more affordable, environmentally friendly heat pumps (Helmy *et al.*, 2019). Many Danish housing associations still generate their heat using fossil fuels like oil and gas (Adam and Alarifi, 2021). Additionally, many plants are outdated and neglected after years of use (World Bank Group, 2022). High energy losses and unnecessary operating costs result from this (Valenza, Caputo, and Calabrò, 2021).

By 2030, to promote novelty, build robust infrastructure, and advance sustainable industrial development, it will be essential to resolve resource limitations, develop, and reinforce the dimensions of emerging nations, and look for new approaches to development issues (World Economic Forum, 2021).

Role of SMEs in India and China

According to Statista, a database company, there are an additional five million SMEs in China yearly, representing a 10% growth rate from the previous year ("Small and Medium Enterprises", 2022) (Table 13.6). China's SMEs are estimated to number over 38 million and contribute over 60% of the nation's GDP and 80% of all jobs (Dewan, 2021).

Table 13.6 Differentiation of SMEs in China and India

S/No.	Chinese SMEs	Indian SMEs
1.	The definition of a SME in China is based on the company's total assets, annual revenue, and employee count.	The employee component is ignored when segmenting business units into small, medium-sized, and large enterprises.
2.	Amount of reserves that these SMEs had to keep on hand to support growth was reduced by the Chinese government's revision of the country's tax laws in 2019.	To enable MSMEs to access the capital market for financing, the Indian government introduced the LLP Act in 2008. As a result, MSME platforms were listed on the BSE and the NSE in 2012.
3.	To aid SMEs, 2018 saw the establishment of the National Financing Guarantee Fund, provides investments or credit loans to them.	The credit guarantee funds trust and the employment generation programme of the prime minister (CGTSME), and MUDRA Loans are just a few of the programmes the Indian government has established to assist entrepreneurs with their financial needs (PMGEP).
4.	China has an estimated 38 million SMEs, according to recent estimates.	There are roughly 63 million or more MSMEs in India overall.
5.	In China, SMEs account for more than 60% of the GDP.	MSMEs contribute 30% to India's GDP.
6.	For the past five years, China has been launching 16,000–18,00 new businesses each day.	India has been able to create about 1000-1100 per day.

(*Continued*)

Table 13.6 (Continued)

S/No.	Chinese SMEs	Indian SMEs
7.	China took its first few steps between 1978 and 1980, a time when the environment for SMEs or other forms of entrepreneurship was also hostile.	The 1990s success of India in the IT services sector encouraged more people to take a similar route.
8.	In comparison to India, China has a longer history of entrepreneurship and small businesses.	Finding ways to increase the number of prosperous Indian entrepreneurs who can inspire others is necessary.
9.	One of the most crucial contributing factors to the development of Chinese SMEs was their singular focus on becoming wealthy as businesspeople.	The goal in the majority of the country, outside of Bangalore and Gurgaon, is to work for the government.
10.	Additionally, China experienced a great deal of policy stability during this time.	In India, where there are many competing goals and there is no consistent policy
11.	China simply has many more cities wherein the ecosystem encourages to invent, tinker, and innovate.	Few cities in India have a thriving ecosystem.
12.	Chinese firms are highly competitive and has a dynamic system.	Too few of Indian firms are competitive
13.	The only way forward is to follow Shanghai's lead, which promotes the development of organic ecosystems in numerous locations.	The only way forward is to create organic ecosystems everywhere, as shown by Silicon Valley, Bangalore.

Source: Authors' own compilation.

Compare this to India, which has 63 million MSMEs hailed as the "growth engines" of the economy and contributes 30% of the nation's GDP. Despite the size, several bottlenecks impede the country's MSME sector's growth and success story.

According to Global Alliance for Mass Entrepreneurship founder Ravi Venkatesan (GAME), China's development offers many lessons that can be applied to other countries. China has established 16,000–18,000 new businesses daily for the past five years. Compared to India, that equates to roughly 1000–1100 per day. The TiE Global Summit 2020 speaker said, "Something very interesting is happening".

Further exploring China's history, Venkatesan noted that the nation took its first few steps between 1978 and 1980 when the environment for SMEs or entrepreneurship was also hostile (Small and Medium Enterprises, 2022). But some things were in its favour. China's history of entrepreneurship and small businesses is longer than India's (Adam and Alarifi, 2021). They have a remarkably robust culture. Some of these individuals reopened their businesses. Despite the challenges, they persisted. As they achieved success, they could lobby the government to alter the established order successfully, and their achievements encouraged others to do the same (Venkatesan, 2022).

The change replicated India's 1990s success in the IT services industry, encouraging more people to take a similar course. It's capitalism from below, led by entrepreneurs who can organise and cooperate with the government rather than by government intervention and policies. It is important to figure out how to encourage others and increase the number of successful Indian entrepreneurs (Venkatesan, 2022).

Main Point of Emphasis

There have also been additional factors that have helped Chinese SMEs grow, chief among them being their singular focus on becoming wealthy (Chandra *et al.*, 2020). Since the 1980s until Xi Jinping took office in 2013, becoming wealthy was China's top priority. They did not imprison anyone during this time, confront their neighbour, or frighten America. Instead, they just focused on the economic agenda and growing wealth.

In addition, China experienced a great deal of policy stability during this time because gaining its business community's and foreign investors' confidence was paramount (Adam and Alarifi, 2021). Such characteristics starkly contrast with India, where numerous goals are at odds with one another, and there is little to no policy stability (Valenza, Caputo and Calabr, 2021). Therefore, if the primary goal is prosperity, significantly more entrepreneurs and thriving SMEs are required than currently. He said this idea must take over and remain the top priority.

In addition, Cultural considerations are crucial in determining the future course (Bhoganadam *et al.*, 2017). For instance, in Bangalore, the emphasis is more on starting a business than in other regions where obtaining a government position is the top priority. Culture has an impact. The most significant factor is that caste or identity does not matter to people in Bangalore or Gurgaon. However, you are urged to create, experiment with, and innovate. Very few cities have a thriving ecosystem because these cultural factors are difficult to duplicate. Simply put, there are many more cities in China with these ecosystems, according to Venkatesan.

Expanding Ecosystems

Then, it would be essential to have more cities and towns where ecosystems exist to boost the sector to activate the growth cycle for SMEs in India (Manikandan, n.d.). In the future, Venkatesan wants to see a sound economic pyramid running India's entire length and breadth. There should be widespread prosperity, many new businesses, and a desire among young people to start their businesses. Even if they fail, they can eventually find employment. In response to a question about where the country should be in ten years, he said, "I hope we can bring that change".

More SMBs on a growth trajectory would pay taxes, borrow money from banks at favourable interest rates, increase productivity, and export goods at competitive prices, among other things, to advance the journey (Lalith Pankaj Raj and Kirubakaran, 2021). Very few companies are competitive and grow to be medium or even large. Therefore, it is advisable to adopt the Chinese model, and the PM's $5 trillion economy will materialise. Additionally, it will generate many jobs, among other benefits.

Venkatesan asserts that it is difficult to unite everyone, including banks, local, state, and federal governments, businesses, and industry associations, but cooperation will be the key to success. One initiative at GAME has been to choose cities where interventions are made that better the ecosystem's ability to function. He used Bangalore, Silicon Valley, and Shanghai as examples to demonstrate his point, claiming that the only solution is to create organic ecosystems everywhere. "This is very multilocal, which is the challenge". In Silicon Valley, it is possible. However, if you leave, it doesn't happen. Shanghai, Silicon Valley, and Bangalore are challenging to copy and paste. But, he added, "I think we are starting to understand what it takes, and the whole point is to work collaboratively" (Table 13.7).

Futuristic Approach of SMEs in Developing Economies

Table 13.7 Futuristic approach of SMEs in developing economies

S/No.	Various futuristics approaches of SMEs
1.	Innovative products, services, and business models will help the SME maintain its financial stability.
2.	Environmental, social, and governance (ESG) objectives will be met by SME business outcomes, and their business models will take both potential positive and negative externalities into account.
3.	SME will excel in its adaptability and resilience, allowing it to recover from setbacks and seize opportunities as the market changes.
4.	The ability to spot opportunities to improve future readiness benefits society, including SMEs themselves, whether it be through job creation, inclusive growth, or sustainable development.
5.	Diversity of social relationships.
6.	Ability to reconfigure.
7.	Ability to redeploy resources.
8.	Flexibility to refine strategy.
9.	Access to valuable resources.

(*Continued*)

Table 13.7 (Continued)

S/No.	Various futuristics approaches of SMEs
10.	Ability to mobilise networks.
11.	Autonomy
12.	Competitive aggressiveness.
13.	To creating jobs, many governments around the world place a high priority on iSME development.
14.	Future venture capital (VC) industry financing may include more funding from iSME projects.
15.	The Fund of Funds for Start-ups seeks to provide start-ups with indirect funding totalling $1.5 billion by 2025, will grow due to SIDBI.
16.	PFIs were able to maintain improving their systems and deepening their understanding of MSME clients. It is due to assurances, many new borrowers were successful to establish credit antiquities, making future loan applications for them less difficult.
17.	SME Finance Policy in Bangladesh will be crucial to improving SME financing.

Source: Authors' own Compilation.

Drivers of Future Readiness

Diverse of social connections: Acquire to heterogenous networks.

Capability to reconfigure: The ability, for instance, to redesign resource chain architecture to increase production to meet demand.

Capacity to repurpose funds: The ability to use currently available material, human, or financial resources for purposes other than those they originally intended for.

Flexibility to modify a plan: The capability of an organisation to gather fresh data and incorporate it in the strategic plan in response to continual alteration of internal or external circumstances.

Access to valuable resources: The efficiency with which a company can acquire new information, funding, and regulatory support.

Capability to mobilise networks: The capacity of organisational members to rely on their business contacts to obtain the required social, financial, or physical resources, especially when time is of the essence.

Self-governance: The extent top management empowers staff to make significant decisions independently.

Aggressiveness in competition: The capacity to take on rivals and gain entry or strengthen one's position in the market.

Many governments worldwide have made the growth of SMEs a top priority because, according to World Bank estimates, 600 million jobs will be needed by

2030 to accommodate the growing global labour force (Chandra *et al.*, 2020). In emerging markets, SMEs are responsible for seven of every ten new jobs (Valenza *et al.*, 2021). Access to financing is a significant barrier to SME growth despite being the second most frequently mentioned obstacle to SMEs' ability to grow their businesses in emerging markets and developing countries (Lalith Pankaj Raj and Kirubakaran, 2021).

Overall stakeholder interviews support the finding that the SME project could help both established and up-and-coming players in the venture capital (VC) industry in future by paying more attention to a pool of money strategy that may include growth capital (Helmy *et al.*, 2019).

Conclusion

The contributions and achievements of SMEs in developing nations can be visible from the following observation. Over 50% of jobs and approximately 90% of businesses worldwide are with SMEs. Up to 40% of the GDP in emerging economies comes from recently founded SMEs (World Bank Group, 2022). These numbers substantially rise when informal SMEs are included (Keskin *et al.*, 2010). The predictions show that 600 million more jobs will be needed by 2030 to meet the demands of a growing global labour force, making the development of SMEs a priority for the international government in many countries. SMEs, which account for seven out of ten jobs in emerging markets, create the most formal jobs (UN Environment Programme, 2022). Accessibility to financing is a significant barrier to SME expansion despite being the next most frequently mentioned hindrance to Small and Medium Enterprises' ability to expand their businesses in developing nations and emerging markets (World Bank Group, 2022).

Profitability is one of a company's most erratic financial indicators because it is affected by internal and external macro factors (Impact of SMEs, 2020). Macroeconomic factors' effect on the profitability of SMEs can be evaluated (Dewan, 2021). Macroeconomic variables like a country's population and number of businesses, FDI, GDP, exports and imports, inflation, unemployment, average salary, taxes paid, and various other factors influence an SME's profitability (Keskin *et al.*, 2010). The monetary success of the companies in Lithuania is dynamic and displays a connection between important elements and commercial success (Pandey, 2022). Most of the designated macroeconomic benchmarks were found to be statistically insignificant and have little to no relationship to corporate profitability, including average wages, inflation, various businesses, and the financial base (Bekeris, 2012).

SMEs and MSMEs have helped greatly in achieving Sustainable Development Goal No. 9, "Industry, Innovation and Infrastructure", of the United

Nations in developing economies. It has contributed to expanding small industrial businesses, developing strong infrastructure, and encouraging research and innovation.

Both India and China, as emerging economies, can achieve economic growth, which will enhance employment and capital formation and boost income and the people's standard of living. But it is necessary to minutely observe the nations' social, political, economic, and cultural perspectives. As far as the applicability of SMEs in the future is concerned, they will prove to be of great economic enhancement if used intelligently by understanding the various pros and cons of the economies. Regarding their financial contribution to developed and developing economies, SMEs are very important, even though different organisations and countries have different definitions of an SME (UNDESA – MSMEs and Sustainable Development Goals Report, 2020). Because they can make decisions quickly, use less money but more skilled labour, and have low management costs, small and medium-sized businesses (SMEs) are now preferred to large corporations in developing countries (Keskin *et al.*, 2010). Large firms have made the idea of "small is beautiful" significant in today's economic climate (Role of SMEs, 2022).

Despite some flaws, SMEs are less vulnerable to economic crises because of their adaptability and flexibility to changing conditions (Bekeris, 2012). SMEs are crucial players in fostering entrepreneurship, innovation, competitiveness, and developing a successful innovation system for developing nations, according to "SMEs vs MSMEs", 2021. Improving SMEs' capacity to benefit from commercial investment opportunities and the environment for their investments benefits their economic performance, spurs growth, and lowers poverty in developing countries (UN Environment Programme, 2022).

SMEs are more adaptable than large corporations in production, marketing, and customer service because they closely monitor the market, understand the needs of their customers, and have strong bonds with their employees (Dewan, 2021). Due to their flexibility, SMEs can handle multiple challenges more effectively and with less harm (Small and Medium Enterprises, 2022). Despite some flaws, SMEs are less impacted by economic crises due to their flexibility and capacity to change with the times (Bekeris, 2012). Additionally, they mitigate the effects of economic crises and serve as a "compressor" (Keskin *et al.*, 2010). SMEs are essential, especially for developing nations (UN Environment Programme, 2022).

Governments have acknowledged that SMEs require specific policies and programmes to survive and grow even in a normal economic environment (Kota, 2018). However, now, the global crisis has been particularly hard on SMEs (Bhuyan, 2016). The fact that SMEs are frequently at risk. During times of crisis, it is crucial to emphasise for several reasons, including (OECD, 2009):

- They are already small, so downsizing is more challenging for them.
- Each of them engages in fewer different types of economic activity.
- Their financial foundation is weaker (i.e., lower capitalisation).
- They either have no credit history or a bad one.
- They have fewer financing options and a greater reliance on credit.

Moreover, the prevailing economic climate has produced benefits for SMEs in developing countries and drawbacks too (Dewan, 2021). In countries with fewer large firms (big business), the potential of SMEs will likely have an impulsive force, as we can predict (The Impact of SMEs, 2020). Coordination and promotion issues in SMEs' activities are caused by a lack of policy decisions and implications though (Kota, 2018). Chronic economic problems in developing countries have had a negative impact on the energy use of these companies (Pandey, 2022). Providing SMEs with the necessary opportunities and guidance has created favourable conditions for developing countries (Role of SMEs, 2022).

Recommendations

After analysing SME's role and contribution, it was found that SMEs also have various disadvantages. The following disadvantages are observed by economists, marketers, governments of various nations, and consumers of goods and services.

Drawbacks

- Although SMEs generate a sizable amount of employment, that employment may occasionally only be temporary since many SMEs fail before they have been in operation for five years. This results in higher unemployment rates.
- In the past, SMEs have drawn criticism for having an alarmingly high bankruptcy rate. If their products or services don't sell, SMEs quickly quit.
- To survive and compete, SMEs occasionally oversupply the market with inexpensive goods and services. This product can temporarily replace the original product, but it frequently falls short of the competition. This destroys the value and reputation of the prospective.
- In addition, SMEs lack the essential capital required to launch and maintain growth after a certain point. The financial crisis is slowly eroding the strength of SMEs.

- SMEs need to innovate to survive. However, the constant pressure to innovate and present new options breeds uncertainty and confusion. Innovation is still the best survival tactic for an SME.
- To succeed, SMEs require an environment that is inspiring and supportive. Political unrest and the government's stringent rules and regulations constrain their capacity for development and growth.
- One decision could lead to a lot of strange things happening. Because of this, risk insurance for businesses is essential. However, SMEs frequently forgo risk insurance for their business because of their tight budgets.
- SMEs may encounter taxation problems if the government does not focus on creating entrepreneur-friendly policies.
- Finding qualified candidates for a specific position is a significant challenge for SMEs. Experienced workers are either unaffordable for SMEs to hire or averse to taking the risk of working for a small business.

SMEs have thus advantages as well as disadvantages. Only simple financing options and business-friendly government regulations can effectively encourage entrepreneurship. Liberal policies motivate would-be entrepreneurs to take calculated risks to benefit themselves and society.

Governments, NGOs, and private organisations must promote SMEs to achieve maximum economic benefits.

Especially emerging and developing economies can achieve benefits through SMEs and MSMEs. The countries with emerging economies are India, Pakistan, Bangladesh, Vietnam, China, Brazil, Nigeria, Mexico, etc.

The functions of SMEs and MSMEs need to be explained to the financially weak and downtrodden citizens, which will help the economic upliftment of a section of society.

The SMEs and MSMEs can bring a positive wave of change in the economies and the resultant factor will be that the economic landscape will be changed.

SMEs and MSMEs can increase capital formation, employment and income, enhancing people's lifestyle and increasing demand. There will be an expansion of business and improvement in international trade. It can bring surplus income to the economies through international trade.

References

Abdulsaleh, A. M., and Worthington, A. C. (2013) Small and medium-sized enterprises financing: A review of literature. *International Journal of Business and Management*, 8(14): 36.

Ackah, J., and Vuvor, S. (2011) The challenges faced by small and medium enterprises (SMEs) in obtaining credit in Ghana (Print).

Adam, N. A., and Alarifi, G. (2021) Innovation practices for survival of small and medium enterprises (SMEs) in the COVID-19 times: The role of external support. *Journal of Innovation and Entrepreneurship*, *10*(1): 1–22.

Adian, I., Doumbia, D., Gregory, N., Ragoussis, A., Reddy, A., and Timmis, J. (2020) *Small and medium enterprises in the pandemic: Impact, responses and the role of development finance*. Washington, DC: The World Bank.

AlQershi, N. (2021) Strategic thinking, strategic planning, strategic innovation and the performance of SMEs: The mediating role of human capital. *Management Science Letters*, *11*(3): 1003–1012.

Bekeris, R. (January 2012) The impact of macroeconomic indicators upon SME's profitability. *Ekonomika*, 91(3): 117–128.

Bhoganadam, S., Rao, N. S., and Dasaraju, S. (2017) A study on issues and challenges faced by SMEs: A literature review. *Research Journal of SRNMC*, *1*: 48–57.

Bhuyan, U. (2016) A study on the performance of micro, small and medium enterprises (MSMEs) in India. *Global Journal of Management and Business Research*, *16*(9): Version 1.0. 33–36.

Chandra, A., Paul, J., and Chavan, M. (2020) Internationalization barriers of SMEs from developing countries: A review and research agenda. *International Journal of Entrepreneurial Behavior and Research*, *26*(6): 1281–1310.

Dalberg. (November 2011) Report on support to SMEs in developing countries through financial intermediaries. https://www.eib.org/attachments/dalberg_sme-briefing-paper.pdf (Accessed 2 August 2023).

Dar, S. A., and Ahmad, N. (2022) Mobile Technology's role in meeting sustainable development goals. *Journal of Technology Innovations and Energy*, *1*(2): 8–15.

Dewan, N. (15 February 2021) Taking a cue from China: How India can help SMEs flourish and prosper. *The Economic Times* (Print).

Di Pippo, S. (2019) Space technology and the implementation of the 2030 agenda. *UN Chronicle*, *55*(4): 61–63.

El Tarabishy, A. (2020) The genesis of the United Nations international name day for micro-, small, and medium-sized enterprises—June 27. *Journal of the International Council for Small Business*, *1*(1): 4–6.

Fakieh, B. (2018). SMEs research: The continuous need to explore the ICT potential, conference paper presented at the 32nd IBIMA Conference, at: Seville, Spain available at https://www.researchgate.net/publication/329013899_SMEs_Research_The_Continuous_Need_to_Explore_the_ICT_Potential

Goyal, S., Agrawal, A., and Sergi, B. S. (2020). Social entrepreneurship for scalable solutions addressing sustainable development goals (SDGs) at BoP in India. *Qualitative Research in Organizations and Management (An International Journal)*, 16 (3and4): 509–529. https://doi.org/10.1108/QROM-07-2020-1992

Hannan, M. A., Al-Shetwi, A. Q., Begum, R. A., Ker, P. J., Rahman, S. A., Mansor, M., and Dong, Z. Y. (2021) Impact assessment of battery energy storage systems towards achieving sustainable development goals. *Journal of Energy Storage*, *42*: 103040.

Helmy, I., Adawiyah, W. R., and Banani, A. (2019) Linking psychological empowerment, knowledge sharing, and employees' innovative behavior in SMEs. *The Journal of Behavioral Science*, *14*(2): 66–79.

Keskin, H., Senturk, C., Sungur, O., and Kiris, H. M. (2010) The Importance of SMEs in Developing Economies (Print).

Kota, H. B. (December 19, 2018) Small Business, big contribution. https://www.dailypioneer.com/2018/columnists/small-businesses–big-contribution.html (10 August 2023).

Lalith Pankaj Raj, G. N., and Kirubakaran, V. (2021) Energy efficiency enhancement and climate change mitigations of SMEs through grid-interactive solar photovoltaic system. *International Journal of Photoenergy, 2021*: 1–19. https://doi.org/10.1155/2021/6651717

Manikandan, S. (n.d.) A Study on Startup and its Impact on MSME in India with Special Reference to Maharashtra State. In *T. John Institute of Management and Sciences (TIMS) organized a 1-Day national conference on "Transforming India through Innovation and Entrepreneurship"* (Print).

Mathai, G. P. (2015) Challenges and issues in micro, small and medium enterprises (MSMEs) in India: A current scenario of economic growth. *Global Journal for Research Analysis, 4*(7): 162–163.

Mavuri, S., Chavali, K., and Kumar, A. (November 2019) A study on imperative innovation eco system linkages to map Sustainable Development Goal 9. At the *2019 International Conference on Digitization* (Print).

Milutinović, R., Stošić, B., and Mihić, M. (2015) Concepts and importance of strategic innovation in SMEs: Evidence from Serbia. *Management: Journal of Sustainable Business and Management Solutions in Emerging Economies, 20*(77): 35–42.

Mondejar, M. E., Avtar, R., Diaz, H. L. B., Dubey, R. K., Esteban, J., Gómez-Morales, A., and Garcia-Segura, S. (2021) Digitalization to achieve sustainable development goals: Steps towards a smart green planet. *Science of the Total Environment, 794*: 148539.

Mpofu, F. Y. (2022) Industry 4.0 in financial services: Mobile Money taxes, revenue mobilisation, financial inclusion, and the realisation of sustainable development goals (SDGs) in Africa. *Sustainability, 14*(14): 8667.

OECD. (June 2017). Enhancing the contributions of SMEs in a global and digitalized economy. Meeting of the OECD Council at the Ministerial Level. Paris, 7–8 June 2017 (Print).

Pandey, P. (29 January 2022) The difference between SME and MSME: Quick guide for better results. https://sabpaisa.in/blog/difference-between-sme-and-msme/ (20 July 2023).

Pasnicu, D. (2018) Supporting SMEs in creating jobs. *Journal of Economic Development, Environment and People, 7*(1): 15–22.

Ramarao, R. (2012) Competitiveness of India's micro and small enterprises through functional competencies: Role in Nation's development. *Vikalpa, 37*(1): 97–112.

Rena, R. (2009). Rural entrepreneurship and development – An Eritrean perspective. *Journal of Rural Development, 28*(1): 1–19.

Singh, C., and Wasdani, P. (2016) Finance for micro, small, and medium-sized enterprises in India: Sources and challenges (Print).

Sivasree, C. H. V., and Vasavi, P. (2020) MSMES in India-growth and challenges. *Journal of Scientific Computing, 9*(2): 126–137.

Tonis, R. (2015) SME's role in achieving sustainable development. *Journal of Economic Development, Environment and People, 4*(1): 41–50.

UN Environment Programme. (2022). Goal 9: Industry, Innovation and Infrastructure. https://www.unep.org/explore-topics/sustainable-development-goals/why-do-sustainable-development-goals-matter/goal-9 (Accessed 10 June 2023).

UNDESA – Report on MSMEs and Sustainable Development Goals. (2020) *Micro – small and medium – sized enterprises (MSMEs) and their role in achieving the sustainable development goals*. (DESA) Department of Economic and Social Affairs (Print).

Valenza, G., Caputo, A., and Calabrò, A. (2021) Is small and medium-sized beautiful? The structure and evolution of family SMEs research. *Journal of Family Business Management.* DOI: 10.1108/JFBM-03-2021-0024

Venkatesan, R. (2022). GAME Global Alliance for Mass entrepreneurship. Retrieved from: https://www.linkedin.com/posts/ravi-venkatesan-ba15b820_ravi-venkatesan-on-mass-entrepreneurship-activity-7077867626286231552-TIwr/

World Bank Group. (2022). *Small and medium enterprises (SMEs) finance*. Washington, DC: The World Bank (Print).

World Economic Forum. (2021) Future readiness of SMEs: Mobilizing the SME sector to drive widespread sustainability and prosperity. https://www3.weforum.org/docs/WEF_Future_Readiness_of_SMEs_2021.pdf (Accessed 10 June 2023).

Part III

Individual BRICS Nations' Perspectives on Entrepreneurship

14 Exploring the Urban Economics of Street Markets in BRICS Nations

The Case Study of Rolêfeira in Araraquara, Brazil

Renan Augusto Ramos and Ndivhuho Tshikovhi

Introduction

The debate on the existing problems in the current world of work gains new layers due to processes such as the precarisation of jobs and productive restructuring in times of neoliberal globalisation (Kalleberg, 2013; Ferreira, 2016; Siegmann and Schiphorst, 2016). However, in the global South, this set of circumstances in work and income is part of previous social and historical contexts, not a direct product of the present time (Munck, 2013; Scully, 2016). The ambivalence of this period, represented by diversity and insecurity, brings these problems to the Western countries that lived through the golden age of full employment (Beck, 2000). Thus, economic diversity is a rising theme in urban studies, representing a theoretical concern that recognises the heterogeneity in urban economic and social practices (Gibson-Graham, 2008; Healy, 2009). The BRICS (Brazil, Russia, India, China and South Africa) are, therefore, fertile ground to develop this research agenda because precarious working and living conditions are widely known and reported in these countries.

The presence of economic diversity in these territories simultaneously produced multiple theoretical methods for understanding the true meaning of these practices in urban spaces. For example, the concepts and theories of the informal and popular economies, as well as the circuits of the urban economy (Hart, 1973; Santos, 2018 [1979]; Hespanha, 2009; Icaza and Tiriba, 2009; Chen, 2012). This broad framework allows for a wide range of discussions that provide, from different scientific areas, the necessary means to analyse the economy in cities. Despite being situated in this plurality in social sciences, the focus is to produce a reading key from the spatial dynamics of urban spaces today, using an urban economic geography perspective to discuss small-scale public space activities.

Several authors have discussed public spaces as a means of socioeconomic integration and as the focus of regulatory policies for their use (Anjaria, 2006; Solomon-Ayeh, King and Decardi-Nelson, 2011; Xue and Huang, 2015; Roever and Skinner, 2016; Álvarez, 2018; Martínez, Short and Estrada, 2018). As mentioned, the current period brings multidimensional challenges that deepen

DOI: 10.4324/9781003475606-18

vulnerable social strata's social and economic reproduction efforts. Various economic initiatives express the various forms of work and income strategies found today linked to the harsh conditions of everyday life. Thus, this chapter contributes to assessing the relevance of public spaces for livelihoods and local urban planning policies. To achieve this objective, a case study with a mixed approach was carried out in the Brazilian city of Araraquara, having as a research site the street market named Rolêfeira.

The chapter has five major sections besides the introduction and conclusion. The first section discusses the multidisciplinary theoretical framework of this study on urban economic geography. Then, we build the two research questions that coordinate the investigation process in this field. The next section shows the empirical location of this research, establishing a discussion based on the street market Rolêfeira. The fourth section presents the chosen approach and the techniques used during the research. The last section underlines the main results of this study, evaluating the role played by the street market as a place of political, economic and cultural interactions in public spaces.

Theoretical Framework

The harsh conditions of work and income directly impact urban spaces in general, and neoliberal globalisation increases challenges for the livelihoods of the less favoured social strata. However, in developing countries like Brazil, these troubled conditions are related to previous factors and not current globalisation (Munck, 2013; Scully, 2016). It is worth mentioning two fundamental historical facts, such as the patterns of urbanisation and industrialisation. Godfrey (1991: 18) states that the rapid urbanisation in Brazil "exacerbated social problems and intensified spatial contrasts in the city". On the other hand, the industrialisation process itself, with high levels of capital, "attracts more and more people but is not able to generate enough jobs" (Santos, 2018 [1979]).

Both phenomena are the backdrop for economic diversity in cities. The everyday economy "comprises many different processes of production, exchange, ownership, work, remuneration, and consumption" (Healy, 2009: 339). Western-centric conceptual models vaguely contributed to a holistic understanding of urban spaces in the global South (Hart, 1973; Santos, 2018 [1979]). How could these BRICS nation's dynamics be correctly understood? The vulnerable population's problems can be a point of departure for this academic discussion. Thus, we propose starting with multidisciplinary urban economic geography studies.

The theory of the circuits explains the urban economy according to the spatial dynamics of cities (Santos, 2018 [1979]). This theoretical framework is based on the historical domain to understand the socio-spatial reality and specificities of the economy in underdeveloped countries[1]. We observe two circuits of the urban economy, the upper and the lower. They are the results of the modernisation context of developing countries during the second half of the 20th century.

Functioning as economic subsystems integrated into the urban space, the circuits "are true communicating vessels" (Silveira, 2013: 70). The upper circuit is represented by activities with high levels of technology, productive techniques and financial support, such as monopoly companies and large banks that coordinate a wide range of relationships in social life today. Nevertheless, the lower circuit represents the adaptation of the economic system to social groups that cannot meet their needs. It consists of small-scale economic activities with capital reduced to a minimum; that is, physical labour is the major asset for these practices.

The interconnections of the circuits cannot be neglected due to the fluid relations of exchange, competitiveness and dominance developed by the upper circuit concerning the lower one. Still, according to the concerns of this chapter, we must draw attention to the lower circuit of the urban economy, as its main rationale is focused on meeting the daily needs of its agents. This circuit is an easy entry for economic occupation in urban spaces (Santos, 2018 [1979]). Another important aspect is related to the vulnerable population's socioeconomic dynamism, highlighting the creative strategies to overcome problems such as widespread unemployment and precariousness.

Although it is the notion of choice in developed countries (Siegmann and Schiphorst, 2016), precarious work can contribute to our discussion, bringing interesting analytical tools. Moreover, this phenomenon is a long-standing feature of developing countries (Munck, 2013; Scully, 2016). The notion of "precarious work is characterised by uncertainty and insecurity" (Munck, 2013: 758). Growing population segments are in precarious conditions in today's capitalism (Scully, 2016; Álvarez, 2018). Ferreira (2016: 7) states that "precarious work is understood as low-quality employment" regardless of formal or informal relationships. In other words, "work-related insecurities have become a common denominator when defining precarious work" (Siegmann and Schiphorst, 2016: 115). Precariousness is related to people's exposure to problems such as social protection, income security, stability, decent working conditions, social dialogue and participation (Ferreira, 2016). We can see that this precarity goes beyond work itself, promoting crises in the social and economic reproduction spheres that affect families and communities (Lee and Kofman, 2012; Kalleberg, 2013).

Hence, precarious conditions provide the source of individual and collective livelihood strategies to overcome socioeconomic exclusion. These limits give rise to several small-scale initiatives to generate work and income in urban spaces. The lower circuit encompasses the issues described above because it is "born and develops as a result of both the dissatisfaction of the demands created by the hegemonic economy and structural unemployment" (Silveira, 2013: 67). The urban poor have always developed "strong social networks and survival strategies of considerable dynamism" (Munck, 2013: 748–749). Thus, cities worldwide, especially in the BRICS, express an economic diversity that organises and reorganises urban spaces, producing different forms of using public spaces.

Research Questions

It is known that any research originates from a general question about a phenomenon of interest (Williams, 2007). The elaboration of a consistent research question provides more assertiveness during the process of investigation (Marconi and Lakatos, 2000 [1982]). It is an organisational strategy for choosing appropriate techniques and methods (Demo, 1995 [1980]). So, the phenomenon of interest is economic diversity in cities. The guiding questions of this research are:

i *What is the relevance of public spaces as places of livelihoods in cities today?*
ii *In what ways can urban planning explore the social and economic potential of public spaces in cities?*

Field Survey Location

A street market named Rolêfeira in the Brazilian city of Araraquara was selected as an empirical location to apply the set of research techniques of our mixed approach. This street market is a place that enables several social-spatial interactions in the city. This street market is the concrete aspect of the aforementioned economic diversity. It highlights the specificities of the everyday economy found especially in cities in developing countries, as well as assessing the politics between local government and small-scale urban activities.

The main objective of this street market is to promote contact between stallholders and potential buyers, building an ecosystem favourable to this set of economic practices. Since 2017, its editions have been organised in various public spaces like sidewalks and squares. However, the current editions occur in a square named "Praça do Faveral". The periodicity is bimonthly when conditions are favourable. Due to the COVID-19 outbreak, the organising committee suspended its events and only returned on 14 August 2022. Until now, there have been 21 editions of this street market in Araraquara.[3]

Method and Techniques

Coherently presenting the method allows assertiveness in the search for answers to any research question. The design of this work was conceived according to the alignment of articulated investigation techniques, which supported a case study with a mixed approach. It is widely known that the exclusive use of statistics can underline shortcomings. To overcome this problem, we developed a mixed approach in our case study in the street market named Rolêfeira. This research design is interesting for simultaneously gathering numerical and narrative data (Williams, 2007). We intended to avoid reductionist views on economic diversity, emphasising the relevance of both data.

The first group of data represented the following classes:

a. Secondary data on work and income in Brazil

b. primary data on stallholders' situation

The national overview was based on work and income indexes such as labour underutilisation, informality and registrations as individual micro-entrepreneurs. On the other hand, the local primary data were organised according to the socioeconomic aspects of the stallholders. This data set showed the composition of problems in work and income today. Therefore, it opened space to understand the complexities at the national level and the local effects in our case study.

The second group of data was collected with two main techniques:

c. Systematic observation in loco

d. Semi-Structured Interviews

Fieldwork provided a means to observe the social-spatial interactions at the chosen street market critically. We focused on sociability based on the economic, cultural, political and symbolic spheres. The interviews were semi-structured with guiding questions for respondents to verbalise their opinions. These highlighted the perception of those related to the investigated phenomenon by giving voice to their personal and political experiences as a resource for understanding the urban economy. In general, these techniques brought the relevance of qualitative data to this research on economic diversity.

Key Research Findings

Theoretical reflection on economic diversity in public spaces and empirical evidence collected during the research allowed for interesting insights into this field. This exploratory study paved an initial way to answer the aforementioned research questions. The systematic observations, articulated with the secondary data and the theoretical framework, provided grounded analysis on multiple socio-spatial and economic practices in the field survey location. Economic diversity is a prevalent phenomenon, ranging from various goods and services. So, there are multiple possibilities for economically using public spaces during the street markets' events. To organise the findings, the chapter profiles the stallholders' small-scale economic practices. Then it explores qualitatively the implications of street markets to urban planning and a broader sociability in public spaces.

Table 14.1 Types of goods traded

Main segments of economic practices			
Handmade crafts		17	38.6%
Food items		13	29.5%
Second-hand clothing items		8	18.2%
Homemade cosmetics		4	9.1%
Beverages		1	2.3%
Others		1	2.3%
	Total sample	44	100%

Profiling These Economic Practices

The initial primary data collected during the research highlighted the main segments of goods traded. The evidence leads us to consider that these activities have a significant presence in the investigated street market due to the low levels of capital involved (Table 14.1). These activities represent an easy entry into the urban economy, as the main resources are part of the agents' daily lives, converting raw materials, household utensils and tools into basic capital and goods. In other words, creativity is an asset employed to turn personal skills or knowledge into an activity capable of providing work and income through a small-scale economic practice.

The second characteristic indicated that more than half of the investigated practices were related to the multidisciplinary debate on informality. In the first place, it is important to bring the idea that not only "the informal economy is a field of study in its own right, drawing an increasing number of scholars from multiple disciplines" (Chen, 2012: 4) but also "represents a broad construct and research domain with significant opportunities for future research" (Webb *et al.*, 2013: 611). Webb *et al.* (2009) provided an interesting way of characterising the informal economy, highlighting its illegal but, at the same time, legitimate aspects. It can be said that this sector produces legal goods and services in unregulated ways. However, the sample as shown in table 14.2 also encompassed registration as an individual micro-entrepreneur. The records of this category drew attention to the aspects of precarious entrepreneurship. This programme is an initiative to formalise informal practices through an entrepreneurial mindset. Although important to access social security benefits, the limited range of earnings opened critics to the mainstream idea of entrepreneurship. To some extent, it is just a new form of precarious strategy for income.

Table 14.2 Level of stallholders' registration

Presence of registration among the economic practices			
No registration		26	59.1%
Register as individual micro-entrepreneur		18	40.9%
	Total sample	44	100%

Table 14.3 Results of economic practices

Economic scale based on monthly earnings			
Up to 500 BRL*		16	36.4%
From 500 BRL to 1,000 BRL		15	34.1%
From 1,000 BRL to 1,500 BRL		6	13.6%
Over 1,500 BRL		7	15.9%
	Total sample	44	100%

* 1 USD = 4.86 BRL on 14 November 2023.

The third characteristic was related to the economic scale. Most initiatives produced less than 1,500 BRL (Table 14.3). The debate on popular economies was a starting point for this topic regarding the tangible expressions of social and economic reproduction. Popular economies are an important segment of the world of work in developing countries. It is also worth mentioning that these economic practices are linked to the daily needs of their agents. They call attention to the "maximisation of well-being and economic reproduction of the groups, rather than the maximisation of profits as the market-oriented capitalist rationality" (Hespanha, 2009: 58). In other words, these work and survival strategies could be understood as "the art of creating favourable conditions to satisfy human needs" (Icaza and Tiriba, 2009: 150). The low monthly income then brought up different possibilities of economic organisation based on principles not exactly associated with financial gains but with the general commitments of household bills. Therefore, they represented the "set of economic activities and social practices intending to ensure the reproduction of social life through the use of one's workforce and available resources" (Icaza and Tiriba, 2009: 150).

The last profile characteristic presented the relevance of these economic practices regarding personal income. Two types of functions were found according to the role played by these initiatives in everyday life: as a complementary or sole source of income. Just over half of the practices have the role of supplementary income. Several implications could be discussed from this information about small-scale activities in public spaces. As Hart (1973: 65) pointed out, "the chronic imbalance between income from wage employment and expenditure needs" highlights the dependence on other combined forms of livelihoods. Multitasking, multiple jobs and informal opportunities were among the possible explanations for these ventures found during the research, also involving the debate on the harsh working and living conditions in developing countries, such as the BRICS. Thus, this data set demonstrated the "willingness of workers to put in long hours on a multiplicity of occupations, both in and out of the organised labour force", to provide the necessary means of social and economic reproduction (Hart, 1973: 66).

Table 14.4 Meanings of economic practices

The role played in personal income			
Supplementary source		23	52.3%
Sole source		21	47.7%
	Total sample	44	100%

These small-scale economic activities take place in urban spaces. It means stating that spatial dynamics cannot be neglected during research in this academic field. To move beyond informality and popular economies, the urban economy's lower circuit is an important analytical key to understanding economic diversity. We mainly use this theoretical framework of urban economic geography because it can integrate other social sciences to reflect on the spatial dynamics of economic processes in cities. The quantitative data on the stallholders' socioeconomic profile expressed these groups' living and working conditions. We described the data in tables and then presented the relationships with the theoretical framework (Table 14.4). Next, we explore the qualitative data collected while researching the Rolêfeira street market.

The Nexus between Politics and Urban Planning

Street vending is, without a doubt, "an important avenue for income generation for those with very low social capital" (Martínez, Short and Estrada, 2018: 1), alleviating problems such as poverty, unemployment and lack of opportunities in conventional jobs. Local governments then play an important role because of their regulatory power over urban planning policies. Several authors critically present the perspective of street vending as a public nuisance due to how shared urban spaces are used (Anjaria, 2006; Xue and Huang, 2015). It is no secret that the right to use public spaces to generate work and income must be ensured (Álvarez, 2018). At the same time, urban policies are a key asset to prevent problems such as traffic jams, obstruction of sidewalks and harassment of vendors. The contradictions between the need to order urban spaces and promote friendly spaces for small local economies represent one of the main issues. The case study conducted in the Brazilian city of Araraquara pointed to an important aspect of this phenomenon. The "Municipal Plan for Creative and Solidarity Economy" is an initiative to create and structure permanent and periodic markets in urban spaces, providing a vibrant environment for small-scale economic practices through urban planning policies. The institutionalisation of street markets seems to be a balancing policy to solve the contradictions. The engagement of civil society and local government policies thus expands the possibilities of facing problems in work and income.

Appropriating Urban Public Spaces

Street economy, expressed by economic activities based on public spaces, "depends on the innovative use of space to survive and flourish" (Solomon-Ayeh, King and Decardi-Nelson, 2011: 20). Roever and Skinner (2016) discussed the importance of the urban poor accessing strategic city spaces. Despite being a significant economic hub for local strategies, our objective was not exclusively to evaluate the Rolêfeira street market for its economic function but to examine its coexistence with other areas of social life. This aspect may represent a strategy to promote broad forms of appropriation of the built environment of cities, including the social, cultural, political and economic dimensions. Watson (2009: 1579) recognised that research on markets "has focused on their economic role" in urban spaces, and Anjaria (2006) underlined the vital role of street markets in the economic and social functions of the city. The evidence collected during our fieldwork drew attention to this very diversity of exchanges between social groups in public spaces. With cultural attractions such as street artists, painters, live musicians and local bands, the potential to promote outdoor leisure activities stands out. They work as an appealing force that provides the necessary means for different social strata's interactions and socio-spatial practices. People interacting in groups, personalised purchase relationships between individuals and vendors, young people talking to each other, and elderly people enjoying themselves with their families are among the main interactions at the street market during the study. In this sense, it is necessary to observe the Rolêfeira not only as an economic space but also as a space where broader sociability is cultivated. Street markets and their broad sociability, therefore, establish new perspectives on appropriating urban public spaces to promote more inclusive cities today.

Conclusion and Further Research

The limits of the conventional labour market represented the lack of capacity to provide salaried jobs, low wages and dissatisfaction with working conditions. Enough theoretical evidence supported the relationships between harsh working conditions and the emergence of multiple income strategies (Hart, 1973; Álvarez, 2018). The chapter then reflected on the spatial dynamics of public spaces as places of work and income for a vast population in today's cities (Anjaria, 2006; Solomon-Ayeh *et al.*, 2011; Martínez *et al.*, 2018). At the same time, we explored the broad social and economic potential of street markets in urban planning policies.

A holistic approach is an important methodological instrument because it demonstrates the complexity of every social phenomenon analysed. The research highlighted a case study conducted at the Rolêfeira street market in

Araraquara, Brazil. Based on multidisciplinary studies in urban economic geography, we first assessed the possibilities of socioeconomic integration by profiling the small-scale activities of the lower circuit (Santos, 2018 [1979]; Silveira, 2007, 2013) and then highlighted the relationships between urban planning and street markets in public spaces. The sample of stallholders evaluated how we could interpret these activities, highlighting the complex situation in the spheres of work and income that was corroborated by the set of national and local data collected. Thus, the chapter drew attention to various viable initiatives for appropriating public spaces by different social strata. The investigated street market represented not the economic, political, or cultural spheres separately but rather a combination of all these aspects – a true overlap demonstrating the pluralism of social-spatial interactions in urban public spaces. The research allowed observing small-scale economic practices using this public space as a visibility channel to trade different types of goods and services.

Finally, economic diversity was one of the main concerns throughout the study. This research agenda points to the multiple forms of economic and social organisation in cities (Gibson-Graham, 2008; Healy, 2009). It is no secret that economic precariousness is a long-known reality in developing countries of the global South (Munck, 2013; Scully, 2016). Thus, we use this theoretical framework of urban studies to present insights into the BRICS themselves. Despite being restricted to a certain place and time, this reflection brings other interesting opportunities for research. Emphasising this issue means recognising a challenging frontier of potential collaborative studies. Therefore, it would be important to encourage comparative scientific studies between cities in BRICS countries to achieve this proposal, using similar methods and techniques during the investigation.

References

Álvarez, M.I.F. (2018) Más allá de la precariedad: *prácticas* colectivas y subjetividades políticas desde la economía popular Argentina. *Íconos* 62: 21–38.
Anjaria, J.S. (2006) Street Hawkers and public spaces in Mumbai. *Economic and Political Weekly* 41(21): 2140–2146.
Beck, U. (2000) *The brave new world of work*. Cambridge, Polity Press.
Chen, M.A. (2012) *The informal economy: Definitions, theories and policies*. WIEGO Working Paper no 1 (Print).
Demo, P. (1995) *Metodologia em Ciências Sociais*. 3a ed. São Paulo: Editora Atlas.
Ferreira, M. (2016) Informal versus precarious work in Colombia: Concept and operationalization. *Progress in Development Studies* 16(2): 140–158.
Gibson-Graham, J.K. (2008) Diverse economies: Performative practices for other worlds. *Progress in Human Geography* 32(5): 613–632.
Godfrey, B.J. (1991) Modernizing the Brazilian city. *Geographical Review* 81(1): 18–34.
Hart, K. (1973) Informal income opportunities and urban employment in Ghana. *The Journal of Modern African Studies* 11: 61–89.
Healy, S. (2009) Economies, alternative. In: *International Encyclopedia of human geography*. Oxford: Elsevier.

Hespanha, P. (2009) Da expansão dos mercados à metamorfose das economias populares. *Revista Crítica de Ciências Sociais* 84: 49–63.
Icaza, A.M.S. and Tiriba, L. (2009) Economia Popular. In: *Dicionário Internacional da Outra Economia*. Coimbra: Almedina.
Kalleberg, A.L. (2013) Globalization and precarious work. *Contemporary Sociology* 42(5): 700–706.
Lee, C.K. and Kofman, Y. (2012) The politics of precarity: Views beyond the United States. *Work and Occupations* 39(4): 388–408.
Marconi, M.A. and Lakatos, E.M. (2000) *Metodologia científica*. 3a ed. São Paulo: Editora Atlas.
Martínez, L., Short, J.R. and Estrada, D. (2018) The diversity of the street vending: A case study of street vending in Cali. *Cities* 79: 18–25.
Munck, R. (2013) *The precariat: A view from the South. Third World Quarterly* 34(5): 747–762.
Roever, S. and Skinner, C. (2016) Street vendors and cities. *Environment and Urbanization* 28(2): 359–374.
Santos, M. (2018) *O espaço dividido: os dois circuitos da economia urbana dos países subdesenvolvidos*. 2a ed. São Paulo: Editora da Universidade de São Paulo.
Scully, B. (2016) Precarity north and south: A Southern critique of guy standing. *Global Labour Journal* 7(2): 160–173.
Siegmann, K.A. and Schiphorst, F. (2016) Understanding the globalizing precariat: From informal sector to precarious work. *Progress in Development Studies* 16(2): 111–123.
Silveira, M.L. (2007) Metrópolis brasileñas: un análisis de los circuitos de la economía urbana. *EURE (Santiago)* 33(100): 149–164
Silveira, M.L. (2013) Da pobreza estrutural à resistência: pensando os circuitos da economia urbana. *Ciência Geográfica* 27(1): 64–71
Solomon-Ayeh, B.E., King, R.S. and Decardi-Nelson, I. (2011) Street Vending and the use of urban public space in Kumasi, Ghana. *The Ghana Surveyor* 4(1): 20–31.
Watson, S. (2009) The magic of the marketplace: Sociality in a neglected public space. *Urban Studies* 46(8): 1577–1591.
Webb, J.W., Tihanyi, L., Ireland, R.D. and Sirmon, D.G. (2009) You say illegal, I say legitimate: Entrepreneurship in the informal economy. *Academy of Management Review* 34(3): 492–510.
Webb, J.W., Tihanyi, L., Ireland, R.D. and Sirmon, D.G. (2013) Research on entrepreneurship in the informal economy: Framing a research agenda. *Journal of Business Venturing* 28(5): 598–614.
Williams, C. (2007) Research methods. *Journal of Business and Economic Research* 5(3): 65–72.
Xue, D. and Huang, G. (2015) Informality and the state's ambivalence in the regulation of street vending in transforming Guangzhou, China. *Geoforum* 62: 156–165.

15 Entrepreneurship for Economic Development and Growth

The Case of Russia in BRICS

Sergei Smirnov and Ndivhuho Tshikovhi

Introduction

In contemporary literature, entrepreneurship is considered one of the most important economic development and growth drivers. This is particularly principal for post-socialist countries of Central and Eastern Europe countries. The State's withdrawal from the economy happened in 1980th, and early 1990th in these countries and this event triggered the dramatic appearance of a newly emerged class of entrepreneurs (Cheberko, 2020; Radaev, 1997). To a large extent, these historical events have determined the following situation – the inconsistent nature and characteristics of contemporary entrepreneurs and entrepreneurship in Russia. In Brazil, India, China, and South Africa, private entrepreneurship has not been prohibited for as long as it was in Russia when it was part of the Union of Soviet Socialist Republics (USSR). China is the only exception, but there was a shorter prohibition period for private initiatives.

Nevertheless, over the three decades since the USSR collapsed, a unique entrepreneurship ecosystem has emerged in Russia and other post-USSR and post-socialism countries of Central and Eastern Europe (Chepurenko, 2017). The path of 30 years of entrepreneurship infancy has not been easy, and it comprises periods of dynamic development that are followed by periods of stricter control and slow-down of independent entrepreneurship formation. The main characteristic to describe the work of independent entrepreneurship in Russia is an unfriendly, unpredictable, and rapidly changing external environment. Unfriendly, unpredictable, and rapidly changing external environments are widely known features of the business climate in Russia. Sometimes, this is compensated for by a raised profit margin. Pass dependency is an important factor that explains the current situation with a hostile business climate. The origins of the distrustful, wary attitude towards independent entrepreneurs can be traced back to the history of the Russian Empire (Cheberko, 2020; Smirnov *et al.*, 2020). Monarchs of the Russian Empire attempted to control the spirit of independent entrepreneurs as they recognised the potential threat of the entrepreneurial community to their autocratic power. Since his enthronement, Tsar Peter, the First

DOI: 10.4324/9781003475606-19

kept industry under his rigorous and autocratic control. The reason for maintaining such control was Peter's military campaigns and the shortage of armaments and ammunition, which could not be produced without the new level of industrial production. The government set requirements on the range, quantity, and quality of manufactured products, and even pricing was set centrally (Cheberko, 2020; Radaev, 1995). Peter the First, designed the system of managed economy, and then during the subsequent centuries, the situation met only minor changes. Based on their beliefs and views, monarchs continued to direct and constrain entrepreneurial activity in the Russian Empire.

The next period of enlargement and further development of private entrepreneurship occurred in the 1830s when a set of laws and decrees were adopted:

- The charter of the bankrupt
- The bill of exchange charter
- The law on joint-stock companies (Cheberko, 2020)

These measures reinforced the economic activity but simultaneously facilitated the entrenched regulatory requirements and deliberate control over entrepreneurs executed by the central and regional authorities. As a result, a cautious attitude towards large independent businesses remains a distinctive feature of the entrepreneurial climate in Russia to this day. During the centuries, it has become a part of national mentality and thus reproduces itself in Russian society till now. Table 15.1 shows the major milestones of private business evolution in Russia.

During the period of the USSR, business initiative was strictly prohibited, and the only entrepreneurs were "shadow" entrepreneurs – "chehoviki" and "farchovshiki", which originated from criminals (Gréen, 2009; Radaev, 1997; Volkov, 2016). During the "perestroika", the former shadow entrepreneurs were the most numerous groups of newly emerged business owners. Close proximity to criminals could not help but influence post-USSR entrepreneurs' behaviour, manners, and business ethics (Gréen, 2009; Radaev, 1997). Conversely, in the 1990s, Russian entrepreneurs were under strong pressure from the criminal and state authorities. This problem was analysed in the research of Volkov (2016). Unfortunately, this criminal connotation has trailed Russian business, albeit weakened. Another source of the input of new entrepreneurs emerged from the cooperators' movement, whose beginnings began several years before the collapse of the USSR (Radaev, 1997). The Soviet cooperators of the late 1980s quite quickly found market niches and became visible in the Soviet economy. They were not closely connected with the criminal culture and better fitted the figure of a classic entrepreneur, which is common in Western countries. In the 1990s, a significant part of this group continued to operate in industries with low entry barriers: trade, transport, catering, and construction work (Barsukova, 1999).

Table 15.1 The evolution of private entrepreneurship in Russia

1861–1917	1917–1921	1921–1929	Late 1930s–mid 1980s	1986–1991	1992–2004	2004–present time
The formation of private business and its growing role in national economic development	Market economy destruction, economic collapse	New economic policy (NEP), private activity returns to the lower levels of the economy	Soviet period, private business was illegal, class of underground entrepreneurs ("tsehoviki") emerged in 1970–the 1980s	The legal emergence of the new type of cooperative, which is almost indistinguishable from the private business	Formal free market economy, entrepreneurial class accumulation, strong influence of criminal practices	From 2004 appearance of State corporations, Growth of State involvement to the Economy, SMEs growth in service industries

Since 2004, a new stage in entrepreneurship development can be discerned. During this period, the state authorities began to play a significant role in economic development (Silvestrov and Zeldner Vaslavskaya, 2010).

This had an impact on the business climate and entrepreneurship. It became more civilised, regulated, and controlled by the state. Since 2004, large state and semi-state corporations, e.g., Rostech, Rosatom, Gazprom, Aeroflot, Russian Railways, United Aircraft Corporation, and United Shipbuilding Corporation, have been recognised as national Champions and turned into main actors in Russian economic development. Business, independent from the state, has continued its growth, but the most profitable sectors and state contracts have come under the control of the largest state corporations (Smirnov and Cheberko, 2018).

According to the official report of the Federal Antimonopoly Service, the state-controlled sector of the economy grew from 35% in 2005 to 70% in 2016. A rather in-depth analysis of Russian entrepreneurship during this period is given in the work of O. Green (2009).

During the subsequent period that lasted from 2014 to 2022 Russian economy was in a precarious state and was facing considerable turbulence induced by the imposition of sanctions and reciprocal countersanctions and a significant decrease in the oil and gas markets. This period was characterised by further restraint of the entrepreneur's community influence on the political and economic institutions, reduction in economic space for independence from the state entrepreneurship, and creeping nationalisation in attractive industries, e.g., banking and insurance, airlines, and construction (Smirnov and Cheberko, 2018). The government has deployed digital technologies that enhanced the effectiveness of tax administration. It impacted the shadow economy's share reduction, increased the effective tax burden, and finally strengthened private business regulation (Smirnov et al., 2020; Smirnov et al., 2021). The state policy in the sphere of entrepreneurship remained controversial, and certain modifications in the statism policy have been implemented. In particular, it adopted the National Project of Small and Medium-Sized Enterprises(SME's) support. According to the project aims, the contribution of SMEs to the country's Gross domestic product (GDP) should rise from 22% in 2017 to 32% in 2024 (National Project, 2020). Due to the national project implementation, the support measures for SMEs became more systematic and adequate. All levels of government have prioritised the analyses, design, and implementation of supportive measures for SMEs

This controversial situation also lasted during the COVID-19 pandemic 2021. Much literature describes the main challenges hindering entrepreneurs' activity, among them usually referring to the biased and unfair work of inspection and law enforcement authorities, which, according to the entrepreneurs' surveys, deter the normal activity of SMEs (Report of Business Ombudsman, 2019–2021). According to the Ombudsman for the Protection of Entrepreneurs' Rights report, 69% of respondents consider doing business in Russia as a puzzling and unsafe process. The share of respondents who report that the Russian legislation system does not effectively protect entrepreneurs from false accusations and unfair claims remains stable at 70.7% in 2019 (Report of Business Ombudsman, 2019–2021).

Also, the share of respondents who do not trust the law enforcement authorities continues to grow. In 2019, it reached 66.7%. Russian entrepreneurship continues to develop despite challenging conditions and an unfavourable business climate. The GEM report 2019 showed a surprising increase in entrepreneurial intentions (GEM, 2022). These metrics soared four times, from 2.2% to 9.8%, and the indicator of total early-stage entrepreneurial activity (TEA) also increased from 5.6% to 9.3% (GEM, 2022). Subsequent reports for 2020–2021 have confirmed achieving a new level of population involvement in entrepreneurship. Quantitative indicators of Russian entrepreneurship are now comparable with other post-socialism countries of Central and Eastern Europe.

Summarising this part, we can conclude that entrepreneurship in Russia remains a state-regulated process as it was during the centuries. The existing political-economic system defines the priorities and instruments of state policies independent from state entrepreneurship. At the same time, global business digitalisation, globalisation, teleworking global socio-economic changes, and the non-observed economy have contributed to the fact that some Russian entrepreneurs learned to keep a low profile to avoid adverse pressures.

The Current State of Entrepreneurship in Russia: Statistics and Comparisons

Divided from the historical part, the situation is quite contradictory. Hence, the question arises – of whether the sustainable and self-sufficient entrepreneurial class has developed in Russia over 30 years of reforms. The result can be compared with other post-socialist countries in transition and with Brazil, Russia, India, China, and South Africa (BRICS) countries. Comparative research on entrepreneurship employs several approaches to compare countries with each other. These approaches involve comparisons based on quantitative and qualitative indicators demonstrating the entrepreneurial ecosystem institutions' maturity level. The Global Entrepreneurship Monitor project has conducted survey-based research on entrepreneurship and ecosystems worldwide for 22 years (GEM, 2022). It provides the data for the organisation of the longitudinal analysis so academics can apply various methodological approaches to studying entrepreneurship at the national level. Russia has participated in this project since 2002. Another source of entrepreneurship and business statistics is the Global Entrepreneurship Index (GEI). It incorporates both individual-level institutional and environmental variables. GEI takes individual-level variables from the GEM survey, and the institutional variables derive from various sources. The Global Competitiveness Index and other World Bank indexes. Entrepreneurship is a complex socio-economic phenomenon, and it is often non-relevant to compare the performance of countries directly. Different world regions have their unique history, progress pace, and inhabitants' mentalities. All these factors contribute a lot to understanding the entrepreneurship ecosystem's current state.

It is considered appropriate to use three groups of countries as a benchmark. The first group is Russia, Belarus, and Ukraine (until 2022), as these Slavonic countries have a similar history. Refer to the comparable indicators in Table 15.1. The second benchmark group was in the Central and Eastern European post-socialist countries (CEEC), which had comparable starting positions after the economic reforms' initiation. Finally, a third benchmark group could be the BRICS countries, the most distant in history but closer in size and importance in the global economy. Below is a summary in Table 15.2 of several indicators of entrepreneurship development in the three Slavic countries.

As mentioned, the differences in SME density are not very large. However, this indicator considers a noticeable share of inactive SMEs, distorting comparisons. The share of inactive entities in three countries is difficult to estimate. Observing the other indicators, we mention Belarus's abnormally high level of entrepreneurial intentions in 2021 (GEM, 2022). The most notable fact – is the high contribution of SMEs to employment and GDP in Ukraine. This characteristic sets the country apart from the group of three Slavic countries and moves it closer to Central and Eastern European countries. Generally speaking, the entrepreneurial ecosystems of the three Slavic countries differ markedly, and it is impossible to cover all differences in the chapter. Unfortunately, no studies on entrepreneurial development exist, even in Russia, Ukraine, and Belarus.

There is noticeably more research comparing Russia with CEEC countries, perhaps because Russia has gigantic territory, is the largest energy supplier, and has global military power. In particular, the work (Chepurenko and Sauka, 2018)

Table 15.2 Entrepreneurship development indicators in Russia, Belarus, and Ukraine

	Belarus	Russia	Ukraine
SMEs Density (2019)*	40.2	38,7	46.3
Employment in SMEs (2019)	34.7%	25.6%	64.6% (2018)
Entrepreneurial intentions (GEM 2022)	24.06%	9.68%	–
TEA (GEM 2022)	13.48%	8.32%	–
Doing Business in 2020 Global rank	49	28	64

* Authors' calculations are based on official statistics (Belstat, 2022; Main economic indicators of Belarus, 2022; Employment in SMEs, 2019; OECD, 2020).

investigates entrepreneurship in transition economies. The chapters focus on a particular country and describe and analyse its major entrepreneurship characteristics. The problem of post-socialist countries in transition attracts the attention of researchers because of its complexity and multidimensional nature. Researchers usually distinguish three groups of countries in transition: the countries of Central and Eastern Europe, Russia, and the other Commonwealth of Independent States [CIS] countries and Baltic countries (Estonia, Latvia, and Lithonia). The paper (Aidis, 2006) notes that a clear distinction can be made between the CEEC and CIS countries in terms of three main dimensions: the environment, the role of the state, and business owner characteristics.

Furthermore, the authors highlighted the low level of knowledge-based entrepreneurship among CIS and CEEC countries. Another paper focuses on analyses of entrepreneurship in the CEEC countries, including Russia, and proposes an original typology of entrepreneurial ecosystems (Chepurenko, 2017). The analysis in this paper is based mainly on 2011–2012 data and de facto confirms previous research that despite the considerable differences in entrepreneurial ecosystems of European transition economies, Russia remains an outsider above them with inexplicable lower indicators of entrepreneurship development. The research on Szerb and Trumbul (2018) is in the same direction as the analysis. The very title of the paper poses the question of whether "Russia is a normal country?" in terms of transition to a free economy and private entrepreneurship. The authors of the paper conclude that – "No". They ascertain the weak development of the institutions necessary for entrepreneurship development and comment on the low quantitative indicators of entrepreneurial activity and the lack of officials' desire to correct this situation. The mentioned studies cover the period up to 2019 and reflect some consensus on Russia's entrepreneurship development.

At the same time, it should be noted that starting from 2019, the GEM reports demonstrate a noticeable change, an increase in entrepreneurial intentions, and TEA. The trend, starting from 2019, is shown in Figure 15.1.

Table 15.3 presents quantitative indicators of entrepreneurship development for several countries in transition and BRICS countries.

The figures help conclude that despite the sharp increase in the entrepreneurial intentions indicator observed in 2019 and confirmed by GEM data for 2020 and 2021, the population's involvement in entrepreneurship in Russia remains lower than in other transition and BRICS countries (GEM 2022). This is probably partly due to worse business framework conditions and low business survival rates. Since the countries are so different in entrepreneurship ecosystems, should governments strive to increase quantitative indicators further, or should we better focus on ecosystem development, increasing the share of voluntary and innovative entrepreneurs?

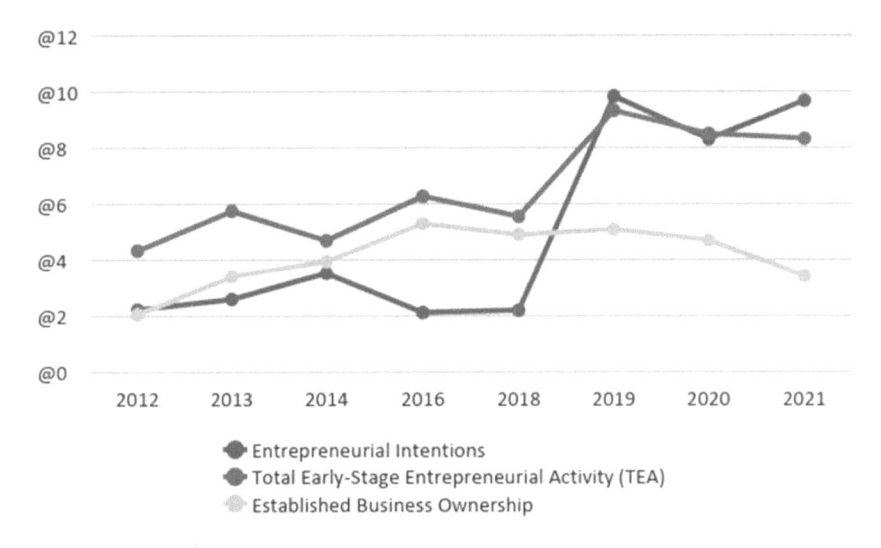

Figure 15.1 Entrepreneurial activity in Russia

Entrepreneurship as a Driver for Economic Development and Growth

The phenomenon of entrepreneurship can be investigated simultaneously through quantitative and qualitative analyses. Quantitative indicators reflect the population involved in the entrepreneurial process, share: of necessity/vulnerable business owners, innovative/traditional ideas for business, of male/female entrepreneurs (GEM, 2022). Qualitative analyses represent the specific qualities of entrepreneurship in the country, framework conditions for doing business, entrepreneur's perceptions, and ecosystem characteristics that foster or hinder the

Table 15.3 GEM's entrepreneurship indicators for particular CEEC, Former Soviet Union countries [FSU], and BRICS countries

Country	Year	Entrepreneurial intentions	Total early-stage entrepreneurial activity (TEA)	Established business ownership
Poland	2021	2.85	2.00	11.06
Bulgaria	2018	3.91	6.00	8.35
Russia	2021	9.68	8.32	3.42
Latvia	2021	17.94	15.13	9.91
India	2021	18.14	14.37	8.51
South Africa	2021	19.96	17.49	5.17
China (2019)	2019	21.42	8.66	9.33
Belarus	2021	24.06	13.48	5.54
Brazil	2021	53.00	20.98	9.95

entrepreneurial process. According to available research, economic, and social development depends primarily on entrepreneurship's qualitative characteristics. In literature, this problem refers to the entrepreneurial paradox (Lafuente et al., 2018).

The less developed countries have a larger share of entrepreneurs in the population, but it does not promote economic development and growth. Entrepreneurship is a driver of economic development, but at the same time, a disproportionate share of entrepreneurs in society only sometimes leads to economic efficiency. Several studies confirm that entrepreneurial activity in rich countries is positively associated with growth and inversely correlated with growth in low-income countries.

Stam et al. (2009) and Valliere and Peterson (2009) have found that high-growth entrepreneurs contribute to growth only in developed countries. The GIM project's head of the research committee also indicated the relationship between the opportunity/necessity entrepreneurship ratio and a country's income. He derived that less developed countries need to strengthen their small- and medium-sized sector before, and then they should focus on the entrepreneurial framework conditions (Acs, 2006). The authors reached the point that the so-called U-shaped curve that reflects the correlation between nascent entrepreneurs and GDP may exist and demonstrate the link between entrepreneurial activity and economic development in the global economy (Acs, 2006). Only the United States stands out in this respect, combining high entrepreneurial activity and high GDP. According to this study, Russia does not lie on this U-curve because it has a low level of nascent entrepreneurship and a low GDP income. However, it should be considered that the chart was based on data from 2005, and since then, the situation has markedly changed.

In another study, the authors note that "empirical evidence is consistent with the view that entrepreneurship can serve as a conduit for the spillover of knowledge, and thereby is conducive to economic growth" (Audretsch et al., 2006). The authors of another paper (Bampoky et al., 2013) conclude that low-income countries need more innovative startups. However, the mentioned research emphasises that more entrepreneurship (higher business creation rates) is not statistically associated with greater economic development. This contradiction between theoretical predictions and empirical findings fuels the entrepreneurship cite examined in this study on the ecosystems of African countries. The scholars confirm the findings on the number of entrepreneurs and economic development in developing countries. Referring to the case of Russia, the situation looks ambiguous. Summarising the above-mentioned research, two ambitious and complementary objectives need to be pursued: coherent entrepreneurial encouragement in society with a focus on highly aspirational and innovative entrepreneurs and simultaneously improvement of the business environment.

On the one hand, according to the GEM report, Russia has already nearly reached the level of other post-socialist countries in terms of quantitative indicators. This is a positive fact because Russia has been lagging deep behind in population involvement in entrepreneurship for the past few years. On the other hand, there are fundamental problems in the entrepreneurial ecosystem: the uneven SMEs spreading in different sectors and regions, the dominance of state-owned companies, and many other problems mentioned above. One future scenario is the rapid growth of necessity entrepreneurship, which often does not lead to economic development, as was demonstrated before. According to GEM reports, Brazil has the highest population in entrepreneurial activity, with total entrepreneurial activity (TEA) of 23%, Panama – 31%, and Colombia – 32%. Respectively, high level of necessity entrepreneurship is a common characteristic of these countries. It is quite possible that Russia will transfer to a similar situation within a few years, which will not prosper but could prevent sustainable, innovative growth.

Returning to the question posed in the remarkable paper of Szerb and Trumbull (2018) – is Russia a normal country? Yes, but it needs more time, like in other FSU, e.g. Belarus and Kazakhstan. Considering the negative scenario, the focus should be on further developing the entrepreneurial ecosystem, encouraging and accelerating technology and digital startups, and creating and developing a new point of digital talent attraction (Strack et al., 2017). Special emphasis should be placed on encouraging the internal intrapreneurship programmes within the large state and semi-state corporations. Large corporations have weak and outdated management systems and hardly need digitisation and digital transformation initiatives.

In recent years state authorities have taken steps in the right direction, conducting more realistic and comprehensive policies aimed at SME support. From 2018 to 2021, many regional initiatives have been launched to support local businesses. These programmes usually provide subsidies, acceleration support, consulting services, co-working places, and special condition loans. These programmes go along with the National Project, which aims to create mass entrepreneurship in Russia (National Project, 2020). One of the supporting measures was the introduction of a special tax regime for the self-employed. This form of entrepreneurship focuses on a specific range of occupations and provides an extremely low tax burden for the self-employed. This measure is not only fiscal but also gives a chance to start a business without obstacles, as self-employed have to install special apps on their phones and operate without accounting. Moreover, a self-employed tax regime creates a prerequisite for shadow entrepreneurs to get out of the shadows.

Another promising direction that can considerably contribute to the entrepreneurial ecosystem development is IT platforms. Currently, "МСП.ru" ("SME.rf") is the country-wide platform that supports entrepreneurs and was launched by "The State Corporation of SME" (National Entrepreneurial platform, 2020). Also, the platform is aimed at entrepreneurs of all "ages" (nascent, young, and established). The special strength is made in startups that enter the market and strive to survive. The platform accumulates all available digital services in one place. For starting a business, it provides marketing data, geo-information about residents and competitive environment, frameworks for business plans, and financial models.

The platform also contains:

- Detailed and well-structured information about supporting programmes that fit particular applicants.
- Documented procedures for participation.
- Online supporting seminars.

The platform has its physical part – named "My Business" (National Entrepreneurial Platform, 2020). Special offices have been launched in all large cities and regions. It provides many offline services for early-stage entrepreneurs who prefer communicating with supporting staff. Centres also administer registration services for individual entrepreneurs, organise company audits, and inform about advisory and financing measures. These centres usually have equipped rooms for free training seminars for people aiming to start their businesses. The platform approach creates facilities for remote entrepreneurs' support and enhances the quality of standardised services crucial in such a large country. In the mid-term, the platform "SME.rf" and offices "My business" can gain popularity and become an essential element of the entrepreneurial ecosystem.

Growing innovative entrepreneurship is another challenging area recognised as the top priority at the state level. According to global indexes (Schwab, 2019), Russian entrepreneurs' and managers' innovativeness has always been low. However, several Innovative Science and Technology Centers (ISTC) have been established as innovative and technological entrepreneurship points following the Silicon Valley model (Smirnov *et al.*, 2018). The ISTC has a special legislative regime with a more favourable taxation burden. Among these, the Skolkovo project is the most reputable. After about 10 years of operation, it had created about 30,000 jobs. In 2020, the quantity of Skolkovo residents reached 2,500 companies (Skolkovo, 2015–2021). Several other similar projects affiliated with major universities are currently underway. For example, the St. Petersburg project "Nevskaya Delta" is implementing in cooperation with St-Petersburg State University. Such projects provide their residents with significant tax benefits: in particular, about 50% lower social contributions rates, zero profit tax, no Value Added Tax (VAT), no property tax, and no customs duties. The effectiveness of such projects is difficult to estimate, but some visible results have already been achieved.

Conclusion

Studies confirm that countries with stronger entrepreneurial ecosystems are developing more dynamically and are more resilient to external shocks. And entrepreneurship may serve as a key driver in unlocking the potential of the Russian economy. An entrepreneurial ecosystem in Russia was established 30 years after the collapse of the USSR. However, it has experienced a mix of sophisticated problems: path dependence, the policy of statism, societal attitudes, political-economic priorities, weak institutions, and a lack of incentives to change this situation. Despite all these problems, entrepreneurship in Russia is developing globally and, at the local level, shows high adaptability and survivability in a challenging environment. The country has almost reached the post-socialist countries of Eastern and Central Europe regarding the population involved in the entrepreneurial process. The share of women entrepreneurs is almost equal to that of men. It is an important advantage that has a positive effect. Historically, Russia demonstrates a very low level of population involvement in the entrepreneurial process. Now, changes are taking place, and a significant increase in entrepreneurial intentions and TEA indicators observed in the country since 2019 indicates a qualitative adjustment in societal attitudes. Entrepreneurial spirit as an endeavour for positive change is highly demanded in the economy and almost all social processes, which Russia needs in the 21st century.

The quantity of started businesses should not be an end in itself. In the context of imposed economic sanctions and the subsequent economic recession, a dramatic increase in the necessity of entrepreneurs is probable. According to contemporary research, innovative entrepreneurship based on emerging technologies, digital trends, and Environmental, Social, Governance (ESG) principles is most desirable. Policymakers and government officials realise the importance of innovative entrepreneurship. The National Project of SMEs assumes a range of initiatives that address innovation: ISTC, industrial parks, and special economic zones. These initiatives are designed to promote innovations and technological entrepreneurship executed by high-aspiration entrepreneurs. However, a low propensity to innovate inherent to Russian entrepreneurs hinders the effectiveness of such initiatives.

Another unfavourable factor is the high proportion of state-owned and semi-state-owned companies, which generally exhibit insufficient innovative behaviour. In this context, internal entrepreneurship has extreme importance as it contributes to the transformation of the large corporations that currently dominate the Russian market. Platform solutions have spectacular potential. The country-wide platform – "SME.ru" has been launched as an e-services portal for entrepreneurs. Given Russia's high degree of centralisation, the single platform combining all e-services in one place becomes an important advantage for the national entrepreneurial ecosystem. The platform capabilities and big data analysis could be explored to conduct longitudinal research on barriers and complaints about unauthorised persecution. The platform potentially gives various opportunities to collect statistics on business termination at different life cycle stages, from nascent to early and established. It also can promote targeted support measures according to predicted enterprise performance. The platform can contribute to tracking growth trajectory and analysing factors of innovative behaviour and business internationalisation. The platform approach can facilitate a new phase of entrepreneurship research and be useful for implementing new quality governmental support policies for innovative and high-aspiration entrepreneurs.

References

Acs, Z. (2006) "How is entrepreneurship good for economic growth?", *Innovations: Technology, Governance, Globalization*, 1(1):97–107. https://doi.org/10.1162/itgg.2006.1.1.97

Aidis, R. (2006) Entrepreneurship in transition countries a review. https://www.academia.edu/9956207/Entrepreneurship_in_Transition_Countries_A_Review (Accessed 30 July 2022).

Audretsch, D., Acs, Z., Braunerhjelm, P. and Carlsson, B. (2006) Growth and entrepreneurship: an empirical assessment. CEPR Discussion Paper No. 5409 https://ssrn.com/abstract=893068 (Accessed 2 July 2022).

Bampoky, C., Blanco, L., Liu, A. and Prieger, J. (2013) Economic growth and the optimal level of entrepreneurship. Pepperdine University, School of Public Policy Working Papers. Paper 46.

Barsukova, S. (1999) Entrepreneurs of different "calls" or the dynamics of the components of entrepreneurial success. Q: where is Russia going? Crisis of institutional systems: century, decade. M., (Print)

Belstat Small and medium business in the Republic of Belarus Figures and facts 2018-2022. https://www.belstat.gov.by/upload-belstat/upload-belstat-pdf/oficial_statistika/2021/infographics_mal_sredn-2021.pdf (Accessed 29 July 2022).

Cheberko, E. (2020) Fundamentals of entrepreneurial activity. History of Entrepreneurship. Moscow, URAIT (Print).

Chepurenko, A. (2017) "Entrepreneurial activity in post-socialist countries: methodology and research limitations", *Foresight and STI Governance*, 11(3):11–24.

Chepurenko, A. and Sauka, A. (2018) "Entrepreneurship in transition economies". Springer International PU

Employment in SMEs: How Far to the Goals of the Strategy-2030? (2019) https://gazeta-bam.ru/media/project_smi3_721/86/d2/62/11/1d/2f/zanyatost-v-malom-i-srednem-biznese-22-iyulya-2019.pdf (Accessed 30 June 2024).

GEM (2022) Global Entrepreneurship Monitor, 2002–2022. http://www.gemconsortium.org/data (Accessed: 24 July 2022).

Gréen, O.S. (2009) "Entrepreneurship in Russia: Western Ideas in Russian Translation". PhD Thesis Printed at Geson Hylte Tryck, Gothenburg

Lafuente, E., Acs, Z. and Szerb, L. (2018) "The entrepreneurship paradox: more entrepreneurs are not always good for the economy – The role of the entrepreneurial ecosystem on economic performance in Africa". SSRN Working Paper Series. https://ssrn.com/abstract=3307617 (Accessed 29 July 2022).

National Entrepreneurial Platform. (2020) SME.rf, "My Business". https://Мойбизнес.рф/Anticrisis (Accessed 29 July 2022).
Main economic indicators of Belarus. National Statistical Committee of the Republic of Belarus. (20228) Main economic indicators of activity of subjects of small and medium business of the Republic of Belarus. 2018–2022 https://www.belstat.gov.by/ofitsialnaya-statistika/realny-sector-ekonomiki/strukturnaja_statistika/osnovnye-pokazateli-deyatelnosti-mikroorganizatsiy-i-malykh-organizatsiy/godovye-dannye/ (Accessed 29 July 2022).
OECD. (2020) Monitoring the implementation of the Ukrainian SME Development Strategy for 2017–2020 (Print).
Radaev, V. (1995) "Two Roots of Russian Entrepreneurship: fragments of History" (Print). "World of Russia", No. 1, p. 159-179.
Radaev, V. (1997) "Transformation of the elites and the formation of the national elite in post-Soviet Russia". The role of the state in the development of society: Russia and international experience. Proceedings of the international symposium. M. RNISiNP
Report of Business Ombudsman (2019–2021) Reports authorised under the President of the Russian Federation for the protection of the rights of entrepreneurs http://doklad.ombudsmanbiz.ru/doklad_2019.html (Accessed 15 July 2022).
National project. (2020) Russian Government National project "Small and medium-sized enterprises and support of individual entrepreneurial initiative" http://government.ru/info/35563/ (Accessed 24 January 2020).
Schwab, K. (2019) "The Global Competitiveness Index". https://reports.weforum.org/global-competitiveness-index-2016-2017/country-profiles/ (Accessed: 30 Jul 2022).
Silvestrov, S. and Zeldner, A. (2009) "State corporations in the economic development of Russia". M: Institute of Economics RAN, 1-32.
Skolkovo. Annual Reports of Skolkovo: 2015-2020 [Online]. Available: https://sk.ru/foundation/results/ [Accessed 29 July 2022].
Smirnov, S., Bobrova, S., Arenkov, I. and Salichova, J. (2021) "Sustainable combinations of distinctive features of innovative firms' business models", *St Petersburg University Journal of Economic Studies*, 37(1):62–83.
Smirnov, S. and Cheberko, E. (2018) "Current stage of entrepreneurship development in Russia from 2014 up To 2017: main issues and trends". Proc. International OFEL 6th International OFEL Conference on Governance, Management and Entrepreneurship. New Business Models and Institutional Entrepreneurs: leading Disruptive Change, Dubrovnik, 344–355.
Smirnov, S., Richter, K., Ekaterina, M. and Galina, I. (2020) On the way to the mass entrepreneurship in Russia: currents state and Trends. 2020 6th International Conference on Information Management (ICIM). https://doi.org/10.1109/icim49319.2020.244687 (Accessed 29 July 2022).
Stam, E., Suddle, K., Hessels, J. and van Stel, A.J. (2009) High-growth entrepreneurs, public policies, and economic growth. *International Studies in Entrepreneurship Series*, 22: 91–110. https://doi.org/10.1007/978-1-4419-0249-8_5
Strack, R., Dyrchs, S., Kotsis, A. and Mingardon, S. (2017) How to gain and develop digital talent and skills. BCG Global. https://www.bcg.com/publications/2017/people-organization-technology-how-gain-develop-digital-talent-skills (Accessed 29 July 2022).
Szerb, L. and Trumbull, W. (2018) "Entrepreneurship development in Russia: Is Russia a normal country? An empirical analysis", *Journal of Small Business and Enterprise Development*, 25(6):902–929.

Valliere, D. and Peterson, R. (2009) "Entrepreneurship and economic growth: evidence from emerging and developed countries", *Entrepreneurship & Regional Development*, 21(5):459–480.

Vaslavskaya, I. (2010) "State corporations in Russia's economic development strategy", *Vestnik of the Institute of Economics of the Russian Academy of Sciences*, 10(2010):157–164.

Volkov, V. (2016) Violent entrepreneurs. The use of force in the making of Russian capitalism. Cornell University Press. Ithaca and London

16 Technological Entrepreneurship and Peculiarities of Its Development in Russia

Nikolai O. Yakushev

Introduction

In the era of digital transformation, entrepreneurship from the socio-economic perspective is the basis for the development of national economies of the BRICS countries. Entrepreneurship, contributing to job growth, is a source of budget revenues in Russia, but more investment in skills, innovation and technology is needed for economic growth and development of territories. However, generally accepted characteristics of entrepreneurship only partially reflect its technological type and the main features in the development of the territory, which becomes even more relevant to the study.

In this regard, this manuscript aims to identify options for the approach to the understanding and characteristics of technological entrepreneurship to understand its current situation and develop effective ways to promote its development in Russia. To realise the goal, the following tasks are solved: to define technological entrepreneurship and its role in the development of the territory; to clarify the approaches to the assessment of technological entrepreneurship for development in Russia; to identify the features of the development of advanced manufacturing technologies in Russia in the context of technological entrepreneurship.

The principles of the systematic approach were used as the methodological basis of the study. To ensure the elaboration of the main aspects of the research objectives, a review of the key principles and characteristics of technological entrepreneurship affecting the problems of the study, including in the context of digital transformation, was carried out. In the course of the study, the methodology of process analysis, tools for interpreting functional dependencies, techniques, and comparison methods were used.

The issues of technological entrepreneurship development in research are considered from the position of transformation of scientific research into the results of applied research (through the participation of commercial entities and business environment institutions), expressed in products and services, distributed according to market principles, and providing new values and desired

DOI: 10.4324/9781003475606-20

benefits to potential customers (Bailetti, 2012; Wyrzykowska, 2012). In addition, technological entrepreneurship touches upon such aspects as intellectual entrepreneurship (Garud and Karnoe, 2003), academic entrepreneurship (Kviatkovsky, 2002), issues of technology transfer and commercialisation (Poznanska, 2014), and knowledge management and high-tech projects (Gianiodis, 2014).

It follows that the economic nature of technological entrepreneurship affects a particular sphere of activity, involving the characteristics of four aspects:

1. Internal entrepreneurship related to technology development in the SMEs sector should focus on identifying market opportunities and commercialising ideas to create economic value (Gorzelany-Dziadkowiec, 2014; Gongming et al., 2014; Bosma and Kelley, 2018). Particular importance is given to creating new ideas and attitudes towards knowledge and new technological solutions, including the company's openness to develop joint projects in the high-tech sector.
2. To own a technological innovation business is determined by an assessment of the potential of real technological capabilities of companies and the development of its necessary elements for the functioning of knowledge, competencies, and technologies, own research services of the company with the implementation of appropriate procedures and methods of distribution, storage, codification, and protection of knowledge (Maysami, Elyasi, Dehkordi, and Hejazi, 2019).
3. Integration of business and science through the organisation of joint work with employees of research institutions, ensuring access of employees to the necessary external knowledge and building a network of links, allowing the exchange of knowledge between the company and its environment (Qing-Lan, Ying-Niao, and Xiao-Min, 2008; Yakushev, 2017).
4. A marketing strategy is at the core of the activity (Butryumova, Karpycheva, Nazarov, and Sidorov, 2015; Khairullina, 2016; Korchagina, Korchagin, and Sycheva-Peredero, 2019;). It involves analysing the market to determine the demand for new products and services, searching for the information necessary to implement new technologies and getting customer feedback on the market offer presented by the company. Active participation of SMEs in the development of technological entrepreneurship is built on the principles of start-up.

Technological Entrepreneurship and Its Role in the Development of the Territory

One of the important economic resources of the region is entrepreneurial activity. At the same time, a special contribution to the economy is made by its technological type. According to some estimates, the contribution of technological entrepreneurship to the world economy is more than 30% of world GDP (as of 2018).

Technological entrepreneurship aims to create a full-fledged chain from the idea (development) to the market realisation of a specific complex product with intellectual value. Essential in understanding entrepreneurship is the norm of part 2 of article 34 of the Constitution of the Russian Federation. It defines entrepreneurship as a kind of economic activity that can be carried out only within its framework. At the same time, an activity aimed at the systematic receipt of some income which is not economic cannot be regarded as entrepreneurship.

In the world, economic thought on entrepreneurship problems significantly contributed to Schumpeter. He described entrepreneurship as a process of emerging new technologies on which new industries and businesses emerged. Schumpeter noted that "entrepreneurship" is not a profession. Hence, it is above professional-specific activities based on innovation, which co-organises the work of other spheres and areas (Schumpeter, 2003).

Problems of perspective planning, formation of enterprise strategy in the development of the territory, and economic activity of firms in the works touched many foreign scientists. These are scientific works of foreign researchers (Ackoff, 1999; Ansoff, 2018; Karloff, 1989; Kotler, 2012; Lambin, 2020; Mescon, 1987; Mintzberg, 1987; Porter, 2008; Thompson, 2023). These works reflect basic theoretical problems and reveal practical issues of entrepreneurship development. Therefore, in these studies, the most important features of entrepreneurship economic scientists include the independence and autonomy of business entities (the entrepreneur is free to make decisions within the legal framework), economic interest (the general purpose of entrepreneurship getting the maximum possible profit, pursuing their interests of high income, the entrepreneur contributes to achieving the public interest), economic risk and responsibility (criminal, economic, social, and political).

The most significant domestic scientific developments in this field were conducted by Abalkin (2010), Bereslavskaya (2005), Boev (2021), Glazyev (2022), Gradov (2014), Efremov (1998), Semenov (2013), and Fatkhutdinova (2021). Their studies emphasised entrepreneurial activity, highlighting the following characteristic: systematic profit making, which is a product of a specific human resource – entrepreneurial abilities.

Consequently, in general, entrepreneurship can be defined as the proactive economic activity of economic actors aimed at making a profit based on their independence, responsibility, and risk.

Meanwhile, as with any economic activity entrepreneurship, its classification features may differ in form, organisational and legal status, relation to property, and territorial features.

The type of entrepreneurship is determined, for example, based on the criterion of belonging to a certain sphere of activity. The Organisation for Economic Cooperation and Development distinguishes four main types of entrepreneurship: trade and commercial (associated with business in the circulation of goods and money), service (provides intangible products), manufacturing (includes the release of industrial and agricultural production of industrial and technical purpose, consumer goods), financial and insurance (as the subject are the purchase and sale of currency values, securities (stocks, bonds), the conclusion of the insurance contract).

In addition, the World Economic Forum distinguishes a special group of specific types of entrepreneurship: social (implementation of solutions to social, cultural or environmental problems) and hybrid (includes several components of different activities in one).

One example of a hybrid type is also technological entrepreneurship, which encompasses manufacturing, based on a shared vision of processes and future changes, as well as the application of technological solutions that include the possibility of making both tangible and intangible products. Entrepreneurship focuses on implementing technological solutions and ensuring their promotion in the market and dissemination in the business environment (Feki and Mnif, 2016). Consequently, it can become one of the key factors in creating modern enterprises' technological and innovative potential. This applies in particular to small and medium-sized enterprises in the regions, which have limited ability to carry out independent research activities due to the need for more resources.

In the studies of foreign scientists' "entrepreneurship" and "technology" are considered the key factors in achieving success and improving the efficiency of modern business, allowing the development of high-tech products (Cassiman, Golovko, and Martínez-Ros, 2010). It also gives modern companies a permanent competitive advantage, mainly due to such positive effects as improving product quality and production efficiency, cost containment, increasing customer loyalty, modernisation of processes, and management methods.

A special role in the research of technological entrepreneurship is given to studying issues related to changes in the economy's structure. Scientists have determined that innovation is not only a defining feature of entrepreneurial activity but also the main factor of economic dynamics, through which new methods of production and marketing of products are initiated and implemented (Ilyin, 2018; Venkataraman, 2004). It was revealed that the most important task for developing innovative businesses is the improvement of financial institutions that ensure the continuity of business project financing and technological infrastructure at all stages of the innovation cycle (Vertakova, 2019; Yakushev, 2020).

A significant role in the development of technological entrepreneurship is played by small and medium-sized enterprises (SMEs), which are characterised by specific quantitative and qualitative characteristics in contrast to large enterprises (Kordel, 2014; Wyrzykowska, 2012). Small and medium-sized enterprises are classified using the unified definition specified in the OECD regulations, taking into account the number of employees (the upper limit is 249 employees), revenues, and the size of assets. In determining the characteristics of technology companies, some scholars (Nicolescu, 2009) emphasise their significant technical and innovative potential, providing a high level of entrepreneurship, speed of decision-making, and close and direct relationship with the business environment. On the other hand, the results of numerous studies (for example, B. Wyrzykowska) indicate that the level of technological entrepreneurship in SMEs is lower than in large enterprises, as the activity of participation in the implementation of innovative solutions decreases with the size of the company (Wyrzykowska, 2012). One of the main disadvantages of technological entrepreneurship in the SME sector is a significant lack of resources, both financial and other (compared to large enterprises), which limits such activities as research and development, investment activities, and as a consequence, the level of involvement of enterprises in the high-tech sector.

The issues of technological entrepreneurship development in the studies are considered from the transformation of scientific research into the results of applied research (through the participation of commercial entities and business environment institutions). The economic impact on the development of territories is not given. At the same time, the presented works contain information on the importance of social responsibility, sponsorship, and grant support of young specialists when localising a company in a certain territory.

In 2016, the Moscow School of Social and Economic Sciences conducted a study identifying groups of potential technological entrepreneurs by region. The largest number is observed in Tatarstan, Moscow, Krasnodar Territory, and Tomsk region. These are regions where the population is focused on starting their own business (especially in the Republic of Tatarstan and Krasnodar Krai) and also demonstrate the most pronounced techno-optimistic attitudes (primarily in the Tomsk region). According to the representative sample survey, the smallest number of potential technological entrepreneurs (600 respondents in the region) stands out in the Leningrad and Yaroslavl regions. At the same time, among the potential technological entrepreneurs, the value of entrepreneurship is the most widespread. Thus, more than half of them would prefer a stable income and confidence in the future to run their own business at their own risk (53% of representatives of this group). In addition, the research results emphasise the trend of declining confidence in institutions, which is most pronounced among the "audience of technological entrepreneurship," indicating the importance of this factor for the modernisation development of the country and regions. As a result, technological entrepreneurship in Russia is considered in the context of socio-cultural and socio-economic factors that ensure innovative development.

Higher School of Economics researchers have also considered the peculiarities of technological entrepreneurship development in Russia (Butryumova et al., 2015). In the study they describe the evolution of technological entrepreneurship in the context of transition economy on the example of a particular region, which has favourable conditions for the development of technological entrepreneurship. Some characteristic features of technological entrepreneurship in the region are highlighted: the most important resources of development are people and knowledge (in the form of intellectual property and experience of participants of the entrepreneurial project); minimisation of external financing; use of niche strategies of development of companies, focus on quality and customer needs. The studied companies in the region focus mainly on the key competencies necessary for entrepreneurship in the technological sphere.

Technological entrepreneurship is considered in the research from different characteristics: legal, managerial, financial, social, cooperative, business environment, commercial relationships, and risk analysis. At the same time, considering the role of technological entrepreneurship in the development of the region will consist of the following key points:

- First, it is the registration of a new subject of economic activity with the localisation of its business in the sector of technology and production of complex products.
- Second, the growth and popularisation of intellectual property and the contribution to increasing the importance of research and development (R&D).
- Third, investment in the knowledge and competence of employees with increasing experience to produce quality products, taking into account the growing needs of the market and the consumer.
- Fourth, the formation of new business models in the form of joint projects and technological alliances, contributing to the development of favourable conditions in the region and cooperation in entering foreign markets.

Thus, the development of technological entrepreneurship (including at the expense of the small and medium business sector) has a significant and positive impact on developing a particular territory, and its economy.

In this case, the goal of technological entrepreneurship should be to increase the level of technological complexity by using the synergistic effect of the interaction of the economic entity between the internal capabilities of the company and the potential of the environment, represented by research and development institutions and structures from the sphere of high technology. A high level of product quality and a market-oriented approach, focused on the use of technological capabilities with the provision of appropriate management decisions, should be taken into account.

Approaches to Evaluating Technological Entrepreneurship for Development in Russia

Russia has created a certain infrastructure and support institutions to develop entrepreneurship in general and technological entrepreneurship in particular. It is represented by science cities, special economic zones, large technoparks, technological platforms, and innovative territorial clusters. For example, to accelerate technological development in Russia, the National Technological

Initiative (NTI) has been developed – a programme of measures to form new markets and create conditions for global technological leadership by 2035. It considers the accumulated scientific and innovation potential and prospects for commercialisation of domestic developments in the following areas: robotics, new production technologies, "smart" energy, intelligent transportation systems, bio- and nanotechnology. Since 2018, the national project "Small and Medium Entrepreneurship and Support of Individual Entrepreneurial Initiative" has been implemented. However, according to a study of the Russian technology entrepreneurship market, the "Startup Barometer," in which experts surveyed more than 530 founders of innovative startups in Russia, many conclusions were made (Maysami et al., 2019). For example, 39% of the respondents said they did not feel the benefit of state development institutions. In addition, 86% of the founders who launched a startup with their own money continue to develop on the proceeds received without external investors. At the same time, the practical implementation of assessing the state of technological entrepreneurship and its contribution to the Russian economy remains insufficient. Therefore, it is important to focus on the transformation of society's entire way of life, down to the values of the population. In this case, it is necessary to search for options to assess technological entrepreneurship, which ultimately reflects the scientific importance and determines the relevance of the task.

Two global indices of competitiveness and innovation can be considered as a potential tool for analysing certain components of technological entrepreneurship and, thus, for determining its contribution to the economy.

Thus, it is possible to determine the ability to compete with other countries in the Fourth Industrial Revolution based on the Global Competitiveness Index (GCI) of the World Economic Forum Schwab (2019). In addition to general economic and specific indicators, the structure of its components includes the level of technological development, business competitiveness, and innovation potential. The study covers about 141 countries in the world economy. According to the 2019 report, the GCI analysis shows that in the current unstable global market conditions, it is extremely important to increase the sustainability of the economy by improving competitiveness and technological development, especially for developing countries.

The top five GCI countries are Singapore, the most competitive economy in the world in 2019, ahead of the United States, which fell to second place, Hong Kong (3rd), the Netherlands (4th), and Switzerland (5th). Russia ranks 43rd (China 28th by comparison) in the world on the GCI, as it did in 2018, despite the improved quality of its research institutions and constant R&D spending (1.1% of GDP). In addition, the problem area remains related to the development level of technology companies, the competitiveness of small and medium enterprises in the international market, and the possibility of their financial support (availability of loans). Therefore, this area remains extremely important for the Russian economy, which requires stimulation of research and development, expansion of financial opportunities for companies, integration of new technologies, and development of appropriate infrastructure.

The Global Innovation Index (GII) is a source for understanding multidimensional aspects of innovation growth (The Global Innovation Index, 2019). It includes 80 detailed indicators for 129 countries to measure the effectiveness of innovation and technology in the economy. According to the report, despite global economic uncertainty, spending on innovation grew in 2019. However, two problems for the economy stand out: public spending on R&D, particularly in advanced economies, is growing slowly or does not show a positive trend at all; risks in technology-intensive sectors due to slower growth of their productivity and the spread of innovation on a global scale are increasing.

According to the GII index, Switzerland, Sweden, and the United States led the way in innovation in 2019, with the latter two moving up in comparison. Following them are the Netherlands and the United Kingdom. Also in the top ten are Germany (8th place) and Singapore (9th place). Russia ranks 46th in the world on the GII index and 31st among European countries, which was also recorded in 2018. However, Russia's position in the world needs to be improved and bigger in several key areas: ICT exports, development of technology companies, development and production of complex products, accumulated innovation policy, investment and export of high technology. As a result, it is necessary to focus in Russia on developing technological entrepreneurship and innovation support in all areas of the economy.

The main feature of technological entrepreneurship should be an increase in the level of technological sophistication of the economy through synergistic effects from the interaction of economic actors in the use of their potential (Sels et al., 2006; Sirilli and Evangelista, 1998; Yakushev, 2017; Vrakking, 1990). In this sense, the characteristic of technological entrepreneurship, inherent in the definition of its attribute, and consists of the interdependence of scientific and technological progress with the selection and development of new products and assets, the focus on the discovery of new opportunities and unique specialists-entrepreneurs of various professional fields, who can implement them; the focus on project activities and investment in startups(Kogan, Papanikolaou, Seru, and Stoffman, 2017; Sels et al., 2006). In addition, it can be analysed as a systematic entrepreneurial activity based on transforming fundamental scientific knowledge into industrially applicable, economically justified and market-demanded technologies (Dasgupta, 2018; Faems, Bos, Noseleit, and Leten, 2020).

Taking the identified signs and characteristics into account, the scholar understands the specific activities to create a complete chain from the idea (development) to the market implementation of a complex product with intellectual value, a feature of which is to increase the level of technological complexity of the economy through the use of synergistic effects from the co-organisation of various factors of production and other market participants.

Of course, there is a question of assessing the level of technological entrepreneurship and its contribution to the state economy. There are different approaches to assessing technological entrepreneurship in foreign and domestic works, but an important area of research remains the definition of its contribution to the economy. Among many studies on this topic (Bailetti, 2012) can be highlighted for its scientific contribution. The author analysed different approaches to the interpretation of "technological entrepreneurship" and the importance of its evaluation in ranking journals published since 1970 (when the First Symposium on Technological Entrepreneurship at Purdue University was held) until 2011 inclusive. The author typologised 93 articles by subject matter and period of publication. Interest in this line of research increased in the 2000s, which was reflected in the fact that from 2000 to 2011, 66% of all articles published since 1970 were published. Bailetti (2012) noted that without an assessment of technological entrepreneurship, it is impossible to work out strategic decisions in the direction of its development.

Here are examples of works by foreign researchers: (Badzinska 2016; Colovic and Lamotte, 2015; Feki and Mnif, 2016; Maysami et al., 2019; Shan, Jia, Zheng, and Xu, 2018) which emphasise the role of assessment of technology entrepreneurship and its particular importance: (a) for small businesses interacting with scientific organisations; (b) for the execution of orders for a certain complex technology; (c) when creating new productions, finding new applications for existing technologies or scientific and technological knowledge; (d) in expanding cooperation for technological change.

The project approach to assessing technological entrepreneurship is also found among domestic researchers. In particular, according to M.V. Khairullina, A.N. Barykin, V.M. Ikryannikov, I.V. Korchagina, R.L. Korchagin, O.V. Sycheva-Peredero, assessment has high importance in the activities of technological companies, which represent the implementation of interrelated technological startups in a particular territory – individual projects to transform scientific knowledge into industrial technology, which can contribute to the economy (Barykin and Ikryannikov 2010; Korchagina et al., 2019).

In general, it is worth noting that in the studies presented above, the assessment of technological entrepreneurship is put in the first place. At the same time, it is worth understanding that technological entrepreneurship cannot be measured only by the generally accepted approach (for example, used in the design documents) by only attributing costs to results. Such a one-sided approach to efficiency assessment sidelines the issue of the degree of correspondence between the planned objectives and the achieved results and, hence, the definition of the contribution of technological entrepreneurship to the Russian economy.

Thus, a relatively recent study (2016) by the global audit and consulting firm Deloitte Touche Tohmatsu on "Soft Skills for Success in

Technology Business" revealed that overcoming the so-called measurement of bottlenecks in understanding economic activity is a critical condition for assessing the impact of entrepreneurship on the economy (O' Mahony and Rumbens, n.d.).

Meanwhile, the existing indicators for assessing the results of technological entrepreneurship and its contribution in Russia do not even reflect the main trends of technological development of the Russian economy shortly (Yakushev, 2020; Yakushev, 2022), which casts doubt on the possibility of intensive development of this sphere of economic activity.

According to the World Bank's Word development indicators, the study focused on foreign experience in the analytical assessment of technological entrepreneurship. Statistical data are collected by country for the following indicators (The World Bank, n.d.; OECD, 2024): export of high-tech products, in total and percentage (high-tech exports); applications for registration of a trademark, by residents and non-residents (trademark applications); applications for patents, by residents and non-residents (patent applications); payments for use of intellectual property (charges).

The International Economic Organisation OECD on Science, Technology and Research and Development statistics include databases (Kogan et al., 2017) dedicated to R&D and S&T performance indicators, such as patents and technology balance of payments, as well as production and S&T impact (patents, technology balance of payments, trade-in high-tech industries). Based on the existing World Bank and OECD indicators, it is possible to assess the development of technological entrepreneurship in the BRICS space, but it is not enough to determine the contribution to the economy.

Russia also uses methods for calculating statistical indicators related to entrepreneurship, used to monitor the implementation of the instructions contained in the decrees of the President of the Russian Federation, in federal laws, regulations and orders of the Government of the Russian Federation (Federal Law, 2023).

Among them are the methods for calculation of indicators (including those relating to the development of technology and entrepreneurship) used to monitor the implementation of the instructions contained in the Decrees of the President of the Russian Federation of 7 May 2012 № 596-606, namely: the share of domestic spending on research and development in gross regional product; share of production of high-tech and knowledge-intensive industries in gross domestic product; share of high-tech and knowledge-intensive industries in gross regional product of the subject of the Russian Federation, the turnover of pro From this list of indicators used there is no direct reference to the assessment of technological entrepreneurship.

In addition, as part of the priority tasks for developing the Russian economy in 2018, the national project "Small and Medium Entrepreneurship and

Support for Individual Entrepreneurial Initiative" was developed and approved (The Russian Government, 2018). In it the following indicators are of great importance.

1. In the federal project "Acceleration of small and medium-sized enterprises":

   - The number of small and medium-sized businesses and self-employed citizens who received support under this federal project.
   - The share of exports of small and medium-sized businesses, including individual entrepreneurs, in the total volume of non-resource exports.
   - The number of small and medium-sized businesses exported with the support of the centres (agencies) coordinating the support of export-oriented small and medium-sized businesses.
   - The number of unique small and medium-sized businesses, which are suppliers of the largest customers determined by the government of the Russian Federation.
   - The number of employed in the organisations of small and medium-sized businesses, which are suppliers of the largest customers, determined by the government of the Russian Federation.
   - The number of newly created and operating small and medium-sized businesses and self-employed, which made significant actions in all information systems under the national project "small and medium-sized entrepreneurship and support of individual entrepreneurial initiative" and improved the revenue indicators and/or the number of employees.
   - The total volume of investment in fixed capital of small and medium-sized businesses that received access to production facilities and premises within the industrial parks and technoparks established in the constituent entities of the Russian Federation on the principles of public-private partnership.

2. The federal project "Popularisation of Entrepreneurship" assesses the number of:

   - Newly created small and medium-sized businesses by the participants of this federal project.
   - Trained in the basics of running a business, financial literacy and other entrepreneurial skills.
   - Trained trainers for the training of target groups using approved methods.
   - Physical persons – participants of this federal project, engaged in the sphere of small and medium-sized businesses, according to the results of their participation in the project.

3 In the federal project "Expansion of SMEs' access to financial resources, including preferential financing":

- The number of micro-loans issued by MFIS to SMEs cumulatively.
- Volume of loans issued to SMEs for the implementation of projects in priority sectors at a subsidised rate, including those secured by the guarantee support within the framework of the National Guarantee System.
- Volume of financial support provided to small and medium-sized businesses.

4 In the federal project "Improvement of conditions for doing business":

- The number of small and medium-sized businesses that use cash registers and have the right not to submit tax returns.
- The number of self-employed citizens who have fixed their status, taking into account the introduction of the tax regime for the self-employed.

Within the national projects under the "International Cooperation and Export and Science," it is possible to note several indicators, which, in one way or another, can reflect the influence of technological entrepreneurship on the economy (Passport of the National Project, 2018; Poznanska, 2014). Among them in the federal project "Export of services":

- The volume of intellectual property payments and business services exports.
- The volume of exports of telecommunications, computer and information services.

In the federal project "Development of scientific and scientific-production cooperation":

- The completed volume of developments ending with the manufacture, preliminary, and acceptance tests of a prototype (pilot batch).
- Increase in the number of large or medium-sized Russian companies involved in the development of technologies, products, and services within the implementation of rec and STI projects (in relation to the base value).
- Increase in the number of patents for inventions obtained with the participation of organisations – participants of recs, as well as STI competence centres within the implementation of projects (in relation to the base value).

Having analysed the basic indicators reflected in the federal projects in the listed national projects "Small and medium-sized business and support of individual entrepreneurial initiative," "International cooperation and export," and "Science," we note the following:

- First, none of the strategic documents refers to the promotion and development of technological entrepreneurship.
- Second, no explicit assessments are showing the importance and contribution to the economy of technological entrepreneurship.
- Third, only two indicators out of the whole mass of the analysed ones, to some extent, allow to indirectly fix the activity of technological entrepreneurship in the territory. These indicators include the total volume of investment in fixed capital of small and medium-sized businesses that have received access to production facilities and premises in the framework of industrial parks and technoparks established in the subjects of the Russian Federation on the principles of public-private partnership; the increase in the number of large or medium Russian companies involved in the development of technologies, products and services within the implementation of REC and STI projects. There are no indicators directly related to technological entrepreneurship in principle.

A certain list of indicators of a general economic nature is used to assess the effectiveness of the leaders of the subjects of the Russian Federation, approved by the Government of the Russian Federation on 17 July 2019, № 915. According to these indicators, in terms of the analysis of the processes taking place in entrepreneurship, it is worth considering the following:

1 (The Constitution of the Russian Federation, n.d.):

- The number of people employed in the sphere of small and medium-sized enterprises (SMEs), including individual entrepreneurs.
- Labour productivity in the basic non-primary sectors of the economy.
- Volume of investment in fixed capital, excluding investment of infrastructure monopolies (federal projects) and budget allocations from the federal budget.
- The number of highly productive jobs in the non-budgetary sector of the economy.

At the same time, only the number of those employed in SMEs, including individual entrepreneurs, is directly related to the monitoring of technological entrepreneurship among the above indicators. However, even this indicator needs to reflect the clear impact of technological entrepreneurship on the development of territories.

According to the ongoing federal statistical observation in Russia, which is a sample document designed to obtain primary statistical data in the prescribed manner, there is a list of forms to collect indicators indirectly related to technological entrepreneurship: the share of organisations engaged in technological innovation, in the total number of surveyed organisations; about the innovative activity of the organisation; about technological innovation of small businesses. In general, these indicators only weakly reflect the area we study and that to a limited extent.

The collection of indicators of innovation activity of the Higher School of Economics mainly reflects the results of statistical surveys that characterise innovation processes in the country's economy (Flanders Investment & Trade Market Survey, 2019). In part, they may have some relation to technological entrepreneurship as well. In the dynamics are presented summary indicators determining the level of development of technological and non-technological innovations, developed in accordance with modern international standards of the OECD and Eurostat. This publication provides statistical data reflecting the innovation activity of organisations of industrial production, several services and other sectors. Meanwhile, it does not allow us to speak in full about the development of technological entrepreneurship and, thus, to make an assessment for its further development.

Thus, the study showed that economic science had not developed an approach to a comprehensive assessment of technological entrepreneurship, which would take into account both its contribution and the level of development, the technological complexity of the economy (Wang, Lu, and Chen, 2008; Xie et al., 2018; Yakushev, 2018). Technological entrepreneurship in Russia can be characterised indirectly only through the analysis of the high-tech business. In 2018, its contribution to the Russian economy was 21.1% of GDP (21.6% in 2017). The three leading regions (Moscow, St. Petersburg and the Moscow region) account for about 38.3% (42.4% in 2017) of the total contribution of high-tech business to the Russian economy (Press-Service, 2019). At the same time, for example, the share of the Vologda region in all Russian values does not exceed one per cent.

Meanwhile, the analysis allows us to conclude that in Russia, the issue of inconsistency of the state statistics system with the goals of managing the development of technological entrepreneurship remains open. Statistical indicators that currently reflect only the key parameters of innovative development of the organisation become available with a significant delay. The structure of statistical evaluation indicators does not quite meet the objectives of the current day able to provide a full assessment of the contribution and development of technological entrepreneurship in Russia.

This problem is confirmed by the fact that the Presidential Instruction of 28 March 2020, № Pr-589 (paragraph 2.6) sets the task of working out the issue of organising statistical monitoring of technological entrepreneurship in Russia (Presidential Instructions, 2020).

The conducted analysis shows the need to correct and amend the Resolution of the Government of the Russian Federation of 16.02.2008 N 79 "On the

Procedure for conducting sample statistical observations of small and medium entrepreneurship" (ed. on 26.12.2017). So, from the author's point of view, it is necessary to make changes in point 6 of the Rules defining the order of conducting sample statistical observations of the activity of subjects of small and medium entrepreneurship. In essence, in paragraph 6, it seems appropriate to add the text: "The unified forms of federal statistical observation of the activities of small and medium-sized enterprises at the end of the year should include information characterising scientific and innovation activity (in particular, the development of technological entrepreneurship)."

At the same time, in our opinion, the approach to the assessment of technological entrepreneurship in Russia should be carried out comprehensively, taking into account the following indicators for statistical data collection:

- The volume of own-produced goods, works and services performed by own forces according to the degree of technological intensity (low, medium, high, with mandatory clarification of what is meant by this).
- The volume of own-produced goods, work and services performed using own in-house capabilities, which were newly introduced or underwent significant technological changes (different from the products previously produced by the enterprise) by sales markets, with a definition of domestic or world markets.
- The volume of goods of own production, works and services performed by own efforts, which underwent improvement (products already produced by the enterprise, produced by using new or improved methods of production) by sales markets with the division of domestic or world markets.
- The costs associated with the process of implementation of new or improved products or services, new or improved processes or methods of production (transfer) of services.
- Costs of implementation of technological solutions by sources of funding (own; funds from federal, regional, local budgets; support funds; foreign investments and others).
- Costs for developing technological solutions according to the sources of funding (own; federal, regional, local budget funds; support funds; foreign investments; and others).

Thus, to understand the situation occurring in technological entrepreneurship, and assess its contribution to the economy at the regional level, it is advisable for the authorities and management bodies responsible for the development of entrepreneurship, including in terms of solving the problem within the national project "Small and medium entrepreneurship and support of individual entrepreneurial initiative," to consider the implementation of the following directions. First, the official consolidation at the legislative level of the concept of "technological entrepreneurship" with the definition of its characteristics has an important practical value in the legal field. Second, it is necessary to develop a methodology evaluating technological entrepreneurship and its parameters, which can be used for analysis, considering the existing Russian and foreign experience of analytical evaluation. With the use of the methodology, there is an opportunity to assess the level of technological entrepreneurship. Third, it is worth considering technological entrepreneurship not only in monetary terms but also with the allocation of specific specialisation and specification in the region based on OKVED. This will give a meaningful reflection of what is happening in technological entrepreneurship in the sectoral context. Fourth, to assess the contribution of technological entrepreneurship in the economy of the country and regions through the developed list of indicators that give a direct assessment. As a result, using unified indicators will make it possible to more quickly determine the contribution and concentration of activity in this activity. Fifth, the results of ongoing scientific research of domestic and foreign scientists should be used to assess technological entrepreneurship. It will strengthen the experience of practical interaction between science and business. Sixth, it is necessary to organise a sociological assessment (surveys, interviews), for example, by the regional business support centre. It will allow people to understand technological entrepreneurship's current state and development in a particular territory.

Features of the Development of Advanced Production Technology in Russia in the Context of Technological Entrepreneurship

This study considered both general and specific issues related to technological entrepreneurship. As a result, our analysis of the scientific literature allows us to bring insight into the definition of advanced production technologies for developing technological entrepreneurship in Russia.

For a better understanding of the essence of advanced production technologies, their importance in the development of business (including technology), and the economy as a whole, it is necessary to lean on materials, positions used in expert activity and realised in practice (Dasgupta, 2018; Yakushev, 2020). So, according to the information of the National Institute of Standards and Technology (NIST, United States), the introduction of advanced production technologies can help companies (including SMEs) and, in particular, those carrying out the business in technological sectors to reach a higher quality of production and innovations. In addition, it can increase the efficiency and productivity of the production process and improve the interconnectedness of supply chains, ultimately making SMEs more competitive in the market and promoting business development in a particular territory (Faems et al., 2020; Sirkin, Zinser, and Rose, 2015; Yakushev, 2021a,b,c; Yakushev, 2022).

In the Boston Consulting Group study "Why Advanced Manufacturing Will Boost Productivity," advanced manufacturing technologies are defined as a set of very flexible, effective tools, considering these production processes (Sirkin et al., 2015). The use of tools comes with positive consequences and impacts the global competitiveness of industries. In addition, as the study notes, advanced manufacturing technologies greatly increase business flexibility, allowing manufacturers in some industries to offer customers the ability to "do things their way," which in turn can stimulate innovation, enable technological entrepreneurship, and allow manufacturers to create new types of products that cannot be produced by spending in traditional processes.

Deloitte, in cooperation with the Competitiveness and Singularity Council of Singularity University (United States), conducted a study on "Exponential manufacturing" (Faems et al., 2020; Exponential manufacturing, 2018). The work emphasises that the ideas and opportunities realised by advanced manufacturing technologies that technology entrepreneurs and other manufacturing companies will use in business, combined with talent and innovation, will determine the success of manufacturing in the future (enterprise, specific region, country, global trends), and can be used to gain competitive advantage in high-tech sectors.

In one of the materials of the Russian non-state development institute "Innopraktika," it is noted that in the world and domestic practice, technological companies are the drivers of innovative growth and the economy as a whole (Yakushev, 2021a). Thus, such companies play a special role in developing and introducing technologies (including advanced production), especially in the conditions of technological development when not only large but also average and small companies have the big flexibility, creativity, and adaptability to changing conditions in the market become actual.

An analysis of the development of advanced manufacturing technologies in Russia in the regions shows the following results (for 2019–2021, the average) (Federal State Statistics Service, 2021). In first place by the number of advanced manufacturing technologies is the Volga Federal District with a total of 76,652 units. The Central Federal District follows it with a total of 77,155 units. The Urals take third place, where advanced production technologies account for 32,260 units. The Northwestern and Siberian federal districts are almost at the same level, with a value of 25,402 and 23,572 units, respectively. At the same time, the main leader in NWFD is St. Petersburg – 10,129 units. The number of advanced production technologies in the Southern Federal District is fixed at 15,805 units. The lowest value for this indicator is observed in the Far Eastern Federal District, which is 10,129 units. At that, the all-Russian level of advanced production technologies equals 33,033 units.

Conclusion, Suggestions, Discussions, and Research Perspectives

In general, the peculiarities of the development of advanced production technologies in Russia in the context of technological entrepreneurship are considered from the perspective of various characteristics: managerial, financial, cooperative, business environment, commercial relations, and risk analysis. At the same time, considering the relationship between technological entrepreneurship and advanced technology will consist of the following key points:

- First, it is the registration of a new economic entity with localisation of its business in the sector of technology and production of complex products.
- Second, the growth and popularisation of intellectual property and contribution to the importance of R and D.
- Third, investment in the knowledge and competence of employees with increasing experience to produce quality products, taking into account the growing needs of the market and the consumer.
- Fourth, the formation of new business models in the form of joint projects, and technological alliances contributes to the development of favourable conditions in the region and cooperation in entering foreign markets.

In this case, the main goal should be the development of technological entrepreneurship to increase the level of technological sophistication of the BRICS economy through the synergistic use of internal company capabilities and the potential of the external environment, represented by development institutions and structures from the high-tech sector.

In Russia, the development of technological entrepreneurship should be carried out comprehensively, taking into account the following characteristics:

- Levels of technological complexity of the economy.
- Contribution of fundamental scientific knowledge into industrially applicable, economically justified and market-demanded technologies).
- Synergy of academic and intellectual potential with commercial organisations implementing new advanced production technologies and innovative business solutions in the market environment.

This requires a change in the basic conditions for the development of technological entrepreneurship in the region with the construction of a new business model in the infrastructure and business support centres on the platform of quality effective solutions (including financial support tools for the possibility of business implementation of advanced technologies).

At the same time, for the development of advanced production technologies in Russia, it is necessary to improve management processes in the sector of technological entrepreneurship.

In the future, this creates a basis for the development of cases, which will make it possible to analyse the situation in technological entrepreneurship in the BRICS space.

References

Abalkin L. (2010) From economic theory to the concept of long-term strategy. *Voprosy Ekonomiki*, (6):4–9. DOI: 10.32609/0042-8736-2010-6-4-9
Ackoff R.L. (1999) Transformational leadership. *Strategy and Leadership*, 27 (1):20–25
Ansoff H.I. (2018) A profile of intellectual growth. *Management Laureates*. Routledge.
Badzinska E. (2016) The concept of technological entrepreneurship: the example of business implementation. *Entrepreneurial Business and Economics Review*, 4 (3):57–72.
Bailetti T. (2012) Technology entrepreneurship: overview, definition, and distinctive aspects. *Technology Innovation Management Review*, 2 (2):5–12.
Barykin A.N., Ikryannikov V.M. (2010) White spots of the theory and practice of technological entrepreneurship. *Management of Innovations*, 3:202–213.
Bereslavskaya V.A. (2005) Production potential in the fulfilment of the strategy for intensive development of enterprises. *Dairy Industry*, (12):48–49.
Boev A.G. (2021) Methodology for the development of key performance indicators and customer satisfaction for the transformation strategy of the industrial complex. *Vestnik Universiteta*, (7):100–112.
Bosma N., Kelley D. (2018) Global Entrepreneurship Monitor. https://www.gemconsortium.org/file/open?fileId=50213 (Accessed 2 June 2023).
Butryumova N.N., Karpycheva S.A., Nazarov M.G., Sidorov D.V. (2015) Research on the evolution of technological entrepreneurship in the Nizhny Novgorod region. *Innovations*, 7 (201):80–89.
Cassiman B., Golovko E., Martínez-Ros E. (2010) Innovation, exports and productivity. *International Journal of Industrial Organization*, 28 (4):372–376.
Colovic A., Lamotte O. (2015) Technological environment and technology entrepreneurship: A cross-country analysis. *Creativity and Innovation Management*, 24 (4):617–628.
Dasgupta M. (2018) Driving innovation through strategic alliances: A framework. *International Journal of Strategic Business Alliances*, 6 (3):130–147.
Efremov V.S. (1998) Business strategy: Concepts and methods of planning. M. Finpress.
Exponential manufacturing (2018). https://www2.deloitte.com/content/dam/insights/us/collections/exponential-manufacturing/DUP_Exponential-Manufacturing.pdf (Accessed 2 June 2023).
Faems D., Bos B., Noseleit F., Leten B. (2020) Multistep knowledge transfer in multinational corporation networks: when do subsidiaries benefit from unconnected sister alliances? *Journal of Management*, 46(3):414–442. DOI: 10.1177/0149206318798037
Fatkhutdinova, A.M. (2021) Transformation of entrepreneurial activity during the crisis. *Theoretical Economics*, 5 (77):50–54.
Federal law "About the development of small and medium-sized business in the Russian Federation" from 24.07.2007 N 209-FZ (last edition). http://www.consultant.ru/document/cons_doc_LAW_52144/ (2 June 2023).

Federal law "About the development of small and medium-sized business in the Russian Federation" from 24.07.2007 N 209-FZ (last edition). http://www.consultant.ru/document/cons_doc_LAW_52144/ (2 June 2023).

Federal Law "On Official Statistical Records and the System of State Statistics in the Russian Federation" of 29.11.2007 N 282-FZ (latest edition). http://www.consultant.ru/document/cons_doc_LAW_72844/ (2 June 2023).

Federal State Statistics Service (2021) Regions of Russia. Socio-economic indicators – 2021 of the Federal State Statistics Service. https://rosstat.gov.ru/folder/210/document/13204 (Accessed 2 June 2023).

Feki C., Mnif S. (2016) Entrepreneurship, technological innovation, and economic growth: Empirical analysis of panel data. *Journal of the Knowledge Economy*, 7 (4):984–999.

Flanders Investment & Trade Market Survey (2019) Compendium of Innovation Indicators: https://www.hse.ru/data/2019/05/06/1501882833/ii_2019.pdf (Accessed 2 June 2023).

Garud R., Karnoe P. (2003) Bricolage versus breakthrough: Distributed and embedded agency in technology entrepreneurship. *Research Policy*, 32 (2):277–300.

Gianiodis P. (2014) Framework for investigating university-based technology transfer and commercialization. *The Routledge Companion to Entrepreneurship*, 14:125–129.

Glazyev S.Y. (2022) Noonomy as the Core of the Formation of New Technological Mode and Global Economic Order. Anthology of Noonomy: fourth technological revolution and its economic, social and humanitarian consequences. Brill, 1:47–68.

Gongming Q., Marcus A., Lee L. (2014) Should small exporting technology enterprises use niche, strategic alliances, or both? *International Journal of Management and Enterprise Development*, 13 (1):21–36.

Gorzelany-Dziadkowiec M. (2014) Intraprzedsiebiorczosc w małych i srednich przedsiebiorstwach. *Studia Ekonomiczne Regionu Lodzkiego*, 12:87–97.

Gradov A.P. (2014) Strategy and tactics for identifying and resolving systemic problem situations in the economy. *π-Economy*, 3 (197):17–27.

Ilyin V.A. (2018) Problems and implementation of the socio-economic potential of territory development: Monograph. Vologda: VolSC RAS.

Karloff B. (1989) Business strategy: A guide to concepts and models. Springer.

Khairullina M.V. (2016) Technological entrepreneurship: Constraints and conditions for development. *Russian Entrepreneurship*, 17 (16):1831–1848.

Kogan L., Papanikolaou D., Seru A., Stoffman N. (2017) Technological innovation, resource allocation, and growth. *The Quarterly Journal of Economics*, 132 (2):665–712.

Korchagina I.V., Korchagin R.L., Sycheva-Peredero O.V. (2019) Estimation of the regional research reserves in the context of economic diversification on the basis of technological entrepreneurship. *Actual Problems of Economics and Management*, 4:56–67.

Kordel P. (2014) Przedsiębiorczosc technologiczna jako mechanizm rozwoju strategicznego organizacji. *Prace Naukowe Uniwersytetu Ekonomicznego we Wrocławiu*, 356:19–28.

Kotler P. (2012) *Kotler on marketing*. Simon and Schuster.

Kviatkovsky S. (2002) Intellectual entrepreneurship and stable economic development in post-socialist European countries. *Problems of Management Theory and Practice*, (3):21–27.

Lambin J.J. (2020) Global corporate accountability. *Symphonya. Emerging Issues in Management*, 1:45–61. DOI: 10.4468/2020.1.04lambin

Maysami A.M., Elyasi G., Dehkordi A., Hejazi S.R. (2019) Toward the measurement framework of technological entrepreneurship ecosystem. *Journal of Enterprising Culture*, 27:419–444.

Mescon T.S. (1987) The entrepreneurial institute: education and training for minority small business owners. *Journal of Small Business Management*, 25 (1):61–66.

Mintzberg H. (1987) The strategy concept I: five Ps for strategy. *California Management Review*, 30 (1):11–24.

Nicolescu O. (2009) Main features of SMEs organization system. *Review of International Comparative Management*, 10 (3):405–413.

O'Mahony J., Rumbens D. (n.d.) Soft skills for business. https://www2.deloitte.com/content/dam/Deloitte/au/Documents/Economics/deloitte-au-economics-deakin-soft-skills-business-success-170517.pdf (Accessed 10 July 2021).

OECD (2024), Researchers (indicator). https://data.oecd.org/rd/researchers.htm (Accessed 06 February 2024).

Passport of the National Project. (2018). International Cooperation and Export. http://static.government.ru/media/files/FL01MAEp8YVuAkvbZotaYtVKNEKaALYA.pdf (Accessed 2 June 2023).

Porter M.E. (2008) The five competitive forces that shape strategy. *Harvard Business Review*, 86 (1):78–93.

Poznanska K. (2014) Przedsiebiorczosc akademicka: cechy i znaczenie w gospodarce swiatowej i polskiej. *Studia Ekonomiczne*, 2014 (183):164–172.

Presidential Instructions (2020) List of instructions from the joint meeting of the Presidium of the State Council and the Council on Science and Education. http://www.kremlin.ru/acts/assignments/orders/63083 (Accessed 10 June 2023).

Press-Service (25 March 2019) National report on the development of high-tech business in the regions of Russia. https://i-regions.org/eng/press-sluzhba/novosti/national-report-high-tech-business-in-the-regions-of-russia-by-ranepa-and-airr (Accessed 20 October 2023).

Qing-Lan Q., Ying-Niao C., Xiao-Min D. (2008) Technology innovation within small and middle enterprises and regional environment. *Scientia Geographica Sinica*, 4:1–7.

Results of Federal Statistical Observations (2022). Results of continuous monitoring of the activities of small and medium-sized businesses. https://www.gks.ru/folder/14477 https://rosstat.gov.ru/small_business_2020 (Accessed 2 June 2023).

Schumpeter J. (2003) Entrepreneurship, style and vision. Boston, MA: Springer.

Schwab K. (2019) The Global Competitiveness 2019 http://www3.weforum.org/docs/WEF_TheGlobalCompetitivenessReport2019.pdf (Accessed 10 July 2021).

Sels L., De Winne S., Maes J., Delmotte J., Faems D., Forrier A. (2006) Unravelling the HRM–Performance link: value-Creating and cost-increasing effects of small business HRM. *Journal of Management Studies*, 43 (2):319–342.

Semenov N. (2013) Economic diversification as a factor in the sustainable development of business structures. *RISK: Resources, Information, Supply, Competition*, (4):87–88.

Shan S., Jia Y., Zheng X., Xu X. (2018) Assessing relationship and contribution of China's technological entrepreneurship to socio-economic development. *Technological Forecasting and Social Change*, 135 (C):83–90.

Sirilli G., Evangelista R. (1998) Technological innovation in services and manufacturing: Results from Italian surveys. *Research Policy*, 27 (9):881–899.

Sirkin H.L., Zinser M., Rose J.R. (2015) Why Advanced Manufacturing Will Boost Productivity. https://www.bcg.com/publications/2015/lean-and-manufacturing-production-why-advanced-manufacturing-boost-productivity (Accessed 10 October 2023).

The constitution of the Russian Federation (n.d.) http://archive.government.ru/eng/gov/base/54.html (Accessed 20 January 2024).

The Global Innovation Index (2019) Creating Healthy Lives–The Future of Medical Innovation https://www.globalinnovationindex.org/gii-2019-report (Accessed 10 July 2021).

The Russian Government (2018) Passport of the national project "Small and Medium Entrepreneurship and Support of Individual Entrepreneurial Initiative." http://static.government.ru/media/files/ualhTsGOc72APotuEQUjhoENhq1qYz4H.pdf (Accessed 2 June 2023).

The World Bank (n.d.) Indicators the World Bank Group. URL: https://data.worldbank.org/indicator (Accessed 2 June 2023).

Thompson B.S. (2023) Impact investing in biodiversity conservation with bonds: an analysis of financial and environmental risk. *Business Strategy and the Environment*, 32 (1):353–368.

Venkataraman S. (2004) Regional transformation through technological entrepreneurship. *Journal of Business Venturing*, 19 (1):153–167.

Vertakova Y. (2019) Prospects for the development of technological entrepreneurship in the machine-building complex. Scientific journal proceedings of the far Eastern Federal University. *Economics and Management*, 1:68–80.

Vrakking W.J. (1990) The innovative organization. *Long Range Planning*, 23 (2):94–102.

Wang C., Lu I., Chen C. (2008) Evaluating firm technological innovation capability under uncertainty. *Technovation*, 28 (6):349–363.

Wyrzykowska B. (2012) Przedsiebiorczosc intelektualna jako kompetencja wspołczesnego menedżera. Zeszyty Naukowe SGGW. *Ekonomika i Organizacja Gospodarki Zywnosciowej*, 100:26–35.

Xie K., Song Y., Zhang W., Hao J., Liu Z., Chen Y. (2018) Technological entrepreneurship in science parks: a case study of Wuhan Donghu High-Tech Zone. *Technological Forecasting and Social Change*, 135:156–168.

Yakushev N.O. (2017) High-tech export of Russia and its territorial specificity. *Problems of Territory Development*, 3 (89):62–77.

Yakushev N.O. (2018) Non-resource exports of the Union State as a factor in the economic development of the territory of Russia and Belarus. *Problems of Territory's Development*, 5(97):41–54. DOI: 10.15838/ptd.2018.5.97.3

Yakushev N.O. (2020) Improving the tools for assessing and managing export activities of SMEs in the region. *Economic and Social Changes: Facts, Trends, Forecast*, 13(3):143–157. DOI: 10.15838/esc.2020.3.69.10

Yakushev N.O. (2021a) Features of the development of advanced production technologies in Russia in the framework of technological entrepreneurship. *The Issues of Territorial Development*, 9(4). DOI: 10.15838/tdi.2021.4.59.2

Yakushev N.O. (2021b) Entrepreneurship in the technological sector: an open question https://scientificrussia.ru/articles/predprinimatelstvo-v-tehnologicheskom-sektore-vopros-otkrytyj (Accessed 10 July 2023).

Yakushev N.O. (2021c) Educational factor in technological entrepreneurship development. *Social Area*, 7(2). DOI: 10.15838/sa.2021.2.29.4 URL: http://socialarea-journal.ru/article/28940?_lang=en (Accessed 10 July 2023).

Yakushev N.O. (2022) High-tech export assessment in Russia's entities and proposals for its development. *Problems of Territory's Development*, 26(2):23–39. DOI: 10.15838/ptd.2022.2.118.3

17 Entrepreneurial Lens into Creative Industries in Russia Post-COVID-19

The Case of Urals Region

Anna Kurumchina

Introduction and Background

For the first time, the theme of cultural industries was considered in 1947 in Adorno and Horkheimer's book The Dialectic of Enlightenment. Philosophical Fragments (Horkheimer *et al.*, 2002). Being representatives of the Frankfurt school, they critically described the role of such cultural industries as cinematography, television, and magazines in capitalist society, demonstrating their dependence on the profit paradigm, segmentation of customers, technical rationality, unification, and standardisation of emotions and information. According to them, in the frame of cultural industries of Western society, the pieces of art are disappearing and replaced by the commercial success formula that consists of standardised cliché or "details" that leads to the disappearing of the live soul from the pieces of art; however, they become understandable, predictable and sell well to a mass audience. Adorno and Horkheimer stressed that only state protectionism in art can still save its freedom from market dictates and customer demand.

Then, in the 1970s the transition to post-industrial society, when industrial production was replaced from the United States and Europe to the eastern countries. After this transition western countries had mostly entertainment industries and services. During this period the creative industries with an accent on individual entrepreneurship and knowledge economy got attention (Luckman, 2017).

The combination of cultural policy and cultural industries got a new impulse of development thanks to the Great Council of London's activities from 1979 to 1986. Three components – micro-entrepreneurship, market, and art – were soldered during this period. This result became considered a territory development driver, leading to increased employment and improved socioeconomic inclusion for any society representatives.

In the Russian Federation, the transition process to post-industrial society started after the collapse of the USSR and the mass destruction of industrial plants. The Middle Urals region is famous for its 300 years of industrial metallurgy history. The world-famous Russian metallurgy plants were built and worked here since 1702. During the 20th century, some of them were destroyed or replaced, but historical plant buildings exist till the present.

As the development of creative industries is a part of the global agenda, the Russian Federation signed the relevant documents and supports spreading the creative industries agenda on its territory.

This rich historical industrial heritage has become a fundament for the uniqueness of Ural creative industries. The Russian government and The Agency for Strategic Initiatives (ASI) developed a programme to renovate such territories. This all-Russian programme transforms the territories of former industrial zones and abandoned buildings. The Middle Urals became a leader of the third stage of the federal project Creative Lab and a pilot region for creative industries. The pandemic was a good period during which we had time to renovate some of them or develop some managerial programmes and projects to implement the ideas of creative industries' clusters.

Problem Statement/Objectives

The pandemic demonstrated that creative and intellectual input into the product has played a significant role in the economy and might be made through digital technologies. These technologies open wide opportunities for disseminating entrepreneurial results worldwide, crossing borders in a new, global, transformed world.

Structural changes caused by the COVID-19 pandemic and the economic, technological, and social accompanying processes forced the states to adopt the Creative Industries Concept, demonstrating its timeliness. The job cuts, on the one hand, and entering the economic arena such categories of employees like women, young people, and disabled persons, on the other hand, demanded alternative ways of employment, and not automated creative industries have been excellent directions to overcome pandemic and changes mentioned above.

The creative industries sector has the potential to create high-added value, making it attractive for entrepreneurs and investors. Many areas of the sector are characterised by a relatively low barrier to entry into the market, which makes it possible for the general population, like women, disabled people etc., to develop their business, allows them to overcome the limitations of development-related to the insufficient volume of the local market and the remoteness of the place of residence of the entrepreneur, to preserve human capital in the regions and municipalities, to ensure balanced territorial development.

These characteristics of creative industries are described as a humanitarian sector of the economy.

It is known that the sector of creative industries provides a significant contribution to the global economy: the average share of the creative industries sector in world gross domestic product (GDP) is 6.6%, and in developed countries, this share reaches 8–12% with an average annual growth of 15%, which significantly exceeds average growth rates of the global economy (this trend is projected to continue in the medium term). But in Russia the potential of the creative economy sector is not enough implemented – the share of creative industries in the country's economy is only 2.23%.

Despite some difficulties caused by the pandemic, it was a period during which our talented and creative entrepreneurs found new opportunities to work and earn money making their input into the growing mentioned share. Our government paid its attention to creative industries at exactly this very moment by initiating a Russian programme to support them.

According to the Spatial Development Strategy of the Russian Federation for the period up to 2025, one of the problems of spatial development of the Russian Federation is an insufficient number of economic growth centres to ensure the acceleration of the economic growth of the Russian Federation. Creative clusters considered in this article in 2023 have become real points of attraction and development of domestic tourism.

Another problem of the spatial development of the Russian Federation also concerns a low level of entrepreneurial activity in most small and medium-sized cities, rural areas, and territories outside the largest urban agglomerations.

Other problems of the creative industries development in Russia as a whole and in the Middle Urals, particularly at the beginning, had three directions, namely:

1 Writing the state and the regional Strategies for the development of creative industries.
2 Development a whole network of creative sites in the region on the territories of former factories and industrial facilities.
3 Business education for creative entrepreneurs and new university educational standards for creative industries.

As a specialist in Cultural Studies, the author of this article wants to stress that culture characterises the development of persons and is associated with the "core" of their personalities and the spiritual world, with the solution of basic issues of the meaning of their existence. So, for us, it is extremely important not only the profit percentage that this sector brings to the regional budget but also the content component of ideas and things used for creating these territories and goods.

We will consider these problems and will demonstrate that the COVID period was a good time for us to implement new business opportunities in the region and provide new employment opportunities in the region. Simultaneously this activity was a result of the manifestation of the essential forces of men, creating a wonderful world around them.

One more peculiarity is that this article has mostly a practically oriented approach rather than a theoretical one.

Literature Review

As we know, the idea of the development of creative industries was caused by profit growth in traditional industrial and financial sectors after the 1970s started slowing down. Now, global investors have only 3% profit or even less as opposed to 7% in the 1970s.

> The world economy has experienced many rapid ups and painful recessions over the past 75 years. But the rise that began in 2010 was lethargic. Until the early 1970s, global growth peaked at 6% or more per year, and after 2008, it averaged at least 4%. Then since then, it has fallen to 3% or less. Global growth, which was only marginally faster than population growth, meant that many of the world's inhabitants experienced zero or negative economic growth. These economic conditions demotivate employees, companies, and the political establishment, as they point to slim chances for improvement.
>
> (Schwab, 2021)

That is why creative industries have been widely recognised as a necessary and significant tool for economic growth and development of territories and industries. The concept of creative industries continued to develop in the 1990s. At the time, the policy of integrated development and promotion of culture, high-tech sectors, and entertainment was introduced by various states. The sector under study is a new group of economic sectors that promote social inclusion, cultural diversification, income generation, trade and innovation, creating economic, and labour advantages in related service sectors and production. Over the past decades, the creative industries have become an important sector of the world economy.

According to the theory, two terms are used: cultural and creative industries. They divide all spheres of cultural production. Traditional, classic culture and folklore belong to cultural industries, and a variety of science and technology, media, music, design, and the modern arts are characterised by creative industries and have become an increasingly important driver of innovation (Badikova and Vasilkovskaya, 2022).

The last sector profoundly impacts the social and cultural aspects of people's lives. According to the United Nations Educational, Scientific and Cultural Organisation (UNESCO), the creative industries generate more than US$2,200 billion in annual revenue worldwide. They are projected to account for more than 10% of world GDP (Mordanov, 2022). Experts from the Organisation for Economic Cooperation and Development (OECD) stressed that the annual growth rates of the indicated sphere range from 5% to 20% in the OECD countries. In the European Union, the share of creative industries in the EU's GDP and employment level is more than 3.0% (Khlystova et al., 2022).

High School of Economics defines creative industries as sectors of the economy, a significant part of the added value of which is formed through creative activity and rights management on intellectual property (HSE University, 2018). This definition is more universal, and many activities can be considered creative. But controversial in this definition is the idea of intellectual property. Some economists criticise it because they consider the restrictive nature of the concept, working in the interests of the capitalist way of making a profit (Simple Numbers, 2021).

In 2011, at the UN General Assembly, the need for a more visible and effective integration of culture into the development policies and strategies at all levels, particularly in the post-2015 Sustainable Development Goals (SDGs), was stated (UNESCO, 2012). Since then, the idea of controlled development of creative industries has been disseminated worldwide among all UN members. Governments started to work on development policies and find Agencies to manage the process.

In 2014, in Florence, the UNESCO's Third World Forum on Culture and Cultural Industries (FOCUS) took place. As mentioned, "Valued at over $620 billion, the global trade in cultural goods and services has doubled over the past decade, demonstrating that culture is a powerful force for economic and social development. Cultural goods and services are not just ordinary merchandise that generate jobs, income, innovation and growth; they also contribute to social inclusion and justice" (UNESCO, 2012). It was very important for the world economy because of the trends examined by the World Economic Forum and mentioned in Prof. Schwab's book (Schwab, 2021).

Unfortunately, a utilitarian view of culture leads to what Adorno and Horkheimer's view mentioned above. According to Kogan (1992), in any practical activity, a person changes the world, and not only really, but also ideally – in his mind. By changing the world, he changes himself, improving his abilities and needs and enriching his knowledge, worldview, and social feelings, such as his social ("essential") forces (Kogan, 1992). Culture embodies a person's spiritual wealth, accumulated knowledge, skills, abilities, and social feelings, which, in the process of creative activity, are embodied in cultural values with social significance. On the other hand, creativity itself is possible only if the individual distributes (masters) the already accumulated cultural values, turning them into his spiritual wealth. Unfortunately, today, the commercialisation of culture is a means of social division: mass commercial cheap culture is for plebs, and classical, expensive cultural goods are for the social elite. From this point of view, creative industries and clusters are sometimes places where social and cultural deviants express their ill fantasies, and commercial approach promotes them like fashionable actual trends. So, the problem of cultural revision arises.

On 20 September 2021, the Russian Government approved Concept #2613-p devoted to the development of creative industries and mechanisms for the implementation of their state support in large and largest urban agglomerations until 2030 (Russian Federation Government, 2021).

This Concept was developed according to the Decree of the President of the Russian Federation dated 24 December 2014, No. 808 "On approval of the Fundamentals state cultural policy and The Spatial Development Strategy of the Russian Federation for the period up to 2025, approved by the Decree of the Government of the Russian Federation dated 13 February 2019 No. 207-r." The main goals of the Concept of the development of Creative Industries are to organise and provide legal status of spontaneous actions in the creative sphere that make their input into the self-realisation of our people and development of their talents, to provide decent, efficient work and successful entrepreneurship, and facilitate the digital transformation.

Special attention was given to the development of creative clusters in Russia because they could provide creative entrepreneurs with places to work and sell their goods, to communicate with each other, and like places that can become platforms for attracting spectators to various performances and territorial development.

Methods and Data Source

The ASI became an implementation operator on this global creative industries agenda in Russia. In 2018, it organised the so-called Rurban project that Rosatom supported (Vasilyeva, 2021).

Rurban is a body with programmes of the Center for Urban Competence of the ASI to promote new projects. It was created in 2018 to develop and apply systematic approaches and models for replication aimed at building urban communities, involving citizens in solving development issues and improving the comfort level of the urban environment, as well as developing the urban economy. One of its projects is called Rurban Creative Lab (Rurban 2021). It is responsible for territorial transformation into creative clusters. Even before the governmental Concept (Gavrilova *et al.*, 2023) was signed, the Rurban Creative Lad initiated a competition based on the results of which regional teams for developing creative clusters were formed. Several regions of the Russian Federation have been chosen for it, namely Irkutsk, Novgorod, Novosibirsk, Ryazan, Samara, Sverdlovsk, Tyumen, Udmurtia, Ulyanovsk, and Khanty-Mansiysk regions.

Why Sverdlovsk region is included in this program?

The Middle Urals region is famous for its 300 years of industrial metallurgy history. The first metallurgy plant was built here in 1630. The world-famous

Russian metallurgy plants were built and worked here since 1702 when Peter the Great initiated the industrial development of Russia. During the 20th century, some of them were destroyed or replaced, but plant buildings exist till the present. This rich industrial heritage nowadays has become a fundament for the uniqueness of Ural creative industries. The Russian government and The ASI developed a programme to renovate such territories. This all-Russian programme is for transforming the territories of former industrial zones and abandoned buildings. Sverdlovsk region is a pilot one for creative industries in Russia.

It is necessary to focus and select as support priorities the types of entrepreneurships based on the use of the results of creative, intellectual activity, regardless of specific types of economic activity, sectors of the economy and (or) share of material (production) component in the final product and service. The government realised the priorities of the activities of public authorities of all levels should be an increase in the share of such entrepreneurship in all sectors of the economy, especially in those identified as promising economic specialisations of the constituent entities of the Russian Federation, as well as the gradual inclusion of creative industries among such specialisations. The development of creative industries, both in terms of value and volume, entails a multiplier economic effect.

The support of creative industries must lead to an increased tax base, increasing the number of new workplaces on local and state levels; reducing disproportions in socio-economic development, and increasing the tourist attractiveness of the territories.

The Russian government instructed regional branches of the Business and Entrepreneurship Support Fund to do their best in implementing these ideas.

The Sverdlovsk Regional Business Support Fund, as a practical-oriented supervisor of the development of the creative cluster in the Sverdlovsk region, approached the task very responsibly. And on 28 February 2021 it initiated the Strategic Session of the Development of the Creative Industries in the Sverdlovsk region.

The main idea of the session was to create a common information field, get answers to questions, form a team of initiators to create a production centre and plan the first steps for developing creative industries in the Sverdlovsk region. The expected results included a ranked list of relevant questions on the topic of creating a production centre; all participants clearly understood the purpose of creation and the essence of the work of the production centre to participate in the work of the centre or not; interested persons can join the team of 18 initiators; the first steps that are necessary for project implementation are outlined; participants understand what is next, what to prepare for; and feel like a part of the project team.

The Minister of Investment and Development of the Sverdlovsk region opened the session.

The participants developed ideas for the cluster, its risks and steps that should be made to achieve the goals. They composed a list of users of the clusters, risks, and steps to overcome risks and attract target users. Much attention was given to the description of the clusters' teams and their supporting motivation. A special impact was made on the planned results and the future image of the creative cluster. And the question of the finance model was considered.

The second meeting organised by the Sverdlovsk Regional Business Support Fund was devoted to discussing the draft law "On the Creative Industries of the Sverdlovsk Region," which took place on 28 May 2021. The aim of the meeting was to present the participants with the law, then answer their questions, and after that, to have a session of developing and collecting their recommendations for the draft. The participants asked the government important questions, for instance, what is the creative product? whether "free artists" are subjects of the creative industries if they are not registered as legal entities. what is the authorised executive body and its functions? etc. In total, the professional community proposed six pages of changes to the thesaurus of the law.

The second topic was the completeness of the support measures provided. And again, professionals in the creative sector asked very productive questions, for instance, who specifically provides consulting support? how the support mechanism is implemented? If there will be different degrees of support depending on the level of development of creative bodies, etc. As a result of the whole session, all 20 pages of suggestions were taken into account and made into law.

These activities demonstrate, on the one hand, the high level of professionalism of creative cluster participants, their openness and desire to work, to create and to develop the region, and, on the other hand, the readiness of the local and federal government to listen and implement ideas from the sector professionals.

Today, there are several creative clusters in Sverdlovsk region. Let's look at everyone closely. The sites in Chernoistochinsk, Nizhny Tagil, and Sysert were the first to be "activated" in the territory of the Sverdlovsk region.

Art Residence in Chernoistochinsk

On the territory of an old Demidov factory in the village of Chernoistochinsk near Nizhny Tagil, a project is being implemented to make a creative space "Art Residence." Its authors are the My Business Center in Nizhny Tagil (created by the Sverdlovsk Regional Business and Entrepreneurship Support Fund, head Sergy Fedoreev) and local entrepreneur Alexander Bykov, who bought the building in 2013 and occupied a small part of it with a furniture workshop.

> After several cultural events that took place in our centre, it became clear to me that creative people have great commercial potential, but it has not been realised. Along with the idea of creating a platform for the sale of

works of art, last year we came up with the idea of creating a creative accelerator, where we will give creative people entrepreneurial competence," says Sergey Fedoreev.

(The First Art Residence, 2020)

The creative cluster in Chernoistochinsk is a space placed on the territory of the former ironworks founded by Akinfiy Demidov in 1726, in the village of Chernoistochinsk, which houses the new museum of platbands "Fancy Balusters." It is an authentic place near the dam of the Chernoistochinsky Pond. Now, it is an unusual and stylish creative space with workshops, an exhibition hall, concert venues, a pottery workshop, its puppet theatre and a souvenir shop.

The Art Residence project was included in the number of projects participating in the 100 City Leaders 2020 programme of the ASI. Tagil's idea entered the top 20. In total, 604 applications from more than 200 settlements in the country were received for the competition.

For these several years of its works, the art residence has developed many activities, its programmes are oriented to promoting the specificity of the local territory – workshops from local artists; lectures from art experts and historians who talk about Demidov, his plants and many other things about this village; celebrate some traditional Slavic and orthodox holidays. The target audiences of the residence are schoolchildren from Nizhny Tagil and Yekaterinburg, weekend travellers and tourists. One of the problems of this residence and the future task is how to involve the local people in the activities of the residence. Its representative, Elena Kirilyuk, is responsible for developing the project.

Creative Factory in Sysert

Another finalist of the federal competition 100 City Leaders 2020 from the Sverdlovsk region was the Creative Factory project in Sysert. This creative cluster is based on the Turchaninov-Solomirsky Ironworks (Figure 17.1). In 2019, one of Demidov's abandoned plants in Sysert became a place for the non-commercial private initiative "Leto na Zavode" (Summer at the Factory). This project demonstrated the creative potential of such zones, and its author presented his project to President Putin. This meeting stressed the extreme importance and significance of the chosen way. The creative cluster "Leto na Zavode" is an important accelerator for the special development of the Sverdlovsk region, and now it is famous on the federal level.

The first buildings of the Turchaninov-Solomirsky plant in Sysert were built in 1732 after iron ore was found here at the end of the 17th century. Until the middle of the 19th century, the enterprise was considered one of the most advanced in the world, but without refurbishment, the plant became very outdated. The Ural industrialists here tried to use cheap labour and did not want to master new methods and technologies. In Soviet times, engines for the famous in

308 *Anna Kurumchina*

Figure 17.1 Souvenirs, Chernoistochinsk

Russia Malyutka washing machine were made here, and with the collapse of the USSR, the plant finally fell into decay.

For the last 30 years, the buildings of the Turchaninov-Solomirsky ironworks in Sysert have been empty, gradually turning into ruins. But in 2018, the entrepreneur Yan Kozhan established an non-governmental organisation(s) (NGO), Sysert Development Agency and gradually initiated several cultural projects: Summer at the Factory, Ural Creative Camp, Purely So, and Touristic cluster. And 2020 the Summer at the Factory project gave the ironworks a second life. During the first season, more than 20,000 people visited the place, and in November 2020, Vladimir Putin paid attention to it. The President of Russia liked the initiative, and Sysert's experience became the starting point for testing this practice in other regions of Russia.

The peculiarity of this place is that it is a seasoned place that works only in summer because the plant premises are not reconstructed yet. They cannot work in winter, although the Sysert Development Agency invited an architect, Narine Tyutcheva, who developed the reconstruction concept. Nonetheless, this process goes slowly.

Despite all difficulties this initiative is in demand with Yekaterinburg and Sysret citizens and tourists, thanks to the governmental support and organiser's energy and resources. It has a wide advertisement that helped attract more than 20,000 people in 2020.

To attract as many people as possible, the organisers cooperate with famous creative teams and celebrities at the federal level. For instance, they provided a platform for the EU-famous and very popular Yekaterinburg Nikolay Kolyada theatre, ballet team Province Dances, etc. All activities were free of charge for the visitors.

This year, the project has found money to make some part of the plant all-season working. The whole budget for the reconstruction is 1 billion rubles.

From sociological and cultural points of view, the development of this project during the pandemic was extremely important for people. The opportunity to meet each other without any restrictions and limits, to visit performances from famous theatre troupes, and to listen to lectures by art and culture researchers were stabilising factors for visitors and gave hope for returning to normal life. Culture and cultural events at this place were a real sphere of freedom and an island of available continuous development of the essential forces of man.

Creative Cluster Samorodok (Prill) in Nizhny Tagil

At the end of 2021, as part of developing creative clusters in the Sverdlovsk Region, the regional government decided to establish a site in Nizhny Tagil. It is based downtown in the building of the former college Samorodok that gave the name to the whole cluster.

> "We chose "Samorodok". The most important factor was the location – the city centre. Since the college, an educational institution was located in the building, I hope the walls will help us. Our task is to carry out high-quality pumping of teams and to create centres for them to be managed by professionals. We plan to upgrade the event agenda related to the development of creative industries: these are various forums, meetings, and festivals", explained Victoria Kazakova, Minister of Investment and Development of the Sverdlovsk Region.
>
> (Tagil City, 2021)

The head of the project and the director of the NGO "Creative Industries and Technologies" Ekaterina Tretyakova, created a really interesting place with a very rich programme. For instance, the day before International Women's Day on March 8, they organised a one-day fair called Garage. The organisers invite self-employed people and entrepreneurs to participate in the fair. The craftsmen who create ceramics, jewellery, clothes and accessories, designers, second-hand shops, vintage online shops, artists, hand makers, and customisers also are invited to participate. The garage sale is a unique opportunity to sell goods of own production, join the concept of smart consumption, which is popular worldwide, give new life to old things, have a good time and buy original gifts for the holiday (Mstrock.ru, 2022). Lots of art and photo exhibitions were organised here.

This cluster's main idea is to unite the creative entrepreneurs of Nizhny Tagil under the umbrella of Samorodok.

As this cluster has existed for one year, it is difficult to get any statistics. But the fact that it works despite today's difficult times stresses its cultural and economic importance and effectiveness. Moreover, because of military operations, all these clusters have a great chance for development. And there is no contradiction. As international tourism and travelling have some objective difficulties for Russian people, it is time for the domestic one. And thanks to Russian rich history and culture there are many places to visit. Therefore, the development of creative industries and clusters started just in time.

Fashion Factory PRO-Textile in Aramil

The former Aramil cloth factory, known as Zlokazovskaya, is included in the network of creative spaces. In 2021, the project received a 2,545,851 Rub grant. from the Presidential Fund for the Support of Cultural Initiatives to create the Overcoat Museum and the "Sun in Threads: Creative Space for Ural Artisans" project.

The history of the development of the cloth factory is an important part of the history of a small town. The factory was the best enterprise in pre-revolutionary Russia for producing textiles; during the Second World War, overcoat cloth was produced here, and every fourth overcoat for the Red Army was sewn here. In the post-war period, until the beginning of the 21st century, the factory was one of the largest enterprises in the textile industry of Russia. Of course, for the Aramil citizens and the nearest settlements, the factory personifies their history and identity. The historical component of the territory unites the projects implemented on this site. The Overcoat Museum and the Art Gallery are open here, providing opportunities for exhibitions, fairs, fashion shows, festivals, concerts, etc.

The implementation of the idea to turn the building of the former enterprise into a venue for a regular regional festival of textile artisans not only draws attention to the historical and cultural context but also unites the efforts of young designers who come up with bright holiday installations and design creative spaces, as well as artisans who create author's collections of clothes, creates a place for discussions, meetings, integration of the creative potential of masters of young and mature age.

The next clusters are located in Yekaterinburg, a Sverdlovsk region capital.

Makletsky House Cluster in Yekaterinburg

This cluster had a principal difference from the previous ones. It was organised and closely linked with the Municipal Museum of the History of Yekaterinburg. The museum's director was the initiator and ideologist of the project, and it was based in one of the museum's buildings.

The House of Makletsky Center for Urban Practices (the project's full name) is a new format of a creative cluster that brings together urban researchers, representatives of the creative industries and activists working with the themes of the city, historical and cultural heritage. The purpose of the cluster is to create an infrastructure for cooperation and implementation of joint projects of organisations, communities, and citizens interested in the study, presentation, and development of Yekaterinburg.

Based on the cluster, there is a resource centre for residents, a family history centre, a coworking space for city initiatives, art residences, a Ural design market, and a podcast space. The cluster is a launching pad for implementing projects for creative and socially active citizens.

This is a joint project of the Museum of the History of Yekaterinburg and the City Initiatives Fund with the support of the Department of Culture of Yekaterinburg.

They chose the Makletsky House at the crossroads of Turgenev and Pervomaiskaya streets to implement the project. The architectural heritage monument used to be the estate of Ilya Zakharovich Makletsky, pre-revolutionary director of the Siberian Trade Bank, public figure and philanthropist. In Soviet times, the House of People's Judges was located here, later – the Regional Institute for the Protection of Children's and Adolescents' Health, and finally, a children's clinic. The main historical two-story house was added on two floors in 1934.

Today, the building has four floors, each with its topic and goal. The first-floor Living Room opened on 6 April 2019, as part of the fourth History Fest. Here, one can learn about the projects of the Makletsky House, drink coffee, listen to lectures and buy local souvenirs. There is also an open library with publications and books about Yekaterinburg and the Sverdlovsk region.

The second floor is a research centre. The floor is beautiful, with a 19th-century fireplace and arched windows overlooking the city. There is an open historical base, and the centre specialists will help you understand the city's and your family's history.

The third floor is a Space for Creative Industries. Studios of musicians and photographers will appear here. Workshops and showrooms of local artists and clothing and decor designers will be next to them.

The fourth floor is a Residence of City Initiatives. The last floor of the house is being transformed into an open co-working space for employees of cultural, social, and other developing city projects.

Part of the centre operates as a residence. People can get a room in the Makletsky House for 6–24 months. In addition, it will be possible to hold your events there.

Unfortunately, this cluster was closed, and the museum archive took over. As a municipal project, more information on why it was closed is required.

"Domna" Creative Cluster in Yekaterinburg

This cluster was initiated in 2021 and has opened its doors in 2022. It houses the front offices of creative structures, a regional production media centre, and a showroom of creative products. The city mayor gave 2500 square metres of building in the central pedestrian historical street of Yekaterinburg for this project. This space is planned to house a shop of local artisans, a collective use centre for clothing production, digital fitting rooms, youth IT coworking, webinars and podcast studios. In addition, the cluster on Weiner st., 16 will become a platform for city, regional, and federal events.

"Domna" occupied the second floor of the building. The reconstruction of the building cost more than 150 million rubles. The Sverdlovsk regional government, the City Administration, and the Sverdlovsk Regional Business and Entrepreneurs Support Fund supervise the project in Yekaterinburg.

It is assumed that the described above sites created in the Sverdlovsk region will be conditionally united into one network, the central link of which will be a creative cluster in Yekaterinburg on Weiner st., 16.

On 20 December 2021, the Governor of the Sverdlovsk region, the mayor of Yekaterinburg and the Head of Sverdlovsk Regional Business and Entrepreneurship Support Fund signed an agreement that legally launched a project to create a network creative cluster on the territory of the Sverdlovsk region with a central site on Weiner st., 16 in Yekaterinburg.

As the idea of developing creative industries and clusters is new, the Middle Urals this chapter describes the process of developing this sector in the region. The main idea is that it is not a spontaneous process but coordinated with the policy of territorial development of the country and the region, getting governmental support at all levels, from regional to federal, with the perspective of international.

Results and Discussion

The situation with COVID-19 demonstrated that creative industries have quickly adopted new business models to operate during a turbulent economic climate. Many creative industries companies have had to transform their operations by changing the operating environment, customer demand, and consumption. The flexibility of creative industries gave a wide range of opportunities for local business development.

On the other hand, such an impetuous transformation of business in the sphere of creative industries in the considered region highlighted the necessity of theoretical and practical education of creative industries entrepreneurs because some of them, especially Heads of creative clusters, have difficulties in management and lack of information about project management, writing grant applications, some business models and juridical questions. Nevertheless, working in such extreme circumstances left no time for long thinking and planning. They were forced to act quickly and efficiently, and the fact that all these creative clusters still work and develop their activities says that it was a fruitful time for doing so.

The importance of renovating old factories' heritage and developing creative clusters in the region is stressed because the new sector got financial and administrative support.

The ideologist of the project for the development of creative industries in the region is the Ministry of Investment and Development of the Sverdlovsk Region, the operator is the Sverdlovsk Regional Business and Entrepreneurs Support Fund. With the assistance of the Fund, the sites are filled with resident entrepreneurs.

The main industrial fair of Russia Innoprom in Yekaterinburg is the main open stage for the meeting and discussion of the sector's development plans. Last, in the 2021 year, at the booth of the Sverdlovsk region, they openly discussed the problems they have in the sector. This 2022 year, the whole day was devoted to the creative industries. The organisers called it Creative Thursday. The panel "Creative Thursday. Experience in the Development of Creative Entrepreneurship in the Urals" was devoted to several questions: network creative cluster of the Sverdlovsk region: sites and their residents; the emergence of new creative clusters in the cities and towns of the Sverdlovsk region; creative cluster as a source of changes in the urban environment; the impact of creative entrepreneurship on the service of domestic and inbound tourism (Events SOFPP., 2022). All heads of the described clusters participated in this panel and shared their experience and results of the year of working.

The author of this chapter is one of the creative cluster heads, too. She is Chief Executive Officer (CEO) of the Agency for Cultural and Science Diplomacy. She focuses the activities on cultural and science projects devoted to creative industries and cultural policies of the Brazil, Russia, India, China, South Africa (BRICS) alliance. In 2021, the Agency for Cultural Diplomacy won the President grant for the online project Meet BRICS Art, devoted to the online art BRICS exhibition and the ten online meetings of professional artists and art researchers on the alliance. The main idea was to get the world acquainted with the alliance's professional artists and form a community of professional artists of BRICS. The project demonstrated the huge importance of cooperation among BRICS creative entrepreneurs. Another direction of the Agency is a School for Cultural Diplomacy for the creative entrepreneurs from BRICS. Now, the Agency plans to develop the idea of including Yekaterinburg city into the BRICS Creative Cities UNESCO. And there are some other projects that the Agency plans to realise next year.

Conclusion

Despite the facts demonstrated above, it is an experiment where the federal government tested the mechanisms of development and support of the humanitarian sector of the economy. Today, they singled out some difficulties that represent tasks that should be solved in the future. Here are some of them.

The concept of creative industries, directly associated with regional and national specifics, differs from country to country, there is no universal applied understanding of creative industries worldwide. As a result, simple, obvious and cross-cutting criteria for all sectors of the economy recognition of companies that belong to the creative sector economy, are absent. Measures of state support (small- and medium-sized businesses, industry, export) are formed for priority industries and the industrial economy and do not consider the specifics of the development of creative industries. In particular, at all levels of government, it stimulates the acquisition of fixed assets and equipment (subsidised interest rates, etc.), but wages are not subsidised, which forms the basis of the costs of the creative economy sector.

Creation innovation support ecosystems, despite their similarity, is oriented exclusively towards technological projects (IT sector, medicine, pharmaceuticals, energy cluster, etc.). Federal, regional and municipal programmes are fragmented and uncoordinated at the expense of those that can be supported. The institutional nature of financial instruments leads to the fact that most promising companies that create products at the intersection of culture, digital technology, and industry are "out of contour" attention of the state.

The tax legislation of the Russian Federation and the system tax administration do not fully take into account the specifics of creative entrepreneurship, namely special mechanisms encouragement of authors, as well as the fact that the circulation of intellectual rights at the stage of creating a product and (or) service does not create an added value. The monetisation of the results of creative work occurs usually at the time of consumption of the final product.

Creative industries collide with the inability to unambiguously determine the optimal mode of taxation of created products and services. For entrepreneurs, the risks of re-qualification of transactions, administrative fines increase, and other sanctions.

The creative industries are critically dependent on the security and efficiency of managing intellectual property. However, the existing modes of circulation of intellectual rights, state registration of transactions with such rights and mechanisms for their protection do not allow for multiplying the number of results. As we said above, the question of intellectual property lies in the sphere of the capitalist paradigm. It is an obstacle to the wide and free dissemination of knowledge, thereby creating artificial barriers to the cultural development of people.

Recommendations

Our recommendations are as follows:

- Creation of territorial infrastructure for creative entrepreneurship of both general purposes, including social and special (professional) infrastructure focused on specific types of creative and (or) entrepreneurial activity.
- Development of a system of knowledge and competencies, both creative and entrepreneurial in nature, including inviting specialists from both Russia and abroad to transfer non-formalised knowledge and skills.
- Formation of an information support system, including, among other things, the possibility of commercial and non-commercial use of elements of historical and cultural, intangible heritage.
- Formation of a financial infrastructure focused on various stages of maturity of creative entrepreneurship, including the "seed stage" (small grants), the stage of ensuring sustainability of the venture and the stage scaling (entering new markets).
- Elaboration of proposals to clarify the mechanisms of taxation, including jointly with the subjects of the Russian Federation, for regional and local taxes and tax administration, taking into account the specifics of creative entrepreneurship in terms of creating and distributing products with a high share of creative work, creating a specialised infrastructure.
- Development of a system of service support for the legal protection of transactions with intellectual property rights and protection of the rights of the results of intellectual activity in online and offline environments, other necessary legal and financial services.
- Creation of ecosystems attractive for the concentration of talents, the implementation of ambitious public and state projects that require active communication and interaction of various people, territories, and institutions.
- Development of export infrastructure – service support expansion of goods and services, promotion of the export of intellectual property rights to global markets.

Such complex attention and efforts aimed at developing the creative sector will be fruitful in the near future.

References

Agency for Cultural and Science Diplomacy. (2020) https://vk.com/cdaekb (Accessed 20 June 2023).

Badikova, T. E., and Vasilkovskaya, M. I. (2022) Creative, creatively, cultural industries: an experience of comparison. Socio-cultural activity: vectors of research and practical perspectives. *Materials of the International Scientific-Practical Conference*, 116–121. https://www.elibrary.ru/download/elibrary_49170169_98568704.pdf (Accessed 20 June 2023).

Events SOFPP (7 July 2022). Roundtable "Creative Thursday". Experience in the development of creative entrepreneurship in the Urals" https://sofp.ru/events//meropriyatiya/kruglyj-stol-kreativnyj-chetverg-opyt-razvitiya-kreativnogo-predprinimatelstva-na-urale/ (Accessed 26 July 2023).

Gavrilova, N., Gershman, M., and Thurner, W. T. (2023) Policy challenges and recommendations in support of Moscow's creative industries – Viewpoints of practitioners, *Creative Industries Journal*, 16 (2): 222–237. DOI:10.1080/17510694.2022.2062946

Horkheimer, M., Adorno, T. W., and Noeri, G. (2002) *Dialectic of Enlightenment*. Stanford: Stanford University Press.

HSE University. (2018) Creative economy of Moscow in numbers. https://measurecreativity.hse.ru/ (Accessed 26 July 2023).

Khlystova, O., Kalyuzhnova, Y., and Belitski, M. (2022) The impact of the COVID-19 pandemic on the creative industries: A literature review and future research agenda. *Journal of Business Research*, 139: 1192–1210.

Kogan, L. N. (1992) Sociology of Culture. Yekaterinburg, UrGU. https://elar.urfu.ru/handle/10995/40853 (Accessed 26 July 2023).

Luckman, S. (2017) *Cultural Policy and Creative Industries*. Routledge EBooks. https://www.taylorfrancis.com/chapters/edit/10.4324/9781315718408-22/cultural-policy-creative-industries-susan-luckman (Accessed 26, July 2023).

Mordanov, M. A. (2022) Characteristics of the state and prospects for creative industries' development during the COVID-19 pandemic time. *Problems of Enterprise Development: Theory and Practice. Collection of Articles of the IX International Scientific-Practical Conference*, 127–132. https://www.elibrary.ru/item.asp?id=48465759 (Accessed 26 July 2023).

Mstrock.ru (14 February 2022). *A garage sale will be held in the creative cluster "Samorodok" on the eve of March 8*. https://mstrok.ru/news/v-kreativnom-klastere-samorodok-nakanune-8-marta-proydyot-garazhnaya-rasprodazha (Accessed 26 July 2023).

Rurban. (2021) https://polisinstitute.ru/rurban (Accessed 22 June 2023).

Russian Federation Government. (2021) The Concept #2613-p devoted to the development of the Creative Industries and Mechanisms for the Implementation of Their State Support in Large and Largest Urban Agglomerations Until 2030. Retrieved on 1 June 2022 from: http://static.government.ru/media/files/HEXNAom6EJunVIxBCjIAtAya-8FAVDUfP.pdf

Schwab, K. (2021) *Stakeholder Capitalism: A Global Economy That Works for Progress, People and Planet*. Hoboken, NJ: John Wiley and Sons.

Simple Numbers. (6 April 2021). *How to barter with other people's ideas (feat. BadComedian)//OlegKomolov.SimpleNumbers* [Video]. YouTube. https://www.youtube.com/watch?v=0_PeL87Gb2s (Accessed 10 September 2023).

Tagil City. (5 March 2020) The first art residence may appear on the squares of the old Chernoistochinsky plant. https://mstrok.ru/news/na-ploshchadyah-starogo-chernoistochinskogo-zavoda-mozhet-poyavitsya-pervaya-v-nizhnem-tagile (Accessed 10 September 2023).

Tagil City. (14 April 2021) Samorodokt, live": A creative cluster will appear in the centre of Nizhny Tagil| https://tagilcity.ru/news/2021-04-14/samorodok-zhivi-kreativnyy-klaster-poyavitsya-v-tsentre-nizhnego-tagila-249725 (Accessed 10 September 2023).

UNESCO. (2012) *Culture: A Driver and An Enabler of Sustainable Development. Thematic Think Piece*. UNESCO. https://www.un.org/millenniumgoals/pdf/Think%20Pieces/2_culture.pdf (Accessed 23 June 2023).

Vasilyeva, V. (2021) *The Rurban. Space Platform Collects the Best Urban and Creative Practices*. Agency for Strategic Initiatives. https://asi.ru/news/178440/

18 The Influence of Entrepreneurship Education on Higher Education Students' Entrepreneurial Intentions and Motivation in South Africa

Ankit Katrodia

Introduction

In South Africa, entrepreneurship is regarded as the panacea to youth unemployment and a major strategy for economic growth (Fatoki and Chindoga, 2011). There is abundant literature regarding the worsening dynamics of youth unemployment and bolstering entrepreneurship education as a possible solution to this problem (Chimucheka, 2014)The shortage of youthful (and successful) businesses is often associated with the symmetrical lack of incentives and conditions to facilitate young entrepreneurs, especially since there are South African examples of young entrepreneurs who have founded companies that have reached millionaire valuations, created dozens of job opportunities, and acted as a stimulus and inspiration for many other young South Africans.

The problem, and therefore the solution, goes back to being that of "mindset", often summarised by a fundamental question, "Are entrepreneurs born, or are they made?" (Kumari, 2018). Many studies and even more experiences show that perhaps there is no clear answer, and there never will be (Kumari, 2018). On the other hand, a series of many gaps remain in the field to be filled, and actions that certainly could spread a much more rooted and widespread entrepreneurial culture from which many more entrepreneurs would be born or at least many more young people would become one (Odeku and Rudolf, 2019). Entrepreneurship today is not treated as a school subject in any type of educational path, or at least not on an ongoing basis. Consequently, young people who graduate from various institutes hardly come out with very clear ideas about the meaning of "doing business" and being entrepreneurs (Odeku and Rudolf, 2019) The historian refers to the British reality, but intuition has a universal value.

Entrepreneurship education not only influences students' intentions but also enhances their motivational factors and self-efficacy beliefs. Fayolle and Gailly (2004) argue that exposure to entrepreneurship education programs can boost students' confidence in their ability to initiate and manage business ventures successfully. This increase in self-efficacy is crucial as it empowers students to

DOI: 10.4324/9781003475606-22

overcome challenges and persevere in their entrepreneurial endeavors. A study by Kedir and Tsegai (2016) found that entrepreneurship education significantly enhances students' perceived desirability and feasibility of entrepreneurship, thereby increasing their intention to pursue entrepreneurial careers. This study attempts to close the knowledge gap by analysing the influence of the higher education system on entrepreneurship intentions and motivation.

Literature Review

The entrepreneurship programmes in South African high schools are based on digital educational modules, through which the participating classes are transformed into entrepreneurial teams and take care of project management, from the concept of an idea to the realisation of the business model, up to the prototype of the product/service. Lastly, "Enterprise in Action", a didactic format of the mini-enterprise, provides that each class is organised as a real company, equipping itself with a managerial structure and operational roles, documents, practices and rules at thein order to develop an idea (Henama, 2018) concretely.

However, the contents of these projects in high schools should be adequately differentiated according to the possible "target groups". It does not make much sense to propose entrepreneurship education activities for adolescents in the second or third grades of lower secondary school to formulate and simulate business creation processes. Entrepreneurship education aimed at young people in adolescence should be considered a tool to improve their ability to take responsibility, face complex decisions and develop a proactive and risk-free mentality. It would make more sense, on the other hand, to "bring" entrepreneurship education paths closer to the more traditional ones to support business creation in the case of adults who have lost a previous job and try to relocate to the labour market as self-employed workers, or in the case of recent graduates who want to start up start-ups (Chipeta, Surujlal, and Koloba, 2016).

When South Africa ended the apartheid regime, it had to rethink its vision of business and trade. After repudiating apartheid and holding its first free elections, based on universal suffrage, in 1994, South Africa had to overcome economic recession and international isolation. Within the framework of a more open political system, the Reconstruction and Development Programme adopted by the new Government in September 1994 set the country on a path that would logically make it an economic giant, thanks to the abundance of its natural resources and the great potential of its industrial base (Lekhanya, 2015).

It soon became clear that it was necessary to eliminate the disastrous legacy that had plunged South Africa into backwardness and international marginalisation in all areas, particularly in terms of investment and foreign trade. One of the architects of the South African commercial power was Faizel Ismail, who held important positions in the Ministry of Commerce and Industry (MCI) of Pretoria from 1994 to 2002, the year in which he assumed the role of representative of his country before the World Organisation of Commerce, in Geneva (Atiase, Mahmood, Wang, and Botchie, 2018).

The new government had to make decisions quickly and speed up the liberalisation process. Labour and unions were part of the new government coalition, but the necessary reforms would entail some job losses, given the high labour force in South African industry. The study concluded that, in an increasingly globalised world, people are still going to lose jobs even if tariff barriers were lowered (Atiase, Mahmood, Wang and Botchie, 2017). South African companies had to modernise. The cheapest products would enter the country, one way or another. The competitors were other developing countries, such as neighbouring countries, whose products occupied a significant part of our consumption basket. It is believed that it was possible to counteract the loss of jobs by showing that, thanks to reforms and openness, we could reduce the cost of living, then very high, and alleviate the difficult situation in which the poor especially found themselves, as a result of the protectionist policies of the past (Ojong, Simba, and Dana, 2021). This was the context in which the reforms were promoted. In agriculture, South Africans had to remove all subsidies and the single marketing mechanism restricting small farmers. Tariffs on textiles, clothing and footwear were cut faster than in other sectors, forcing manufacturers to seek markets abroad. South Africa also had to provide supply incentives and encourage all companies to turn to foreign markets and start exporting, which meant conducting research and development activities and training their staff. In addition, Small and Medium-Sized Enterprises (SMEs) need to be helped to establish themselves abroad, for example, by promoting and facilitating their participation in international trade fairs, to present their products and gain marketing experience (Ojong, Simba and Dana, 2021). The private sector was used to being protected from foreign competition, and our companies did not collaborate, not even to promote exports. They all waited to see what the other would do (Ratten and Jones, 2018). They did not understand the process of globalisation and mistrusted other countries, perhaps because of South Africa's international isolation (Ojong, Simba and Dana, 2021).

What is an Entrepreneur's Education, and Why is it Important?

Entrepreneurship consists of skills that can be learned, and the main objective of the European Commission is to support entrepreneurial education, enhancing its importance at all levels, from primary school to university and beyond (Van der Westhuizen, 2017). Young people from high schools benefit from entrepreneurship paths, regardless of whether they become entrepreneurs because these educational activities allow them to develop important transversal skills, which are also useful in looking for work and in their career guidance path. Indeed, starting from an agrarian-based economy, the Irish adopted high technologies to modernise and transform their production with enormous dedication and work (Kanonuhwa, Rungani, and Chimucheka, 2018).

They had made enormous efforts to attract investment and simultaneously developed exports. And they had made large investments in education, thinking of the sectors that would be the most important in the country's economic future. Sweden and Finland also showed the importance of linking export promotion with attracting foreign direct investment (Odora, 2015). In New Zealand, it can be seen how a company culture could be changed. Clearly, the task had not been easy at all, but they managed to convince their private sector that New Zealand companies had to unite to prevail in foreign markets for the benefit of all, without depending on the government but rather using it as a facilitating agent than as the main actor in the promotion process. An important effort was the creation of sectoral export councils, and soon, the entities willing to lead this process stood out in the private sector (Kanonuhwa, Rungani and Chimucheka, 2018).

Results and Discussions

Entrepreneur Education for Developing Nations Like South Africa

Currently, South Africa ranks third among all the economies on the African continent, with a Gross domestic product (GDP) of US419.02 billion (2022). Cultural wealth must be added to economic wealth: South Africa has a great diversity of languages, with up to 11 official languages, and has inherited the inspiration of a historic leader like Nelson Mandela. The South African economy continued to recover in 2018 and 2019 thanks to the notable improvement in the agricultural and mining sectors, the latter favoured by a simultaneous increase in global demand for minerals and prices. Overall, this is less progress than the average in recent years (Chipeta, Kruse, and Surujlal, 2020). The main factor that will weigh down the pace of activity is political uncertainty, which will weigh negatively on investment decisions. The country strives to move towards a more egalitarian and socially committed society. In short, it is a dynamic and young town that looks to the future with a focus on education and development (Soni, 2014).

From a commercial point of view, the European Union member countries occupy the first positions, behind China and the USA. South Africa exports metals, machinery and transport equipment to Europe, while it imports automobiles, chemicals, manufactured goods and oil from the EU. Since 2004, the European Investment Bank (EIB) has supported the development and economic activity in South Africa with loans and equity investments worth more than €2.5 billion. The volume of projects approved in 2014–2017 amounts to 440.9 million euros. In all this commercial flow, Spain participates as a partner with a consolidated presence and growing importance (Soni, 2014).

Taking advantage of the good harmony between the Spanish and South African business cultures is a great opportunity, and not only because of the growing importance of the country's economy, South Africa is, in addition to being a large market in itself, the gateway to the countries of Southern Africa. Most of the companies in the region conduct their business from Johannesburg, the African continent's great financial and economic hub. South Africa has historically been the largest investor in all the neighbouring countries, with productive commercial activity, especially in the banking, insurance, telephone, consumer and agricultural sectors (Chikanda and Tawodzera, 2017).

The Role of Government and Higher Education Institutions in Promoting Entrepreneurship in South Africa

South Africa is the starting point for any regional commercial activity or establishment. With the help of good advice and support in high schools, entering the country can provide the Spanish company with an adequate platform for operations throughout the Southern African region. In the difficult reality of the African country, media education and literacy may be the only refuge left to achieve educational progress and offer practical solutions based on the participation of citizens to inform and motivate a large mass of people with low levels of training and income (Urban and Chantson, 2019).

In South Africa, there are several local obstacles, namely the need for teachers to maintain their motivation levels, discipline problems and school absenteeism, lack of parental attention to the student's learning environment, and the overwhelming relationship between directors and teachers with the departmental administration. But this absence of concrete plans, in light of a system plagued by patronage, must be understood in a particular context of racial, class and gender inequalities (Ojong, Simba and Dana, 2021).

Having young students, particularly in Africa, who are educated in the media is essential to achieving any economic, social and political development. If young people are media literate, they can analyse information and use it to acquire more skills and competencies. The media have to recover their fighting mission, robust, without fear, offering a speech that can be trusted, with a continuous process of inclusion of all the colour ranges of society to complement the curricula that have been based on incorrect information to reduce the digital divide (Tengeh and Nkem, 2017).

Students' Entrepreneurial Intentions and Motivation in South Africa

According to Locke and Latham (2004), motivation includes internal and external action triggers. It also influences three different aspects of action: choice, effort, and persistence. Entrepreneurial action is also strongly correlated with entrepreneurial intention (Carsrud and Brännback, 2011). Self-acknowledged convictions by people that they intend to launch new business ventures are referred to as entrepreneurial intention (Thompson, 2009). Beginning with the search, evaluation, and exploitation of opportunities (Shane, Locke, & Collins 2003) the entrepreneurial process begins with entrepreneurs who have needs and goals they wish to fulfil by starting a new business. These needs and goals can differ from one entrepreneur to the next (Naffziger *et al.*, 1994; Shane *et al.*, 2003). These objectives and requirements serve as the main impetus for entrepreneurs to launch a business (Carsrud and Brännback, 2011; Gollwitzer and Brandstätter, 1997). According to Naffziger *et al.* (1994), entrepreneurs start the entrepreneurial process expecting to achieve both intrinsic and extrinsic goals or outcomes.

Entrepreneurs' motivation, based on the value they place on the perceived rewards associated with the behaviour, determines whether they will engage in entrepreneurship (Fayolle and Gaily 2004). The motivation of social entrepreneurs affected their awareness of unmet needs and opportunity recognition, according to Yitshaki and Kropp's (2011) research. Depending on the results realised from participating in the process, entrepreneurial motivation plays a key role in all stages of the entrepreneurial process and can help keep entrepreneurs committed to their businesses (Naffziger *et al.*, 1994; Carsrud and Brännback, 2011).

The entrepreneurial process is full of risks and challenges that may make it difficult for someone to decide to take action (McMullen and Shepherd, 2006). Entrepreneurs must, therefore, possess high levels of perseverance, self-assurance in their capacity to face and overcome obstacles, and conviction that acting entrepreneurially will enable them to achieve the results or rewards they value (Zanakis, S.H., Renko, M. & Bullough, A. (2012). Enhancing entrepreneurial intention and motivation is therefore essential for economic growth in terms of the emergence and expansion of new businesses that would result in employment opportunities for young people and the unemployed.

In terms of education and personal development, entrepreneurship is a valuable skill that develops creativity and self-confidence. Entrepreneurial culture aims to drive innovation and create the conditions for leadership and ongoing success. Train flexibility and adaptation to change (Crush and Ramachandran, 2014).

Various Strategies to Support Entrepreneurs

Due to the popularity of social media, there has been an increase in entrepreneurial activity in South Africa. There are several strategies through which one case supports the entrepreneurs. Buying directly from local enterprises and businesses, in one case, contributes to the growth and strengthening of the economy. The jobs of the enterprises are maintained and possibly new jobs are built. In most cases, businesses bet on offering sustainable and environmentally friendly products.

If one chooses to buy products from these enterprises in South Africa, they also contribute to caring for the environment. Unique, original and special gifts are achieved. Whoever receives a detail bought from an enterprise has something different, which has been made with dedication and, in some cases, personalised (Littlewood and Holt, 2018).

The main thing is to buy from local businesses in South Africa, neighbourhood stores, artisans, and farmers in the plaza. Buy from start-ups that use social networks as a showcase. Support the businesses of friends and family, helping them to make them known to more people, through their own social networks, for example. If one has knowledge of digital marketing, digital platforms, and online payments, one can offer free help to achieve its implementation in enterprises that have not yet taken the step to digital. Recommend products that have been purchased from entrepreneurs (Littlewood and Holt, 2018).

The new wave of entrepreneurship in South Africa has directed various sectors to seek sustainability alternatives for their businesses, whether it is creating new products, adapting their business ideas to current needs or exploring digital and home tools. For example, furniture businesses for houses, places to disconnect and surround yourself with nature, and details to celebrate special dates, among others. Companies should be encouraged to expand their activity to global markets. Those entrepreneurs who aspire to market their products or services on the largest possible scale will be the ones who stand out. Nowadays, thanks to new technologies, it is possible to share or request practically everything through numerous online applications: accommodation (Airbnb), vehicles (Uber and Lyft), and videos (YouTube). Reaching global markets overnight is already a reality – without much logistics or investment required (Littlewood and Holt, 2018).

Conclusion

This study sought to understand the influence of entrepreneurship education on higher education students' entrepreneurship intention and motivation in South Africa. It established that although significant efforts are being put in place to motivate learners to become entrepreneurs, they are not enough to ignite entrepreneurship intention and motivation. Several factors have been observed to come in the way of entrepreneurship intention and motivation, including personal traits and external factors such as lack of funding, failing small entrepreneurship ventures, government policies and various others. The government should take a deliberate strategic stance to do everything within its power to fully support entrepreneurial activities to significantly reduce youth unemployment in South Africa. South African entrepreneurship institutions need to be more proactive in advancing the innovative business ideas of the youth by offering the necessary skills, support and knowledge to turn the ideas into sustainable reality.

References

Atiase, V., Mahmood, S., Wang, Y. and Botchie, D. (2018) Developing entrepreneurship in Africa: Investigating critical resource challenges. *Journal of Small Business and Enterprise Development*, 25(4):644–666. DOI: 10.1108/JSBED-03-2017-0084

Carsrud, A., & Brännback, M. (2011). Entrepreneurial motivations: What do we still need to know? *Journal of Small Business Management*, 49(1):9–26. https://doi.org/10.1111/j.1540-627X.2010.00312.x

Chikanda, A. and Tawodzera, G. (2017) Informal entrepreneurship and cross-border trade between Zimbabwe and South Africa (rep. i-41). Waterloo, ON: Southern African Migration Programme. SAMP Migration Policy Series No. 74.

Chimucheka, T. (2014) Entrepreneurship education in South Africa. Mediterranean. *Journal of Social Sciences*, 5(2):403.

Chipeta, E.M., Kruse, P. and Surujlal, J. (2020) Effects of gender on antecedents to social entrepreneurship among university students in South Africa. *International Journal of Business and Management Studies*, 12(1):18–33.

Chipeta, E.M., Surujlal, J. and Koloba, H.A. (2016) Influence of gender and age on social entrepreneurship intentions among university students in Gauteng Province, South Africa. *Gender and Behaviour*, 14(1):6885–6899.

Crush, J. and Ramachandran, S. (2014) Migrant Entrepreneurship, Collective Violence and Xenophobia in South Africa (rep., pp. 1–41). Waterloo, ON: Southern African Migration Programme. SAMP Migration Policy Series No. 67.

Fatoki. and Chindoga, 2011. The entrepreneurial intention of undergraduate students in South Africa: The influences of entrepreneurship education and previous work experience. *Mediterranean Journal of Social Sciences*, 5(7):294.

Fayolle A. & Gailly B. (2004), Using the theory of planned behaviour to assess entrepreneurship teaching programs: A first experimentation, IntEnt2004 Conference, Naples (Italy), 5–7 July.

Gollwitzer, P. M., & Brandstätter, V. (1997). Implementation intentions and effective goal pursuit. *Journal of Personality and Social Psychology*, 73(1):186–199. https://doi.org/10.1037/0022-3514.73.1.186

Henama, U.S. (2018) Disruptive entrepreneurship using Airbnb: The South African experience. *African Journal of Hospitality, Tourism and Leisure*, 7(1):1–16.

Kanonuhwa, M., Rungani, E.C. and Chimucheka, T. (2018) The association between emotional intelligence and entrepreneurship as a career choice: A study on university students in South Africa. *SA Journal of Human Resource Management*, 16(1):1–9.

Kedir, A. M., & Tsegai, D. (2016). The impact of entrepreneurship education on entrepreneurial intentions of university students in Ethiopia. *Education + Training*, 58(2):219–236.

Kumari, N. (2018) Entrepreneurs are Made, Not Born. SSRN: https://ssrn.com/abstract=3143973 or DOI: 10.2139/ssrn.3143973 (Print).

Lekhanya, L.M. (2015) The role of universities in promoting social entrepreneurship in South Africa. *Journal of Governance and Regulation* (Print). June 2015 4(3):67–71.

Littlewood, D. and Holt, D. (2018) Social entrepreneurship in South Africa: Exploring the influence of environment. *Business and Society*, 57(3):525–561.

Locke, E. A., & Latham, G. P. (2004). What should we do about motivation theory? Six recommendations for the twenty-first century. *The Academy of Management Review*, 29(3):388–403.

Malebana, M.J. (2021) The effect of entrepreneurial motivation on entrepreneurial intention of South African rural youth. *Academy of Entrepreneurship Journal*, 27:1–14.

McMullen, J. S., & Shepherd, D. A. (2006). Entrepreneurial action and the role of uncertainty in the theory of the entrepreneur. *Academy of Management Review*, 31(1):132–152. doi:10.4337/9781783479801.00007

Naffziger, D.W., Hornsby, J.S., & Kuratko, D.F. (1994). A proposed research model of entrepreneurial motivation. *Entrepreneurship Theory and Practice*, 18(3):29–42.

Odeku, K.O. and Rudolf, S.S. (2019) An analysis of the transformative interventions promoting youth entrepreneurship in South Africa. *Academy of Entrepreneurship Journal*, 25(4):1–10.

Odora, R.J. (2015) Integrating product design and entrepreneurship education: A stimulant for enterprising design and engineering students in South Africa. *Procedia Technology*, 20(2015):276–283.

Ojong, N., Simba, A. and Dana, L.P. (2021) Female entrepreneurship in Africa: A review, trends, and future research directions. *Journal of Business Research*, 132(C):233–248.

Ratten, V. and Jones, P. (2018) Bringing Africa into Entrepreneurship Research. In African Entrepreneurship (pp. 9–27). Cham: Palgrave Macmillan.

Shane, S., Locke, E. A., & Collins, C. J. (2003). Entrepreneurial Motivation. *Human Resource Management Review*, 13:257–279.

Shane, S and S. Venkataraman. (2000). The Promise of Entrepreneurship as a Field of Research. *The Academy of Management Review*, 25(1):217–226.

Soni, P. (2014) Entrepreneurship policy in South Africa. *Arabian Journal of Business and Management Review*, 3(10):29–43.

Tengeh, R.K. and Nkem, L. (2017) Sustaining immigrant entrepreneurship in South Africa: The role of informal financial associations. *Sustainability*, 9(8):1396.

Thompson, E.R. (2009) Individual entrepreneurial intent: Construct clarification and development of an internationally reliable metric. *Entrepreneurship Theory and Practice*, 33:669–694. https://doi.org/10.1111/j.1540-6520.2009.00321.x

Urban, B. and Chantson, J.J.T.J. (2019) Academic entrepreneurship in South Africa: Testing for entrepreneurial intentions. *The Journal of Technology Transfer*, 44(3):948–980.

Van der Westhuizen, T. (2017) Theory U and individual entrepreneurial orientation in developing youth entrepreneurship in South Africa. *Journal of Contemporary Management*, 14(1):531–553.

Yitshaki, R., and F. Kropp (2011). "Becoming a social entrepreneur: Understanding motiva-tions using life story analysis," *International Journal of Business and Globalisation* 7(3):319.

Zanakis, S.H., Renko, M. & Bullough, A. (2012). Nascent entrepreneurs and the transition to entrepreneurship: Why do people start new businesses? *Journal of Developmental Entrepreneurship*, 17(1):1–25.

19 Towards an Aggressive Economic Growth

Promoting Entrepreneurship as a Catalyst for Development in South Africa

Gilbert Motsaathebe and Ravinder Rena

Introduction

The coalition of Brazil, Russia, India, China, and South Africa (BRICS) provides opportunities for economic growth, development, and expansion of business investment for organisations operating in the Global South. However, despite this clear advantage, some of the countries in the Global South (refers to Africa, Latin America and the Caribbean, Pacific Islands, and Asia, excluding Israel, Japan, and South Korea) continue to struggle with economic growth and instead actively create welfare states where much of the population depends on the state for their well-being. In South Africa, for example, almost half of the population lives on social welfare (South African Social Security Agency, 2023). According to the South African Social Security Agency's 2022/2023 Annual Report, "approximately 31% (more than 18 million grants) of South Africa's population depend on the social assistance programme". South African Social Security Agency (SASSA) Annual Report, 2023: 18). This was once again reiterated by President Cyril Ramaphosa when "We are the only African country giving grants to almost half its population. There is no other country in Africa that takes of its people as we do in South Africa" (Ramaphosa 2023 cited in Madisa and Amashabalala, 2023). The country provides free housing and various types of government grants to a category of people who are incapable of earning a living wage. The problem with this model is that it is not sustainable as most people rely on the government, placing a huge burden on the fiscals instead of playing an active role in the country's economic development. To this end, the government has been trying to create jobs and alleviate poverty and inequality. However, this has not been attainable. COVID-19 complicated the situation even more. In addition, the country has also been marred by corruption, endemic state capture and failure to address the triple legacy of poverty, inequality, and unemployment. It has been downgraded many times by international rating agencies.

The purpose of this conceptual chapter is twofold. Firstly, it identifies key catalysts that are integral in promoting economic growth in South Africa.

Secondly, the chapter uses a systems approach. It draws on the example of the Asian Tigers to offer a comprehensible model for implementing what it sees as the key catalysts of economic growth and development in a country marred by sluggish economic growth such as South Africa.

The Asian Tigers are a group of countries comprising Hong Kong, Singapore, South Korea, and Taiwan. They successfully reconfigured their economies in the 1960s by focusing on manufacturing and exports to bring about exponential economic growth. The chapter argues that South Africa, facing a serious problem of unemployment, inequality, and poverty, could follow the Asian Tigers' example to turn the situation around. According to the latest statistics, the country is currently experiencing the highest unemployment rate since 2008 (Stats SA, 2021). These results "are reflective of a struggling economy suffering high job losses and high levels of economic inactivity, exacerbated by the COVID-19 pandemic lockdown restrictions and, more recently, the July 2021 social unrest that some parts of the country experienced, which led to some businesses being permanently closed".

Against this background, the chapter examines various factors that could help stimulate economic growth and put the country on a firm development path. We argue that, with parastatals that are increasingly failing (e.g. Transnet, Eskom, and South African Airways [SAA]), South Africa will require a sound economic system to turn the situation around. Many factors could help invigorate the economy. For this chapter, we focus on only three of these factors that we have identified, namely: Prioritisation of Entrepreneurship, thriving Small and Medium Enterprises (SMMEs) and well-managed parastatals.

Despite evidence that entrepreneurial drive, well-intentioned and managed parastatals and SMMEs could contribute significantly to economic growth, very little attention has been paid to these key drivers (see Gupta, Guha and Krishnaswami, 2013). This chapter addresses this important gap. The specific objectives of this chapter are:

1 To critically analyse the current situation that deems South Africa a welfare state and suggest a shift that prioritises entrepreneurship in growing the economy meaningfully.
2 To propose coordinated implementation of what we see as the three catalysts of economic growth and development, namely: Prioritisation and support of entrepreneurship, thriving SMMEs and well-managed parastatals.

It is assumed that meaningful economic growth in South Africa hinges on the entrepreneurial drive, well-functioning parastatals and viable SMMES. Like entrepreneurship, SMMEs are very important in the economy. Literature indicates that this sector contributes immensely to the Gross domestic product (GDP), creates jobs, provides skills, and contributes to the manufacturing and exporting of goods. Hence, we strongly argue for prioritising entrepreneurship as a vehicle to grow the economy aggressively. We attempt to answer why SMMES are failing in South Africa. What are the challenges? The chapter is structured as follows: The context of the study with a focus on SMMEs and Entrepreneurship, the role of Parastatals, analysis of the current situation, Lessons from the Asian Tigers, conclusion and recommendation.

Literature Review

Analysis of the Strategy of the Government

Ever since the dawn of democracy in 1994, the country has been busy addressing the triple legacy of poverty, unemployment, and inequality. This has remained unattainable. Even its attempt to provide low-income houses, called Reconstruction and Development Programme (RDP) houses, has not been effective. Many of those who applied for these houses more than 20 years ago are still waiting to receive them due to several issues that include corruption. According to the *Sunday World* newspaper, "Corruption has become widespread, particularly in the granting of low-income housing subsidies, selection of building contractors and allocation of completed RDP houses, while many government officials have also been accused of allocating houses to close relatives, illegal immigrants and members of their political affiliation".

What is clear, however, is that the country's economy is badly managed. This is evident when one looks at the status of the parastatals, which ought to be strategic economic drivers. Government departments and parastatals continue to have wasteful and fruitful expenditures. The Presidency Annual 2021 Report painted a bleak picture regarding these parastatals. Many of these organisations experience problems of underperformance or total loss-making and desperately struggle to stabilise, develop a competitive edge and return to acceptable levels of profitability.

> Our detailed recommendations in the parastatals' management reports can only succeed if the entities have sound internal control environments and effective governance structures and processes. This links directly with some of the initiatives the government is implementing to strengthen the governance of Parastatals, including establishing a Presidential State-Owned Enterprises Council.
> (Auditor-General's 2021 report cited in the Presidency Annual Report 2020–2021)

According to official sources, "the South African economy contracted by an estimated 7.2% in 2020" (South Africa Yearbook, 2021). The same source paints a bleak picture when coming to unemployment. This was further exacerbated by COVID-19 lockdowns and other factors, including unreliable electricity supply, which resulted in multiple power outages that disrupted economic activities. The government continues introducing several strategies to deal with this concerning state of the country. The latest is the Economic Reconstruction and Recovery Plan, which was introduced late in 2020. This was introduced largely in response to the devastating impact that the COVID-19 has and is also aligned with the National Development Plan (NDP) that has been in force since 1996 to eradicate poverty and social and economic inequality by 2030. Described as a "broad vision for sustainable industrialisation and economic development and transformation in South Africa and, by extension, Africa" (South Africa Yearbook 2020/2021), the NDP's vision is expressed specifically in terms of specific priorities. Key amongst these priorities is economic transformation and job creation. Poverty and lack of employment are big problems in South Africa. Hence, economic transformation and job creation are key priorities for the country. This is because, during the apartheid years in South Africa, the majority of the population was economically dispossessed.

All departmental plans are required to align with the NDP. The President and Deputy President are designated champions of the Plan. Although the NDP sounds good on paper, it is clear, given the current trajectory, that it will not be able to eradicate poverty by 2030. It is already 2022, and we are only eight years from 2030. After 1994, the South African economy had great prospects with positive economic growth until 2008, when the world markets collapsed due to the massive decline in the value of US homes and subsequent stresses to the world markets. That great recession lasted from 2007 until 2009, leaving many countries struggling to return to their former glory. South Africa never made a commendable economic recovery from that meltdown.

The drive to eradicate poverty and reduce inequality is further driven through another mechanism called "Operation Vulindlela". Loosely translated as "open the path", Operation Vulindlela was established in 2020 as a joint initiative of The Presidency and National Treasury, which is intended to accelerate the implementation of the Economic Reconstruction and Recovery Plan by accelerating priority structural reforms. It is based on similar delivery unit initiatives in countries such as the United Kingdom and Malaysia (South Africa Yearbook, 2021). However, a cursory review shows that this operation is misdirected and tends to focus more on ancillary issues, such as the rolling out of digital communication infrastructure that will do little to address the fundamental problems of slow economic growth, poverty and inequality in the country.

There is also a Department of Trade, Industry, and Competition, formed due to the merger between the former Economic Development and Trade and Industry departments. It is essentially tasked with spearheading economic development in the country. The department, among others, provides "financial support to stimulate and facilitate the development of businesses" (DTIC, 2022). The Department of Trade Industry and Competition (DTIC) strives for "A dynamic industrial, globally competitive South African economy, characterised by meaningful economic transformation, inclusive growth and development, decent employment and equity, built on the full potential of all citizens" (DTIC, 2022). Whether this vision is being realised is another question.

Then there is the Department of Public Enterprises (DPE) established in 1994 to champion and direct the restructuring of State-Owned Companies (SOCs) and ensure their optimal economic and developmental impact. South Africa has many parastatals. They include the Development Bank of Southern Africa (DBSA). Independent Development Trust, Industrial Development Corporation of South Africa, the South African Broadcasting Corporation, the South African Forestry Company (SAFCOL), South African Nuclear Energy Corporation, the South African Post Office, Telkom, Transnet, the SAA, the South African Express Airways, Denel, the SAFCOL, and Alexkor.

The DPE is mandated to ensure that these enterprises contribute to realising the government's strategic objectives, as articulated in the NDP, Medium Term Strategic Framework (MTSF-2019-2024) and the Reimagined Industrial Strategy. "Well-governed and financially sustainable public entities play a vital role in national development" (South Africa Yearbook, 2021). The NDP sets ambitious goals for poverty reduction, economic growth, transformation, and job creation. The private sector has a major role in achieving these objectives (National Planning Commission, 2011). However, many of these companies have experienced losses and suffered from corruption and mismanagement. As a result, they have routinely been bailed out by the government and become an unnecessary liability to state financial resources instead of *vice versa*. The COVID-19 lockdowns exacerbated the situation; for example, it is reported that the Agricultural Development Bank of South Africa (Land Bank) defaulted on its debt obligations (South Africa Yearbook, 2021). This is worrying because the Public Finance Management Act (PFMA) of 1999 regulates financial management in all public entities. It requires parastatals to generate sufficient financial resources from their operations to meet all obligations and deliver on their respective mandates. However, this has not happened.

Theoretical Framework: A Systems Approach

Theoretically, a system approach is deemed suitable to explain the integrated way in which the key drivers identified in this chapter must be applied. A systems approach means we view these key elements of aggressive economic growth as interrelated and interdependent. As such, it provides a good framework for applying these key drivers and growing the economy systemically. According to OECD (2017:09) Systems approaches:

> Call for constant adjustment throughout the policy cycle, with implications for how institutions, processes, skills and actors are organised. Because they focus on outcomes, systems approaches require multiple actors

within and across levels of government to work together. Administrations must develop a vision for a desired outcome to effect system change, define the principles according to which that future system will operate, and start implementing interventions to transform the existing system into the future system.

(OECD 2017:09)

From the systems perspective, the South African economy is viewed in this chapter as a system that consists of various sub-systems that must all operate in unison to ensure success. As part of a whole all subsystems are required to consistently operate optimally because if one part of the system is not functioning optimally, the entire system will be adversely affected. Thus, the government should pay serious attention to ensure that the three catalysts (prioritisation and support of entrepreneurship, thriving SMMEs and well-managed parastatals) become effective.

Premising the application of the key catalysts within the systems approach can assist in ensuring well-coordinated efforts across all three key catalysts and sub-systems that will bring about the desired success. Thus, the systems approach enables us to develop a model for implementing key catalysts.

Methodological Approach

It is worth reiterating from the onset that this is a conceptual paper that assesses the current situation through a literature review, which includes relevant documents and policies to make suggestions for future applications. The documents consulted for this research were: NDP; Stats SA, various journal articles, books, and reports. These documents were deemed appropriate because they provided insights into the current socio-economic situation in South Africa and some of the policies intended to obviate the challenges confronting the country. Such documents were crucial in informing the novel expedient suggested in this chapter. As Wilson-Jones points out, "Conceptual papers are thought-provoking papers that challenge current thinking and practice and propose new approaches and models for application. True to its conceptual gist, this chapter maps the way for the future using "the available data and text to gain information related to the problem at hand" (Rahman and Khondkar, 2020:14). The information gained from the documents and available data perused provides a compressible context that enables conceptualists to come up with workable suggestions that are strategic. To ensure the effective implementation of the suggestions, the chapter employs the Systems Approach, as mentioned earlier. Using a systems approach is very relevant to the situation in South Africa as it "helps governments to confront problems that holistically traverse administrative and territorial boundaries" (OECD 2017:09).

The Criticality of the Systems Approach

Entrepreneurship as a Catalyst to Sustainable Economic Growth

Entrepreneurship is a key factor in promoting economic development, innovation, competitiveness and job creation, yet little is known about the skills required for successful entrepreneurship (see Gupta et al., 2013). Krackhardt (1995:53) suggests that "people who are entrepreneurial take advantage of opportunities to acquire added value for themselves or their firm". Thus, he highlights the behaviourist view of entrepreneurship, something which Pinchot (1985) labels as intrapreneurship, emphasising the skills and attributes of individuals involved in entrepreneurial ventures, as well as the dichotomy of what refers to as corporate entrepreneurship, which attaches more premium to an organisation's characteristics. While Mason and Brown (2014) insist on the importance of an entrepreneurial ecosystem in bringing about economic growth. They described it as:

> "a set of interconnected entrepreneurial actors (both potential and existing), entrepreneurial organisations (e.g. firms, venture capitalists, business angels, banks), institutions (universities, public sector agencies, financial bodies) and entrepreneurial processes (e.g. the business birth rate, numbers of high growth firms, levels of 'blockbuster entrepreneurship', number of serial entrepreneurs, degree of sellout mentality within firms and levels of entrepreneurial ambition) which formally and informally coalesce to connect, mediate and govern the performance within the local entrepreneurial environment"
>
> (Mason and Brown, 2014:04).

However, Isenberg (2014) submits that it is important to thoroughly understand the "entrepreneurship ecosystem" as an economic development strategy and debunk some of what he sees as misconceptions about this notion. While Liguori et al. (2019) observed that favourable entrepreneurship ecosystems are thought to drive business and innovation, they argued that a commonly accepted measure of entrepreneurial ecosystem favourableness is yet to be developed.

GDP was above 1% from 2000 to 2007, with the highest in 2001 (estimated at 4%) and the lowest in 2003 (about 1%). 2007–2009 registered a sharp decline from a positive 3% to a negative 2.5%, coinciding with the global economic recession and leaving its footprints in South Africa. The GDP improved from 2010 to 2018 but remained negative and stood at approximately −1% by 2018. This improvement was still way below the neutral level and the historical average of 2.6% observed between the years 2000 to 2007.

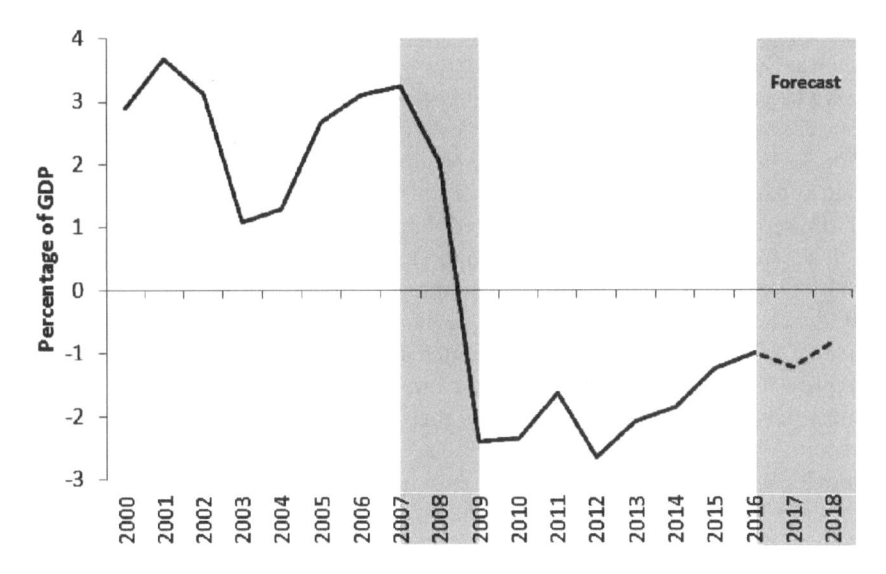

Figure 19.1 The general trend of GDP from the year 2000 to 2018.
Source: South African Reserve Bank (2018:42).

The Role of SMMEs in the Economy

Small, Medium, and Micro Enterprises are generally accepted as playing an important role in expanding the domestic economy and presenting new opportunities for job creation in economies of nation-states worldwide (Machacha, 2002; Haase, Lautenschläger and Rena, 2011). According to (Gordon, 2003; Maksoud and Yousef, 2003; Rena, 2009), the small business sector is responsible for 60–70% of employment creation in first and third-world countries, respectively. The latter view is supported by Ntsika (2009:16) that Small, Medium, and Micro Enterprises are important inputs in generating employment and overall economic growth in many countries. The small business sector has attributes like other firms; however, SMMEs cannot be compared with large companies due to the unique nature of operations and the general ecosystem.

The small business sector contributes towards the much-needed economic certainty and the allocation of all activities that produce goods and services in a country. Small, Medium, and Micro Enterprises have high numbers in any economy. These businesses have the capacity to innovate, can easily breathe life into new ideas and are linked to major companies through the umbilical cord of subcontracting (Kroon and Moolman, 1992:129).

SMMEs are poverty reduction pillars and job creators in many economies globally (Rena, 2009). SMME are not only viewed as providing opportunities to those who cannot find gainful employment in the formal economy but are generally viewed as creators of wealth (Riley, 1993:11). In Africa, nation states such as South Africa, Egypt, Morocco, Kenya, Uganda, Botswana, and Tanzania have taken conscious decisions to support the small business sector. The small business sector, which constitutes 95% of countries affiliated with the Organisation for Economic Cooperation and Development (OECD), has also been identified as playing a critical role in member states' economic growth (OECD, 2017).

Entrepreneurship is growth-oriented. Entrepreneurs take risks to grow. They utilise resources effectively, identify opportunities, develop innovative solutions to problems, create new markets and employment, and consistently acquire new skills. They participate actively in the economic growth of their respective countries. Therefore, they need to be supported and encouraged if the country hopes to grow its economy aggressively. A country serious about growing its economy must develop policies and incentives that promote entrepreneurship. In their report, Meyer and Meyer (2022) feel that South Africa is not doing enough to provide an enabling environment for entrepreneurship. Their view is supported by the National Entrepreneurship Context Index, which ranks South Africa as the 6th worst-performing country globally regarding entrepreneurial support. However, Saul Molobi, a former South African government official, insists that the country has made a concerted effort to empower its citizens economically. "Government has developed progressive policies, laws, and regulations as tools to drive socio-economic transformation" (Molobi, 2022:no pagination). He was referring to many policies that the government introduced. However, we argue that the efforts were not sufficiently coordinated, so we believe a more systematic approach is required.

As part of the entrepreneurship ecosystem approach, Motsaathebe (2022) insists that entrepreneurship needs to be a compulsory subject in any African country, given the continent's potential in terms of its minerals and many untapped opportunities. He disagrees with Isenberg's (2014) suggestion that formal education in entrepreneurship may not lead to more successful entrepreneurship, saying that Isenberg's observation is not based on any empirical data. Furthermore, in a study conducted in 2011, Motsaathebe (2011) stressed that there was a need for an education that was responsive to the country's needs. Hence, the argument for entrepreneurship to be made a compulsory educational subject with be the right move to enable more South Africans to become economically active instead of relying on government welfare.

An attempt to quantify the SMME sector in South Africa should be taken with caution as it is very difficult to give an accurate number of the SMME sector due to the complexities of the ecosystem of the SMME sector characterised by business that operates in the formal economy and others existing in the informal economy. The complexities are also exacerbated by a lack of uniformity in the scientific methodologies used by various research institutions to study the sector (Berry *et al.*, 2002:13–14). The table above indicates that the North West Province is ranked number seven (7) in South Africa regarding the total

Table 19.1 Number of SMMEs per Province in South Africa

SMMEs	Number Quarter (2008Q1)				Number (2015Q2)			
	Total	Formal	Informal	Other	Total	Formal	Informal	Other
Total	2 182 823	666 501	1 420 933	95 389	2 251 821	667 433	1 497 860	86 528
W/Cape	223 933	114 976	95 212	13 745	230 324	110 107	110 188	10 030
E/Cape	218 865	56 579	154 631	7 655	197 366	50 670	141 739	4 957
N/Cape	29 894	11 450	11 768	6 676	20 611	8 534	9 058	3 019
FS	114 949	31 040	76 127	7 783	96 846	26 224	60 816	9 806
KZN	418 406	102 591	289 347	7 783	373 434	74 976	283 165	15 293
NW	109 860	25 817	76 855	7 188	112 856	27 430	79 153	6 273
GP	687 556	270 093	405 180	12 283	785 321	306 231	465 100	13 989
MP	193 259	29 760	156 814	6 685	185 399	35 208	141 129	9 063
Limpopo	186 101	24 193	155 001	6 907	249 663	28 054	207 512	14 098

Source: Stats SA, BER.

number of SMMEs. Table 19.1 also indicates that the total number of SMMEs in the North West Province increased between 2008 and 2015.

For example, the table indicates that in Quarter 1 of 2008, the North West Province had 25 817 SMMEs operating in the formal economy and 76 855 SMMEs in the informal economy. In total, the North West Province had 109 866 SMMEs in 2008. Table 19.1 also indicates that the North West Province 2015 had 27 430 SMMEs operating in the formal economy and 79 153 SMMEs operating in the informal economy. In 2015, the province had 112 856 SMMEs operating in both the formal and informal economies, respectively.

Entrepreneurship is growth-oriented. Entrepreneurs take risks to grow. They utilise resources effectively, identify opportunities, develop innovative solutions to problems, create new markets and employment, and consistently acquire new skills. They participate actively in the economic growth of their respective countries. Therefore, they need to be supported and encouraged if the country hopes to grow its economy aggressively. A country serious about growing its economy must develop policies and incentives that promote entrepreneurship.

The SMME Sector in South Africa

In the context of South Africa, the classification of the SMME sector is provided in the 1995 White Paper on National Strategy for the Development and Promotion of Small Business and the National Business Act of 1996. The NBA of 1996, Table 19.2 as amended in 2004, classifies the SMME sector as follows:

Micro-enterprise is classified as a business with 5 or fewer employees and a turnover of not more than R150 000 per annum. These micro-enterprises operate in both the formal and informal economy of South Africa. Other characteristics of micro-enterprises are that generally, businesses do not qualify for Value Added Tax because of their small size, they are businesses that are managed by the owner(s), and informal operational and accounting systems also characterise them. In other sectors of the economy, such as construction, manufacturing, electricity, and mining, the limit of micro-enterprises is 20 workers.

Very small businesses hire between 1 and 10 workers and have a turnover ranging between 400 000 and 500 000, but the turnover is determined by industry classification. Depending on industry classification, the total assets value of the very small business is not more than 500 000.

Medium-sized businesses hire between 50 and 100 employees with the exclusion of industries such as construction, manufacturing, mining and electricity. Medium-sized businesses have more than one management layer with significant devolution of power. Specialisation in terms of labour is one of the defining characteristics of medium-sized enterprises. Medium size business ventures also have a total asset portfolio value of not less than R7.5 million and an annual turnover of not less than R6 million and not more than R25 million as per industry sector. Critically, medium-sized enterprises are defined by legislation as companies that operate in the formal economy.

Small enterprises are established compared to very small and micro enterprises. The business models and operations of small enterprises are complex. Small enterprises employ between 11 and 50 employees and are also characterised by a turnover that ranges from R2 million to R6 million. Small enterprises' total asset portfolio in terms of value is not more than R2 million and does not exceed R4.5 million.

Table 19.2 Schedule of SMMEs by the NSB Act of 1996

Sector or subsector in accordance with the Standard Industrial Classification	Size or class	Total full-time equivalent of paid employees Less than:	Total annual turnover Less than:	Total gross asset value (Fixed property excluded) Less than:
Agriculture	Medium	100	R4.00 m	R4.00 m
	Small	50	R2.00 m	R2.00 m
	Very small	10	R0.4 m	R0.40 m
	Micro	5	R0.5 m	R0.10 m
Mining and Quarrying	Medium	200	R30.00 m	R18.00 m
	Small	50	R7.50 m	R4.50 m
	Very small	20	R3.00 m	R1.80 m
	Micro	5	R0.15 m	R0.10 m
Manufacturing	Medium	200	R40.00 m	R15.00 m
	Small	50	R10.0 m	R3.75 m
	Very small	20	R40.00 m	R1.50 m
	Micro	5	R0.15 m	R0.10 m

(*Continued*)

Table 19.2 (Continued)

Sector or subsector in accordance with the Standard Industrial Classification	Size or class	Total full-time equivalent of paid employees Less than:	Total annual turnover Less than:	Total gross asset value (Fixed property excluded) Less than:
Electricity, Gas, and Water	Medium	200	R40.00 m	R15.00 m
	Small	50	R10.00 m	R3.75 m
	Very Small	20	R4.00 m	R1.50 m
	Micro	5	R0.15 m	R0.10 m
Construction	Medium	200	R20.00 m	R4.00 m
	Small	50	R5.00 m	R5.00 m
	Very small	20	R2.00 m	R2.00 m
	Micro	5	R0.15 m	R0.15 m
Retail and Motor Trade and Repair Services	Medium	100	R30.00 m	R5.00 m
	Small	50	R5.00 m	R2.50 m
	Very small	10	R3.00 m	R0.50 m
	Micro	5	R0.15 m	R0.10 m
Wholesale Trade, Commercial Agents, and Allied Services	Medium	100	R50.00 m	R8.00 m
	Small	50	R25.00 m	R4.00 m
	Very small	10	R5.00 m	R0.50 m
	Micro	5	R0.15 m	R0.10 m
Catering, Accommodation, and other Trade	Medium	100	R10.00 m	R2.00 m
	Small	50	R5.00 m	R1.00 m
	Very small	20	R1.00 m	R0.20 m
	Micro	5	R0.15 m	R0.10 m
Transport, Storage, and Communications	Medium	100	R20.00 m	R5.00 m
	Small	50	R10.00 m	R2.50 m
	Very small	10	R 2.00 m	R0.50 m
	Micro	5	R0.15 m	R0.10 m
Finance and Business Services	Medium	100	R20.00 m	R4.00 m
	Small	50	R10.00 m	R2.00 m
	Very small	10	R2.00 m	R0.40 m
	Micro	5	R0.15 m	R0.10 m
Community, Social, and Personal Services	Medium	100	R10.00 m	R5.00 m
	Small	50	R5.00 m	R2.50 m
	Very small	10	R1.00 m	R0.50 m
	Micro	5	R0.15 m	R0.10 m

Source: National Small Business Act of 1996.

The problem with the current setup in South Africa is that the country is creating a population of consumers and not producers. The country is well endowed with natural resources; however, these resources are not being put to good use due to the current education system that is producing graduates who lack the entrepreneurial streak required to exploit the resources replete in the country. For instance, South Africa has one of the largest gold reserves in the world Table 19.3. According to the Mineral Council of South Africa (2022), the Witwatersrand Basin

Table 19.3 Table of Mineral Resources in South Africa

Minerals	South Africa's Production Capacity
Platinum	Number one largest producer of platinum in the world by a significant margin, with a production of between 148 and 112 metric tons per year.
Manganese	Boasts the largest known deposit of manganese and the country is a leading producer of manganese globally.
Palladium	The world's second-largest producer of palladium.
Iron Ore	The 5th largest exporter of Iron Ore in the world.
Chrome ore	Boasts 72% of the world's chrome reserves. Together with Kazakhstan, South Africa hosts 95% of the world's chromium reserves.
Diamond	Ranks among the top 10 diamond producers globally.
Coal	Produces over 250 million tons of coal every year and according to Africa Mining IQ (2022), over 90% of the coal consumed in Africa is produced in South Africa.
Gold	Over 50% of all gold reserves are found in South Africa with the Witwatersrand Basin remaining the largest gold resource in the world, according to Africa Mining IQ, 2022.
Steel	The second largest steel producer in Africa after Egypt. South Africa produces 5.7 million metric tons of crude steel annually.

Source: Authors' Own.

remains the world's largest gold resource, and South African gold only accounts for 4.2% of global gold production.

In addition to the minerals on the table, the country also boasts a range of other important minerals such as vanadium, titanium, and several other lesser minerals (South African Mining 2022), yet the country still fails to transform the lives of mining host communities economically. It has also failed to rehabilitate disused mines, leading to a problem of what has come to be known as the *Zama* phenomenon, characterised by illegal mining by individuals. The country is still struggling to provide an adequate electricity supply and has been characterised by consistent power outages.

Although the country, through its Department of Mineral Resources and Energy, has long focused on transforming mining and rehabilitating unused mines, many mining shafts have been left unattended and have now been taken over by *Zama Zamas*. This has affected the economic capacity of citizens. Many of these citizens depend on government social welfare for their livelihoods. According to the World Bank (2022), South Africa remains one of the world's biggest spenders on social welfare. While commendable, the welfare services are not a solution to the country's economic and social issues because they are not sustainable and do not address the fundamental issues of poverty, unemployment and economic inequality.

Thriving SMMEs

Small, Medium and Micro Enterprises (SMMEs) are widely acknowledged as playing a key role in economic growth. However, countries such as South Africa have not yet realised the importance of creating a conducive environment for thriving SMMEs. SMMEs are important players in the economy of the country. For example, recent reports show that SMMEs in the country employ about 60% of the country's workforce and contribute 34% to the country's GDP (IFC Unseen Sector Report, 2021). However, there is still a problem of creating a meaningful, conducive environment and capacity building for SMMEs, which will help the country develop economically. Part of this problem is identifying the pattern of growth they follow so that all SMMEs are capacitated along all stages of their growth to become more sustainable and boost the country's economic agenda significantly. As Gupta *et al.* (2013) note, "there is a dearth of literature on finding patterns of growth followed by the small and medium enterprises". The information in this chapter will go a long way in closing this gap.

According to Ngcobo and Sukdeo (2015), some of the problems that SMMEs encounter in South Africa include dwindling government support, constraining government policies and regulations, scarcity of enabling information, and poor level of awareness of government support programmes and lack of communication between the government and SMMEs. Our chapter argues that the government needs to take these issues seriously and meaningfully address them to create an enabling environment for SMMEs to thrive. We argue that the Asian Tigers' trajectory provides a great example of how the three key drivers that we have identified could be applied.

What Lessons Can Be Draw from the Asian Tigers?

The Asian tigers consisting of Taiwan, South Korea, Hong Kong, and Singapore provide a good example of how South Africa could try to grow its economy aggressively. Hong Kong started its economic development trajectory by focusing on the textile industry. Singapore, South Korea, and Taiwan started their industrialisation by focusing on manufacturing and exporting different types of manufactured goods. In all these countries, government intervention by way of providing incentives for local manufacturers was critical. This resulted in massive industrialisation that addressed problems of unemployment and economic stagnation by creating much-needed jobs and growing the manufacturing sector considerably, particularly in Taiwan and South Korea. Today, South Korea and Taiwan are the world's biggest manufacturing countries while Hong Kong and Singapore are financial hubs. These countries developed so rapidly. It is also worth mentioning that they did not do it alone as they also benefited from the support of other countries such as the US, which had a vested interest because their developed economy had an economic spill-over effect for the United States. According to CFI (2022), these countries mostly benefited from international exchange assistance from the United States.

For various reasons, most African countries, including South Africa, have seen their development hampered since their independence. Be it copper, crude oil, uranium, and even diamonds, Africa has a vast array of natural resources on this continent which makes stagnation in development for most countries and eventually leads to Dutch disease.

For example, Zambia's economy, in recent times, declined as the result of steep decreases in the international price of copper, higher prices of oil and industrial inputs, falling copper production, economic and public sector mismanagement, and postponement of adjustment, which led the country into heavy debt.

Whatever the biggest factor of the country's decline may be, we must find pragmatic ways to overcome what is plaguing our beloved continent. One solution could be to look at the progress of the Asian Tigers, who are largely driven by the Confucius culture. "Asian Tigers" is the name given to the four Asian economies of Hong Kong, Singapore, South Korea, and Taiwan. These countries underwent rapid industrialisation and maintained exceptionally high growth rates (over 7% a year) between the early 1960s and 1990s. By the early 21st century, all four had developed into high-income economies, specialising in areas of competitive advantage. How did these countries do it?

Economic success among the Asian Tigers was achieved through key policies imposed by governments, such as policies with a deep focus on exports. These countries focused on export-oriented industrial development to richer countries. They also encouraged human capital development in that their citizens should develop specialised skills to improve productivity. This kind of policy can fill in labour gaps in certain sectors to reduce the number of jobs foreigners take in African countries. Singapore's economic ascension is nothing short of remarkable for a country that lacks territory and natural resources. By embracing globalisation, free-market capitalism, education, and imposing strict pragmatic policies, the country has overcome its geographic disadvantages and become a leader in global commerce.

The country was strategic in the way in which it embraced globalisation. They used multinationals to educate their domestic, unskilled workers in information technology, pharmaceuticals and electronics. This paid great dividends for them. By 1990, they had gone from merely exporting textiles, garments, and basic electronics to engaging in wafer fabrication, logistics, biotech research, pharmaceuticals, integrated circuit design, and aerospace engineering.

It would be a giant leap if African countries could increase exports of tertiary products and not only natural resources. Regarding trade, these countries adopted exchange rate policies favouring exporters, export incentives and selective tariff protection; financial repression, slowing financial sector development and consumer lending to provide cheap financing to industry – for exports.

For all the natural resource wealth we have in Africa, we too should aim to improve the terms of trade about our exports. Many African countries cannot utilise these natural resources to turn them into finished goods due to a lack of advanced industrial technology. The least that can be done is to improve our terms of trade regarding exports. The policies and trade treaties like the African Continental Free Trade Agreement in Africa cannot be sustained until the policies are implemented for the benefit of African nations, and the actual losses will catch up even if terms of trade do not deteriorate further. The complacency engendered by the relatively high GDP growth rates is misplaced, given the very rapid rate of population growth in Africa, both in absolute terms and compared to other global regions. Given many African countries' fragile fiscal positions and mounting debts, these policies are only possible if the economy adjusts to a sustainable path.

The African governments can increase subsidies for local businesses. This will encourage their growth and, hopefully, the quality of local services and goods. This allows policymakers to increase the number of taxpaying businesses long-term, especially if they cannot improve the terms with foreign businesses.

If Africans, can instil this kind of productivity in our people, it will go a long way towards our multi-faceted development as a continent. People respect each other's time, space, and efforts when you live by such means. The goal should be to end up living in communities that are well looked after, working in places where people are always pragmatic, productive and time-sensitive, and have high social capital among our people.

The countries also made a considerable investment in education, particularly the education that is relevant to the country's needs in terms of the resources they had at their disposal. The other area in which the Asian tigers demonstrated success was leadership and management. Unlike South Africa, which is often marred by problems of corruption and poor leadership, the Asian Tigers had a decisive and visionary leadership that was not in the position of power to enrich them but to serve as "servant leaders". They also focused on well-thought-out economic policies that support exponential growth. Thus, the hallmarks of their success were marked by:

- Massive industrialisation
- Manufacturing and export
- Great leadership
- Well-educated population

However, the Asian Tigers did not just grow their economies without problems. As the markets reached saturation points, it meant that the export markets would suffer because there came a time when they could not keep up creating employment like they did when they relied on a large workforce to manufacture products for their foreign export markets due to a lack of demands. In addition, the Asian Financial Crisis of 1997 also affected them significantly. The crisis was caused by the collapse of the currency exchange rate, which started in Thailand and quickly affected the rest of Asia (CFI, 2022).

Conclusion

This chapter highlighted the possible impact of Entrepreneurship-driven growth in South Africa. The chapter further highlights the significance of well-functioning parastatals and thriving SMMEs in growing the economy aggressively. We argue that the current *status quo* is detrimental to growth and development. Furthermore, we argue that well-positioned institutions are ideal for required economic growth. Therefore, South Africa must employ a more systematic approach to growing the economy and addressing the triple challenge of poverty, unemployment and inequality. We strongly advocate for a methodological application of what we see as the key triple catalysts, i.e., robust entrepreneurship, well-managed parastatals and an enabling environment for SMMEs to thrive and create more jobs, contribute to the economy and empower more people to own the means of production rather than having them as consumers.

References

Gordon, G. (2 September 2003) SME survey. *Sunday Times Business*.
Gupta, P. D., Guha, S., and Krishnaswami, S. S. (2013) Firm growth and its determinants. *Journal of Innovation and Entrepreneurship*, 2(15):2–14. https://doi.org/10.1186/2192-5372-2-15
Haase, H., Lautenschläger, A., and Rena, R. (2011) The entrepreneurial mind-set of university students: A cross-cultural comparison between Namibia and Germany", *International Journal of Education Economics and Development*, 2(2): 113–129.
Isenberg, D. (2014) What an Entrepreneurship Ecosystem Actually Is, Havard Business Review. https://hbr.org/2014/05/what-an-entrepreneurial-ecosystem-actually-is (Accessed 20 April 2022).
Krackhardt, D. (1995) Entrepreneurial opportunities in entrepreneurial firms: A structural approach. *Entrepreneurship Theory and Practice*, 19(3):53–70.
Kroon, J., and Moolman, P. L. (1992). *Entrepreneurship*. Potchefstroom University for Christian Higher Education: South Africa.
Liguori, E., Bendickson, J., Solomon S., and McDowell, W.C. (2019) Development of a multi-dimensional measure for assessing entrepreneurial ecosystems, *Entrepreneurship and Regional Development*, 31(1–2): 7–21. DOI: 10.1080/08985626.2018.1537144
Machacha, L. (2002) Impact of information technology on small and medium enterprises (SMEs) in Botswana, in K. Kimppa (ed.), Proceedings of Expanding the Horizons of

African Business and Development. *The International Academy of African Business and Development International Conference*, Port Elizabeth, South Africa, 3–6 April 2002, pp. 277–282.

Madisa, K., and Amashabalala, M. (2023 January 06) Half of South Africa's population are 100% dependent on state welfare. *SowetanLive*. https://www.sowetanlive.co.za/news/south-africa/2023-01-06-half-of-south-africas-population-are-100-dependent-on-state-welfare/ (Accessed November 2022).

Maksoud, S. S., and Yousef, M. A. A. (2003) *Information and Communication Technology for Small and Medium Enterprise in Egypt*. SME Development Unit-Ministry of Foreign Trade, 1–15.

Mason, C., and Brown, R. (2013) Creating good public policy to support high growth firms, *Small Business Economics*, 40, 211–225.

Mason, C., and Brown, R. (2014) "Entrepreneurship ecosystems and growth-oriented entrepreneurship", Report for the OECD LEED Programme, Paris.

May, R. (2014) Implementing a leadership development program for your business. *Journal of the Knowledge Economy*, IX, 137–146.

Meyer, N., and Meyer, D. (2022 16 February) The South African entrepreneurial ecosystem and enabling environment is not supporting new and established entrepreneurs as it should. https://www.dailymaverick.co.za/article/2022-02-16-entrepreneurship-is-a-key-economic-driver-ramaphosas-sona-2022-offers-glimmers-of-hope/ (Accessed 18 June 2023).

Mineral Council of South Africa. (2022) Minerals Council Strategic Goals and Objectives. https://www.mineralscouncil.org.za/ (Accessed 2 July 2023).

Molobi, S. (2022 22 April) Publisher's comment: Towards developing an empowering ecosystem for enterprise development, *Jumbo Africa Online*.

Motsaathebe, G. (2011) Journalism education and practice in South Africa and the discourse of the African renaissance, communication, *Journal of Communication Theory and Research*, 37(3): 381–397.

Motsaathebe, G. (2022) Africa hundred years from now: A Rhetorical and Futurological Inquiry, Keynote address delivered at the biennial conference of the Association of African Rhetoric held in Nairobi, Kenya on 20–22 July 2022, *Jumbo Africa Online*. https://www.jamboafrica.online/verbatim-prof-gilbert-motsaathebe-africa-hundred-years-from-now-a-rhetorical-and-futurologist-inquiry/ (Accessed 10 June 2023).

National Planning Commission. (2011) *National Development Plan – Vision 2030*. Pretoria, Government of South Africa. https://www.nationalplanningcommission.org.za/National_Development_Plan#:~:text=The%20NDP%20aims%20to%20achieve%20the%20following%20objectives%20by%202030%3Aandtext=Focusing%20on%20key%20capabilities%20of,Building%20a%20capable%20and%20developmental (Accessed 9 October 2023).

Ngcobo, S., and Sukdeo, R. (2015). Challenges facing SMMEs during their first two years of operation in South Africa. *Corporate Ownership and Control*, 12(3–5), 505–512. https://doi.org/10.22495/cocv12i3c5p2

Ntsika Enterprise Promotion Agency. (2009) National Small Business Act: Ntsika Enterprise Promotion Agency: Nominations. https://www.gov.za/documents/notices/national-small-business-act-ntsika-enterprise-promotion-agency-nominations-09-jul (Accessed 19 January 2018).

OECD. (2017) *Systems Approaches to Public Sector Challenges: Working with Change*, Paris: OECD Publishing. https://doi.org/10.1787/9789264279865-en (Accessed 25 November 2022).

Pinchot, G. (1985) *Intrapreneuring: Why You don't Have to Leave the Corporation to Become an Entrepreneur*. New York: Harper and Row.

Rahman, M. M., and Khondkar, M. (2020) Small and medium enterprises (SME) development and economic growth of Bangladesh: A narrative of the glorious 50 years. *Barishal University Journal of Business Studies*, 7(1): 09–24.

Rena, R. (2009) Rural entrepreneurship and development – An Eritrean perspective. *Journal of Rural Development*, 28 (1):1–19.

Riley, T. (1993) Characteristics of and Constraints Facing Black Businesses in South Africa: World Bank Discussion Paper on the Economy of South Africa No 5.

South Africa Year Book. (2020/2021) https://www.southafrica-usa.net/consulate/yearbook_2021.html (Accessed 22 March 2023).

South African Social Security Agency Annual Report. (2022/2023) https://static.pmg.org.za/SASSA_2022-23_Annual_Performance_Plan.pdf (Accessed 15 July 2022).

Stats SA (2021) The South African economy sheds more than half a million jobs in the 3rd quarter of 2021. https://www.statssa.gov.za/?p=14922#:~:text=quarter%20of%202021-,The%20South%20African%20economy%20sheds%20more%20than%20half%20a%20million,2nd%20quarter%20of%202021 (Accessed 11 February 2023).

The Presidency Annual Report 2020–2021. https://www.thepresidency.gov.za/sites/default/files/The%20Presidency%20Annual%20Report%202020-2021.pdf (Accessed 10 October 2023).

Index

Note: Page references in *italics* denote figures and in **bold** tables.

2030 Agenda for Sustainable Development 230

Aatmanirbhar Bharat Abhiyaan 52–54
Abalkin, L. 279
Academy of Management Annals 102
Acs, Z. J. 162, 163
action plans 22
Adorno, T. W. 299, 303
Adusei, M. 166
advanced production technology in Russia 292–293
advertising: and COVID-19 133; SMMEs 23–24
Aeroflot 265
Africa: COVID-related infection rates 31; SMEs 221
The Agency for Strategic Initiatives (ASI, Russia) 300, 304–305, 307
aggressive economic growth 326–342
Agricultural Development Bank of South Africa (Land Bank) 330
Ahmed, H. M. S. 100
Ahmed, Y. A. 100
Al Buraiki, A. 60
Alessa, A. A. 58
Alexkor 330
Al Mamari, S. 98–99
Almodovar-Gonzalez, M. 162, 166
Anjaria, J. S. 259
Aparicio, S. 162, 166
Arenius, P. 175
"Arthashastra" 152–153
artificial intelligence (AI) 90, 150
Art Residence, Chernoistochinsk 306–312

Asian Development Bank (ADB) 48, 101
Asian Financial Crisis of 1997 342
Asian Tigers 327, 339–342
Australia, SMEs in 221
Autio, E. 162, 166

Bakhtiar, S. 100
Banu, S. 18, 20, 26
Baporikar, N. 61
Barykin, A. N. 285
Beach, D. 205
Behera, M. 18, 24
benchmarks 156–157
Bereslavskaya, V. A. 279
Berry, A. 35
Bharat Petroleum Corporation Limited (BPCL) 152
Boev A. G. 279
Boos, N. 69–70
Boston Consulting Group 293
Bouazza, A. M. 11
Boucas da Silva, D. L. 23–24, 25
Brändle, L. 128
Brazil, Russia, India, China and South Africa (BRICS nations) 1, 154; causal factors launching cooperation in ICAP 213–214; challenges and opportunities in 3–4; COVID-19 pandemic in 2–3; documental analysis of cooperation in ICAP 209–213; entrepreneurship 154–156; future research directions 215–216; Innovation Cooperation Action Plans 204–216; perspectives on entrepreneurship

4–5; recommendations 215–216; STI Development within 206–209; urban economics of street markets in 251–260
Brewer, P. 137
Brown, R. 332
Bruyat, C. 109–110
Burki, U. 215
business models 11–12, 21, 89–90, 312–313; Akshaya Patra Foundation 157; digitally enabled hyper-local 103; inclusive 104, 105; innovative 95, 132; MSME 235; offline 20; online 20, 24; SMMEs 25
Buzulukova, E. 10, 23
Bykov, Alexander 306

Cabinet Committee of India 95
Caboz, J. 135–136
carte-blanche 113
C-CAMP COVID-19 Innovation Development Accelerator (C-CIDA) 103
Central Public Sector Enterprises (CPSEs) 152
CFI 340
Chakuzira, W. 110, 112
Chandra, A. 218
Chang, W. J. 67
Chavan, M. 218
Chen, M. Y. 188
Chernova, C. 18
China 42; entrepreneurs and COVID-19 spread 58; GDP 86; government support on SMEs 86–88, *87*; *Regulations on Guaranteeing the Payment of Small- and Medium-sized Enterprises* 85; SMEs in 221, **236–237**, 236–238
China Industry Research Network 43
China Securities Regulatory Commission 186
China Stock Market & Accounting Research (CSMAR) database 182, 186–187
Chinese Research Data Services (CNRDS) database 182
Chinese SMEs 41–42; and COVID-19 pandemic 75–91; cut and deferment measures 80–82; entrepreneurship 90; future development of 88–90; government support 86–88, *87*; labour support 83–84; overview **76–77**, 76–78; stable employment 83–84; strengthen and improve financial support 82–83; supportive policies launched for 80–86
commercial hair salons 68
Company and Intellectual Property Commission (CIPC) 65
Company Statutory Documents 65
Competitiveness and Singularity Council of Singularity University (United States) 293
competitive SOEs 184, 196, **196**
Confederation of Indian Industry (CII) 222
Confucius culture 340
consumer tastes: SMMEs 24
Cornell University 213
correlation coefficient matrix 190–191, **191**
costs: consumer borrowing 81; finance 17, 83; fixed costs (FC) 119–121; SMMEs 25; total costs 119; variable costs (VC) 119
COVID-19 pandemic 1; barriers for youth entrepreneurs 118–123; in BRICS nations 2–3; and Chinese SMEs 75–91; impact on Indian exports 49–52, *50–52*; impact on SMEs 58, 60–63; impact on SMMEs in BRICS nations 9–27; infection rate in Africa 31, **32–33**; managing 115–116; and MSMEs 43–46, 100–102; rescue package barrier 122; and restaurant entrepreneurs 127–141; SME rescue packages **117**; vs. SMEs 115; and SMMEs in South Africa 31–39; and sustainability of Indian MSMEs 41–55
Creative Cluster Samorodok (Prill) in Nizhny Tagil 309–310
Creative Factory project in Sysert 307–309
creative industries: annual revenue worldwide 302; High School of Economics defining 303; in Russia post-COVID-19 299–315
Creative Industries Concept 300
Creative Lab 300

Credit Guarantee Fund Trust to Medium and Small Enterprises (CGTMSE) 53

Dai, R. 20–21
debts relief finance scheme: requirements 65–66; for SMEs in South Africa 64–66
Deen-Swarray, M. 68
Deloitte 293
Deloitte Touche Tohmatsu 285
Demidov, Akinfiy 307
Denel 330
Denyer, D. 12
descriptive statistics **190**, 190–191
developing economies/nations: contributions of SMEs in 224–229, **225**, **227–228**; entrepreneur education for 320–321; futuristic approach of SMEs in 239–240, **239–240**; higher wealth creation for 153–154
Development Bank of Southern Africa (DBSA) 330
Dey, M. 20
The Dialectic of Enlightenment. Philosophical Fragments (Adorno and Horkheimer) 299
Diaz-Casero, J. C. 166
digital capabilities 89
digital technologies 136–137
Directorate General of Commercial Intelligence and Statistics (DGCIS) 44
Disaster Management Act (South Africa) 36, 59
Diswas, P. 20
Djukic, M. I. 166
Dladla, L. G. 17, 18
documental analysis in Innovation Cooperation Action Plans 209–213
"Domna" Creative Cluster, Yekaterinburg 312
Donga, G. 127
Doran, J. 163, 164, 175
Duan, Z. M. 193
Dube, K. 129
Duggappa, V. 18, 20, 23
Dynamic Ordinary Least Squares model 164

economic development: entrepreneurship as driver for 269–272; entrepreneurship for 262–274
economic diversity 260
economic growth: aggressive 326–342; entrepreneurship as catalyst to sustainable 332; entrepreneurship as driver for 269–272; entrepreneurship for 262–274
Economic Reconstruction and Recovery Plan 329
economy: role of SMMEs in 333–338, **335**, **336–337**, **338**; street 259
Edcon and Comair 116
Edomah, N. 9
Efremov, V. S. 279
Electronics System Design and Manufacturing (ESDM) 104
Emergency Credit Line Guarantee Scheme (ECLGS) 53
emerging economies: entrepreneurship and economic growth in 161–176; overview 161–164; quantitative measures of entrepreneurship 164–167
employee health and safety, and SMMEs 21
Employees Provident Fund Organisation (India) 54
employee well-being and welfare 25–26
Employers Organisation for Hairdressing, Cosmetology and Beauty (South Africa) 66
empreneurs 113
"Enterprise in Action" 318
enterprise innovation: mixed ownership reform of 191–193, **192**; and top management governance 192
enterprises: "Little Giant" Enterprises 87; state-owned 181–200; *see also* specific types
entremployees 112–113
entrepreneur education 317–320; for developing nations 320–321; and higher education students in South Africa 317–323; in South Africa 320–321
entrepreneurial action 22
entrepreneurial intention 321–322
entrepreneurial mindset 22

348 *Index*

entrepreneurs: activities 114–115; business opportunity barrier 118–119; in COVID-19 pandemic 67; COVID-19 pandemic barriers for youth 118–123; COVID-19 pandemic rescue package barrier 122; cycle *111*; financial barrier 119–121; Indian 95–105; psychological barrier 122–123; social 112; typologies in South Africa 111–115; various strategies to support 322–323
entrepreneurship: BRICS nations perspectives on 4–5; as catalyst for development in South Africa 326–342; as catalyst to sustainable economic growth 332; defined 109–110, *110*, 162; as driver for economic development/growth 1, 269–272; and economic growth in emerging economies 161–176; governance in 147–159; growth-oriented 334, 335; history 149–150; indicators **168–169**, **171**; post-COVID-19 era in South Africa 108–125; post-COVID-19 opportunities 123, **123–124**; potential of India in 150; quantitative measures of 164–167; re-defining 109–115
E.ON 235
equity balance 181–200
Estupinan, X 100
eThekwini Declaration 207
Europe: biotechnology-related fields 234; COVID-related infection rates 31; SMEs 221
European Commission 319
European Investment Bank (EIB) 320
European Union 303; member countries 320
Eurostat 290
existential issues, SMMEs 26

Fairlie, R. W. 113
"Fancy Balusters" 307
Farinha, L. 162
Farooque, M. 99
Fashion Factory PRO-Textile in Aramil 310
Fatkhutdinova, A. M. 279
Fayolle, A. 317

Federal Insurance Contributions Act (FICA) 65
Feng, L. 193
Fernandez-Portillo, A. 162, 166
Ferreira, M. 253
Ferreira, P. 162, 175
financial support, and SMMEs 16–19
Five Alert Level System (FALS) 135
For Entrepreneurs Only (Wilson) 123
formal businesses *vs.* informal businesses 68
Fossen, F. M. 113
Fourth Industrial Revolution 283
Frankfurt School 299
Fritsch, M. 165
Fubah, C. N. 26, 60
futuristic approach of SMEs in developing economies 239–240, **239–240**

Gaba, A. K. 162, 164–165, 175
Gaba, N. 162, 164–165, 175
Gailly B. 317
Gates, Bill 149
Gazprom 265
Giones, F. 58
Glazyev S. Y. 279
Global Alliance for Mass Entrepreneurship 237, 239
Global Competitiveness Index (GCI) 266, 283
Global Competitiveness Report (GCR) 213
Global Entrepreneurship Index (GEI) 266
Global Entrepreneurship Monitor (GEM) 163, 165, 266
Global Innovation Index (GII) 213, 284
globalisation 9, 103–104, 154, 157–158, **227**, 251–252, 266, 319
Global Market Research Company 36
Global North 205, 215
Global South 204, 215, 326
Goal 9 of the SDGs 229
Gomes, S. 162, 175
governance: background 148–149; in BRICS entrepreneurship 154–156; in entrepreneurship 147–159; good 156; and New World Order 157–158, *158*; overview 147
government-financed SME agencies 225
government institutions 152; and entrepreneurship in South Africa 321

Government of India (GOI) 41;
  Aatmanirbhar Bharat Abhiyaan 52–54;
  policy initiatives by 52–54; schemes
  introduced for upliftment MSME **98**
government procurement tenders 19–20
Gradov A. P. 279
Great Council of London 299
Gross Domestic District Product (GDDP)
  150
Gungah, V. 166
Gupta, P. D. 339

Haeffele, S. 67
Haidilao Hot Pot 79
Hall, A. 68
Hansen, E. G. 12
Harbin Pharmaceutical Group 89–90
Hart, K. 257
Herfindahl-Hirschman Index (HHI) 196
Hermes, N. 165
higher education institutions: and
  entrepreneurship 321; in South Africa 321
Hindustan Petroleum Corporation Limited
  (HPCL) 152
Ho, Y. P. 166
hobbypreneurs 112
Hobson, A. 67
Hockey, J. 68
Hong Kong 339
Horkheimer, M. 299, 303

Ikryannikov, V. M. 285
inclusive/sustainable industrialisation
  230; SMEs 230
Independent Development Trust 330
index of industrial production (IIP) 102
India: Aatmanirbhar Bharat Abhiyaan
  52–54; challenges/policy
  recommendations for MSMEs 54–56;
  classification of MSMEs 95–96,
  96; emerging economies 244; and
  entrepreneurship 150–153; expanding
  ecosystems 238–239; GDP and
  MSMEs 95, **96**; GDP growth in **101**;
  government-financed SME agencies in
  225; impact of COVID-19 on MSMEs
  44–46, *45*; lockdown in 41; number of
  persons employed by MSMEs in **46**,
  46–49, *47*, *48*; percentage of MSMEs
  in 221–222; promotion of MSMEs 41;
  SMEs in **236–237**, 236–238

Indian Companies Act 151
Indian entrepreneurs 95–105;
  COVID-19 pandemic and MSMEs
  100–102; digital transformation
  102–103; inclusive and sustainability
  models 104; inter-professional
  collaboration 103; localisation
  103–104; mental well-being 104;
  research study 102; trends and
  perspectives of 102–104
Industrial Development Corporation of
  South Africa 330
industrialisation 233, 252, 329; inclusive
  and sustainable 230; maintainable
  229; massive 339, 341; rapid 340; re-
  industrialisation 108
Industrial Revolution 149
industry 218–244
informal businesses: *vs.* formal businesses 68
information technology (IT) 150
infrastructure 218–244; digital 24;
  Internet 214; media 134; modern 150;
  physical 113; resilient 230; social 17,
  183; technological 24, 280
innovation 89, 218–244; enterprise
  191–193, **192**; and mixed ownership
  reform 191–193, **192**; restaurant
  entrepreneurs (South Africa) 139;
  SMEs 230
Innovation Cooperation Action
  Plans: causal factors for launching
  cooperation in 213–214; documental
  analysis of cooperation in 209–213
innovation level of state-owned
  enterprises 181–200
Innovative Science and Technology
  Centers (ISTC) 272
*Institut Européen d'Administration des
  Affaires* (INSEAD) Business School
  213
Inter-American Development Bank 218
interest rates, SMMEs 19
International Finance Cooperation 220;
  Global SME Finance Facility 220
International Financial Institutions (IFIs)
  219
International Labour Organisation (ILO)
  43, 55
International Monetary Fund (IMF) 41,
  133, 149
inter-professional collaboration 103

invention, and MSMEs 234
Iqbal, B. A. 9
Irfan, M. 18
Isenberg, D. 332, 334
Ismail, Faizel 318

Jaén, I. 127
Jaipur Declaration 211
Japan: government-financed SME agencies in 225; SMEs 221
Jaunky, V. C. 166
Jiang, X. Y. 193
job creation, and SMEs 219
Jobs, Steve 149
Johannesburg Stock Exchange (JSE) 61
Julien, P.-A. 109–110

Kalacheva, O. N. 17, 20, 25
Kalidas, S. 65–66
Kar, B. 100
Karatayev, Sergei 149
Karlan, D. 165
Kautilya *see* VishnuGupta
Kedir, A. M. 318
Khairullina, M. V. 285
Khan, F. 60
Khan, M. 98–99
Khan, M. I. 99
Khanna, S. 61, 100
Kim, J. 130
Kłopotek, M. 68
Kogan, L. N. 303
Korchagin, R. L. 285
Korchagina, I. V. 285
Krackhardt, D. 332
Kropp, F. 322
Kuckertz, A. 128

Latham, G. P. 321
Lensink, R. 165
Lepojevic, V. 166
"Leto na Zavode" (Summer at the Factory) 307
lifepreneurs 112
Lightelm, A. A. 59
Liguori, E. 332
Liñán, F. 127
"Little Giant" Enterprises 87
Liu, Y. G. 187
loans: organisations making 220–221; repayments, SMMEs 19

localisation 103–104
lockdowns: COVID-19 impact on SMEs during 62–63; salons and nail bars sustainability during 63–64
Locke, E. A. 321
Luo, H. 198

Ma, X. X. 187
Ma, Z. 20, 21
Madubela, A. 134
Magwentshu, N. 65–66
"Make in India" 152
Makletsky, Ilya Zakharovich 311
Makletsky House Cluster in Yekaterinburg 311–312
Mandela, Nelson 320
Marcotte, C. 163
Maritz, A. 67
marketing, and SMMEs 23–24
Mason, C. 332
Matenda, F. R. 161
Mbovane, T. 66
McCarthy, N. 163–164, 175
"МСП.ru" ("SME.rf") 271–273
McLellan, N. F. 17
Medium and Small-Scale enterprises (MSMEs): benefits of 222; business models and solutions achieving SDGs 235; challenges/policy recommendations 54–56; changing business practices 235; contribution to Indian economy 44; and COVID-19 pandemic 43–46; encouraging invention 234; Gross Value Added (GVA) 97; issues affecting 222–223; number of persons employed in India **46**, 46–49, *47*, *48*; percentage, in India 221–222; role in India *44*; role of 42; sole proprietorship register as 222
Meesho 103
Meet BRICS Art 313
Menon, Shiv Shankar 152
mental well-being 104
Meyer, D. 334
Meyer, N. 334
micro-enterprise 335–336
Mineral Council of South Africa 337
minimum government engagements 152
Ministerial Advisory Committee (MAC) 135
Minniti, M. 175

Index   351

mixed ownership reform: and enterprise innovation 191–193, **192**; of SOEs 191–193, **192**
Mkhonza, V. M. 18
Mkhumane, L. 58–59
Mladenovic, J. 166
Modi, Narender 151, 154
Mohammed, A. 99
Molobi, Saul 334
monopolistic SOEs 184, 196, **196**
Moos, M. 26, 60
Moscow School of Social and Economic Sciences 281
Motsaathebe, G. 334
Moyo, M. 68
MSMED Act 95
MSMEs SDG Accelerator Programme of UNDP 235–236
Mzini, L. B. 17

Naffziger, D.W. 322
Nagi, I. 129
National Bank for Rural Development (NABARD) 53
National Business Act of 1996 335
National Development Plan (NDP) of South Africa 36, 329
National Entrepreneurship Context Index 334
National Housing Bank 53
National Institute of Standards and Technology (NIST, United States) 292
National Smaill Industries Corporation (NSIC) 221
National Small Business Act 36
Neklyudova, N. 18
networking, and SMMEs 24–25
New Development Bank (NDB) 211
New World Order 157–158, *158*
Ngcobo, K. 63
Ngcobo, S. 339
Njanike, K. 9
Nombembe, P. 63–64
Non-Banking Financial Companies (NBFCs) 220
non-technological SOEs 185–186, **198**, 198–199
North-Eastern Development Finance Corporation (NEDFi) 221
Ntsika Enterprise Promotion Agency 333

O'Connor, M. 163–164, 175
Odusola, A. 58–59
Ombudsman for the Protection of Entrepreneurs' Rights report 265
Omonona, S. 18, 20, 22–23, 26, 61
Oni, O. 18, 20, 22–23, 26, 61
online services 67–69
"On the Creative Industries of the Sverdlovsk Region" 306
operating subsidies 21
"Operation Vulindlela" 329
opportunity-driven entrepreneurship 112
Ordinary Least Squares regression model 165
Organisation for Economic Co-operation and Development (OECD) 147, 213–214, 279, 290, 302, 330, 334
organisations, and loans 220–221
Overcoat Museum 310

Pakistan: emerging economies 244; GDP growth in **101**; SMEs 221
Palm, K. 136
Palsgaard 235
partnerships, and SMMEs 24–25
part-timers 112
Paul, J. 218
PayNearby 103
Pedersen, R. B. 205
Peterson, R. 166, 270
Pikoos, T. D. 63, 68
Pinchot, G. 332
Policy for the Promotion of Employment Creation Programmes (PPECP) 148
politics and urban planning 258
precariousness 253
Presidential Fund for the Support of Cultural Initiatives 310
principal component analysis (PCA) 169–170, 172
private entrepreneurship in Russia **264**
Process Tracing 205
profeneurs 113
promotions, and SMMEs 23–24
Province Dances 309
Public Finance Management Act (PFMA) of 1999 330
Puthusserry, P. 23, 26–27
Putin, Vladimir 307–308

352 Index

Qin, J. D. 198
Quiros-Alcala, L. 71

Rajagopaul, A. 65–66
Ramaphosa, Cyril 31, 129, 133, 326
Rashid, N. H. 166–167
Rathore, U. 61, 100
Razumovskaia, E. 22
Reconstruction and Development Programme (RDP) 328
regional marketisation development 184–185, **197**, 197–198
Regional Rural Banks (RRBs) 220
Regulations on Guaranteeing the Payment of Small- and Medium-sized Enterprises (China) 85
re-industrialisation 108
"*Research Report on the Impact of COVID-19 on Small and Medium-sized Enterprises and Countermeasures*" 78
Reserve Bank of India 54
resilient infrastructure, and SMEs 230
Restaurant Association of South Africa (RASA) 135
restaurant entrepreneurs (South Africa): certainty 131; challenges faced by 133–136; and COVID-19 127–141; decision-making for 131–133; financial challenges 134; good hygiene and sanitization 137–138; innovative practices 139; kerbside pickup 138; lack of government support 136; lockdown restrictions 134–136; overview 127–129; retrenchment of employees 138; risk 131–132; strategies to overcome effects of COVID-19 136–139; uncertainty 132–133; use of deliveries 137
retrenchments, and SMMEs 26
revenue schemes, and SMMEs 25
RGS Nordic 235
Riom, C. 99
Robertson, N. L. 69
Robinson, V. 68
robustness test 193, **194–195**
Roever, S. 259
Rolêfeira street market, Araraquara, Brazil 251–260; economic practices 256–258, **256–258**; field survey location 254; method and techniques 254–255; nexus between politics and urban planning 258; research findings 255–259; research questions 254; theoretical framework 252–253; urban public spaces 259
Roman, A. 161
Rosatom 265, 304
Rostech 265
Roy, A. 18, 20
Rupert, Johann 118
Rurban Creative Lab 304
Rurban project 304
Russia 262–274; advanced production technology in 292–293; The Agency for Strategic Initiatives (ASI) 300, 304–305, 307; creative industries in 299–315; current state of entrepreneurship in 266–269; entrepreneurship and economic development/growth 269–272; evaluating technological entrepreneurship in 282–292; National Technological Initiative (NTI) 282–283; post-COVID-19 299–315; private entrepreneurship in **264**; "Startup Barometer" 283; statistics and comparisons 266–269; technological entrepreneurship 278–282
Russian Empire 262–263
Russian Federation: Concept #2613-p 304; Spatial Development Strategy of 301
Russian Railways 265
Rusu, V. D. 161

Sahasranamam, S. 102–103
Sahoo, P. 17
Sajan, E. L. 17, 18
salons/nail bars: metrics of running 69–71, **70**; operated during lockdown restrictions 69; sustainability during lockdowns in South Africa 63–64; unable to access public sector funding 66
Sanchez-Escobedo, M. C. 162
Sanya Declaration 206
Saptanga Theory (VishnuGupta) 151–152
Sarkisian-Artamonova, A. A. 17, 20, 25
Savrul, M. 162
Schaltegger, S. 12
Schwab, K. 283, 303

Science, Technology and Innovation (STI) 205
scientific recovery support strategies 88–89
SDGs 229; 12 Indicators and 8 Targets for 230–231, **231**; MSME business models and solutions achieving 235
Sebby, A. G. 137
Second World War 127, 310
Semenov, N. 279
"servant leaders" 341
"shadow" entrepreneurs 263
Shambare, J. 110
Shanghai Zaitu Network Technology 89–90
Shaw, Kendall 137
Sheresheva, M. 10, 23
Sibanda, M. 161
Siberian Trade Bank 311
Sifolo, P. P. S. 18
Singapore 339
Sitharaman, Nirmala 152
size of business in SMEs 219–223
Skinner, C. 259
small, micro, and medium enterprises (SMMEs) 339; business models 21; in China 10; classification of 35; combating strategies for 22–26; COVID-19 pandemic impact on 9–27; data analysis 15; data collection 12–14, **13**, **14–15**; demand and supply 20–21; digital transformation 20; employee health and safety 21; factors affecting the survival and growth of 36; financial and technical support 16–19; general policy recommendations 22; government support initiatives for 36–38; Indian 10; interest rates and loan repayments 19; mitigation of COVID-19 impact 31–39; payments to 19–20; policy responses 15–22; role in the economy 333–338, **335**, **336–337**, **338**; schedule, by the NSB Act of 1996 **336–337**; in South Africa 335–338; subsidies and obligations 21; tax rates 20
small and medium enterprises (SMEs) 220–222, 319; Africa 221; Australia 221; in China 221, **236–237**, 236–238; contribution in developing economies 218–244; contributions in developing nations 224–229, **225**, **227–228**; contribution to job creation 219; credit lines 229; debts relief finance scheme in South Africa 64; drawbacks 243–244; drivers of future readiness 240–241; effects of COVID-19 on 58, 60–63, 75, 115; Europe 221; expanding ecosystems 238–239; findings and analysis 224–229; futuristic approach in developing economies 239–240, **239–240**; Goal 9 of the SDGs 229; inclusive/sustainable industrialisation 230; in India **236–237**, 236–238; innovation 230; Japan 221; literature review 219–223; Pakistan 221; research methodology 223–224; research phases 223–224; resilient infrastructure 230; size and scope of 114; size of business in 219–223; in South Africa 116–118, **117**; space technologies crucial to 229–241; and start-ups 222; targets 230–231; United States 221; widely distributed in other nations 221
Small and Medium Enterprises Development Index (SMEDI) 78
Small Enterprise Development Agency (SEDA) 35
Small Enterprise Finance Agency (SEFA) 64
small enterprises 336
Small Finance Banks (SFBs) 221
small industrial companies 233–234
Small-Scale Development Bank of India (SIDBI) 53, 220–221, 228–229
Small-Scale Industrial Enterprises (MSME) financing 234
Smart, P. 12
smartpreneurs 113
social change 156–157
social entrepreneurs 112
soft loans 64
sole proprietorship register as MSME 222
South Africa: analysis of strategy of government 328–330; and Asian tigers 339–342; COVID-19 impact on SMEs during lockdowns 62–63; criticality of systems approach 332; debts relief finance scheme for SMEs 64–66; declining GDP growth 34–35;

declining trade volume 35; Department of Health 59; economic impact of COVID-19 34, 60; economic stimulus package 31–34; entrepreneur education for 319–321; entrepreneurship and sustainable economic growth 332; entrepreneurship in post-COVID-19 era in 108–125; entrepreneurs typologies in 111–115; higher education institutions in 321; informal sector 58–59; literature review 318–320, 328–330; methodological approach 331–342; mineral resources in **338**; role of SMMEs in economy 333–338, **335**, **336–337**, **338**; salons/ nail bars sustainability during lockdowns 63–64; SMEs in 116–118, **117**; SMMEs and COVID-19 31–39; strategies to support entrepreneurs 322–323; students entrepreneurial intentions/motivation 321–322; theoretical framework 330–331
South African Airways (SAA) 327, 330
South African Broadcasting Corporation 330
South African Express Airways 330
South African Forestry Company (SAFCOL) 330
South African Nuclear Energy Corporation 330
South African Post Office 330
South African Social Security Agency's 2022/2023 Annual Report 326
South Africa SME Finance Association (SASFA) 61
South Korea 80, 326–327, 339–340
space technologies, SMEs 229–241
Spaza shops 59, 65, 121
Spur Corporation 134
Stam, E. 166–167, 270
start-ups and SMEs 222
statehood 151–152
state-owned enterprises (SOEs): competitive 184, 196, **196**; control variables 188; correlation coefficient matrix 190–191, **191**; dependent variable 187; descriptive statistics **190**, 190–191; empirical results 190–193; heterogeneous analysis 196–199; independent variables 187–188; literature review/research hypotheses 182–186; mixed ownership reform and innovation 182–184; mixed ownership reform of 191–193, **192**; model specification 188–190; monopolistic 184, 196, **196**; non-technological 185–186, **198**, 198–199; regional marketisation development 184–185, **197**, 197–198; research design 186–187; robustness test 193, **194–195**; sample selection and data sources 186–187; technological 185–186, **198**, 198–199; variable selection and measurement 187–188
Statistical Methods for the Division of Large, Medium, and Small Enterprises 76
Sternberg, R. 167
STI Development within BRICS 206–209
Stoica, O. 161, 162
Stork, C. 68
Storr, V. H. 67
strategies: combating for SMMEs 22–26; scientific recovery support 88–89; SMMEs 23
street economy 259
street markets: in BRICS nations 251–260; urban economics of 251–260
street vending 258
students: entrepreneurial intentions 321–322; entrepreneurial motivation in South Africa 321–322
Su, J. 25
Su, W. 10–11, 18, 20, 21, 22
subsidies/obligations: operating 21; and SMMEs 21
Sukdeo, R. 339
Sun, Y. 25
Sunday World newspaper 328
Suresh, B. H. 18, 20, 26
survivalist entrepreneurship 112
sustainability models 104
Sverdlovsk region 304–306
Sverdlovsk Regional Business Support Fund 305–306
Sycheva-Peredero, O. V. 285
Sysert Development Agency 308, 309
Szerb, L. 162, 163, 268, 271

Index 355

Tahir, M. 215
Taiwan 56, 327, 339–340
Tammy Taylor Nails 64
Tang, T. J. 187
Tanzania: government-financed SME agencies in 225; small business sector in 334
tax rates, and SMMEs 20
technological entrepreneurship 278–282, 292–293; for development in Russia 282–292; evaluating 282–292; and peculiarities of development in Russia 277–295
technological SOEs 185–186, **198**, 198–199
technology: SMMEs 24; support, and SMMEs 16–19
techpreneurs 113
Telkom 330
Thompson, A. 69
Ticketpro Dome 62–63
Tobak, S. 115
Tongdun Technology Co., Ltd. 90
top management governance 181–200
Tranfield, D. 12
Transnet 330
Tretyakova, Ekaterina 309
Trumbull, W. 268, 271
Tsar Peter 262–263
Tsegai, D. 318
tuck shops 59
Turchaninov-Solomirsky Ironworks 307
Turkey, and government-financed SME agencies 225
Tyutcheva, Narine 309

Ufa Declaration 208
Ullah, Z. 99
Ullah Khan, S. 99
UN Conference on Trade and Development (UNCTAD) 152
Unemployment Insurance Fund (UIF) 66
unemployment subsidies 84
United Aircraft Corporation 265
United Nations: 12 Indicators and 8 Targets for SDG 9 230–231, **231**; General Assembly 303; SDGs 229
United Nations Development Programme (UNDP): MSMEs SDG Accelerator Programme of 235–236

United Nations Educational, Scientific and Cultural Organisation (UNESCO) 302; Third World Forum on Culture and Cultural Industries (FOCUS) 303
United Nations Industrial Development Organisation (UNIDO) 233–234
United Shipbuilding Corporation 265
United States: government-financed SME agencies in 225; SMEs 221
unpaid vacations, and SMMEs 26
Urals Region 299–315; Art Residence in Chernoistochinsk 306–312; literature review 302–304; problem statement/ objectives 300–302; *Sverdlovsk region* 304–306
urban economics: in BRICS nations 251–260; of street markets 251–260
Urbano, D. 162, 166
urban planning 258
urban public spaces 259

Valdivia, M. 165
Valero, A. 99
Valliere, D. 166, 270
Van Stel, A. 166, 167
Vashisht, A. 95
Vatavu, S. 161, 165
Venkatesan, Ravi 237–239
very small businesses 336
VishnuGupta 151–153
Volkov, V. 263
Vyas, M. 102

Wahono, R. S. 37
Watson, S. 259
Webb, J. W. 256
Wei, M. H. 188
Wennekers, S. 166, 167
White Paper on National Strategy for the Development and Promotion of Small Business (1995) 335
Wijewickrama, E. 99
Wilson, H. 123
Wind database 182, 186–187
Wong, P. K. 166
World Bank 60, 149, 218, 229, 240, 266, 338; Word development indicators 286
World Bank Enterprise Surveys 234

356 *Index*

World Economic Forum 104, 213, 280, 283, 303
World Health Organisation (WHO) 13, 115
World Intellectual Property Organization 213
World Organisation of Commerce, Geneva 319
World Trade Organisation (WTO) 35
Wyszomirski, M. 67

Xiao, D. 25
Xi Jinping 186, 238

Yan Kozhan 308
Yekaterinburg Declaration 206
Yekaterinburg Nikolay Kolyada theatre 309
Yitshaki, R. 322

Zaki, I. M. 166–167
Zama Zamas 338
Zdnet 99
Zhang, L. R. 193
Zheng, G. J. 187
Zlokazovskaya (Aramil cloth factory) 310